Transnational Cooperation

TRANSNATIONAL COOPERATION

An Issue-Based Approach

Clint Peinhardt and Todd Sandler

University of Texas at Dallas

OXFORD
UNIVERSITY PRESS

Oxford University Press is a department of the University of Oxford.
It furthers the University's objective of excellence in research, scholarship,
and education by publishing worldwide. Oxford is a registered trade mark
of Oxford University Press in the UK and in certain other countries

Published in the United States of America by
Oxford University Press
198 Madison Avenue, New York, NY 10016,
United States of America

Cataloging-in-Publication data is on file at the Library of Congress

9780199398607 (hbk.)
9780199398614 (pbk.)

9 8 7 6 5 4 3 2 1

Printed in the United States of America on acid-free paper

To Anne Dutia and Jeannie Murdock

CONTENTS

LIST OF TABLES AND FIGURES

Tables

Figures

PREFACE

Transnational, regional, and global challenges abound in today's interdependent world and require cooperation among countries. In some instances, multiple countries must jointly address a contingency (for example, the spread of an agriculture pest); in other cases, countries in the same geographical region must act in concert to alleviate a concern (for example, acid rain); and in still other scenarios, all countries of the world must work together to achieve an outcome (for example, curbing climate change). The need for transnational cooperation among countries will grow in importance as globalization increases cross-border exchanges of a desirable and undesirable nature. The exchange of knowledge and culture is desirable, while the exchange of pollutants or financial instability is undesirable. Population growth also places stresses on the planet that make one country's problems adversely impact the welfare of other countries, thereby increasing the need for transnational cooperation. For instance, deforested hillsides in one country may result in flooding or climate change in a neighboring country. Civil conflict in one country may create refugee flows that affect neighboring countries. With huge daily flows of financial capital, countries' economies and fortunes are closely interdependent.

Transnational cooperation or the action by two or more sovereign countries to promote their common good has seen both successes and failures in recent decades. Thus far, actions to check climate change, resulting from atmospheric accumulation of greenhouse gases, have been a cooperation failure despite some hopeful signs at the December 2014 meeting of the Conference of Parties to the Kyoto Protocol in Lima, Peru. The eradication of smallpox in 1979 and the near eradication of polio are clear transnational cooperation successes. The allocation of geostationary orbital slots and electromagnetic spectrum frequencies to satellites is another transnational cooperation success. Other such successes include deployment of tsunami early-warning systems, regulation of air corridors for commercial flights, a universal set of weights and measures, creation of the United Nations, deployment of effective peacekeeping operations, and the reduction in ozone-layer-depleting substances. So the big question for this book is what factors promote or inhibit transnational cooperation. In those cases where the required cooperation is not forthcoming, we need to discern what actions or institutions can overcome barriers and further transnational cooperation.

To pursue our study of transnational cooperation, we rely, in part, on elementary game theory, bolstered by concepts from economics, political science, and political economy. We assume no prior knowledge of game theory; all game-theoretic concepts, tools, and analyses are explained in detail for the uninitiated reader. These concepts are reinforced with myriad examples and repeated throughout the book. Transnational cooperation requires strategic interaction among countries and other key agents (for example, multilateral institutions, multinational firms, nongovernmental organizations, and public-private partnerships) that is best captured by the tools of rational interactive choice, or game theory. This rational interactive choice may or may not result in desirable outcomes. The celebrated, and overused, Prisoners' Dilemma leads to very undesirable outcomes, but other game forms are often associated with better outcomes. Economic concepts, such as markets, market failures, public goods, the commons, and externalities, also play an important role in our analysis. We are very interested in elucidating the role and importance of institutions. Such institutions can fundamentally affect the success of transnational cooperation and have assumed novel forms in the current era of globalization.

The book commences with four chapters that lay the foundation for the analysis. This is followed by a rich set of issue-based chapters that consider foreign assistance, global health, sovereignty, leadership, international trade, global finance, civil wars, terrorism, drug trafficking, money laundering, rogue states, nuclear proliferation, climate change, ozone-shield depletion, and other topics. We know of no other book that addresses such a rich set of topics of current importance with an elementary but firm theoretical basis.

This book has a number of other unique features. First, the book's authors include a political scientist and an economist, both of whom possess a firm grounding in both disciplines. Second, the book relies on paired comparisons to clarify the subtleties of transnational collective action. These comparisons allow us to ask a host of questions. For example, why has the world been so successful at curbing ozone shield depletion but so unsuccessful at reducing climate change? This is the case even though both issues involve global public goods with similar attributes. Another question concerns whether failed states pose a greater security threat than rogue states. Yet another question involves why the prognosis for cooperation differs between sulfur-based acid rain and nitrogen-based acid rain. Understanding these and many other paired comparisons in this book will allow the reader to learn that simple maxims—for example, fewer participants promote successful collective action—do not necessarily hold and why. Third, our book focuses on collective action and cooperation at three levels of aggregation: the global, regional, and transnational levels. Most books either focus on global or regional cooperation without comparing and contrasting these two types of collaborations. Much can be acquired by distinguishing between global and regional cooperation and the requisite institutions involved at these two levels of aggregation. Fourth, the book concerns both economic and political issues. Sovereignty and leadership would not be considered in an economic treatise of transnational cooperation, while international trade and market failures are unlikely to be examined in a political science analysis of transnational cooperation. We intend this book to be a true treatise in political economy by treating both political and economic concerns with adequate care, skill, and insight.

The current book is much more than an updating of Sandler's *Global Collective Action* (Cambridge University Press, 2004). Much has happened since 2004 to the exigencies confronting the world. This means that many topics not found in the earlier book (for example, sovereignty, leadership, failed states, financial crises, drug trafficking, money laundering, nuclear proliferation, and others) are included in the current book. Moreover, many topics in *Global Collective Action* are not in *Transnational Cooperation*. By including a political scientist as an author, the current book has more appeal to readers interested in international relations and public policy, while retaining its appeal to readers in economics. Any chapters in *Transnational Cooperation* that partially overlap with topics in the earlier book have been completely redrafted and updated. *Transnational Cooperation* is a new book. Compared with *Global Collective Action*, this new book is much more reader friendly and accessible, with finer details now placed in footnotes for the interested reader. The current book contains many more examples and references than the earlier book. Unlike *Global Collective Action*, *Transnational Cooperation* has much to say about regionalism, which is growing in importance.

We owe a tremendous debt of gratitude to many people. Iman Shamseldin typed and retyped various drafts of Sandler's chapters. We have profited from insightful comments from five anonymous reviewers on various drafts. We received excellent counsel and encouragement from Scott Parris, the senior economics editor at Oxford University Press (OUP). We also appreciated the efforts of the production staff at OUP, who transformed the typescript into a book. We acknowledge an intellectual debt to our many co-authors of our articles addressing related issues as those covered in the book. Peinhardt thanks his UTD colleagues—Jonas Bunte, Brandon Kinne, and Banks Miller—for many discussions about his issue chapters and for their support during the writing. He is also grateful to Adam Yeeles for help with the map in Chapter 9. Sandler thanks Jeannie Murdock, Justin George, and Khusrav Gaibulloev for helping with the indexes, diagrams, and related matters. This project succeeded because of the support of our respective wives, Anne Dutia and Jeannie Murdock, and the understanding of our children.

Dallas, Texas
January 2015

Clint Peinhardt
Associate Professor of Political Science,
Public Policy and Political Economy

and

Todd Sandler
Vibhooti Shukla Professor of Economics
and Political Economy
University of Texas at Dallas

CHAPTER 1

Transnational Cooperation

Transnational cooperation or successful collective action involves two or more countries working together to achieve an outcome that is more difficult and, in some instances, impossible to obtain through independent efforts. For example, a global standard of weights and measures requires universal consensus—no country can unilaterally declare such a standard. Generally, transnational cooperation is motivated by mutually beneficial payoffs to the cooperating countries. Historically, transnational cooperation involved military alliances, such as the Triple Entente and the Triple Alliance prior to World War I, the Allies and the Axis during World War II, and the North Atlantic Treaty Organization (NATO) and the Warsaw Pact during the Cold War.[1] Other historical examples concerned curbing transfrontier pollution—for example, the resolution of the Trail Smelter dispute between Canada (the polluter) and the United States, which set the precedence for the "polluter pays principle" of environment compensation. For some time, countries have assisted one another during natural disasters, which is a form of collective action. Assisting nation-states hope that others will come to their assistance when they are in need of help.

The world is beset with myriad global, regional, and transnational challenges of varying degrees that require some form of transnational collective action by two or more countries. At the global level, these challenges include curbing climate change, monitoring the heavens for planetesimals, installing safeguards against financial crises, tracking the outbreak of contagious diseases, annihilating transnational terrorist organizations, eliminating human trafficking, isolating new viruses, eradicating infectious diseases, and developing best medical practices. Regionally, challenges encompass

---

1. On these alliances, see articles by Conybeare, Murdoch, and Sandler (1994) and Conybeare and Sandler (1990), which investigated burden sharing within these alliances based on data on allies' contributions to defense.

ameliorating acid rain, forestalling the spread of invasive species, maintaining watersheds, monitoring the intensity of hurricanes, limiting bank runs, caring for refugees, quelling political violence, and installing tsunami-alert systems. Bilateral challenges include illegal immigration, river pollution, surface ozone, drug trafficking, and cross-border criminal activities.

If we can see into the future, what do we need to know to treat transnational challenges effectively? Our efforts would be greatly enhanced if we knew beforehand what challenges are the most persistent, so that society can take palliative actions immediately against these exigencies. This insight means that scarce resources can be allocated to where they are most needed. Problems that have self-ameliorating mechanisms should not be addressed. Since we cannot truly see the future, we can do the next best thing and apply our understanding of collective action to anticipate these persistent problems.[2] To act decisively, we must second-guess tomorrow's challenges that are either not currently experienced or recognized. This necessitates, in part, thinking about the consequences that new technologies in the development stage or other novel contingencies may have on the environment, human health, the economy, security, and social well-being. This foreknowledge allows us to act sooner, thereby limiting the extent of the harm and reducing the expenditure of palliative resources. Additionally, we must learn which of today's challenges are overblown—for example, invasive species may face natural forces that keep population levels in check once a threshold is reached. Finally, society must have the forethought to develop the requisite infrastructure to alleviate today's and tomorrow's transnational challenges. This infrastructure may require a rotating committee of scientists, drawn from multiple disciplines, to spot these challenges at an incipient stage. Additional monitoring technologies are needed to assist these scientists—for example, atmospheric observatories on Mauna Loa on the island of Hawaii monitor carbon dioxide and other chemicals in the stratosphere. Provision of this infrastructure hinges on international cooperation, founded on transnational and intergenerational awareness, which has surfaced during the twentieth century as countries recognize their interdependencies.

The financial crisis of 2008, which resulted in the "great recession," underscores today's interdependency of countries worldwide. This crisis originated in the United States because of a housing bubble funded in part by subprime mortgages given to borrowers with inadequate incomes to repay the loans.[3] These borrowers were attracted because the loans required little or no money

2. The foundation of the study of collective action began with Mancur Olson's seminal 1965 study. Other noteworthy contributions include Hardin (1982), Marwell and Oliver (1993), and Sandler (1992).
3. There is a copious amount of material on the financial crisis of 2008; for a succinct summary, see Britannica (2009).

down and had initially low interest rates. After a couple of years, the interest rates on these subprime loans became outrageously high. Clauses in these loans did not allow the borrowers to refinance at a lower interest rate, so they had little choice but to default on their loans, which had been sold by the original lender to mortgage-buying institutions. As house prices plunged in some markets in 2007, many recent home purchasers now owned houses with values of less than their mortgages. In reaction, some borrowers defaulted on their loans. Countrywide Financial Corporation, which at the time was the largest mortgage lender in the United States, was a casualty of the financial crisis. Two government-chartered institutions—Fannie Mae and Freddie Mac—which held many more mortgages, lost hundreds of billions owing to defaulted loans. The financial crisis spread to investment firms, such as Bear Stearns, Lehman Brothers, and Merrill Lynch, whose portfolios contained large amounts of mortgage-based securities whose value evaporated with defaulted loans.

The financial crises in the United States spread to Germany, Japan, China, and elsewhere as U.S. imports declined, thereby underscoring how countries' fortunes are integrally tied in today's world with its huge daily flows of financial capital. The recession was especially deep and long lasting because banks became reluctant to lend out money. Commerce hinges on businesses' ability to secure short- and long-term loans. Questionable loan practices in the United States had ripple effects throughout the world markets as liquidity dried up. Subsequently, debts in some European Union (EU) countries— Portugal, Spain, Ireland, Italy, and others—affected stock prices and the speed of recovery in the United States. Given that the Chinese and EU economies have become huge, crises there also reverberate globally. Poor financial practices in key economies can adversely affect economies everywhere. The 2008 recession blindsided the world despite the accumulated experience and knowledge from past financial crises.

MARKET FAILURES AND THE NEED FOR COLLECTIVE ACTION

Markets permit the voluntary exchange of goods and services, guided by prices and profits. Market economies function best when property rights are defined and protected, competition is rigorous, and market information is plentiful. Moreover, markets must be complete, so that anything with value (negative or positive) is traded. Property rights are claims of ownership, written or implicit, that give the owner control over a good's benefits. Laws define property rights, police enforce these rights, and courts adjudicate disagreements over these rights. Quite simply, markets allow for the voluntary exchange of property rights by sellers and buyers; in so doing, prices reflect the value of what is being exchanged. Competition requires a large number of small buyers and sellers, so that no one has a measurable influence on price. If buyers and sellers are informed about prices, profits, and market opportunities, then market information is sufficient for efficient exchange. Finally, markets are complete when no producer or consumer has negative or positive consequences on others that go uncompensated. This last requirement is a tall order, since consumption and production activities may have consequences, not captured by the transaction's price. Until U.S. federal laws outlawed smoking in the workplace, secondhand smoke imposed significant uncompensated costs on nonsmokers not reflected in the price of cigarettes.

In a well-functioning market, prices signal to buyers and sellers where to buy cheaply and where to sell for a profit, respectively. According to Adam Smith and classical economists, individuals are guided by an "invisible hand" to an efficient outcome, where resources gravitate to their most-valued use. The beauty with markets is that there is little or no need for explicit coordination. If governments provide defense, a justice system, education, and infrastructure, then markets will achieve an efficient allocation of resources. However, income distribution may be undesirable because individuals with few marketable skills may starve. Also, unanticipated shocks to the system may result in instabilities, such as financial crises. At the national level, governments are still needed to redistribute income and address instability even when markets work efficiently.

Let us ignore redistribution and instability concerns for the time being and briefly consider how markets can fail to direct resources to their best use, which is a primary concern of this book. Markets may fail in this goal when property rights are not defined or enforced. If, for example, ownership is in common, then property rights in commonly utilized resources are not defined in such a way as to allow for trade. Open-access commons or "common property" involves such valuable things as the atmosphere, where people and firms have dumped their waste products—for example, sulfur emissions from coal-fired power stations. Until the Law of the Seas Treaty, countries could not legally protect their coastal fisheries located some miles offshore, thereby encouraging overfishing by fishing vessels from other countries without regard to the sustainability of the stock. Market failures can also stem from information imperfections. If, for example, an employer cannot monitor workers' effort, then low output on a given day may be due to laziness or random events, such as an Internet outage or substandard raw materials, beyond their control. Laziness must be punished, but this is not the case for randomness. When information is imperfect, resources do not necessarily find their best use because the link between effort and reward is broken. The notion of incomplete markets—another cause of market failure—is tied to externalities, or an uncompensated interdependency. Externalities result in third-party benefits or costs that are not taken into account by the price, thereby distorting resource allocation so that too little of some activities and too much of other activities are produced or consumed based on the output's value. For example, fall leaves are burned even though the particulates harm local residents, especially those with asthma, who would gain from a more benign means of disposal.

The study of market failures is the subject of Chapter 3. For now, we need to emphasize that to address such failures often requires effective collective action at the country or international level, depending on the extent of the benefits or costs. If they spill over borders, then transnational collective action may be needed, as in the case of transfrontier pollution. Collective action is justified because the underlying market failure means that a judicious intervention may make society better off.[4]

FOUR LEVELS OF COLLECTIVE ACTION

Collective action or the efforts of two or more agents to accomplish a goal with mutual benefits may occur on at least four levels. Global collective action involves the collaborative efforts of few or many countries, resulting in benefits experienced by a large expanse of the planet. Some global collective action requires efforts by most countries, because nonparticipants can undo some of the progress of the participants. Consider actions to eliminate safe havens for terrorist organizations. Even a few countries offering sanctuary can undo the concerted efforts of much of the world's countries to deny safe haven. In the case of climate change, failure of China or India to reduce their greenhouse gas emissions can greatly limit the outcome to curb such emissions. In other global collective action scenarios, a few countries or even a single country can "privilege" the world with benefits.[5] The U.S. Centers for Disease Control (CDC), with the help of relatively few countries, privileges the world with actions to isolate new viruses and bacteria, and to track outbreaks.[6]

Regional collective action is associated with well-defined regions, whose basis can be founded on geographical (for example, sub-Saharan Africa), geological (a seacoast), geoclimatic, cultural, or historical considerations. Two or more countries in a region must initiate regional collective action, as in the control of acid rain or a pest infestation. In Chapter 4, we will see that

---

4. Market failure opens the door for welfare-improving collective action, where at least one individual is made better off without harming anyone. There may even be instances where everyone can be made better off by some corrective action.

5. This notion of privilege, where one agent provides the collective good for everyone, was due to Olson (1965).

6. The CDC and its unique role in global collective action were discussed in Sandler and Arce (2002). The CDC must rely on the country of origin to help in its collection of the pathogen.

regional collective action is not necessarily easier to achieve than global collective action, despite the greatly reduced number of countries gaining benefits from such action.

Transnational collective action benefits two or more countries. Bilateral collective action, which is prevalent today, falls far short of the regional variety. Many trade and pollution agreements are bilateral in nature. In some instances, transnational collective action may concern geographically separated countries, as in the fight against river blindness (Onchocerciasis), which infects people in sub-Saharan Africa, the Arabian Peninsula, and isolated parts of Central and South America. In other instances, transnational cooperation may require a level of technology possessed by relatively few countries—as in the case of space exploration—thereby limiting participation.

As mentioned earlier, collective action may be needed at the country level for concerns devoid of cross-country implications. At subnational levels, collective action is provided by state, provincial, and local jurisdictions. Most countries contain literally thousands of such jurisdictions—for example, county governments in the United States or local councils in England.

At each level, there are different actors, which are discussed in greater detail in Chapter 4. These actors have been multiplying in recent years with the growth in the number of nongovernmental organizations (NGOs), charitable foundations, and private-public partnerships. The key thing to remember is that the catalysts for cooperation are not always countries at the global, regional, and transnational levels. For example, the Gates Foundation is trying to address a cure for and more effective controls of malaria, which adversely impacts people in tropical developing countries. Additionally, infrastructure requirements differ at each level, as do the impediments to and promoters of cooperation.

WHY IS THE NEED FOR TRANSNATIONAL COLLECTIVE ACTION INCREASING?

Transnational spillovers are easier to spot given advances in remote sensing and terrestrial monitoring technology. Thus, the spread of deserts, pollutants, diseases, pests, and deforestation can be readily tracked. Advancements in social media allow for the tracking of ideas and revolutionary rhetoric among countries. The need for transnational cooperation is also fostered by the breakup of countries following World War II. As a consequence, country-level problems became international concerns—for example, the Czech Republic and Slovakia generated benefit and cost spillovers for one another after the breakup of Czechoslovakia. The dissolution of the Soviet Union resulted in myriad transfrontier interdependencies after the breakup that had been internal to the Soviet Union prior to the breakup.

Technology also drives transnational dependencies and the need for transnational collective action. Consider the creation of chlorofluorocarbons (CFCs) as a refrigerant and cleansing agent. This substance is blamed for creating a hole in the stratospheric ozone layer, which protects life on the planet from harmful ultraviolet radiation.[7] Technology also gave us personal computers and the Internet, which are now vulnerable to computer viruses and worms, control of which has transnational implications. When applied to agriculture, technology was behind the Green Revolution, which not only increased crop yields but also insidious pollutants that befouled the air, atmosphere, rivers, lakes, and groundwater. Advances in communication—another technology-driven outcome—bolster the dissemination of scientific and medical breakthroughs worldwide. Technological advances in air travel promote commercial, social, and other global and regional ties, while allowing deadly diseases to be disseminated near and far in a matter of days. The Ebola outbreak in 2014 serves as a graphic example. Technology will play a huge role in future collective action by bringing down the cost of collaboration—just think about Skype, which allows for face-to-face global communication among scholars.

In 2012, the population on Earth surpassed the seven billion mark. Population growth also drives transnational spillovers and the need for transnational collective action to address the disposal of wastes, the transmission of diseases, the growth of poverty, and the stresses on the planet's ecosphere. The heating of the atmosphere from greenhouse gases is one of the most worrying manifestations of this seemingly unchecked population expansion. Quite simply, increases in population create pollutants that surpass the *carrying capacity* of various environments to absorb pollutants without adverse consequences. These pollutants do not respect political boundaries, thereby imposing transnational externalities on other countries. Population growth will result in greater demands being made on finite resources, such as drinking water, in some parts of the world. These demands on limited resources can erupt in conflicts, which generate their own cross-border consequences in the form of refugees, disruption to resource flows, heightened uncertainty, collateral damage, and rebel activities. To resolve such externalities, transnational and even global (for example, UN peacekeeping) collective action may be mandated.

Globalization may also motivate an enhanced need for transnational cooperation. In essence, globalization primarily manifests itself in terms of increased cross-border trade and financial capital flows. Enhanced

---

7. The relationship between CFCs and ozone shield depletion was addressed in Benedick (1991), Congleton (1992), de Gruijl (1995), and Murdoch and Sandler (1997).

exchanges among countries may be intended or unintended in today's globalized economies. The exchange of final goods, resources, and services is intended, while the exchange of computer viruses or financial crises is unintended. The linkage of countries through commerce, technology, communication, and transportation means that countries are more susceptible to transnational externalities, which may, at times, require collaborative actions of two of more countries to assuage. For example, the staging of terrorist attacks in foreign capitals to capture headlines means that venue countries, where the attacks occur, are drawn into the affairs of other countries. These venue countries may be motivated to work with countries hosting the terrorists in order to eradicate the group. Another example involves more integrated capital markets resulting in financial crises at times being exported abroad, as in the 2008 U.S. financial crisis.

Regionalism characterizes greater exchanges among a more localized set of countries, which, as in the case of globalization, may result in more externalities and the need for transnational cooperation. Given spatial propinquity, regionalism may be a more efficient engine for generating cross-country externalities. Nearby countries share watersheds, airsheds, river basins, forests, mountain ranges, and other natural conveyors of externalities. At the regional level, economies can be more susceptible to externalities than would be true of more spatially disperse countries, none of which possesses a major economy. Spatial proximity may unite countries through cultural and historical ties, thereby promoting externalities.

TRANSNATIONAL COOPERATION: WHAT IS AND IS NOT POSSIBLE?

There are some simple intuitive rules of thumb with respect to the feasibility of transnational cooperation. First, countries are more willing to cooperate when confronted with challenges with dire consequences. If a new deadly plague threatens humans, countries will be quick to try to pool research facilities and talent to ameliorate the threat. This is particularly true if the disease affects both rich and poor countries alike. Second, countries must understand a problem before joining others to take decisive collective action. If sufficient uncertainty surrounds a transnational contingency, countries will likely wait until this uncertainty is resolved before committing themselves to a costly path of action that may be difficult to change at a later date. The Montreal Protocol on protecting the ozone layer came into existence shortly after the hole in the ozone layer was discovered and scientists established an indisputable link between CFCs emissions and ozone shield depletion.[8] As more knowledge about ozone depleters was obtained, other ozone-shield-depleting chemical substances were banned or restricted. Third, countries are more inclined to form loosely tied local and regional collectives than tightly linked global collectives. For example, NATO allies must be unanimous on key decisions; unanimity maintains an ally's autonomy on security commitments that really matter.[9] This unanimity decision rule keeps NATO loose, because any ally can block a distasteful policy unless duly compensated. If large collectives are needed to address a problem with spatially dispersed consequences, then multiple regional collectives can forge loose linkages through networks—see Chapter 4. Fourth, bilateral agreements are common, especially between contiguous countries or trading partners. Agreements between just two countries generally have less negotiation costs than agreements among a larger number of countries. These smaller negotiation costs bolster finding a consensus. With more countries, each can hold out for some benefits or concessions in the agreement, which then delays framing and ratification. Fifth, regional development banks and multilateral institutions (for example, the World Bank) can facilitate collective action at the regional and global levels, respectively. Customs unions, which promote trade within partners, can also foster collective action with respect to regional concerns.

Countries are loath to enter tight linkages, except for important exigencies, such as pending war or an environmental catastrophe. We do not envision a single global state or a tightly knit federation like that in *Star Trek* because countries place a huge value on their autonomy.[10] Moderately tight regional collectives, such as the EU, have been plagued by difficulties as countries have had to regulate autonomy over important fiscal decisions due to mandates issued by the collectives. In recent years, citizens of debt-ridden EU countries have rioted over stringent public-spending directives coming from the EU. We also believe that countries can no longer behave in a natural anarchic state devoid of agreed-upon standards of behavior. This is clearly rectified by international infrastructure that facilitates exchange. International transportation and communication networks have had to address a number of collective action concerns—maintenance of system interoperability, avoidance of accidents and mishaps, definition of jurisdictional rights, and promotion of competitive practices.[11] In international shipping, the International Maritime Organization oversees international trade and

8. See Benedick (1991) on the politics associated with the Montreal Protocol on protecting the ozone layer.

9. For a detailed description of the institutional structure of NATO, see Sandler and Hartley (1999).

10. The importance of autonomy was discussed in Sandler (2004) and Sandler and Cauley (1977).

11. Zacher (1996) is an excellent source on these collective agreements.

mandates conventions regarding accident avoidance, innocent passage, pollution, and other issues. Civil aviation is regulated by the International Civil Aviation Organization, which, among other regulations, makes pilots communicate in English. The International Telecommunication Union (ITU) allocates frequency bands of the electromagnetic spectrum to various specific purposes and institutes rules to limit interference. Interoperability is also bolstered by ITU rules that require the adoption of standardized equipment.

Countries abide by these international regulatory bodies because countries gain greatly in terms of safety, convenience, and commerce. The adoption of behavioral standards augments international exchanges, communications, transportation, and interactions, with relatively little sacrifice of autonomy. Even before these international regimes, countries already had similar regulations at home (for example, allocation of electromagnetic bandwidth for emergency and other uses), so that universal standards did not mean much departure from the status quo. Such conventions really impacted the behavior of firms and individuals, while paving the way for larger gross national product, which benefits countries agreeing to these regimes. In fact, such regimes freed participating governments from having to institute their own standards and altering them over time. Technological advances in communication and transportation require the updating of such regimes periodically. The relative ease by which these regimes came into being readily illustrates that collective action, even at the global level, is possible. Another example of successful global collective action is the eradication of smallpox in 1979 after vaccination achieved herd immunity, whereby new cases among unvaccinated individuals stay in check.

FACTORS PROMOTING TRANSNATIONAL COLLECTIVE ACTION

Drawing from the seminal work of Mancur Olson (1965) on collective action, we can identify facilitators and inhibitors of collective action. This action is usually easier to achieve among a small number of agents, which likely explains the plethora of bilateral agreements. Although small numbers facilitate collective action, such numbers are not sufficient for successful results. In Chapter 2, we shall investigate the Prisoners' Dilemma, in which even two agents fail to achieve an ideal outcome owing to perverse incentives. Another rule of thumb is that like-minded countries with similar means are more apt to work collectively to address a common problem. Homogeneous tastes among countries dictate that individual countries will view the associated benefits and costs from acting collectively in the same manner. When countries possess similar means, they are less inclined to try to shift the burden to the richer countries, since there are no such countries in the set that is contemplating action. This attempt to shirk among countries of diverse incomes may keep any country from acting, unless the net gain from taking the initiative alone is positive, in which case a country then "privileges" the others with the required actions. During the early years of the Cold War, the U.S. nuclear deterrent kept the Soviet Union from expanding further westward and, in so doing, single-handedly kept Western Europe free.

Selective incentives, in which countries obtain some country-specific benefits from collective action, can motivate participation, especially when these gains cannot be achieved independent of the collective action. Tied foreign aid can provide donor-specific benefits (for example, an agreement for the donor's military bases in the aid-recipient country), while helping the world to eliminate some abject poverty. Institutional rules can, in fact, bolster collective action by offering selective incentives—for example, donor-specific recognition given to donors who give an amount beyond some institutionally imposed threshold. Recurring transactions among countries can also foster collective action as countries come to depend upon one another, while forging trust. In a similar vein, past collective action may promote future collective action. Thus, countries linked by security relationships, such as alliances, are apt to work together on environmental and other problems. Collective action is also bolstered if payoffs are immediate and certain. If countries must wait decades for a payback, then collective action is less likely to ensue. This follows because a certain amount of money is worth more today than the same amount decades into the future, so tomorrow's paybacks must be much larger than today's payout or costs to warrant action today. We have earlier indicated that uncertainty inhibits collective action, which is also true of uncertain benefits. Obviously, large payoffs from collective action promote such action when costs are modest. Finally, the presence of a leader country that plays a major role in the contingency is a favorable catalyst for collective action in terms of leading by example.

PAIRED COMPARISONS

A unique feature of this book is its use of paired comparisons as a learning device for clarifying the subtleties of collective action successes and failures. The rough rules of thumb for success, listed in the previous section, are not always predictive of the prognosis for transnational collective action. Consider the cases of ozone shield depletion and climate change.[12] Both problems impact every country and require collective action on the part of many heterogeneous countries. In addition, both issues can result in catastrophic consequences if left unchecked. Despite these similarities, the world has

12. These two issues are addressed in Chapter 12. Also see Barrett (1999) and Sandler (2004).

made great strides in addressing ozone shield depletion by limiting the production and consumption of ozone-shield depleters, while the world has achieved little success thus far in curbing greenhouse gas emissions. Carbon dioxide continues to accumulate relatively unabated in the atmosphere. What subtle considerations distinguish these two collective action concerns? This is addressed in Chapter 12.

There are many other such paired comparisons throughout the book. Why was smallpox eradicated in 1979, while polio still poses a threat? We will learn in Chapter 6 that the answer rests on differences in herd immunity, the role of conflict, and the type of polio vaccine being used. Other paired comparisons include the following: Why is sulfur-based acid rain a more difficult regional collective concern to address than nitrogen-based acid rain?[13] Why are volatile organic compounds (VOCs) more difficult regional pollutants to control than either type of acid rain? In addition, why does financial capital flow more freely than trade, when both flows can make all participating countries better off? Why are infectious diseases more difficult to address than noninfectious diseases, when the former diseases pose the greater threat of negative transnational spillovers? What are the similarities and differences between fighting international crime and curbing transnational terrorism? Both issues require a huge amount of international cooperation in terms of sharing information, pooling law enforcement resources, coordinating border control, and allowing extradition. Do failed states (for example, Somalia) present a greater threat to global security than rogue states (for example, North Korea)? In this regard, why has the world united against some externalities from failed states, such as piracy, but been much less united against some externalities from rogue states, such as nuclear proliferation? Answers to such questions would provide much insight into the promotion of world security.

These are a small sampling of paired comparisons that can teach us much about transnational cooperation. Another comparison is between regional and global collective action. Even though regional collective action involves fewer countries than global collective action, the latter can for some contingencies face a better prognosis. Yet another paired comparison concerns domestic and transnational terrorism.

ORIENTATION OF THE BOOK

This book presents an analysis of transnational cooperation or collective action that stresses basic concepts and intuition. Unlike other books on

---

13. Murdoch, Sandler, and Sargent (1997) analyzed the underlying collective action differences between these two types of acid rain.

similar topics, we ground our analysis in a solid game-theoretic foundation, in which rational actors maximize (minimize) desirable (undesirable) outcomes, subject to constraints. We do not judge rationality based on the desirability of the objectives pursued; thus, we consider terrorists, who account for their constraints appropriately, as rational even though we do not condone the killing of innocent people to achieve a political goal. Rationality results in predictable behavior. Game theory reminds us that these rational actors must account for the responses by other rational actors. Game theory concerns *strategic rational action*,[14] where each agent (player) tries to second-guess the response of its allies or adversaries. Over the last decades, game theory has assumed a large role in the analysis of international interactions in economics and political science.

Our game theory presentation is at an elementary level that presumes no previous game-theoretic exposure by the reader. We are interested in basic concepts, such as the key components of a game (that is, the players, the available actions, and the associated payoffs) and the notion of equilibrium. At equilibrium, no player wants to choose a different strategy or action if given the opportunity to do so. We rely on games in normal or matrix form for two or more players. In the latter case, we often assume identical players, which may be countries, to display the game's underlying implications without unnecessary complexity. Our presentation is almost devoid of mathematics, except for some elementary algebra. We relate a variety of game forms to collective action concerns. While the famous Prisoners' Dilemma is germane to numerous transnational collective action dilemmas, many other types of games are more descriptive of other action impediments.

The book is aimed primarily at lower- and upper-level undergraduates. We keep the language nontechnical to appeal to freshmen and sophomores. Important terms are carefully introduced and illustrated. Throughout the book, we rely on myriad examples that are relevant in today's world. These examples involve international trade and finance, the environment, health, sovereignty, leadership, crime, and political violence.

This book should also appeal to graduate students interested in real-world examples. Our analysis draws many comparisons and contrasts among diverse collective action concerns, which enable graduate students to identify issues worthy of future research and dissertations. The book will interest not only policy makers, but also practitioners concerned with foreign aid, global health, security, and other problems. People working at multilateral institutions and NGOs should find the book enlightening.

Given its breadth of topics, the book is relevant to many disciplines, including political science, economics, public policy, social science, and law.

---

14. Our characterization of game theory agrees with that of Dixit, Skeath, and Reiley (2009), which is an excellent introduction to game theory.

Within economics, it has much to say on topics relevant to public economics, institutional economics, international trade, public choice, environmental economics, defense economics, urban economics, regional studies, and international finance. In political science, topics contained herein are germane to world politics, international organizations, international relations, security studies, and international political economy.

PLAN OF THE BOOK

The remainder of the book contains 12 chapters. Chapters 2 through 4 contain the theoretical foundation, with Chapter 2 devoted to an introduction of game theory applied to collective action. Chapter 3 introduces market failures—public goods, externalities, common property, and asymmetric information—and their role in the need for international cooperation to correct inefficient resource allocation. In Chapter 4, the notions of subsidiarity and jurisdictional responsibility are investigated. In so doing, we contrast and compare globalization, regionalism, and transnationalism. This chapter also introduces the key agents or players at the transnational level.

In the second part of the book, we investigate many issues using the theoretical framework of the first part of the book. Chapter 5 considers sovereignty, leadership, and U.S. hegemony. Although sovereignty works against collective action as countries stubbornly cling to their autonomy, leadership promotes collective action as countries set an example for others. It is essential that key countries are the leaders if successful collective action is to result. This was the case in banning ozone depleters, because the primary producing and consuming countries led the offensive. Chapter 6 considers foreign aid and global health as two separate but interrelated topics. These issues are intertwined, in part, because the populations of poor countries provide ideal hosts to pathogens. Moreover, health concerns hold back development regardless of the amount of aid. In Chapter 7, we present the case for free trade as a public good and the need for collective action solutions to the commitment problem surrounding protectionism. Various attempts, both successful and unsuccessful, to limit trade barriers are addressed. In Chapter 8, international financial crises are discussed, along with measures, such as the three Basel Capital Accords, to inhibit future crises. Essential linkages between trade and capital flows are examined. The roles of key institutions—the International Monetary Fund (IMF) and central banks in major economic powers—are analyzed with respect to promoting financial stability.

The next three chapters investigate the darker side of globalization and regionalism. Chapter 9 concerns international crime, which is partly tied to enhanced transactions, communications, and transportation. This chapter focuses on drug trafficking and money laundering as our paired comparison.

The International Criminal Police Organization (INTERPOL) and other multilateral institutions have an important role to play in coordinating collective action in fighting international crime and terrorism. In Chapter 10, we consider political violence in myriad forms—terrorism, insurgencies, revolutions, and civil wars. Important comparisons and contrasts among these forms of political violence are drawn, especially in regard to the efficacy and possibility of transnational cooperation. Chapter 11 investigates rogue and failed states and their role in piracy, hosting terrorist groups, and nuclear proliferation. These problems are some of the most difficult to address through international cooperation.

Chapter 12 considers environmental contingencies and the record with respect to collective action. This action has taken the form of international treaties. Global, regional, and bilateral environmental problems and their prognoses are investigated. Many interesting paired comparisons are put forward.

In Chapter 13, we conclude by considering recent attempts to prioritize global challenges. With limited international resources to combat global crises, the world needs some sort of prioritization. Our prioritization comparison relies on international public opinion surveys, the UN Millennium Development Goals, and past Copenhagen Consensus.[15] We highlight the many difficulties associated with such a counterfactual thought-experiment, which hinges on what would happen in the absence of action. We then argue that collective action theory provides a means of prioritizing by going after crucial problems with poor collective action prognoses. We conclude the chapter with scenarios of the future of global politics, focusing on different groups of actors and their ability to push and pull states and international government organizations (IGOs) to act.

15. The challenges were prioritized for 2008 in Lomborg (2009).

CHAPTER 2

Principles of Collective Action and Game Theory

A s indicated in Chapter 1, collective action arises when the efforts of two or more agents are needed to achieve an outcome that cannot be accomplished through independent actions. Agents may be individuals, organizations, countries, multinational firms, or some other entities. For instance, a trade boycott to punish a country for state-sponsored terrorism or nuclear weapons proliferation requires the collective efforts of most countries to succeed. Even a few key defector countries that supply the boycotted country's needs can severely limit the effectiveness of the boycott. This is a real concern because defectors can amass large profits by breaking the boycott. A similar example is action by the global community to eliminate safe havens for a terrorist group, since even one defector country that provides such a haven can greatly compromise the actions of all other countries.[1] As a general rule, collective action that calls for wide participation is more challenging to attain than such action on the part of fewer states. This general principle is valid in many, but not all, situations. For example, some forms of global collective action can be fostered by multilateral institutions, such as the United Nations and the World Bank, that possess the requisite infrastructure and membership to promote cooperation on a global scale. In special instances, an action with global benefits can be achieved through the efforts of one country that has a huge stake in the sought-after outcome. Thus, the United States supports its Centers for Disease Control (CDC) to monitor disease outbreaks and identify new pathogens in order to safeguard U.S. citizens at home and abroad.[2]

---

1. Lee (1988) discussed this type of problem under the guise of paid riding.
2. On the CDC, see Sandler and Arce (2002) and Sonntag (2010).

In many cases, the need for collective action is tied to the provision of pure public goods, whose benefits are nonrival *and* nonexcludable. A good's benefits are *nonrival* when a unit of the good can be consumed by one individual without detracting in the slightest from the consumption opportunities still available for other individuals from the same unit. If sulfur pollution is reduced within the vicinity of a city, then everyone within this environment benefits from the cleaner air. One person's breathing the cleaner air does not diminish the experience of others who breathe the improved air. If a country manages through missile launches or a spaceship tug to divert the approach of an earthbound asteroid that would have wreaked widespread havoc and destruction, then all would-be impacted countries would experience nonrival benefits. The tracking of hurricanes provides nonrival benefits to everyone in the storm's path as protective measures are taken. At times, nonrival benefits are equated conceptually with *zero* additional (marginal) cost in extending consumption of the good to another user. For the diverted asteroid, there is no additional cost associated with the diversion for larger populations in its destructive path. The second characteristic of a pure public good is *nonexcludability* where, once provided, the public good's benefits are available to payers and nonpayers alike. Reducing pollution and diverting an asteroid offer nonexcludable benefits, while the tracking of hurricanes provides excludable benefits. The latter follows because the country launching the satellite can withhold data from other countries.

Nonexcludability results in free riding as potential users wait for others to provide the good, whose benefits they can then consume free of charge. Nonrival benefits mean that exclusion is not warranted, because exclusion reduces social well-being by denying consumption opportunities to potential consumers who derive a positive benefit at no costs to society, once the good is provided. The dilemma for society is then how to provide a pure public good if the provider cannot recoup its costs by charging a price. In some cases, government provision, financed by taxes, may be an option for a public good, whose benefits stay within the country's territory. For international or transnational public goods, sovereign governments may need to cooperate to provide such goods, whose benefits are nonexcludable and nonrival to two or more countries. Since the publication of Mancur Olson's (1965) *The Logic of Collective Action*, the provision of public goods epitomizes the collective action problem. In fact, public good provision is just one type of collective action concern; others involve externalities (uncompensated interdependencies within and among countries), common property, and other market failures (see Chapter 3).

Pure public goods differ fundamentally from private goods, whose benefits are excludable and completely rival among users. As such, private goods can be exchanged through markets as prices equate the quantity demanded with the quantity supplied. An individual's consumption of a unit of a private good exhausts the consumption opportunities of that unit. Moreover, the enforcement of property rights eliminates the possibility of a free ride. Unless the private good generates harmful or beneficial effects on others and no compensation is paid, there is no need for collective action for these goods.

The provision of a pure public good demonstrates that *individual rationality is not sufficient for collective rationality.* That is, rational individuals[3] may provide a deficient level of the public good. Problems are magnified when the individuals are powerless to improve this inefficient outcome owing to perverse incentives, as we will see when we relate the provision of public goods to the Prisoners' Dilemma game. For public goods and other collective action concerns, one agent's choice is tied to those of other agents, which is why game theory becomes germane. That is, how much one person wants to contribute to a public good depends on how much others contribute because all consume the same amount, given nonrivalry and nonexcludability of benefits.

[margin handwritten note: Contrary to the expected]

INTRODUCING GAME THEORY

"Game theory is the science of rational behavior in interactive situations" (Dixit, Skeath, and Reiley, 2009, p. 5). As a consequence, game theory assumes that a player maximizes an objective—say, utility—subject to constraints that include the anticipated actions of the other player(s). In a noninteractive situation, a consumer decides how to spend his/her income on two private goods so as to get the highest satisfaction level. In this standard problem, the objective is utility and the constraint is the budget constraint, where income equals the expenditure on the two private goods whose prices are given. This consumer problem involves no game theory because the individual's choice is not affected by the choices of other individuals in an explicit interactive framework. Although determined by the actions of all buyers and sellers, competitive market prices are fixed or outside of the control of a single individual; that is, the influence of a single buyer or seller on the market price is negligible. Next, suppose that the individual is purchasing a private good *and* a pure public good at fixed prices. The purchase of the public good by others then affects the individual's choices. Moreover, the individual's own choice of the purchase of the public good impacts how much the other individuals will

---

3. In economics, individual rationality rests on four basic tenets. First, more of a good is desired to less. Second, tastes are consistent—that is, an individual, who prefers basket A to basket B and also prefers basket B to basket C, must then prefer basket A to basket C. Third, all baskets can be ranked one to another. Fourth, an individual maximizes his/her utility subject to a budget constraint, where expenditures equal income.

choose to provide. The purchase of a public good is, thus, an interactive situation that involves game theory. This is true for a two-country military alliance, such as the Israeli-US alliance, where each country's military choices are not independent of those of its ally.

There are four identifying characteristics of a noncooperative game, in which players act independently.[4] First, the set of players must be specified, which for the North Atlantic Treaty Organization (NATO) includes the 28 current allies. Second, the strategy sets, one for each player, must be identified. For alliances, this can be the military expenditure decision of each ally. When contemplating a trade boycott, each potential participating country possesses two strategic actions: join or do not join the boycott. Third, the resulting payoffs for the players' strategic combinations must be ascertained based on some payoff formula. Fourth, a behavioral assumption is needed that maintains the assumed rationality of the players. Rational players' behavior are predictable. These four ingredients are the "rules of the game," which also encompasses such things as the order of plays—sequential or simultaneous—which is part of the strategy sets.

A final distinction is between cooperative and noncooperative games. A noncooperative game has each player acting on his/her own. In contrast, cooperative game theory involves players acting in unison as a coalition to maximize some joint gain that is subsequently divided among coalition members. The devil is in the details because how to divide the collective gain is never clear and can be done in various ways. Even though this book is about transnational cooperation, we rely exclusively on noncooperative game theory for a number of reasons. First, all cooperative games can be expressed as a noncooperative game. Second, a noncooperative game can encompass cooperative or mutually beneficial outcomes along with mutually deficient outcomes. Third, by eschewing cooperative games, we do not have to impose a payoff division assumption that can always be subject to question. Fourth, countries cherish their sovereignty and rarely form tight, enforceable ties with other countries that allow the collective to act as one, as required by cooperative game. For example, NATO allies must vote unanimously on key policies (for example, membership expansion or changes in military doctrine), thereby effectively preserving members' sovereignty.[5] As such, NATO is a loose alliance because allies can block undesirable policy changes or decisions. Fifth, cooperative games require a good deal of algebra, which we can avoid by staying with a noncooperative game representation.

---

4. For more in-depth treatments of game theory, the reader should consult Binmore (1992), Dixit, Skeath, and Reiley (2009), and Watson (2002).
5. On the structure of the NATO alliance, see Sandler and Hartley (1999).

We illustrate most of our collective action games in terms of a matrix, accounting for the players, their strategic choices, and each strategic combination's payoffs. Often, we strip the game down to two players, each of whom possesses just two possible strategic moves. When this is done, the game can be fully illustrated by a 2×2 matrix. This matrix representation is also called the normal or strategic form of the game. If the payoffs are ranked or ordinally displayed for each player, where 4 is assigned to the greatest payoff, 3 to the next largest payoff, 2 to the second smallest payoff, and 1 to the smallest payoff, then there are 78 distinct 2×2 game forms.[6] Despite all of these distinct games, the lion's share of attention in international relations has been focused on the Prisoners' Dilemma, to which we now turn.

PRISONERS' DILEMMA

We illustrate the Prisoners' Dilemma as a two-country—A and B—public good contribution game. Each country can either contribute nothing or else one unit to the public good, whose benefits are experienced by both nation-states. To compute the payoffs associated with the four strategic combinations, we must indicate the benefits and costs associated with the contributions to the public good. Suppose that each unit of the good costs the ith contributor 10, denoted by $c_i = 10$. Further suppose that each unit contributed gives 7 in benefits ($b_i = 7$) to both players, regardless of the contributor, owing to nonexclusion and nonrivalry of benefits. The resulting payoffs are displayed in matrix a in the upper portion of Figure 2.1. The left-hand payoff in each cell is that of country A, whereas the right-hand payoff in each cell is that of country B. Country A is termed the row player, while country B is called the column player, so that the two rows represent A's strategies and the two columns denote B's strategies.

When no one contributes, there are no benefits or costs, so that payoffs are 0 to both countries, as displayed in the upper left-hand cell in matrix a in Figure 2.1. If country B contributes alone, then B nets -3 ($= 7 - 10$) as provision costs of 10 are deducted from B's derived benefits of 7, while country A gets a free ride worth 7 in the upper right-hand cell in matrix a. When roles are interchanged, so that A contributes a unit of the public good and B free rides, the payoffs are reversed in the lower left-hand cell in matrix a. Finally, if both countries contribute a unit, then each receives 4 $\left[= (2 \times 7) - 10 \right]$ as aggregate benefits of 14, gained by each country from the two contributed units, are reduced by each country's provision costs of 10. If we compare the corresponding payoffs in the first row for country A with those for A in the second

---

6. This is established in an important article by Rapoport and Guyer (1966).

a. Contribution Prisoners' Dilemma, $b_i = 7$, $c_i = 10$

	B Do Not Contribute	B Contribute
A Do Not Contribute	Nash 0, 0	7, −3
A Contribute	−3, 7	4, 4

	B Do Not Contribute	B Contribute
A Do Not Contribute	Nash 2, 2	4, 1
A Contribute	1, 4	3, 3

b. Ordinal representation of Prisoners' Dilemma

Figure 2.1
Prisoners' Dilemma

row, then A has an obvious choice to contribute nothing, insofar as the associated payoffs are larger than those for contributing a unit. That is, 0 is a larger payoff than −3, and 7 is a larger payoff than 4. Similarly, the logical strategy for B is also not to contribute, given the symmetry of the game. We say that each country has a *dominant strategy* not to contribute, because this strategy provides a higher payoff regardless of the other player's choice. From, say, A's viewpoint, its payoff is greater by not contributing regardless of which column is chosen by B. In matrix a, both countries' dominant strategy is not to contribute. Rationality predicts that a player will seize its dominant strategy and eschew a *dominated strategy* that provides a smaller payoff for each of the other player's choices. In matrix a, contributing is the dominated strategy.

The mutual no-contribution strategy combination in matrix a is a *Nash equilibrium from which neither player would unilaterally alter its strategy* if given the opportunity. If, at this equilibrium in matrix a, country A (or B) alone changes to contributing a unit, then A's (B's) payoff is reduced from 0 to −3. Alternatively, a Nash equilibrium can be described as each player selecting its best response to the other player's best response. In a Prisoners' Dilemma, the best responses are the dominant strategies, whose mutual use results in the Nash equilibrium.[7] This Nash equilibrium is deficient since mutual contributions would make both players better off; hence, a Prisoners' Dilemma results in a collective action failure at its Nash equilibrium.[8] Moreover, individual rationality of playing one's dominant strategy results in this collective action failure. At the Nash equilibrium, both players regret their independent actions. If the players could agree to cooperate and contribute, then both would be better off by 4 over the Nash equilibrium. However, at the mutual contributions outcome, each would be tempted to stop contributing unilaterally—renege on its agreement—to seek the largest payoff of 7. These are the perverse incentives that were mentioned earlier.

To display the hallmark of the Prisoners' Dilemma, we convert the cardinal payoffs in matrix *a* to the corresponding ordinal payoffs in matrix *b* in Figure 2.1. Thus, the payoff of 7 is assigned an ordinal rank of 4, the second-best payoff is given an ordinal rank of 3, the third-best is assigned an ordinal rank of 2, and the smallest payoff is given an ordinal rank of 1. This transformation of payoffs results in matrix *b*, which preserves not only the dominant strategy (since 2 > 1 and 4 > 3), but also the Nash equilibrium. Only one of the 78 possible 2 × 2 ordinal games has this precise form.[9]

Before we take up the *n*-player version of the Prisoners' Dilemma, it is instructive to review this game, which received its name from the great mathematician, Albert Tucker. Tucker envisioned two individuals who are apprehended near the scene of an armed robbery, which carries a maximum prison sentence of 20 years. A search of the suspects' car turns up an unregistered handgun, which carries a prison sentence of two years. The state has no reliable eyewitness to place the suspects at the crime, so conviction depends on one of the prisoners confessing to the crime. The district attorney separates the suspects and offers them the following deal: if one of them confesses, then the confessor gets no jail time and the other suspect gets the maximum 20-year sentence. If, however, both confess, they each receive a reduced 10-year sentence. Thus, the strategy set includes *not confess* and *confess*. In a 2 × 2 matrix, confess is analogous to the not contribute (noncooperative)

7. The intersection of dominant strategies, if one exists for each player, yields a Nash equilibrium, but a Nash equilibrium need not be the intersection of dominant strategies. In fact, a 2 × 2 normal-form game can have a Nash equilibrium without either player possessing a dominant strategy, as will be true for the chicken game, which we encounter later.

8. The mutual contributions payoffs are said to Pareto dominate the no-contribution outcome given that the well-being of both players improves when both contribute compared to when neither contributes.

9. If the two strategies were interchanged in the rows and columns, then the distinguishing feature of the Prisoners' Dilemma would have the (3, 3) and (2, 2) payoffs switched along the main diagonal and the 1s and 4s interchanged along the off-diagonal. This alternative array of payoffs still identifies the Prisoners' Dilemma.

strategy, while not confess is analogous to the contribute (cooperative) strategy. Given these payoffs, it is then easy to show that matrix *b* applies when confess is substituted for do not contribute and do not confess is substituted for contribute. The dominant strategy is to confess even if both are guiltless of the robbery owing to the perverse incentives manufactured by the clever district attorney.

The Prisoners' Dilemma characterizes many two-country collective action concerns. Examples include the arms race between the United States and the Soviet Union during the Cold War, which is later discussed. Another example involves two countries confronted with a third country that sponsors terrorism directed at the two countries. Each targeted country would prefer that the other targeted country retaliates against the state sponsor, since the free-rider country gains some benefits without putting its own soldiers in harm's way. The state sponsor would sustain the most damage if both targeted countries joined in the punitive attack, which makes the state sponsor end its sponsorship. An attack by only one targeted country may be insufficient for this outcome, but will direct future attacks to the retaliator country. No retaliation by either targeted country results in the state sponsor carrying on as usual so that each country has the risk of future attacks. In this scenario, the free-rider country gets the largest ordinal payoff, followed by the payoff associated with mutual retaliation, where both retaliators must sustain costs to get the benefits. The sole retaliator receives the smallest ordinal payoff because the terrorist threat is not fully eliminated and will be solely redirected at the retaliator in the future. This was the situation when the United States sustained the 9/11 attacks, years after its retaliatory strike against al-Qaida in Afghanistan. The second-smallest ordinal payoff is tied to mutual nonretaliation. Thus, this scenario may possess the ordinal payoffs of matrix *b*, where "retaliate" replaces "contribute" and "do not retaliate" replaces "do not contribute" in matrix *b*. Pollution scenarios can also fit the Prisoners' Dilemma, as can many other two-country public good scenarios, such as punishing a rogue country, eradicating an infectious disease, or annihilating a common threat.

We now extend the analysis of the Prisoners' Dilemma to n players, where n may correspond to eight countries contemplating reducing emissions of their greenhouse gases (GHGs), which can trap solar energy in the atmosphere thereby warming the earth's climate. Each of the eight countries is viewed as having two strategies: cut GHG emissions by 15% or not cut GHG emissions by 15%. The latter means that the country takes no action to limit its emissions. Cutting emissions by 15% is assumed to yield 7 in benefits to the country taking action as well as to each of the other seven countries. This follows because reducing emissions is a pure public good with nonrival and nonexcludable benefits. Benefits are cumulative so that if three countries reduce emissions, then each country experiences 21 $(= 3 \times 7)$ in benefits. To cut its

	0	1	2	3	4	5	6	7
Country i Does Not Cut GHGs by 15%	Nash 0	7	14	21	28	35	42	49
Country i Does Cut GHGs by 15%	-3	4	11	18	25	32	39	Social Optimum 46

Figure 2.2
Eight-country Prisoners' Dilemma, $b_i = 7$, $c_i = 10$

GHG emissions costs a country 10. For simplicity, we assume that all countries are identical, facing the same $b_i = 7$ and $c_i = 10$. Even though our representation is highly stylized, it captures basic principles associated with such multiplayer contribution games.

In Figure 2.2, the columns refer to the actions of the other seven states, and the two rows denote the strategy of the ith representative state. The payoffs listed in each of the sixteen cells are those of country i, based on its emission reduction decision and those of the other countries. In the top row, country i does not curtail its GHG emissions and, thus, free rides on the actions of some or all of the other seven countries. If no country limits its carbon footprint, then country i receives no gain, indicative of no free ride. If, however, country i does not act but one country reduces its emissions, then country i gains 7 at no expense to itself. In the top row, every reducing country confers a benefit of 7 on country i, so that it receives 14 from two reducers, 21 from three reducers, and so on. Country i's maximum gain of 49 comes from its inactivity, coupled with seven other countries lowering their emissions. In the bottom row of Figure 2.2, country i cuts its emissions by 15%, with or

	0	1	2	3	4
Country i Does Not Cut GHGs by 15%	Nash 0	7	14	21	28
Country i Does Cut GHGs by 15%	-3	4	11	18	Social Optimum 25

Figure 2.3
Five-country Prisoners' Dilemma, $b_i = 7$, $c_i = 10$

without similar cuts from others. When country i limits emissions alone, it nets –3 as its costs of 10 overwhelms its benefits of 7. If country i's actions to cut emissions are joined by one other country, then country i gains 4, which equals its gross benefits of 14 ($= 2 \times 7$) less its own costs of 10. In computing gross benefits, we must remember that each reducing country confers 7 in benefits to the eight-country collective. The other net payoffs for country i in the bottom row are calculated in an analogous fashion, in which net payoffs equal 7 times the number of reducers (including country i) less 10 in costs.

The dominant strategy for this eight-country contribution game is for country i not to cut GHG emissions, insofar as the payoffs in the top row exceed the corresponding payoffs in the bottom row by 3, which is the difference between c_i and b_i. As country i and, thus, the other seven countries play their dominant strategy of not reducing GHG emissions, a Nash equilibrium results with no action whatsoever and a payoff of 0 to all eight countries. At this equilibrium, country i will not unilaterally switch to being a reducer because $0 > -3$. By symmetry, this is true for all the other seven countries. The social optimum corresponds to all eight countries cutting their emissions, thereby giving each country a net payoff of 46. The payoff of 49, where there are seven activist countries and one free rider, does not yield the social optimum with greatest aggregate payoff. At the true social optimum, the aggregate gain is 368 ($= 8 \times 46$). When, however, country i receives 49, the other seven countries each receive just 39 as each of these activist countries are joined by six other activist countries. In this scenario, the aggregate payoff is 322, which equals 49 plus 273 ($= 7 \times 39$).[10]

This game is representative of the climate change dilemma, as we will show in Chapter 12. Despite the Kyoto Protocol calling on countries to reduce GHG emissions, atmospheric accumulation of GHGs continues at an alarming rate (Biello, 2013). Another scenario involves countries contemplating punitive actions against a country that allegedly used chemical weapons on its own people. Other examples may include ending a foreign civil war, finding a cure for malaria, or keeping a rogue state from acquiring nuclear weapons. As the difference between c_i and b_i increases, the incentive to act decreases. A way forward may exist when countries are not symmetric and one or more countries view b_i as exceeding c_i, so as to act on everyone's behalf. But even this scenario may face insurmountable roadblocks if the free riders take actions to exacerbate the problem. For example, as a shared environment becomes cleaner, other

10. This game representation can accommodate any number of identical players. For n players, there must be $n-1$ columns to represent the actions of the countries other than i. If $c_i > b_i$, then the dominant strategy is to do nothing, resulting in a Nash equilibrium where no country acts. The social optimum involves all n countries acting for a per country gain of $nb_i - c_i$ and an aggregate gain of $n^2 b_i - nc_i$. Given that the Nash equilibrium is associated with an aggregate benefit of 0, we see that the deficiency of the Nash equilibrium increases with the group size for a pure public good, which is one of the tenets of collective action.

countries may increase their pollution, thereby offsetting some or all of the improvements.

What are some potential ways forward? One conceivable way would be to reward action by an amount greater than 3 $(= c_i - b_i)$ in Figure 2.2. If this reward is, say, 4, then every payoff in the bottom row will exceed the corresponding payoff in the top row by 1 (not displayed), thereby transforming cutting emissions into the dominant strategy. When this occurs, the social optimum with a payoff of 50 $(= 46 + 4)$ for country i is the Nash equilibrium, since $50 > 49$. An alternative means to accomplish this outcome would be to punish inaction by a penalty greater than 3, so that each payoff in the top row of the transformed Figure 2.2 (not displayed) becomes less than the corresponding payoff in the bottom row. Once again, country i and, hence, the other countries would cut emissions, so that the social optimum becomes the Nash equilibrium.

Unfortunately, each of these two "fixes" is beset with its own collective action problem. The reward solution to overcoming free riding begs the question because the presence of a reward mechanism acts like a pure public good, whose benefits are themselves nonexcludable and nonrival, thereby posing its own Prisoners' Dilemma. Moreover, some unspecified entity must come up with the 32 in payments to reward the eight countries. We note that this reward payment or bribe increases with the difference between c_i and b_i and with the number of countries. The punishment solution suffers from the need for an enforcer, who then privileges everyone with a free ride on the enforcement mechanism. North Korea's continual defiance of the Nuclear Nonproliferation Treaty has been met with universal condemnation, but no enforcer has taken effective action to date. Iran appears to be following the North Korean path to nuclear weapons. In the Iranian case, Israel and the United States may view their $b_i - c_i$ from independent action as positive and take decisive action if and when Iran's nuclear weapons development surpasses some threshold. Asymmetry or heterogeneity of gains may motivate enforcement in select situations.

It is instructive to reinvestigate the multi-country Prisoners' Dilemma of Figure 2.2 for a different size collective. This we do in Figure 2.3, where there are five identical countries, each of which gains 7 from independent action at a cost of 10. Country i's payoffs in the 10 cells match those in the corresponding cells in Figure 2.2. Moreover, an identical analysis finds the Nash equilibrium where no country acts and the social optimum where all countries must act. At this social optimum, the payoff to country i is 25 and the aggregate gain for the collective is 125. Hence, the shortfall or inefficiency of the Nash equilibrium is reduced to 125 from 368 when contrasting the five- and eight-country cases. This comparison highlights a general principle of collective action, first emphasized by Olson (1965), that the suboptimality of noncooperative behavior increases as the number of countries (agents) increases. This principle hinges on $c_i > b_i$ and symmetry of players.

COLLECTIVE ACTION AND PRISONERS' DILEMMA GAMES

What is the relationship between collective action and Prisoners' Dilemma games? Are they one and the same? The answer is important in understanding collective action and its role in international relations. This relationship has not always been expressed correctly in the literature. For example, Hardin (1982, p. 25) stated that "Indeed, the problem of collective action and the Prisoners' Dilemma are essentially the same."[11] I agree that every Prisoners' Dilemma gives rise to collective action failures, as seen in the last section. The rational pursuit of one's dominant strategy results in a Nash equilibrium with deficient payoffs for the collective.

It is the reverse statement—all collective action failures are Prisoners' Dilemmas—that is false. In fact, most collective action failures do not correspond to a Prisoners' Dilemma. To illustrate, consider a situation where each of two potential contributors—A and B—can supply one or no units of a pure public good; but, a minimal threshold of two units must be achieved before a benefit of 10 is received by both players. Contributing a unit costs 5. The situation is illustrated in the top matrix in Figure 2.4. The absence of contributions results in a payoff of 0 for players A and B. If just A or B contributes a unit, then the contributor suffers the cost of 5 without any gain for a net payoff of –5, while the noncontributor obtains no free-rider benefits, since the two-unit threshold has not been met. Finally, if both A and B contribute a unit of the public good, thereby meeting the threshold, then each receives a net payoff of 5 $(= 10 - 5)$. There is no dominant strategy, insofar as $0 > -5$, but $0 < 5$. There are, however, two Nash equilibria corresponding to the diagonal cells in matrix a,[12] where each player matches the other's strategy. Thus, both A and B either give no units or both give one unit. As always, neither player would unilaterally change strategy at the two Nash equilibria, since $0 > -5$ and $5 > 0$ for both players at the respective equilibria. This normal-form matrix is known as an *assurance* game, where each player wants to be assured that the other will contribute if he/she contributes. Without this assurance, a contribution would be wasted. In an international relations scenario, an assurance game would apply if two countries confront a common enemy that neither can defeat independently. However, the countries can defeat the enemy by pooling their forces. During the summer fire seasons, Western states in the United States must pool their firefighters to suppress the largest blazes, such as the 2013 Yosemite and Idaho fires. An assurance game may also correspond to two or more neighboring countries mounting sufficient effort against an invasive species.

11. Despite this erroneous statement, the Hardin (1982) book is excellent and is particularly useful in its extended discussion on conventions and norms.
12. These equilibria are known as pure-strategy equilibria, in which each player chooses a single strategy and does not randomize between strategies. There is also a mixed-strategy Nash equilibrium for this assurance game, which is beyond the scope of this elementary treatment.

B

A	0 units	1 unit
0 units	Nash 0, 0	0, –5
1 unit	–5, 0	Nash 5, 5

a. Assurance game – minimal threshold of 2 units

B

A	0 units	1 unit
0 units	0, 0	Nash 7, 4
1 unit	Nash 4, 7	4, 4

b. Coordination game – only first unit counts

B

A	0 units	1 unit
0 units	–4, –4	Nash 7, –3
1 unit	Nash –3, 7	4, 4

c. Chicken game, $b_i = 7$, $c_i = 10$

Figure 2.4
Some alternative game forms for collective action

likely course

The collective action prognosis for the assurance game is more hopeful than that for the Prisoners' Dilemma because one of the Nash equilibria is the social optimum.[13] Because there is no dominant strategy, the required coordination between the two players may not be achieved when both act simultaneously and independently. This quandary can be circumvented if one player assumes a leadership role and contributes. Once the other player sees this leadership, it is then in the follower's interest to contribute as well. To illustrate, consider the top matrix in Figure 2.4. Assume that A contributes a unit before B makes a decision. Then player B is induced to contribute because a payoff of 5 is better than the 0 payoff associated with not contributing. Quite simply, free riding is not a viable option. In the Prisoners' Dilemma, leadership in terms of contributing offers the smallest payoff to the leader; in Figure 2.1a, such a leadership role gives a net payoff of –3 to the leader as the other player free rides. In contrast to Prisoners' Dilemmas, the sequence of moves matters in an assurance game, where the leader provides incentives for the other player to mimic the displayed behavior. A would-be leader can demonstrate intent by assuming actions to bind oneself to a course of action. In a conflict situation, this signal of intent may take the form of amassing troops and weapons on the border of a country to be invaded. In an assurance game, a contract to contribute is self-enforcing or incentive compatible once one player initiates the agreed-upon action.

Next consider a different game in the middle matrix of Figure 2.4. For this *coordination game*, only the first unit of the public good supplied yields a benefit of 7 to both players at a cost of 3 to the contributor. If neither contributes, there are no gains; if, however, both players contribute, each nets 4 as unit costs of 3 must be paid by both. The second unit contributed results in wasted resources because this unit generates no additional benefits. This situation applies to uncovering intelligence, breaking a code, finding cures to diseases, discovering new medical practices, or infiltrating a criminal organization; once the task is accomplished, additional efforts provide no further gains. A dragon only needs to be slain once! In Chapter 3, this contribution situation is indicative of *best-shot public goods*. The displayed coordination game has no dominant strategy, but possesses two Nash equilibria on the off-diagonal, where one player contributes and the other free rides. Since both Nash equilibria are social optima, one might wonder why there may be a collective action failure. The required coordination may not ensue as players act independently; that is, both may wait for the other to act or both may act in unison. In the latter scenario, some resources are wasted. Thus, countries may duplicate efforts in uncovering intelligence or in infiltrating the same transnational criminal organization. The asymmetric payoffs at the Nash equilibria are at the

13. On assurance games, see Barrett (1994), Runge (1984), Sen (1967), and Sandler (1992, 1997, 1998).

heart of the potential coordination failure as one player sits back hoping that the other will act, thereby giving the player a greater payoff. Leadership can result in the requisite coordination.

Next suppose that there are 10 countries in a similar situation—for example, only a single country must act for every country to gain. Moreover, any contribution beyond the first unit results in wasteful duplication. The coordination problem involves more countries, and this may pose a greater collective action dilemma. In practice, this coordination is accomplished by relying on the most capable country to initiate action in a world with heterogeneous players (countries). In some peacekeeping missions, the largest share of the task has fallen on the nearest capable country. For example, Australia assumed a leadership role in UN peacekeeping mission in the Solomon Islands, Timor-Leste, and Bougainville, Papua New Guinea.

In the bottom matrix in Figure 2.4, the *chicken* version of the contribution game is displayed and serves as a useful paired comparison to the Prisoners' Dilemma. This underlying game assumes that each contributed unit gives 7 in benefits for both players at a cost of 10 for the contributor. The payoffs in matrix *c* of Figure 2.4 match those in matrix *a* of Figure 2.1, except for the no-contribution outcome in the upper left-hand cell. If no one contributes in chicken, then each player sustains a penalty of –4 in matrix *c* of Figure 2.4. Chicken requires the payoff for the no-contribution outcome to have the smallest ordinal payoff. These dire consequences can be avoided if someone acts. The game is named "chicken" because each player would like to hold out so that the other player acts (or "chickens out"). This chicken scenario may apply to the stockpiling of antidotes against a potential biological attack directed at two countries. The absence of any stockpiling can be disastrous for both countries. If one country acts alone and possesses sufficient antidotes for the exposed population, then the stockpiling country may still lose when provision costs outweigh the benefits. Another example can be two in-peril communities sandbagging against a pending flood, where the height of the sandbags is the quantity of the public good. Yet another example may be a tsunami early-warning system, where action is the deployment of monitors at sea. The more deployed monitors, the better the protection for both countries. No monitors spell disaster, while some monitors may be a savior for the free riders.

In the chicken game, there is no dominant strategy. There are two Nash equilibria on the off-diagonal, where the player that free rides gets the largest ranked payoff.[14] If a country assumes a leadership role and credibly signals no

---

14. The classic storyline has two cars driving directly towards one another from opposite directions. If neither swerves, then both die and sustain the lowest-ranked payoff. If one driver swerves (chickens out) and the other holds the course, then the swerver receives the second smallest payoff, while the intrepid driver obtains the largest-ranked payoff. If both drivers swerve, then each gain the second-best payoff because neither is braver than the other.

action, then it can secure the greatest payoff for itself. Unlike assurance where leadership requires action to obtain the large benefit, leadership necessitates inaction (not contributing) in chicken to obtain the large benefit. When *A* becomes the leader in matrix *c* and does not contribute, *B* has no choice but to contribute since a loss of 3 is preferred to a loss of 4. In an assurance game, leadership results in the social optimum, which is not necessarily the case in chicken. Unlike the Prisoners' Dilemma where leadership has no real effect, leadership in chicken avoids the worst outcome for both players.

Next, we consider two additional game forms that may describe some international relations scenarios and collective action concerns. In the top matrix of Figure 2.5, the ordinal representation of the *hero* game, also known as the *apology* game (Rapoport and Guyer, 1966), is displayed. Hero is a coordination game with no dominant strategy and two Nash equilibria on the off-diagonal. Both Nash equilibria are desirable; however, they provide a large payoff for the player *who does not act*. The actor is the "hero" since this player unselfishly

A \ *B*	Do Not Act	Act
Do Not Act	2, 2	Nash 4, 3
Act	Nash 3, 4	1, 1

a. Hero (Apology) game – ordinal form

A \ *B*	Do Not Act	Act
Do Not Act	2, 2	Nash 3, 4
Act	Nash 4, 3	1, 1

b. Benevolent chicken game – ordinal form

Figure 2.5
More alternative game forms

supplies a greater reward for the other player. A coordination failure can still ensue if both act simultaneously or neither acts. This pattern of payoffs is also applicable to issuing an apology, where the one who receives the apology is better off than the one who issues the apology. Both parties issuing apologies result in the worst outcome, followed by neither issuing apologies.[15] Hero can apply to a diplomatic row where one country can greatly improve the situation by issuing an official apology. In a conflict, an ally acknowledging friendly fire can be represented by a hero game, which applied to the second Gulf War involving U.S. and UK forces. In literature, O'Henry's short story, "Gift of the Magi," has the pattern of payoffs in the top matrix, where mutual gift giving resulted in the smallest payoffs being realized!

In matrix *b* in Figure 2.5, a *benevolent chicken* game in ordinal form is displayed, where the Nash equilibria are the social optima that can be achieved by leadership on the part of the player who acts alone. In contrast to hero, the acting player does best. If both players try to act simultaneously, then the smallest payoffs result in a collective action failure. Because the acting player gains relatively more, both players may try to lead with terrible consequences. Benevolent chicken may correspond to a pest infestation scenario, where unilateral aerial spraying helps both parties, with the greatest payoff to the player directing the spraying. If both players spray, then there is too much spraying with dire health consequences.

We conclude this section with the ordinal form of a game that has no Nash equilibrium involving the exclusive choice of one of two available strategies.[16] In Figure 2.6, the upper left-hand cell looks attractive, but row player *A* will act unilaterally to improve its payoff from 3 to 4. The lower left-hand cell is also not a Nash equilibrium because column player *B* will act unilaterally to move to the mutual-action cell in the lower right-hand corner. In this latter cell, row player *A* will stop its action to improve its payoff from 1 to 2. Finally, in the upper right-hand cell, *B* will unilaterally end its action so that we are back to where we began. There is an endless cycle with no strategic combination serving as a Nash equilibrium. There are many other configurations of 2×2 ordinal payoffs that result in no equilibrium. In such situations, leadership cannot achieve a desired outcome and collective action failure looms large.

These examples should suffice to emphasize that a wide variety of games are associated with potential collective action failures, thereby requiring some kind of institutional or other arrangement to keep these failures from occurring. As simple as these games are, they embody the essence of many real-world examples.

15. The hero (apology) game can also have payoffs in the diagonals switched so that mutual inaction is the worst outcome.
16. There is a mixed-strategy equilibrium if this game had cardinal payoffs.

		B	
		Do Not Act	Act
A	Do Not Act	3, 3	2, 1
	Act	4, 2	1, 4

Figure 2.6
No-equilibrium game in ordinal form

REPEATED PRISONERS' DILEMMA

We return to the Prisoners' Dilemma game. Suppose that two countries are deciding troop deployments to a civil conflict that could jeopardize the supply of raw materials. Keeping these supplies flowing is the underlying pure public good. To ensure that a Prisoners' Dilemma applies, we assume that the net difference between *individual* benefits and costs from deploying peacekeepers is negative. If this interaction takes place just once, then the expected outcome is like that of Figure 2.1, where neither country sends peacekeepers. Next suppose that the identical game is played twice in sequence. In both rounds, the countries choose not to send peacekeepers. This follows because far-sighted countries look ahead to the second period and realize that the dominant strategy is to do nothing, given that there is no tomorrow at this vantage point. With no action anticipated in the second (last) period, the dominant strategy in the first period is also not to send peacekeepers since none will be sent in the ensuing period. In fact, for any fixed number of known periods, the likely outcome of the game is for no peacekeepers to be sent by the two countries in any of the rounds of play. In essence, countries view the game from the last known period and choose their best (dominant) strategy in that period. Then the countries "fold the game back" and choose their dominant strategy in the next-to-last period and so on. This bodes badly for peacekeeping, which the United Nations realized when it tried to field and finance troops for peacekeeping missions in the 1950s and early 1960s. To rectify the problem, the United Nations instituted mandatory assessment accounts to finance future missions after December 1973 (Sandler and Hartley, 1999, pp. 99–102).

In the real world, there are repeated Prisoners' Dilemmas that have better prognoses. If there are an endless number of tomorrows, then each player's dominant strategy may be to provide the public good or to cooperate in every period, especially when the future is highly valued. For example, owners of houses along a common lake cooperate to pay to have the duckweed eliminated each summer even though a Prisoners' Dilemma applies. This follows because failing to cooperate may elicit a punishment from the other players that results in long-term losses that are greater than the immediate gain from defecting. The classic example follows from a tit-for-tat strategy where each player begins by cooperating (that is, contributing a unit of the public good) until one's counterpart stops supplying the public good.[17] Following such a defection, the player will stop providing the public good until the other player cooperates again. That is, the tit-for-tat strategy is to mimic the opponent's strategy from the previous period. Such dynamic strategies, with their threat-backed inducement to cooperate, may result in successful collective action. Institutional arrangements promote the permanency of interactions over time, thereby fostering collective action. Spatial propinquity can also promote a sense of permanency among nearby countries. Long-lived institutions display their date of founding prominently to remind members that members' interactions are here to stay, so that cooperative actions have significant paybacks now and into the future. Continual interactions give rise to norms and social conventions, whose legitimacy rests on their ability to limit transaction costs (as roles are learned and expectations are formed) and their effectiveness fosters the group's well-being.[18]

Next, consider a game with an unknown endpoint, so that the game or interaction may continue with a given probability in the next period. For this scenario, the players cannot merely imagine themselves at the end of the game and devise a multiperiod strategy that is best in the last period and each preceding period. The game cannot be folded back period by period starting in the final period. When the length of the game is unknown, a tit-for-tat strategy, which punishes defectors, can overwhelm any immediate gain from defecting and trying to obtain a free ride. The greater the likelihood that the game will continue in the ensuing period, the greater the likelihood that players will cooperate to avoid punishment.

Repeated games are an important consideration for the other game forms—for example, assurance, chicken, and hero. In each instance, games with either no endpoint or an uncertain one may result in the cooperative outcome with threat-based multiperiod strategies.

<hr>

17. On repeated plays of Prisoners' Dilemma, see Axelrod (1984) and Sandler (1992, Chapter 3).
18. Norms and social conventions are discussed by Hardin (1982) and North (1990).

GENERAL PRINCIPLES OF COLLECTIVE ACTION

The roots of the general rules of thumb for collective action stem from the immensely important *The Logic of Collective Action* (hereafter *Logic*) by Olson (1965). This work on groups' ability to fail or succeed in collective endeavors altered thinking in economics, sociology, anthropology, law, and political science (especially international relations) on group behavior (Taylor, 1987). Prior to the publication of *Logic*, the general feeling was that groups promoted the collective well-being even when the individual agents acted independently of one another. *Logic* distilled simple principles to guide thinking about collective action. Olson (1965) aimed to formulate basic principles that held in most, but not all, circumstances. In fact, Olson's reliance on simple maxims with little or no qualifying conditions was, in large part, behind the book's success. These maxims could be simply stated and easily understood by many disciplines, thereby giving the book wide appeal. Olson's rules of thumb with their unstated assumptions taunted researchers to find exceptions, a practice that continues today. Even though there are notable exceptions to these rules or principles, they are valid in many key situations that correspond to essential real-world examples. In addition, Olson's propositions could be empirically tested. Logic had impeccable timing since it came at a time when many disciplines began focusing on group behavior.

As displayed in Table 2.1, Olson's general rules of thumb for collective action can be grouped into three categories: size propositions, group composition propositions, and institutional recommendations.

The first size proposition indicates that large groups may have difficulty in forming. This implies that collective action to clean up a lake, shared by three countries, is generally easier to accomplish than a collective action problem such as averting climate change, which requires supporting action by every country on the planet. The first size proposition follows, in part, because potential participants can better discern the net gain from their actions when only a few agents are involved. For global interactions, potential participants have a more difficult time in calculating what their actions will or will not accomplish. Consider U.S. efforts to reduce its carbon footprint. The effects of U.S. actions to curb emissions may be counterbalanced by growing GHG emissions by China and India, which are not currently obligated to cut GHG emissions by the Kyoto Protocol. Organizing costs also work against the formation of large collectives to address common contingencies. In practice, this latter concern can be circumvented by starting with small collectives at a local or regional level and later linking these collectives geographically. The cost to mount an effort to keep a local Wal-Mart from a neighbor is much cheaper and easier than to get an amendment to the U.S. Constitution approved. The latter requires two-thirds approval of the U.S. Congress and involves organizing collective action throughout the United States.

Table 2.1. Collective action: Some general rules of thumb

Size propositions:

- Large groups may not provide themselves with a collective good because such large groups may have difficulty forming.
- The larger the group, the greater the inefficiency associated with independent behavior.

Group composition propositions:

- Exploitation hypothesis: Larger members (those with the greater endowments) bear a disproportionate burden of collective provision.
- Heterogeneous groups are more likely to achieve some level of collective action.
- Homogeneous groups are more apt to form.

Institutional recommendations:

- Collective failures may be overcome through selective incentives that provide individual gains.
- Collective action failures may be overcome through institutional design—for example, a federated structure or cost sharing.

Source: Olson (1965) and Sandler (1992).

In the case of independent action, the second size proposition indicates that suboptimality increases with the size of the group. This proposition is nicely illustrated by a comparison of the five- and eight-country Prisoners' Dilemmas in Figures 2.2 and 2.3. For five countries, the suboptimality associated with the Nash equilibrium is a loss of 125 compared to the social optimum, while for eight countries, the suboptimality associated with the Nash equilibrium is a loss of 368 compared to the social optimum. When players are identical, the extent of suboptimality generally increases with group size, which tends to hold for pure public goods.

We next turn to group composition propositions. Collectives may be homogeneous where all members possess identical tastes and income, or heterogeneous where members have different tastes and/or income. In practice, both kinds of collectives exist. The members of a yacht club or a board of directors are likely to be homogeneous, while allies in a military alliance (for example, NATO) or a customs union are heterogeneous.

The first group composition proposition indicates that the large rich members are apt to shoulder a disproportionately large burden of collective provision. Olson and Zeckhauser (1966) first noted this tendency for the NATO alliance in the 1950s and 1960s by showing that the allies with the largest gross domestic product (GDP) devoted the greatest share of their GDP to military expenditures. Given that the bigger allies have the most to lose from an attack and also more income to allocate to defense, these large allies will choose sizeable defense expenditures. If, moreover, defense is purely public among allies, then the small allies may have much of their defense needs covered by the larger allies' defense spending (Sandler, 1993). This leads to an *exploitation hypothesis* whereby the large allies are exploited by the small allies through free riding by the latter. Consider a generic pure public good provision. If the public good is "normal" in the sense that its purchase increases with an agent's income, then the richest agent will supply the largest amount of the good, followed by the next richest, and so on, provided that tastes are the same. In fact, contributors can be rank ordered from highest to lowest based solely on income;[19] thus, the large, rich agents carry the burden of the collective provision for the small, poor agents. The validity of the exploitation hypothesis hinges on tastes correlating with income. Suppose, instead, that a poor agent has a stronger demand for the public good than that of a richer agent. In this scenario, the small, poor agent may carry a disproportionately greater burden for the large, rich agent. Consider the Israeli-U.S. alliance, where Israel has much more to lose from a Middle East conflict than the United States, thus leading Israel to allocate a much larger portion of its GDP to defense than does the United States. If, moreover, the small ally has a marginal cost advantage in supplying the public good,[20] then this too may turn the exploitation hypothesis on its head, so that the small contributes a relatively larger portion of its GDP to the public good.

The second composition proposition in Table 2.1 indicates that heterogeneous collectives are more likely than equal-sized homogeneous collectives to achieve some level of the collective action or the provision of a public good. This heterogeneity in tastes and/or endowments augments the likelihood that some member, typically the richest and most interested, will gain a sufficiently large share or amount of the collective benefit to provide the public good for the group. That is, one or more members may gain enough to privilege the entire group with the public good. In the early 1950s, the United States carried the overwhelming defense burden of the NATO alliance, especially when the United States built its strategic nuclear arsenals (Russett, 1970). The United States emerged from World War II with little war damage compared to its European NATO allies, thereby leaving the United States in a position to lead regarding the alliance. In scanning the heavens for asteroids and other potential extraterrestrial threats, the United States assumes the lion's share of the burden given its resources and monitoring capabilities. When every country possesses the same means and tastes, no country may experience sufficient benefits to supply the group with the collective action.

19. This is established by Andreoni (1988), Bergstrom, Blume, and Varian (1986), and Cornes and Sandler (1996).
20. Marginal costs are the additional costs of another unit of output.

For initial formation of the collective, group homogeneity proves support-ive because common like-mindedness means that agreements can be reached with minimal transaction costs. If, for instance, all potential participants of a proposed collective possess identical preferences and income, then all want the same provision level and there is little to barter over. In addition, such homo-geneity makes it easy for potential members to identify one another at the ini-tial formation stage. It is not uncommon to see like-minded agents with similar tastes form collectives—for example, rich people are more apt to want exclu-sive country clubs that have immaculate fairways despite the high price tag. Homogeneity can also be partly based on spatial considerations, leading to the rise of regionalism and its associated collectives such as customs unions and defense pacts. At its formation, the G-7 (the United States, the United King-dom, France, Germany, Italy, Canada, and Japan) included the most influential (capitalist) industrial states. These countries were beset with similar problems that made a loose consultative union attractive. This union has grown in size over the years, giving way to the G-10 and G-20.

The third set of general rules of thumb concerns overcoming collective action failures. Olson's *Logic* suggested two pathways to more effective col-lective action. First, selective incentives or private inducements can moti-vate individual action for the collective. Consider charitable contributions to a city's symphony. Large contributors are often rewarded with season tickets or recognition in the printed program of each concert. The hope is that these private rewards, when coupled with the public good reward of having a better local symphony, may induce a larger contribution. For international rela-tions, a hegemon may become the world's cop because it then has more input in setting the world's agenda. The latter is the selective (private) incentive. In regards to foreign aid, donor countries' selective incentives often take the form of conditioned aid that provides some donor-specific benefits—for ex-ample, hiring and paying for the donor country's technical assistance. A tropical country receives private inducements for preserving its rain forest owing to ecotourism, natural beauty, watersheds, climatic benefits, fruits, and nuts. This preservation also yields global collective benefits from seques-tering carbon and preserving biodiversity. The greater is the portion of these private inducements as a share of total benefits, the greater will be the agent's motivation to contribute to the collective action (Cornes and Sandler, 1996; Sandler, 1977). If, moreover, the private inducements are complemen-tary to the public benefits,[21] then the greater is the individual's inducement

21. Complementary goods or gains give a consumer larger benefits when consumed together. Thus, season tickets to the symphony will be more valuable as the orchestra's quality improves through contributions. Such complementarity works against free riding because increased contributions by others will induce individuals to increase their own contributions to gain better tickets to an improved orchestra (Cornes and Sandler, 1994). These prime tickets are tied to one's largess.

to contribute (Cornes and Sandler, 1984, 1994). In fact, greater contributions by others may induce a contributor to give more owing to complementarity. Thus, complementarity may reverse the free-rider tendency. More recently, selective incentives are discussed in terms of *joint products* (see Chapter 3), in which a collective activity yields two or more outputs that vary in their degree of publicness. If one of these jointly derived outputs is private to the provider, then this private output is the selective incentive that motivates individual action. For example, an ally's military expenditure fosters not only alliancewide protection (a public benefit to the alliance), but also provides natural disaster relief and National Guard protection (private benefits to the provider).

Second, the design of institutional structures can overcome collective action failures. In *Logic*, Olson focused on the use of federated structures that bolster closer contact among participants in small subgroups where individual actions are easily recognized. The *Logic* discussed national labor unions, which rely on a federated structure where much of the fund-raising is done by the local chapters. The same is true of nationwide charities, such as the United Way, which depends on local groups and communities for raising funds. Institutions can also impose thresholds to change the underlying game from a Prisoners' Dilemma to an assurance game, which possesses a more favorable collective action prognosis. The promise of the transformed assurance game can be realized by institution-promoting leadership. Cost-sharing is another effective institutional design innovation for inducing collective action as shown in the next section.

COST-SHARING AND SUCCESSFUL COLLECTIVE ACTION

We now return to the contribution game in Figure 2.1a, which is a classic Prisoners' Dilemma where $b_i = 7$ and $c_i = 10$ for two players, each of whom can contribute one or no unit of the pure public good. For the cost-sharing scenario, we maintain the benefit per unit contributed at $b_i = 7$ for the contributor and the other agent. The difference is that provision costs are shared *regardless* of the provider so that $c_i = 10/2 = 5$ for both players on each contributed unit.

The associated cost-sharing game is displayed in Figure 2.7, where the payoffs in the diagonal cells are identical to those in the top matrix of Figure 2.1 because cost-sharing has no impact on the net payoffs when either no one contributes or both contribute a unit of the public good. In the mutual-contributions cell, each player nets 4 as benefits of 14 on the two units are reduced by the shared costs of $10 [-2 \times (10/2)]$. The off-diagonal payoffs are influenced by cost-sharing where both players receive the gross gain of 7, reduced by their shared cost of $5 (= 10/2)$, so that both players net 2 regardless

	B	
	Do Not Contribute	Contribute
A Do Not Contribute	0, 0	2, 2
A Contribute	2, 2	Nash 4, 4

Figure 2.7
Cost sharing and Prisoners' Dilemma, $b_i = 7$, $c_i/2 = 5$

of their role. There is no longer an inducement to free ride because one gets charged proportionally for the contribution of the other player. With cost-sharing, the social implications of one's decision are "internalized" as the externality from each contribution has its own payment. The dominant strategy is now to contribute since $2 > 0$ and $4 > 2$ for each individual. Moreover, the Nash equilibrium is the social optimum of mutual giving.[22] This game is known as *harmony* or *no-conflict* because there is no collective action failure. There are many alternative forms of the harmony game, given cases of ordinal ranked payoffs from 4 to 1 (Rapoport and Guyer, 1966). This suggests that there are many institutional arrangements for achieving this desirable outcome.

Cost-sharing would also transform the *n*-person Prisoners' Dilemma of Figures 2.2 and 2.3 into harmony games, where contributing is the dominant strategy for all *n* players and the Nash equilibrium is the social optimum. Cost-sharing is used by the United Nations to pay for peacekeeping missions, following the establishment of assessment accounts by Resolution 3101 of the UN General Assembly (Sandler and Hartley, 1999). Most international organizations rely on cost-sharing to finance the institution's operations, as does INTERPOL through members' assessments (Sandler, Arce, and Enders, 2011). Typically, the cost-sharing formula assesses each member either based on its ability to pay (for example, a country's GDP) or its position in the institution (for example, a permanent UN Security Council member) rather than equally. The total assessment on the members is, however, based on the organization's scale of operations, which determines its budget or costs. Even though each member is assessed differently, each must view its net gain to be positive or else it would exit the institution. In effect, staying in is a dominant strategy

22. This cost-sharing fix works provided that $b_i > c_i / 2.$

despite the cost-sharing so that a harmony game results. NATO also instituted cost-sharing to finance its infrastructure and its military and civil structures (Sandler and Forbes, 1980).

PRISONERS' DILEMMA AND CHANGING CIRCUMSTANCES

We now consider an arms race between two enemy countries or alliances—denoted by A and B. During the Cold War, A represents NATO, while B represents the Warsaw Pact. In the top matrix of Figure 2.8, the game is displayed in terms of ordinal payoffs. The smallest payoff is from unilateral disarmament, while the largest payoff is from unilateral armament. The former makes the ally vulnerable to defeat, while the latter gives the ally a tactical advantage. Mutual increases in armaments result in the second smallest payoff because money is spent but neither ally gains an edge. The second largest payoff comes from mutual disarmament since money is saved and neither ally

		B	
		Arm	Do Not Arm
A	Arm	Nash 2, 2	4, 1
	Do Not Arm	1, 4	3, 3

a. Arms race as a Prisoners' Dilemma

		B	
		Arm	Do Not Arm
A	Arm	Nash 2, 2	3, 1
	Do Not Arm	1, 3	Nash 4, 4

b. Arms race as an assurance game

Figure 2.8
Two forms of arms races

becomes more vulnerable. This is a classic Prisoners' Dilemma that results in an arms race, as characterized the Cold War for decades.

How can this deficient outcome be addressed? In 1985, Mikhail Gorbachev instituted a policy of glasnost to openly discuss economic, political, and other reforms within the Soviet Union. Glasnost and perestroika (restructuring) resulted in greater contact between the Soviet Union and the United States. The economic stresses caused by decades of the arms race made both countries, particularly the Soviet Union, come to realize that mutual arms reductions would result in the largest payoffs, followed by those for unilateral arms increase. This realization and changes in payoff perceptions developed because Gorbachev and Reagan came to trust one another. Each country had sufficient missiles and warheads to cause unacceptable damage to its counterpart many times over. Mutual arms reduction would save resources without increasing vulnerability. The end outcome was the START I Treaty and reductions to Soviet and U.S. warheads and launchers. As such, the assurance matrix in Figure 2.8 applied, in which the 4s and 3s are switched compared to the Prisoners' Dilemma. The social optimum was achieved when Gorbachev took a leadership role in announcing verifiable arms reductions. Thus, the Prisoners' Dilemma can be addressed when circumstances change and the players view their payoffs differently.

MULTIPLE EQUILIBRIA IN AN n-PLAYER CHICKEN GAME

Return to the contribution game in Figure 2.2 and replace the 0 in the upper left-hand cell with −4. This changed payoff transforms the game into an n-player chicken game where no action spells disaster that can be avoided by one country curtailing its emissions. The Nash equilibrium is now for a single country to reduce its GHG emissions, because this country receives a higher payoff by staying in this role given that −3 > −4. That is, the country will not unilaterally want to change its action. The social optimum continues to involve all countries cutting their emissions. There are now n Nash equilibria, each with a single country reducing its pollution. To avoid disaster necessitates finding a single savior country. This might seem easy, but we must remember that a more preferred position is still to free ride on the efforts of the savior. If one country provides the required disaster-avoiding action, then all other countries are better off free riding since the associated payoff of 7 exceeds being the second savior, which gives a payoff of 4. Countries must decide independently whether or not to reduce emissions. Collective action may fail from two causes. First, every country may sit back hoping for some other country to act to avoid the dire consequences of no one acting. This is a coordination problem. Consider a victim of a brutal attack screaming for help outside an apartment complex in the middle of the night. Would the cries bring a savior? Often they do not.[23] Second, the Nash equilibrium, if achieved, avoids the worst payoff but does not achieve the social optimum, whose payoff is well above the Nash equilibrium.

The second, but not the first, concern is ameliorated if we change the chicken game somewhat to require, say, four countries to act to avoid disaster. Now, the Nash equilibria are the cases where four countries out of the total supply the required action. Once four countries act, the fifth is better off free riding so that the social optimum, which is nearer to the Nash equilibria, is not achieved. (Only when all countries must act to supply the public good to avoid a disaster will the social optimum be achieved in an n-country chicken game.) The four-country chicken game involves having precisely four countries act when each knows that too small of a group will suffer the costs of their actions without concomitant benefits. There are two potential fixes: (1) devise an institutional scheme for getting the required participation, and (2) provide refunds to countries when the threshold for diverting disaster is not reached. Another means would be to announce the number of countries pledging action, analogous to what the United States did prior to the Gulf War in 1991. In these examples, institutional design matters.

In reality, chicken-type coordination problems are frequently solved by the asymmetry of the players. Consider the response to the use of chemical weapons by Syria in 2013. The overwhelming might of the United States places it in a unique position to threaten to launch a military strike to deter future use of such weapons by Syria or other countries.[24] Once again, we see how asymmetry can provide some collective action.

CONCLUDING REMARKS

This and the next two chapters set up the theoretical framework for the issue-based application chapters to follow. We hope to convince the reader that elementary game theory can put the complex phenomena of transnational collective action failures and successes into better perspective. Game theory offers a simple organizing principle for understanding the myriad facets of collective action. By understanding the perverse incentives associated with some collective action concerns, countries can take measures to reverse these incentives through far-sighted institutional design. Effective collective action

23. Dixit, Skeath, and Reiley (2009, pp. 282–286) analyzed a real-life situation of murder in Kew Gardens, New York in 1964. Thirty minutes of screams brought no one to help even though at least 30 people heard the screams. The appearance of even one person would probably have scared away the assailant!

24. Apparently, subsequent use of chemical weapons by Syria did not invoke the U.S.-pledged military strike, thereby hurting future U.S. credibility.

is possible, as demonstrated by past successes in addressing the stratospheric ozone-depletion problem or eradicating smallpox.

We also distilled some essential rules of thumb regarding collective action. In the process, we highlighted some of the implicit assumptions required of these maxims. Understanding these assumptions can enlighten policy makers to engineer institutional innovations that foster collective action at the local, transnational, regional, and global levels.

CHAPTER 3

Market Failures and Collective Action

In a competitive market environment,[1] Adam Smith (1976) believed that individuals' pursuit of their self-interests will result in a desirable outcome for the entire economy. This uncoordinated display of selfishness leads the economy by an "invisible hand" to a social optimum, from which it is not possible to improve someone's well-being without hurting someone else's well-being.[2] In an ideal competitive setting, changes in tastes and/or technologies will set in motion the required adjustments in prices and profits to equilibrate the quantity demanded and the quantity supplied in each and every market. These adjustments would be quick and rather costless, provided that some underlying assumptions are fulfilled. Moreover, no explicit coordination is then needed among buyers and sellers as the invisible hand does its magic.

A key underlying assumption is that governments must enforce and protect *property rights* or claims of ownership, required for market exchange. These property rights vest the owner with the control of any benefits and the responsibility for any costs associated with a product or service. With property rights assigned and enforced, Smith saw very limited roles for government. These roles involve providing defense, education, and some other infrastructure, such as roads, bridges, and sewers. In advanced societies, Smith would surely have included the provision of airports, the assignment of the electromagnetic spectrum, the designation of air-traffic corridors, the tracking of new diseases, and the assignment of orbital slots for satellites. Adam Smith did not worry about income distribution, economic stability, or

---

1. A competitive market requires the following assumptions: (1) a large number of small sellers, (2) a large number of small buyers, (3) perfect mobility of buyers and sellers, (4) perfect (complete) knowledge, (5) a homogeneous product, and (6) unrestricted entry and exit of sellers. These assumptions mean that the forces of supply and demand give rise to a price that each firm views as given and unaffected by its sales.

2. Such a position is known as a *Pareto optimum*.

economic growth. Competitive markets may be associated with poverty among those with limited skills, but Smith did not have much to say about this concern. Although bad practices or pessimistic expectations can result in economic downturns or financial crises, Smith did not wrestle with these dynamic issues.

What can go astray in Smith's flawless ideal? Markets can fail when prices and profits do not direct resources to their most-valued use. As a result, socially inferior outcomes follow, from which resources can be reassigned to improve society's well-being. These *market failures* may stem from a number of causes. First, markets may be incomplete where some exchanges are not priced even though costs and benefits are present. This is the case for an *externality* or uncompensated interdependency. If, for example, my wood-burning fireplace pollutes my neighbor's air and I am not required to compensate for the damages, then I am not truly assuming all of the costs of my fireplace from a social viewpoint. This will lead me to pollute more than had I been made to account for these third-party effects. Second, markets may not be competitive, which Smith fully realized. Third, the presence of pure public goods poses a concern, because a worthwhile activity may not be provided or else undersupplied owing to free riding. Fourth, property rights may be owned in common with inadequate means to limited access.[3] In other instances, property rights may not be enforced, as is true in some failed states. Fifth, information may be incomplete so that buyers and sellers are not fully informed about a transaction—for example, a buyer not knowing about cheaper prices or reliability issues with the product. Sixth, there may be market distortions, such as tariffs that restrict free trade (see Chapter 7). Even taxes used to finance government activities, including the provision of public goods, may distort the operation of markets.

The presence of market failures may give rise to the need for collective action for some pure public goods, as previously shown in Chapter 2. Market failures may occur not only within states but also among states. For the former, a country's government may address the problem, while for the latter, countries' governments or some international organization or agreement may have to coordinate action. The latter can take the form of a supranational structure (for example, the World Trade Organization), a treaty, a summit, or an ad hoc agreement. Currently, there are many supranational institutions at the global and regional level (see Chapter 4). Addressing market failures among states brings us into the realm of international relations. Of course, the study of international relations encompasses many political and diplomatic issues, such as setting up diplomatic missions or recognizing new states that do not involve market failures.

3. Open-access commons are analyzed by Ostrom (1990), Ostrom, Gardner, and Walker (1994), and Sandler and Arce (2003).

The primary purpose of this chapter is to explore the various market failures and their requisite collective action, if any, within and among countries. A secondary purpose is to emphasize that not all potential causes of market failures require explicit policy intervention. Corrective policy is costly so that the gain in efficiency from such policy must justify its costs. Some market failures may be self-correcting, while others may be too costly to correct. In the former case, two countries with coal-fired power plants along a common border may come to realize that it is in their mutual interests to reduce acid-rain-inducing sulfur emissions. If, however, an externality causes relatively little inefficiency, but is costly to control, then no remedial action may be best. For public goods, we shall see that the three dimensions of publicness—nonrivalry of benefits, nonexclusion of nonpayers, and the aggregation technology[4]—determine the need and the form of intervention. It is essential to resist broad generalizations with respect to market failures and the need for collective action. For example, we shall see that club goods, which are a type of public good, require no explicit corrective action. A tertiary purpose of this chapter is to apply game theory to our study of market failures. We begin with a paired contrast between pure public goods and private goods. This is followed by a survey of the many kinds of collective goods. We next analyze the aggregation technology of public goods and its implications for collective action. Externalities and incomplete information are then considered, prior to our concluding remarks.

PURE PUBLIC GOODS VERSUS PRIVATE GOODS

Since pure public goods were defined in Chapter 2, only a brief recap is needed here. Pure public goods possess nonrival and nonexcludable benefits. Nonrivalry means that there are no costs to extend the good's consumption to another person, so that the incremental cost of accommodating another user is zero. To limit consumption of a nonrival good through charges or barriers makes society worse off because the added consumption gains are costless to achieve. Hence, everyone should be permitted to consume a nonrival good. The issue then becomes how to finance the nonrival good if charging for its services and excluding nonpayers is inefficient.[5] The second property of public goods involves nonexcludability. Nonexcludability results in free riding because there is little reason to pay for a pure public good, which is freely

---

4. The aggregation technology indicates how individual contributions determine the overall level of the public good available for consumption (Hirshleifer, 1983; Cornes and Sandler, 1984).
5. An individual will refuse to pay for the nonrival good if his/her gain is less than the user fee associated with the exclusion mechanism.

available once provided. Hence, both properties of publicness may result in a market failure, where a valued activity is either not provided or underprovided. As shown in Chapter 2, pure public goods are often associated with Prisoners' Dilemma or chicken games, particularly when each unit contributed bolsters the total in an additive or cumulative fashion and the benefits per unit, b_i, is less than the costs per unit, c_i.

As a paired comparison, consider a private good, whose benefits are completely rival and excludable. When a piece of pie—a private good—is diligently consumed, there is nothing left for someone else to consume. Moreover, property rights protection ensures benefit excludability for the private good. If, therefore, someone wants the private good, then it must be purchased. Individuals can exchange private goods in markets. In contrast, pure public goods cannot be exchanged since benefits are nonrival and nonexcludable. Once someone supplies the pure public good, there is no further possibility of exchange where the provider is necessarily compensated because benefits are freely available.

A simple game representation of a private good brings out the stark strategic differences between it and a pure public good. Suppose that a unit of a private good gives the user a benefit of 8 at a cost of 4. Unlike pure public goods, $b_i - c_i$ must be positive for a pure private good, or else there is no incentive to purchase it. Remember that a unit of the private good does not provide benefits to others. In Figure 3.1, we display the normal-form game for the private good, where players A and B can each buy one unit or no units. If neither player buys a unit, then each receives 0. If, however, only A purchases a unit, then A receives a net gain of 4 $(=8-4)$, while B receives 0. The payoffs are reversed if only B buys a unit. When both purchase a unit, each nets a payoff of 4. There is no gain from free riding owing to exclusion. The dominant strategy for both players is to purchase a unit, which results in the Nash

		B	
		0 units	1 unit
A	0 units	0, 0	0, 4
	1 unit	4, 0	Nash 4, 4

Figure 3.1
Private good where $b_i - c_i > 0$, $b_i = 8$, $c_i = 4$

equilibrium to this harmony game. Trade in private goods between individuals is a harmony game, which is true of free trade between countries (see Chapter 7). The Nash equilibrium is also the social optimum, which distinguishes private goods from pure public goods. For pure public goods, there is a strong strategic component because anyone's purchase of the public good helps other individuals. In contrast, there is no strategic component in private good exchanges under competitive conditions. Recall from Chapter 2 that harmony games are not strategic. One player's gain is independent of the choice of the other player: in Figure 3.1, the player's payoff of 0 or 4 only depends on his/her action.

The nomenclature of public and private goods is somewhat misleading. Some private goods may be publicly provided—for example, free milk to schoolchildren. In addition, some types of public goods, such as parks, may be privately or publicly provided, especially if exclusion is possible. Highways are publicly and privately provided, while universities can be public or private. Thus, we must remember that private and public refer to the properties of the goods and not how they are provided. Technology can sometimes influence a public good's properties and, therefore, its classification. For example, technology may transform a nonexcludable public good into an excludable one. Encryption can limit which ships receive lighthouse signals to curtail free riding. Once exclusion is feasible, institutional arrangements can designate who gets a public good's benefits.

MYRIAD COLLECTIVE GOODS

To highlight the importance of the two standard properties of publicness, we investigate the collective action implications of five classes of collective goods. There are many types of public or collective goods, so that these five types are by no means exhaustive; however, these five varieties represent many of the most important types of collective goods.

Impurely public goods—some rivalry but no exclusion

Rivalry in terms of crowding or congestion changes a pure public good into an impure public good. Crowding is a detraction in a public good's quantity or quality as more individuals use the good. Consider neighboring allies whose contiguous borders constitute a front that is threatened by an enemy alliance. With conventional weapons, rivalry takes the form of a thinning of forces. That is, as troops are concentrated along a portion of the front, other portions are left relatively less protected (Sandler, 1977). Another collective good example is the electromagnetic spectrum, where the use of similar or nearby frequencies can result in interference or noise, which is signal congestion. Policing is also subject to crowding in the form of thinning of police protection or crime deterrence. In the alliance and police examples, the afforded protection is nonexcludable but subject to rivalry. This is also the case of the electromagnetic spectrum, which can be accessed by users but is subject to congestion.

Rivalry means that extending consumption of the public good to more users results in a nonzero cost. As such, there are now grounds for excluding users, since there is a crowding externality imposed by one user on other users. These nonzero costs of use mean that the consuming group must be exclusive, leaving out those users whose marginal gains from use are less than the concomitant congestion that their consumption causes. Unfortunately, nonexclusion does not permit this limitation on group size, and this then results in overuse and a market failure. Society is better off excluding those users whose derived benefits do not exceed the negative crowding impact of their consumption. Another example of such a good is the control of an invasive pest that threatens alternative locations. With limited resources, action to curtail the pest in one area limits the offensive elsewhere owing to resource thinning.

A variety of game forms may apply to this kind of collective good. For pest control, a coordination game, such as chicken, may apply where some action is anticipated, but who will act and by how much is uncertain and must be negotiated or decided among the threatened countries. If the consequences of inaction are sufficiently severe for each threatened country, than an assurance game may be relevant with matching actions when the pest is mobile and easily capable of moving to a neighboring country.

Group size is a real concern in regards to collective action for this class of impure public goods. As the number of actors grows, overuse and underprovision are anticipated to worsen, given increasing congestion concerns and greater free-riding incentives. Group size inhibits collective action as increased crowding limits an individual's share of the collective benefit, so that fewer individuals discern a gain from providing the good. The exploitation hypothesis[6] may be turned on its head because larger users cause the most congestion, thereby limiting benefits to the small users. That is, the large users' crowding places a greater burden on the small user. When these larger agents are the primary supplier of the collective good, the utilization burden must be compared to the opposing supply burden to ascertain the net exploitation, if any. Some public provision may be required to address these collective action concerns.

6. The exploitation hypothesis indicates that the small individuals place a greater burden of the good on the large individuals.

Impurely public—full exclusion and no rivalry

We now turn to an excludable impure public good that displays no rivalry. The provision of an early-warning system, say, for tsunamis or other such catastrophes is such a good. Another instance is hurricane tracking provided by satellites. These satellites see into the hurricane to ascertain its intensity and rainfall potential. For both examples, the collected information can be withheld from nonsubscribers to the satellite's information. Another example is a database, which allows corporations to judge terrorist or political violence risks in countries where they may base operations. Yet another example would be pay-per-view television programs, which are excludable but not congestible. The exclusion mechanism serves to eliminate strategic behavior by forcing some users to pay for the good. If there is no cost from extending use, then exclusion is suboptimal because potential users, who gain from the good's benefit, are denied access when the subscription price exceeds their marginal willingness to pay. Because it costs society nothing to give access to these users in the absence of crowding, social well-being falls as exclusion is practiced. If, however, exclusion is not practiced, then funding the good is problematic.

As group size increases, the extent of suboptimality rises when exclusion is practiced because there will be more excluded potential users. The exploitation hypothesis is generally not relevant for these goods insofar as the large agents are more likely to be able to afford the subscription fees. In general, group composition is less of a concern except on equity grounds. Subsidies for poorer users may be needed to extend use and reduce inefficiency. In aid programs, donors can subsidize poor countries so that they can partake in these excludable public goods (Kanbur, Sandler, and Morrison, 1999).

Club goods

Club goods are a particular type of impure public good, whose benefits are excludable *and partly rival.* Such goods may involve a small (for example, an intimate nightclub) or large number of consumers (for example, a toll road). Access to club goods is blocked by exclusion mechanisms that are virtually costless to operate.[7] The existence of partial rivalry in the form of congestion is essential for deploying the exclusion mechanism and forming a club where only members have access. Unlike the last class of impure public goods, a member's use implies a congestion cost on other users that justifies keeping out those individuals whose gain from membership does not equal or exceed

7. If exclusion costs are not nominal, then the efficiency gains from employing the exclusion mechanism must exceed the associated costs.

the crowding costs imposed on other users. Examples of club goods within and among countries abound. Within countries, club goods include toll roads, health clubs, movie theaters, swimming pools, and golf courses. At the international level, club goods involve transnational parks (for example, the Great Barrier Reef), the Suez and Panama Canals, satellite communication networks, and remote-sensing services. In the latter case, collecting data on one area of the planet crowds out training a satellite's instruments on other locations. Since communication satellites have capacity and interference concerns, congestion costs exist.

Club goods can be provided by club members, financed through tolls imposed on users based on the crowding costs that their use creates.[8] Since crowding is heavier during peak-use periods, then the toll can be varied accordingly. Clubs allow members to cooperate to provide the shared good, so that strategic considerations are not generally pertinent. Efficient provision of the club good is achieved through a toll mechanism that accounts for the crowding that each visit imposes on the membership. If the number of potential members exceeds the optimum membership size for the club, then new clubs can form to accommodate the population of potential members. A university is a club for its students, whose toll consists of tuition. When a state's population grows, the state university system opens up new campuses or new clubs.

Clubs can accommodate members with identical or different tastes. Consider a club with heterogeneous members, whose tastes and incomes differ. The club would charge the same toll per use or visit based on the congestion costs imposed on others.[9] Members with a greater demand for the club good would visit more often and pay more in total tolls. Thus, the club is able to get members to reveal their preferences for the club good through the number of visits. For a satellite communication network, heavier users send and receive more signals, which can be monitored and charged accordingly. This is also the way that Internet providers desire to charge for downloaded information. The collected tolls not only finance the club good, but they also pay for the good's maintenance and eventual replacement. The presence of club goods underscores that some collective goods can be provided privately and that such goods need not involve market or collective action failures. Clubs embody cooperative games where members work in unison through a deceptively simple institutional arrangement.

On the international scene, club goods have grown in number as technological innovations allow for more efficient monitoring and exclusion. Members can

8. For a fuller treatment of clubs and club goods, consult Berglas (1976), Buchanan, (1965), Cornes and Sandler (1996), Sandler (2013a, b), and Sandler and Tschirhart (1980, 1997).

9. As such, the tolls internalize the crowding externality, thereby achieving allocative efficiency.

be multinational firms, countries, international organizations, private-public partnerships, or charitable foundations. A global communication satellite network, such as INTELSAT, includes all of these kinds of members along with others. At the regional level, there is a push for regional infrastructure, such as interstate highways and inland waterways, to promote regional commerce (Estevadeordal, Frantz, and Nguyen, 2004; Sandler, 2013a; Shearer and Tres, 2013). Such infrastructure projects are frequently club goods, subject to congestion and monitoring.

Joint product collective goods

Joint products refer to an activity that gives rise to multiple outputs whose degree of publicness varies. As such, jointly produced outputs can be purely public, impurely public, private, a club good, or something else. Joint products imply bundling where multiple outputs occur simultaneously. There are myriad instances of joint products. Defense spending by allies in a military alliance can protect a common front (an impure public good), provide national guard (a country-specific good), patrol the country's coastline (another country-specific good), or deter an enemy attack against the alliance (an alliancewide pure public good). Country-specific outputs are private to the ally from the alliance's viewpoint, but are public within the alliance. The Amazon rain forest provides global public benefits (species diversity and carbon sequestration), club good benefits (ecotourism), localized public benefits (watersheds, erosion control, and local climate effects), and private benefits (fruits and nuts). Joint products stem from education as the student receives private benefits (an education and a diploma), while society benefits from a more educated population. The latter justifies public subsidies and support of higher education. Peacekeeping missions also generate joint products—private benefits to the conflict region and public benefits in terms of greater stability to neighboring countries and the world at large. Foreign aid involves joint products in terms of recipient-specific reduced poverty, donor-specific gains, and global gains. The donor may benefit from conditions placed on the aid, while the world may gain a healthy host population, less susceptible to diseases that may spread worldwide.

For joint products, myriad game forms apply depending on the mix of excludable to total benefits associated with the outputs. Suppose that a large share of these benefits are excludable in the form of private or club goods. In this scenario, a harmony game is germane where the dominant strategy is to support contributing, not unlike trading a private good. If, instead, the largest share of outputs is purely public, then Prisoners' Dilemma and chicken games are pertinent. Since a wide variety of outputs can be mixed, other game forms—hero, assurance, and coordination—may apply.

With joint products, the prognosis for effective collective action hinges on the activity's ratio of excludable benefits to total benefits.[10] As this ratio approaches 1, the share of excludable benefits dominates, enabling markets and clubs to allocate resources efficiently to the activity's provision. In contrast, a ratio of 0 implies purely public outputs, free riding, and suboptimal provision. Joint products may even imply overprovision when jointly produced public bads, such as pollution, arise from the activity. Ratios between 0 and 1 allow for a wide range of outcomes.

Institutions can be engineered to bolster the share of contributor-specific joint products, thereby motivating effective collective action. For instance, the United Nations vests permanent Security Council members with veto power in approving peacekeeping missions. These members pay a greater assessment of these missions' costs so that the veto allows them to disapprove missions that they view as less important or unnecessary (Sandler and Hartley, 1999). As such, they can exercise a private benefit. Similarly, the International Monetary Fund (IMF) provides a larger block of votes to members, who have disproportionate power in providing IMF loans. This greater voting privilege is a donor-specific benefit that motivates enhanced support of the IMF.

Provision of joint products is bolstered if the private and public outputs are complementary so that each output enhances the consumer's derived satisfaction from consuming the other jointly produced output. That is, complementary goods are best consumed together. Bundling is particularly efficacious for the provision of complements. If an activity produces private and pure public outputs that are complementary, then increases in the activity provided by others will increase the public good spillovers. These spillovers, in turn, induce an individual to provide more of the activity as a means to get more of the complementary private good. Bundling through joint products means that the spillover recipients cannot obtain the contributor-specific benefit unless they support the collective action. The presence of a jointly produced private benefit acts like property rights that motivate action; complementarity reinforces this desire to support the collective action.

OPEN-ACCESS COMMONS

A commons shares features that are similar to a nonexcludable impure public good. A key difference is that the impure public good is provided, while an open-access commons is typically a nature-provided input (for example, a fishery or a jungle tract) that can be exploited or used by anyone. Like the impure public good, the use of the open-access commons gives rise to congestion costs

10. On the influence of this ratio on optimality, see Sandler and Forbes (1980), Sandler and Hartley (2001), and Sandler and Murdoch (2000).

that affect all other users. Unlike the impure public good, potential users are also impacted, since the quality of the commons can be degraded, thereby limiting future options of would-be users. In more advanced treatments, intertemporal consequences of today's use on tomorrow's users are analyzed. When species are being harvested, this intertemporal impact may result in species extinction.

The open-access commons (henceforth, the commons) provides a paired comparison with a pure public good, which possesses nonrival and nonexcludable benefits. The open access that is associated with commons may be physically determined, culturally based, or institutionally set. Open access to the oceans beyond some coastal resource zone is institutionally based on the Law of the Seas Treaty, while open access to watersheds or the stratospheric ozone layer is physically determined. Institutional rules regulate access to air-traffic corridors, orbital slots in geostationary space, or the electromagnetic spectrum. In some scenarios, the commons can be viewed as a fixed input that is jointly exploited: for example, hunters use a common hunting area. The hunting ground is the fixed input with a given amount of game at a point in time, and the hunters' weapons and time are the variable inputs used to harvest the animals. Other examples include sending cattle out to a common pasture or having boats ply a fishery. In the fishery, as more boats harvest the fish stock, the crew of each boat must expend more effort to land a given catch. This increased effort is the crowding externality, reflective of the partly rival commons. Each boat is not anticipated to account for the crowding that it creates for other boats. These independent actions lead to overharvesting, which is a market failure.

Although the commons game shares some of same characteristics as the public good contribution game, there are key differences. This is brought out in Figure 3.2,[11] where we present a five-person contribution game and a five-person commons game. In the top matrix, the contribution game is depicted and is analogous to the eight-person contribution game, previously displayed in Figure 2.2 with different values for b_i and c_i. In matrix a of Figure 3.2, representative individual i has two possible strategies: (1) do not contribute, or (2) contribute one unit of the public good. Each contributed unit gives a benefit of 6 to the contributor and each of the other four potential contributors. If i does not contribute and if, moreover, no one else contributes, then i's payoff is 0. When i does not contribute but one other individual contributes a unit, then i receives the free-rider benefit of 6. In the top row of Figure 3.2a, i receives 12 if two others contribute a unit apiece, 18 if three others contribute a unit apiece, and 24 if four others contribute a unit apiece. Next consider i's

11. Some literature treats the two situations as having identical strategic properties (Ostrom, Gardner, and Walker, 1994), while other literature highlights subtle, but important, strategic differences (Sandler and Arce, 2003).

contribution payoffs. When i contributes alone, the net payoff is -2 or the difference $b_i - c_i \; (=6-8)$. If i contributes and is joined by one other, then i's net gain is $4 \left[=(2\times6)-8\right]$. The other payoffs in the bottom row are computed in a similar fashion. For representative player i, the dominant strategy, indicated by the arrow, is not to contribute, because each payoff in the top row is greater than the corresponding payoff in the bottom row by 2. The Nash equilibrium is for no one to contribute as all individuals exercise their dominant strategy, thereby yielding a total payoff of 0 for the collective. As discussed for an analogous case in Chapter 2, the social optimum is for all five persons to contribute for a total gain of $110 \; (=5\times22)$. The underlying game is a Prisoners' Dilemma. Increasing the number of persons from five would create a greater gap between the Nash and social optimum payoffs.

In matrix b of Figure 3.2, an analogous five-person pasture commons game is displayed, where we have reversed the values of the benefit and costs associated with individual action, so that $b_i = 8$ and $c_i = 6$. This reversal is needed so that action—grazing one's cattle—is individually rational with a net positive payoff. Each farmer has two strategies: not to graze or to graze one's herd. Grazing one's cattle imposes a public cost of 6 on everyone, including the farmer whose cattle are put out to pasture. In the top row of matrix b, we display i's payoff if i's herd is not allow to graze the commons. When no one uses

	Number of contributors other than i				
	0	1	2	3	4
→ i Does Not Contribute	Nash 0	6	12	18	24
i Contributes	−2	4	10	16	Social Optimum 22

a. Five-person contribution game, $b_i = 6$, $c_i = 8$

	Number of farmers other than i whose cattle graze in commons				
	0	1	2	3	4
i Does Not Graze	Social Optimum 0	−6	−12	−18	−24
→ i Grazes	2	−4	−10	−16	Nash −22

b. Five-person commons game, $c_i = 6$, $b_i = 8$

Figure 3.2
Five-person symmetric representations

the commons, i's payoff is 0. For each farmer who uses the commons, i's payoff falls by 6—that is, it is –6 for one user of the commons, –12 for two users of the commons, and so on. If i solely exploits the commons, i's net gain is $2\ (=8-6)$. When i's cattle are joined by another farmer's herd on the commons, i nets $-4\ \left[=8-(2\times6)\right]$. The other payoffs in the bottom row of matrix b are computed in a similar fashion. The dominant strategy is to exploit the commons since the payoffs in the bottom row are greater than the corresponding payoffs in the top row by 2. As all farmers exercise their dominant strategy, the Nash equilibrium results in a loss of 22 for each farmer. At this Nash equilibrium, no farmer will unilaterally alter his/her strategy since $-22 > -24$. The five-farmer collective nets –110 at this equilibrium. In matrix b, the social optimum corresponds to where no one exploits the commons. As in the public good contribution game, this is a Prisoners' Dilemma. Moreover, the gap in payoffs between the Nash equilibrium and the social optimum worsens as the number of farmers increases. For example, this gap is a loss of 168 for six farmers and a loss of 238 for seven farmers.

Even though both games are Prisoners' Dilemmas whose Nash equilibrium's suboptimality worsens with group size, there are some essential differences between these games. The two games differ because benefits are public and costs are private in the contribution game, while costs are public and benefits are private in the commons game. In Figure 3.2, we see that the positions of the Nash equilibrium and the social optimum are reversed in the two games. In the contribution game, no one acts, while the desired outcome is for everyone to act; in the commons game, everyone acts, while the desired outcome is for no one to act (Sandler and Arce, 2003). Thus, public policy must encourage action for pure public goods and discourage action for commons. Another difference cannot be seen in Figure 3.2 owing to our assumed symmetry of players. For heterogeneous individuals, there is a strong tendency for the small to exploit the large in contribution games. This follows because large, rich contributors have a greater demand for the pure public good, thereby affording a larger free ride to small, poor individuals. Next consider a commons with two fishing firms. Suppose that the large firm has 100 boats in its fleet, while the small firm has just 10 equal-sized boats. In this example, the large firm will cause 10 times as much congestion costs as the small firm and, in so doing, will disproportionately exploit the commons. As such, Olson's (1965) exploitation hypothesis is turned on its head so that the large exploits the small.

Summary

Table 3.1 summaries the six cases of collective goods reviewed in this section. For each type, the table provides two examples, the strategic implications, and the provision prognosis. Clearly, different kinds of collective goods demand

Table 3.1. Collective goods: Examples, strategic implications, and provision prognosis

Good Type	Examples	Strategic Implications	Provision Prognosis
Pure Public	• Reducing ozone shield thinning • Eradicating a disease	Prisoners' Dilemma or chicken game may apply.	Undersupplied and need for public provision. General collective action principles hold for many cases.
Impurely public with some rivalry but no exclusion	• Defending a perimeter • Utilizing the electromagnetic spectrum	A wide variety of game forms apply, including a coordination game, where some provision is anticipated if the agents can decide who will supply the good.	Some supply is anticipated, but the good is overused and undersupplied. Size principles hold, but not all of the composition principles hold. Some public provision is needed.
Impurely public with full exclusion but no rivalry	• Early-warning system • Hurricane tracking and intensity alerts	Exclusion eliminates strategic considerations and forces some individuals to reveal a preference. Those whose willingness to pay is too small are excluded despite the absence of crowding costs.	Inefficiency results because people with positive benefits are excluded. Size principles remain a concern, but composition principles are less germane. Subsidies to the poor may reduce inefficiency.
Club goods	• Transnational parks • Remote-sensing services	In a club, there are no strategic considerations. Members cooperate to provide a shared good, where visits are monitored. Tolls finance the shared good.	Optimal provision results as crowding externality is internalized through tolls. Taste differences are revealed through visitation rates and are charged accordingly.
Joint products	• Military alliance • Preservation of rain forests	A wide variety of game forms are relevant, including assurance, depending on the mix of excludable to total benefits. Dominant strategy may even be to contribute if share of private benefits is sufficiently large.	Ratio of excludable to total benefits is the key consideration. As this ratio approaches 1, efficiency results. General collective action principles hold more fully as this ratio approaches 0. Institutional design must emphasize these excludable benefits.
Open-access commons	• Fishery • Hunting ground	Prisoners' Dilemma with a dominant strategy to exploit the commons.	Size principles apply, however, exploitation is turned on its head—the large exploits the small.

different remedial action and/or institutional design. Not all collective goods are created equal. This table serves as a ready reference for the specific applications discussed throughout the book.

AGGREGATION TECHNOLOGY AND PUBLIC GOODS

Since 1983, a third property of publicness—the aggregation technology or social composition function—influences the prognosis for public good provision.[12] The aggregation technology indicates how individual contributions affect the overall level of the public good that is available for consumption. This property influences individuals' incentive to contribute to the public good, thereby affecting the strategic implications surrounding the provision of the public good. In particular, this technology determines whether the public good provision of others can offer a free ride, or whether one's own provision adds to the level of the public good. The aggregation technology also influences whether a redistribution of income among contributors and potential contributors can impact the overall provision of the public good.

Traditionally, a *summation* technology of aggregation had been assumed where each unit contributed to the public good adds identically and cumulatively to the total level of the good that is available for consumption. In matrix *a* in Figure 3.2, a summation technology is implicitly assumed, so that five units provided gave five times the benefits of a single unit. Thus, each contributed unit augments consumption and its associated benefits in an additive fashion. Curbing global warming depends on decreasing the atmospheric accumulation of greenhouse gases (GHGs). If each of six nations cuts its GHG emissions by 100 tons, then the overall reduction in new emissions is 600 tons. If, likewise, each of these nations manages to absorb 100 tons of accumulated emissions by planting forests, then the overall influence on GHG accumulation is additive. A summation aggregator also applies to cleansing a lake of a pollutant. Overall removal of the pollutant corresponds to the sum of everyone's effort. Other summation examples include charitable contributions or foreign aid, both of which ideally have a cumulative effect on reducing poverty.

With a summation aggregator, each contributor's efforts to the pure public good are perfectly substitutable for those of other contributors. Summation paves the way for free riding, since one person's contributions to the public good have precisely the same marginal impact on what can be consumed as anyone else's contributions. Summation is a necessary ingredient to the

12. On aggregation technologies, see Arce and Sandler (2001), Cornes (1993), Cornes and Sandler (1984), Hirshleifer (1983), Kanbur, Sandler, and Morrison (1999), Sandler (1998), Vicary (1990), and Vicary and Sandler (2002).

so-called neutrality theorem, which says that redistributing income *among contributors* has no influence on the total amount of the public good even when contributors' tastes differ.[13] It was once believed that if the state taxed a low contributor or took money from a low contributor and gave the collected money to a high contributor, then the overall level of the public good would increase. We now know that this effort would merely raise the public good contributions of the income recipient by precisely the amount of reduced contributions of the taxed individual. To achieve an increased amount of the public good, society must *draw income from a noncontributor*, who cannot by definition reduce contributions to the public good. Neutrality also applies to redistributing income among countries contributing to a pure public good that adheres to the summation aggregator.

Two game forms are associated with a pure public good abiding by a summation aggregator. The first is the Prisoners' Dilemma when $b_i - c_i < 0$, and the second is chicken if the absence of a contribution gives a negative payoff smaller than $(b_i - c_i)$. The Prisoner's Dilemma results in underprovision of the pure public good, while the chicken game results in unequal burden sharing if someone provides the good. If the necessary coordination is not achieved, then dire consequences result in the absence of provision.

We next turn to a weakest-link aggregator where only the smallest effort determines the level of the public good. During a conventional war, consider a contiguous front for five states facing an approaching enemy army. The country's border with the least fortification will be the most vulnerable, thereby determining the protection (a transnational public good) afforded to the five states. Action to limit a transnational terrorist group's funding abides by a weakest-link aggregator, as does tracking the diffusion of a disease or plague. In the latter example, the least-vigilant effort determines how well the health authorities respond to the threat posed by the disease. Other weakest-link examples include curbing the spread of revolutions, keeping a secret, or securing airports against skyjackings.

The hallmark of weakest-link public goods is matching contributions, because there is no gain from providing beyond the smallest contribution level. Larger contributions merely used up scarce resources without increasing the amount of the public good available for consumption. For weakest-link public goods, there is no incentive to free ride since the smallest contribution is then zero so there are effectively no units to consume, no matter what others provide. Remember that the smallest contribution determines the overall amount of the public good.

13. Neutrality and its requirements are discussed by Bergstrom, Blume, and Varian (1986), Cornes and Sandler (1984, 1985), Sandler and Posnett (1991), and Warr (1983). Shibata (1971) first discovered neutrality.

		q_B 0	1	2
	0	Nash 0, 0	0, –3	0, –6
q_A	1	–3, 0	Nash 3, 3	3, 0
	2	–6, 0	0, 3	Nash 6, 6

Figure 3.3
Weakest-link public good with three contribution strategies

Figure 3.3 depicts a 3×3 game matrix for weakest link where country *A* or *B* can each contribute 0, 1, or 2 units to the public good, denoted by q_A and q_B, respectively. Suppose that each unit contributed costs 3. If the smallest contribution is one unit, then each country receives 6 in benefits prior to the costs of 3 being deducted; if, however, the smallest contribution of the players is two units, then each country receives 12 (or 6 per matched unit) in benefits prior to the costs of $6\ (=3\times2)$ being deducted. In Figure 3.3, no contributions give 0 in payoffs to both countries; a one-unit match results in 3 in net payoffs to both countries; and a two-unit match offers 6 in net payoffs to both countries. If country *A* contributes a unit and country *B* does not contribute, then *A* nets –3 and *B* gets 0 insofar as the overall level of the public good is zero. There is no gain to free riding. These payoffs are reversed for the two countries when *B* contributes one unit and *A* does not contribute. If, say, one country provides two units and the other provides just a single unit, the larger provider nets $0\ (=6-6)$, which equals the benefits from the matched unit minus the provision costs of 6 from the two units, while the smaller provider gets $3\ (=6-3)$, which equals the benefits from the matched unit minus the provision costs of 3 from one unit. The remaining payoffs in the matrix are computed in a similar fashion for this assurance game (see Chapter 2 on such games), with three Nash equilibria of increasing desirability along the main diagonal. These equilibria involve matched contributions. The most advantageous outcome corresponds to two matched units. If, however, country *A* can only afford one unit, then the resulting equilibrium has both countries giving a single unit unless the richer country chooses to support the contribution of the poorer country (Vicary and Sandler, 2002).

In real life, many contribution levels of the public good are possible for weakest-link public goods, where the actual outcome hinges on the purchasing capacity of the countries. When countries have similar tastes *and* means, they desire the same amount of the public good. As such, the Nash equilibrium will be the social optimum and full transnational cooperation is achieved. When, however, these tastes or spending capacities do not match, then the richer country can bolster the contributions of the poorer one to raise the latter's provision to a more acceptable level for both countries. This support can take the form of income or in-kind transfers. Thus, for example, the U.S. Centers for Disease Control can send monitors into poor countries to gauge the dispersion of a disease outbreak. The neutrality concern of pure public goods does not apply—that is, income redistribution from the rich to the poor will raise the level of the weakest-link public good as the poor can contribute an amount after the transfer that is more in line with the desired amount of the rich (Sandler, 1997, 1998; Vicary, 1990).

A related aggregator is weaker link, where provision levels above the minimum add progressively less to the overall level of the public good. Thus, there are some benefits from unmatched units, but these benefits decline as the amount of these unmatched units increases relative to the smallest contribution level. A weaker-link aggregator opens up more possible equilibria including those not involving matching behavior, which brings back some free-rider incentives. Consider the 3×3 game matrix in Figure 3.4, where each contributed unit again costs 3. Matched units give 6 in benefits before costs are deducted, so that the diagonal cells are identical to those in Figure 3.3. If one country provides one unit and the other free rides, then the single unmatched unit gives 3 in benefits to both countries, which nets 3 for the free rider and $0 (=3-3)$ for the contributor. Next consider one country providing two units and the other providing no units. The two units give 4 in total benefits to both countries, so that the free rider receives a payoff of 4 and the provider only receives $-2 \left[=4-(3\times2)\right]$ as costs of 6 are deducted. Finally, if one country provides two units and the other country provides one unit, then the matched unit gives 6 in benefits to both countries and the unmatched unit gives another 3 in benefits to both countries. The country that provides one unit nets $6 (=6+3-3)$, while the country that provides two units nets $3 \left[=6+3-(3\times2)\right]$. There are seven Nash equilibria in Figure 3.4, which includes the three matching outcomes. For this example, the "unmatched" equilibria occur when only one provision unit separates the highest and lowest contributors. Such equilibria allow for enhanced collective action possibilities, because perfect coordination is not required for a weaker-link aggregator. If an "unmatched" equilibrium results, the richest country will normally provide the greatest number of units of the public good. The focus or best equilibrium (social optimum) is where the greatest number of matched units are contributed, but this equilibrium might not be feasible when incomes are unequal.

		q_B		
		0	1	2
q_A	0	Nash 0, 0	Nash 3, 0	4, –2
	1	Nash 0, 3	Nash 3, 3	Nash 6, 3
	2	–2, 4	Nash 3, 6	Nash 6, 6

Figure 3.4
Weaker-link public good with three contribution strategies

Weaker-link examples abound. Eliminating an invasive pest from neighboring countries is a weaker-link public good, as is educating the public about disease transmission. Sterilizing hospitals is another weaker-link public good. Weaker-link public goods give rise to a variant of an assurance game, where leadership by one country alone is not sufficient for obtaining the best outcome. If, say, country A leads with two units, then the outcome can have B providing one or two units. Income redistribution should generally be in the direction of the poorer country.

We consider four additional important aggregators associated with public goods. For the threshold aggregator, the overall contribution level for the public good must surpass a set amount before benefits per unit are realized. Thresholds are involved with peacekeeping missions, where too small of a contingency of peacekeepers is unable to separate belligerent sides. Since a disastrous deployment of UN peacekeepers to the Congo in the 1960s, UN peacekeeping forces are no longer dispatched unless a sufficient capacity is surpassed (Sandler and Hartley, 1999). Another threshold example is forest-fire suppression in the western United States. Depending on the size of the conflagration, the authorities in charge of fire suppression determine the necessary contingent of firefighters, so that lives are not lost and the fire can eventually be brought under control. Of course, random factors such as sudden wind-direction changes can still lead to tragedy. Some charitable campaigns abide by a threshold if a certain goal must be funded.

In matrix a of Figure 3.5, we display a simple threshold public good example, where each country can give one unit or no units of the good at a cost of

	B	
	0 units	1 unit
A 0 units	Nash 0, 0	0, –5
1 unit	–5, 0	Nash 5, 5

a. Public good: two-unit threshold aggregator

	B	
	0 units	1 unit
A 0 units	0, 0	Nash 10, 5
1 unit	Nash 5, 10	5, 5

b. Public good: best-shot aggregator

	B	
	0 units	1 unit
A 0 units	0, 0	2, 0
1 unit	Nash 1, 3	Nash 3, 3

c. Public good: weighted sum

Figure 3.5
Three alternative aggregators for public good contributions

5 per unit. Benefits of 5 per contributed unit do not occur until two units are provided. If country A provides a unit, but country B gives nothing, then there are no benefits because the threshold is not attained, so that A nets -5 and B gets 0. The payoffs are reversed when roles are switched. When both countries contribute a unit, the threshold is achieved and each country receives $5 \left[=(5 \times 2)-5\right]$ as the benefits from two units are reduced by the costs of 5. This is an assurance game with Nash equilibria along the main diagonal. The preferred equilibrium is attained if A or B assumes a leadership role and contributes a unit. If further units of contribution are allowed, then the tendency is for the Nash equilibrium to remain at the minimal threshold. This follows because contributing beyond the threshold often involves benefits on the next unit that are less than the associated costs from each individual's viewpoint. In the depicted game, a country views another unit beyond the threshold as netting it nothing. Even with more countries, there is a strong tendency to gravitate to the threshold contribution (Sandler, 1992).

A fifth useful aggregator is best shot where only the largest effort determines the level of the public good. If six countries provide 0, 2, 5, 8, 9, and 11 units, respectively, then the overall level of this best-shot public good is 11. A best-shot public good with alternative provision levels could involve the highest score on a standardized test by which a school's prestige is judged. The school's prestige is the best-shot public good. If, however, the best-shot public good is either achieved or not, then the largest effort is most likely to provide the public good. Best-shot public goods include discovering cures for diseases, infiltrating a criminal network, mapping the human genome, deciphering a code, or discovering an asteroid on a collision path with earth.

In matrix b of Figure 3.5, we display a 2×2 game for a best-shot public good, where $b_i = 10$ on just the first unit and $c_i = 5$ on each unit. Countries A and B can contribute 0 or 1 unit to the public good. If neither country contributes, there is no payoff to either. The initial unit contributed, which is the best shot, generates 10 in benefits for both countries at a cost of 5 to just the provider. In this scenario, the best-shooter country gets 5 as costs of 5 are subtracted from benefits of 10, while the free rider receives 10. When both countries contribute a unit, the second unit is redundant and provides no benefits, so the payoff in the bottom right-hand cell of matrix b is 5 for both countries. This is a coordination game where efforts are coordinated so that only the best shooter comes forward. The Nash equilibria in the off-diagonal cells are social optima. Leadership by either country to do nothing or to contribute results in the optimum when both countries possess equal capabilities. If capabilities are unequal, then there are grounds for redistributing income to the more capable country, so that the best-shot public good is achieved. Often, this necessitates redistributing income to the richer countries. This unequal-capacity case is not displayed in Figure 3.5.

A less extreme form of best shot is better shot, where effort below the largest adds progressively less to the public good level. Developing the polio vaccine was a better-shot public good because the Salk inactivated vaccine was preferred to the Sabin live-attenuated vaccine. Nevertheless, Sabin's oral vaccine had its applications, where it required less skill to administer—for example, in developing countries with poor healthcare infrastructure. Better-shot public goods also involve antibiotics, some of which are more effective than others against bacteria. The less effective ones can be used on patients who cannot tolerate the more effective antibiotics or who are less infected. Other better-shot public goods include developing health treatment regimes, deploying second lines of defense for repelling incoming missiles, and developing a new generation of fighter jets. If there are more than two levels of provision, better-shot public goods may involve Nash equilibria away from the extreme corner cells on the off-diagonal (Arce and Sandler, 2001). In such cases, many additional Nash equilibria may result, as in the case of weaker-link public goods. Any income redistribution must be to the richer country to ensure that the best form of the good is provided.

Our final aggregator is weighted sum, for which weights are applied to the individual contributions before summing them to ascertain the overall level of the public good available for consumption. Weighted sum generalizes summation, which corresponds to unit weights. With non-unit weights, one country's provision to the public good is not a perfect substitute for some other country's provision, thereby reducing free-riding incentives. This reduction encourages provision. Weighted-sum public goods include reducing acid rain, monitoring the planet from alternative vantage points, or controlling a spreading pest. In the case of acid rain, sulfur or nitrogen deposition on country i is a weighted sum of emissions at home and in other countries, where these weights are the share of the emitting countries' pollution deposited on country i. Upwind countries' emissions possess greater weights. These weights are determined by wind direction, the countries' relative positions, their sizes, storm patterns, and other factors.

Consider matrix c in Figure 3.5, in which a unit provided by country A gives 6 in benefits to itself and just 3 in benefits to country B, while a unit provided by country B gives 5 in benefits to itself and just 2 in benefits to country A. Further suppose that each unit costs 5. If just B contributes, then A receives a free ride worth 2, while B nets 0 $(=5-5)$. When roles are switched, B receives 3 in free-rider benefits, while A nets 1 $(=6-5)$. If both countries contribute, then A receives 3 $(=6+2-5)$ and B also receives 3 $(=5+3-5)$. This particular game has two Nash equilibria in the bottom two cells of matrix c.[14] The social optimum is only ensured if country B leads by providing one

14. In this particular example, A's contribution yields 9 in total benefits, with A receiving 2/3 of the total and B receiving 1/3 of the total. A similar calculation for B's contribution gives 5/7 of the total benefits to B and 2/7 of the total benefits to A.

	B	
	0 units	1 unit
A — 0 units	0, 0	2, –1
A — 1 unit	Nash 3, 3	5, 2

Figure 3.6
Alternative weighted-sum public good

unit, or else both countries play their dominant strategy to contribute a unit of the public good. In any case, the more desired Nash equilibrium has a good prognosis.

Weighted-sum public goods are associated with a wide range of game forms, as suggested by the alternative game matrix in Figure 3.6. A unit of the public good provided by country A now yields 8 in benefits to itself and 3 in benefits to country B, while a unit provided by B gives 4 in benefits to itself and 2 in benefits to country A. Once again each unit costs 5. The payoff calculations follow the same procedure as before. In Figure 3.6, country A has a dominant strategy to contribute—unlike country B, which has no dominant strategy. Country B will reason that country A will play its dominant strategy and the Nash equilibrium will result. Virtually any game form is possible depending upon the weights associated with countries' strategic payoffs. If income redistribution is used to achieve a more desirable outcome, then income should be directed to the contributors whose provision benefits others and itself by the most. Consider a pollution scenario where a country's action impacts itself the most. The equilibrium will then likely be along the main diagonal and countries are motivated to curb their own pollution—that is, transnational cooperation is encouraged despite pollution spillovers to other countries (see Chapter 12).

By way of summary, Table 3.2 indicates the seven aggregators discussed in this section, along with two examples for each, their strategic implications, and their provision prognosis. There are many other aggregators, but we highlight the most important ones. On balance, the recognition of aggregators other than summation provides three crucial insights: (1) the possibility of cooperation hinges, in part, on the aggregator; (2) income redistribution to encourage provision depends on the aggregator; (3) the desirability of the Nash equilibrium relates to the underlying aggregator.

Table 3.2. Alternative aggregation technologies for pure public goods

Aggregation Technology	Examples	Strategic Implications	Provision Prognosis
Summation: Public good levels equal the sum of individual contributions	• Curbing global warming • Reducing lake pollution	Prisoners' Dilemma or chicken if $b_i - c_i < 0$	Undersupply or the need to coordinate efforts to avoid dire consequences.
Weakest link: Only the smallest effort determines the public good level	• Limiting terrorist funding • Tracking the diffusion of a disease	Assurance	Matching behavior with optimal results if agents possess identical tastes and income.
Weaker link: Provision levels above the minimum add progressively less to the overall level of the public good.	• Eliminating pests • Educating the public about disease transmission	Variants of assurance	Outcomes in addition to matching behavior. Some undersupply is anticipated in many cases.
Threshold: Good must surpass a threshold for benefits to be received	• Peacekeeping • Fire suppression	Assurance	Threshold often reached and outcome may be near to optimal.
Best shot: Only the largest effort determines the public good level	• Discovering cures for diseases • Infiltrating a criminal network	Coordination	Results may give efficient outcomes, especially when a leader nation with sufficient resources exists.
Better shot: Effort below the largest adds progressively less to the public good level	• Polio vaccine • Developing treatment regimes	Variants of coordination	Undersupplied or efficiently supplied.
Weighted sum: Each contribution can have a different additive impact	• Reducing acid rain • Monitoring the planet from different vantage points	Wide variety of game forms	A wide variety of outcomes are possible, with suboptimality being less of a concern.

EXTERNALITIES

An *externality* is an important source of market failure, which involves an uncompensated interdependency among two or more agents. Such externalities abound at the international level. When an accident at a country's nuclear power plant releases radioactive material into the air or oceans (for example, the Fukushima Daiichi nuclear power plant meltdown following the March 11, 2011 earthquake in Japan), a *transnational externality* is experienced. The 2011 Japanese earthquake also triggered a tsunami, which created huge debris fields in the oceans that washed up on the West Coast of North America. Other transnational externalities include pollution from coal-fired power plants or refugees fleeing a civil war. Countries that generate negative externalities do not typically compensate for the damage that they cause. For accidents and/or pollution, this lack of compensation means that countries are not motivated to take appropriate actions to minimize their impacts on other countries. Consider transboundary pollution associated with producing some product. Without being responsible for the pollution consequence inflicted on others, firms will produce too much from a social viewpoint. This follows because the firm considers only its (private) production costs and not the damage that its production imposes on others, which constitutes social costs. In contrast, an external benefit or positive externality may result; for example, when some country eliminates an international crime cartel that operates in many countries. For positive externalities, too little of the action is expected because private, not social, benefits motivate the country taking action. If, however, other affected countries were to compensate the country taking the action, then a greater level of action would ensue.

Externalities arise because costs or benefits imposed on others are not part of the agent's calculus when deciding the level of an activity. As a consequence, a misallocation of resources results where too little or too much of an activity takes place from a social viewpoint. For externalities, price does not direct resources to their most-valued use, so a market failure occurs. There are a number of ways to address externalities. First, a tax or subsidy that accounts for the external costs or benefits, respectively, can be assigned to the externality generator.[15] This is known as *internalizing the externality*. Second, if there are few parties—say, two—to an externality, then the externality generator and recipient can bargain with one another to a mutually agreeable outcome that accounts for social consequences.[16] Third, a government or a supranational

---

15. In the case of external costs (benefits), the tax (subsidy) is set equal to the marginal external costs (benefits) at the point where marginal social costs equal marginal social benefits.

16. This bargained solution follows the Coase (1960) theorem, where an optimum is achieved no matter who—the externality generator or the recipient—is assigned the property rights to the externality.

body (an international government organization) may fix the activity at a more desirable level. For instance, United Nations' peacekeeping operations have brought greater stability to some conflict-ridden regions. The United Nations Environmental Program has helped monitor transboundary pollutants, which resulted in treaties that curbed pollutants. The World Health Organization has assisted in ameliorating the consequences of some diseases and have helped to achieve herd immunity through vaccination for other diseases.

Externalities are closely related to pure public goods, with externalities being more inclusive. Every pure public good is an externality, but most externalities are not pure public goods. The latter follows because externalities may effect as few as a single person. In contrast, the contributions of each provider of a public good affect the other agents' well-being. Moreover, public goods generally imply substitutability among agents' actions that do not necessarily characterize externalities. This is best brought out by a *unilateral externality*, where one agent's action impacts another agent's well-being but not the reverse. An upstream firm pollutes the waters of a downstream firm but not vice versa. Unilateral externalities are generally difficult to address since the externality recipient has no leverage (other than a bribe) over the generator to alter its behavior. This leverage is more relevant to a *reciprocal externality* where, say, two parties generate and receive an externality from one another. There are, for example, instances of transboundary externalities where one country is downwind to but upstream from another country. Thus, these countries can trade concessions on river pollution for concessions on air pollution.

When transfrontier pollution involves a large number of countries, treaties may be formulated and ratified to curb the pollution. We shall see in Chapter 7 how trade agreements address transnational externalities arising from tariffs imposed on imports. Like myriad kinds of public goods, externalities are associated with a wide variety of game forms and, therefore, possess varied prognoses for success. At the international level, supranational and regional organizations are ideally positioned to correct transnational externalities.

ASYMMETRIC INFORMATION AND MARKET FAILURES

Asymmetric information involves one party to a transaction being more informed than another. A market failure may arise as some relevant costs or benefits are inevitably left out of the marketplace. Suppose that a house has many large rat snakes in the attic that prowl the house at night devouring rodents. Further suppose that the house is put on the market. The seller knows about the snakes but fears that disclosing information about the serpents in the rafters would hurt the selling price and so keeps this knowledge to herself.

When the house sells, the price may be too high or too low. The price is too high for a buyer who greatly fears snakes (even useful ones), but the price is too low for a buyer who loves snakes and hates rats. At any rate, the house price does not reflect this important attribute, thereby distorting price. Asymmetric information limits price as a signaling mechanism, and this curbs the operation of the invisible hand.

Asymmetric information involves many transnational externalities. Consider a transnational terrorist group given safe haven in some failed state. The group knows its true strength but the countries that the group targets often do not know the group's strength. Without this knowledge, threatened governments may assign too few resources to eradicating the group if they view it as rather small, as the United States assessed the size of al-Qaida prior to 9/11 and the U.S.-led invasion of Afghanistan in October 2002 (Enders and Sandler, 2012). Asymmetric information is also tied to pure public goods. If governments knew each benefit recipient's true valuation of the public good, then the governments would know how much to provide. Asking the recipients to reveal their true valuation does not work because to reveal the truth may raise their taxes for the good. Incentives work against being truthful.

Asymmetric information arises from two distinct causes—*hidden action* and *hidden type*. In the case of hidden action, the uninformed party cannot observe the action of the informed party. Suppose that ten states form a common insurance pool against earthquakes and forest fires. The associated insurance coverage involves not only a response to managing the crisis after its occurrence, but also partial compensation for the losses. Possessing the insurance may alter incentives for preventative measures—building earthquake-resistant buildings—and clearing undergrowth in forests. These actions may be hidden from the other states joining the pool. A *moral hazard* problem evolves because the insurance reduces incentives to be vigilant, thereby raising the risks to the pool's members. To reduce moral hazard, the insurance pool can raise deductibles in order to place more of the costs of poor choices on the party who makes these choices. The insurance can also use screening devices to elicit pertinent information from the more informed party. Screening may request detailed records on past catastrophes, building codes, and forest-management programs.[17] Sovereignty limits revelation of information on, for example, transfrontier pollution and nuclear weapon development. The development of remote sensing and other monitoring technologies is curbing some hidden action—for example, the ability to ascertain the state of forests from satellite imaging.

17. Employers use candidate's past academic degrees as a screening device for reliable employees.

A second form of asymmetric information concerns the presence of two or more types of agents to a transaction or two or more qualities of goods offered for sale, where the true type is known to one party but not to the other. Suppose that five countries are bargaining over a common pollution problem, where some countries value the cleanup more than others. Countries do not want to reveal their true type because this will leave them with a greater share of the cleanup bill. Next consider a government that confronts a terrorist group, whose members may be moderate or hard line. If most members are moderates, then the government would have to make fewer concessions; however, it is in the group's interest to appear more hard line.[18] If the group's moderates accept a government's offer, then the hard liners may form a splinter group, as was true of the Abu Nidal Organization which splintered from the Palestine Liberation Organization (PLO). Hidden types are often associated with an *adverse-selection* problem in which bad risks drive good risks away. The terrorism example is a case in point. In used car markets, "lemons" force reliable cars out of the market into trades among friends and family (Akerlof, 1970). This follows because most buyers cannot determine whether a used car is reliable or not. Thus, buyers limit their offers, thereby undervaluing reliable cars and forcing them from the market. Actions that reveal pertinent information can reduce the adverse-selection problem. Recent UN-led efforts to monitor pollution can inform countries about whether neighboring countries are high or low polluters, thereby fostering treaty formation and ratification.

CONCLUDING REMARKS

This chapter first shows that there are myriad market failures that require collective action at the transnational level. Second, these collective action problems are associated with a variety of game forms, thereby resulting in different prognoses for effective transnational collective action. Third, not all public goods imply the same policy remedies. Transnational club goods can, for instance, be efficiently supplied with tolls that account for congestion and preference differences through visitation charges. Fourth, the third property of publicness—the aggregator technology—is a crucial consideration in assessing whether transnational collective provision will be successful or not. Weakest-link and best-shot public goods have better prognoses than those public goods abiding by a summation technology. Fifth, accounting for the

18. The group may signal being hard line by engaging in some heinous attacks. *Signaling* is a strategy of the more informed player that reveals advantageous information for its goals to the less informed player. Thus, a weak terrorist group may spend all of its resources in initial attacks to appear stronger than it is (Lapan and Sandler, 1993).

aggregator technology opens the way for new policy instruments such as income redistribution to address public good underprovision. Sixth, institutional choices can influence the properties of publicness and, therefore, the prognosis for transnational cooperation. The rich variety of market failures makes for a wide range of palliative actions. Seventh, to conserve on policy resources, it is essential to know when these market failures are self-correcting, as in the case of some weakest-link public goods.

CHAPTER 4

Transnational Public Goods: Taxonomy, Institutions, and Subsidiarity

The interest in transnational public goods (TPGs), which affect two or more countries, has grown in recent decades for a number of reasons. First, current concern with globalization augmented the importance of TPGs.[1] Globalization underscores the prevalence of cross-border flows of all types, including the spillover of benefits and costs among countries associated with TPGs and transnational externalities. That is, globalization involves more than the growth of international trade and financial capital flows, because it also concerns the transfers of ideas, knowledge, and computer viruses. To address these TPGs' spillovers and transnational externalities, myriad institutions—global governance networks (for example, International Civil Aviation Organization and International Maritime Organization), multilateral institutions, nongovernmental organizations (NGOs), charitable foundations, and multistakeholder institutions (for example, Global Fund—see Sridhar and Woods, 2013)—have taken actions. Second, technology continues to create novel TPGs and transnational public bads (TPBs)—for example, ozone-shield-depleting chlorofluorocarbons. Third, enhanced terrestrial and extraterrestrial monitoring capabilities allow countries to spot TPGs and TPBs and their consequences. Fourth, the Balkanization of countries in Africa, Asia, and Europe may transform national public goods (NPGs) into TPGs. Fifth, the new regionalism fosters the willingness of countries to invest in regional infrastructure, such as waterways, interstate highways, and regional electricity grids, which represent regional public goods (RPGs).[2]

---

1. The link between globalization and TPGs can be found in Kaul and Conceição (2006), Kaul et al. (2003), Kaul, Grunberg, and Stern (1999), and Sandler (1997, 2004).

2. On the new regionalism, see Dodds (1998), Estevadeordal, Frantz, and Nguyen (2004), and Stålgren (2000).

An essential distinction among TPGs can be drawn based on the good's range of spillovers. TPGs affect more than a single country, while global public goods (GPGs) impact most of the globe, as in the case of the preservation of species or the diversion of an asteroid on an earth-bound trajectory. RPGs provide benefits to some defined region, and transregional public goods (TRPGs) supply benefits to countries in two or more regions (for example, actions to curb malaria). The prognosis for each of these classes of TPGs depends on factors that either promote or inhibit the good's provision. With respect to TPGs, there is a jurisdictional issue as to what is the appropriate institution that should finance or provide the public good. Should, for example, RPGs be provided by regional or multilateral global institutions? This brings up the notion of subsidiarity, where the jurisdictional range of the institution is chosen to match the corresponding spillover range of the TPG (Sandler, 2004, 2013a). As shown later, there are grounds, in some instances, from departing from a strict adherence to subsidiarity, so that some RPGs should be financed or supported by multilateral institutions.

The purpose of this chapter is to investigate how best to provide TPGs, which possess vastly different ranges of spillovers as well as diverse characteristics. Since we are interested in how to support public good provision, the next section reviews two basic taxation/payment principles for financing public goods that can be applied at the supranational level. The ensuing section offers some examples of public goods with varying spillover ranges and the institutions that facilitate their provision. This section is followed by a discussion of considerations that promote or inhibit the provision of GPGs and public goods with more limited ranges of benefit spillovers. Next, we assess the supply prognosis for TPGs based on a taxonomy that combines the aggregation technology with three basic categories of TPGs—pure public, impure public, and club goods. The remaining three sections investigate subsidiarity, indicate institutional design principles, and offer concluding remarks, respectively.

FINANCING PUBLIC GOODS: BENEFIT VERSUS ABILITY-TO-PAY PRINCIPLES

Within nations, the public or government sector serves two primary purposes: redistribute income and correct market failures. By redistributing income, the public sector attempts to correct abject poverty and establish a safety net for those who experience hardships. In a market economy, people may fall on hard times owing to a lack of skills, physical impairment, or recession. The public sector addresses market failure primarily by providing public goods and ameliorating externalities.

To achieve these objectives, two key principles guide taxation or revenue collection at the national level, and these principles can be applied to address similar concerns at the supranational level. The benefit principle charges recipients of public good benefits according to their derived gain. At the supranational level, this means that countries that receive benefits from a TPG are charged accordingly. This can pose significant difficulties in the case of pure public goods, because there is no way to exclude nonpayers. Moreover, countries may not be forthright when asked about their derived benefits, because they know that they will be charged based on their answer. It is in a country's interest to underreport their true derived benefits in order to shift more of the provision costs on to other countries. The benefit principle, however, escapes this problem and works perfectly well for club goods. By charging users a fee based on their frequency of visits, clubs force members to reveal their true preference for the shared good through visitation rates.[3] For example, ships from a country that uses the Panama Canal pay a fee that accounts for the associated crowding that each transit causes. Countries with more shipping interests and needs will use the canal more often, pay more fees, and gain greater benefits than countries with less shipping interests. The transit fees go to maintaining the canal and upgrading it over time. Most regional infrastructure—for example, bridges, interstate highway systems, communication networks, and integrated energy transport networks—can be operated as clubs with the benefit principles being applied through user fees. The Initiative for the Integration of Regional Infrastructure in South America, started in 2000 by 12 South American countries, ties these countries' infrastructure together to promote regional commerce (Costa, 2012). The financing of such an initiative can be through club user fees.

The second principle of taxation is based on an agent's ability to pay; a larger gross domestic product (GDP) reflects a greater ability to pay. For TPGs that are not club goods, this second principle is easier to administer because the supplying institution only needs to ascertain a recipient country's GDP and not its derived benefits. GDP is reported annually by the International Monetary Fund, the World Bank, and other institutions. In practice, many multilateral organizations use the member countries' GDP as a primary means to assign assessments to underwrite the public goods and other services that they provide. The United Nations bases its annual membership fees in large part on GDP. The International Criminal Police Organization (INTERPOL) largely supports its efforts to promote international police cooperation through membership fees based on member countries' GDP. Among its many public goods, INTERPOL maintains databases on suspected terrorists, fugitives, and stolen and lost travel documents that member states can check against passports at

---

3. Phone networks are clubs that also operate on the benefit principle of financing. These networks force subscribers to reveal their type through the plan that they purchase. Subscribers with a high demand for phoning will purchase an expensive plan with more minutes of calling time.

borders to keep their homelands more secure (Sandler, Arce, and Enders, 2011). For UN peacekeeping, member countries' assessments are based on income and status (Durch, 1993; Mills, 1990). The latter partly accounts for the benefit principle, since the five permanent members of the Security Council pay higher assessments than countries with comparable GDP. These permanent members have veto power over "undesirable" peacekeeping missions; hence, these countries support missions that further their strategic and economic interests.

Insofar as there is no recognized supranational government for collecting taxes from countries, the financing of GPGs and other TPGs is done on an ad hoc basis through membership and user charges (Held and McGrew, 2003). Since the early 1990s, the growth of regionalism has given rise to regional collectives that can impose some taxes to redistribute income or to provide RPGs—the EU is a prime example. The ability of regional collectives to tax is rather limited, especially when compared with government spending at the national level by member states. Countries cherish their fiscal autonomy and are not inclined to sacrifice much revenue to supranational collectives at any level, including the regional level. However, situations will arise when countries will see that collective action at the regional level can provide benefits beyond the requisite costs. In these cases, participation is voluntary because the country sees a net benefit in paying its assessments or fees.

If membership fees are not used to support a TPG, other means may apply. A rich country may see sufficient net benefits from its unilateral support to privilege other countries—for example, the U.S. Centers for Disease Control and Prevention (CDC) provides outbreak surveillance and isolates new pathogens. CDC's actions supply GPGs. The United States funds this institution because it believes that these efforts yield sufficient health safeguards in the United States to warrant the costs. Essentially, the United States is greatly worried about pathogens originating from other parts of the world causing huge health risks at home. Past examples include HIV/AIDS and Severe Acute Respiratory Syndrome (SARS). With air travel, new diseases can travel the globe within days. In addition, countries can combine efforts to supply a TPG, such as NATO's actions to address peacekeeping needs in the Balkans and elsewhere (Sandler and Shimizu, 2014). In other cases, neighbors can jointly finance infrastructure (for example, the Chunnel joining France and the United Kingdom) and recoup its costs through user fees. Neighbors can confront a common contingency, such as forest fires, invasive species, pollution, or flooding, given their united needs and interests. Another way to finance a TPG is through country-based taxes so that countries do not have to relinquish their taxing authority to supranational entities. To meet reductions in the use of CFCs mandated by the Montreal Protocol, countries collected their own taxes on CFCs as these substances were curtailed. The same would be true of a carbon tax on greenhouse gas emissions to curb climate change. Transnational environmental treaties rely on ratifiers to use their taxes to meet targeted reductions. In summary, there are myriad means that collectives apply to finance TPGs.

SOME INSTITUTIONS AND THEIR PUBLIC GOODS

Institutions have come into existence at the global, transregional, regional, and country levels for providing public goods and addressing externalities. Before we introduce a few of these institutions, the defining characteristics of these four levels must be made clear. Obviously, global institutions contain a large share of the world's countries as members. If membership is available to all countries worldwide that fulfill certain requirements, then the institution is global. In contrast, the member countries of regional institutions must be from a well-defined region. The regional basis may be geological—for example, countries along a river, or on a plain, or along a seacoast. In other cases, region may be geographically based in terms of a continent or well-defined geographical location, such as Central America or the Balkans. Geoclimatic considerations may define a region as countries with similar growing conditions for crops, thereby potentially profiting from agricultural research findings. In particular, the Regional Fund for Agricultural Technology (FONTAGRO) underwrites agricultural innovations within Latin America. In other instances, a region may be politically based—for example, communist countries in Eastern Europe prior to the fall of the Berlin Wall. Customs unions may be the political basis, in which member states permit free trade within the unions, but impose a common tariff on nonmembers. Cultural similarities, such as language or ethnic heritage, may be the regional basis for institutions. Finally, historical factors may define a region stemming, for example, from past colonial ties as in the Commonwealth of Nations. These regional considerations *also apply* to the defining spillover range of RPGs.

Transregional institutions contain member countries from two or more distinct regions. For instance, the Initiative for the Integration of Regional Infrastructure in South America includes countries from distinct Latin American regions to foster interstate commerce. The Global Environmental Facility (GEF) promotes sustainable development through environmentally friendly programs supported by grants. These environmental efforts (for example, to foster biodiversity, curb climate change, and stem desertification) are directed at developing countries in regions throughout the world. Similarly, the Consultative Group for International Agricultural Research (CGIAR) bolsters agriculture-based technological advancement in developing countries. Neither the GEF nor the CGIAR underwrites efforts in the developed countries, so that these organizations do not support actions globally. Their funding is, however, supported by developed countries and other interested parties. Thus, these organizations provide a network tying regions to the provision of public goods with various ranges of spillovers.

Finally, country-based institutions are financed within a single country even though the organization's missions may involve the provision of public goods at various levels of spillovers. This is true of the CDC and the Pasteur Institute. The latter French institution isolates new pathogens and develops health-based knowledge that constitutes public goods.

In Table 4.1, we selectively display global, transregional, regional, and country-based institutions and some examples of the public goods that they supply. We have already discussed most of the global and transregional institutions listed.

At the regional level, we include three important common markets—the EU, Mercado Común del Sur (MERCOSUR), and the Andean Community of Nations (CAN). MERCOSUR currently includes Argentina, Brazil, Paraguay, Uruguay, and Venezuela as full member states. It not only promotes free trade within the union, but also intends to facilitate the movement of labor and capital among members. As is true for the EU, MERCOSUR wants to integrate some macroeconomic, taxation, and other policies over time (Berrettoni and Lucángeli, 2012). CAN is a customs union that currently includes Bolivia, Colombia, Ecuador, and Peru. Members want CAN to become a common market and have initiated action to permit free movement of citizens among member states. Both MERCOSUR and CAN are interested in supplying RPGs and NPGs that bolster member countries' development.

Among regional institutions, the Association of Southeast Asian Nations (ASEAN) currently has 10 member countries that cooperate economically and politically. Its missions include the furtherance of free trade, human rights, environmental protection, security, and infrastructure (Wescott, 2004). As such, ASEAN provides TRPGs, RPGs, and NPGs. To the extent that ASEAN acts to curb greenhouse gas emissions, it may also offer a GPG. The Central American Electricity Interconnection System (SIEPAC) provides an RPG in the form of electricity reliability. SIEPAC and FONTAGRO are two instances of regional institutions that supply an RPG. The table also lists regional development banks that help finance regional development through loans and grants (Estevadeordal, Frantz, and Nguyen, 2004). Key development banks include the African Development Bank, the Asian Development Bank, and the Inter-American Development Bank. Currently, these banks have an important role to promote regional infrastructure that can further development. Like the World Bank, these regional development banks not only offer knowledge, but also they foster financial stability and, in so doing, supply public goods with a variety of spillover ranges.

Finally, Table 4.1 lists two country-based institutions, discussed earlier, that provide myriad public goods. Of course, there are many additional institutions that could have been included in the table at various levels. An interesting feature of some of the institutions listed is that they supply public goods with multiple ranges of spillovers. Thus, in many cases, the jurisdictional range of the institution does not match the type of public goods provided. That is, the United Nations, the World Bank, and the World Health Organization supply

Table 4.1. Global, transregional, regional, and country-based institutions and their public goods

	Examples of public goods
Global institutions	
United Nations	Peacekeeping, foreign assistance, global governance, knowledge; provides GPGs, TRPGs, RPGs, NPGs
World Bank	Foreign assistance, financial stability, knowledge, health; provides GPGs, TRPGs, RPGs, NPGs
World Health Organization	Health public goods at global, transregional, regional, and national levels
INTERPOL	Fighting transnational crime at global level
Transregional institutions	
Initiative for the Integration of Regional Infrastructure in South America (IIRSA)	Integrates energy, transport, and telecommunication networks to foster interstate commerce; promotes TRPGs, RPGs, NPGs
Global Environmental Facility (GEF)	Promotes sustainable development through environmentally friendly programs
Consultative Group for International Agricultural Research (CGIAR)	Fosters agricultural-based technological advancement; provides TRPGs, RPGs, and NPGs
Regional institutions	
European Union (EU)	Provides regional infrastructure, governance, best practices, security, income redistribution, and environmental protection; offers GPGs, TRPGs, RPGs, and NPGs
Mercado Común del Sur (MERCOSUR)	Promotes regional free trade; offers RPGs, NPGs
Andean Community of Nations (CAN)	Promotes regional free trade; offers RPGs, NPGs
Central American Electricity Interconnection System (SIEPAC)	Provides electricity reliability, an RPG
Regional Fund for Agricultural Technology (FONTAGRO)	Offers common-pool financing for agricultural innovation, an RPG
Association of Southeast Asian Nations (ASEAN)	Provides regional free trade, human rights, environmental protection, security, and infrastructure; offers TRPGs, RPGs, and NPGs
Regional Development Banks	Finances infrastructure, offers knowledge, promotes financial stability; provides TRPGs, RPGs, NPGs

continued

Table 4.1. (continued)

	Examples of public goods
Country-based institutions	
Centers for Disease Control	Offers outbreak surveillance, isolation of new pathogens, knowledge; provides public goods at all levels
Pasteur Institute	Offers isolation of new pathogens, knowledge; provides public goods at all levels

GPGs, TRPGs, RPGs, and NPGs. At times, regional institutions may promote GPGs and TRPGs beyond their jurisdictional mandate. We will return to this observation when discussing subsidiarity.

PROGNOSES ON THE PROVISION OF NPGS, RPGS, TRPGS, AND GPGS

Supplying the four classes of public goods with different spillover ranges confronts diverse challenges. As such, each pair (for example, NPGs and GPGs) can make for interesting pairwise comparisons. NPGs yield benefits primarily confined to the country's territory. Examples of NPGs include a country's justice system, its national guard, its police, its infrastructure, and its primary schools. Some NPGs—a national park—attract foreign visitors, thereby yielding spillovers beyond the country's territory. Of the four classes of public goods, NPGs have the most favorable prognosis, because countries possess proper incentives to supply these goods. This follows because no other country will provide these NPGs and the goods' benefit primarily enrich the country's citizens. Moreover, the central government makes provision decisions primarily in light of the NPG's benefit recipients whom it represents. If financing is a problem, then a developing country has an incentive to obtain loans from the World Bank, regional development banks, donor countries, or other institutions. NPGs are complementary to RPGs, TRPGs, and GPGs (Ferroni and Mody, 2002). For instance, a country's education attainment—an NPG—is necessary to promote good health and sustainable environmental practices, whose benefits spill over to other countries. In addition, a country's security forces can not only maintain peace within the country, but can also promote regional stability, an RPG. The main inhibitor of NPGs is a lack of finances—poor countries may be constrained in their ability to obtain the necessary financing. In Table 4.2, we list the three promoters and the sole inhibitor of NPGs, along with promoters and inhibitors for the other three public goods.

RPGs confront more challenges to their provision than NPGs and GPGs. In RPGs' favor, the rise of regionalism and customs unions can facilitate provision.

Table 4.2. Factors promoting and inhibiting NPGs, RPGs, TRPGs, and GPGs

National Public Goods (NPGs)

- Incentives favorable for countries to provide NPGs (promote)
- Loans from development banks, multilaterals, and donors can be taken out by countries (promote)
- NPGs complementary to RPGs, TRPGs, and GPGs (promote)
- Countries may lack finances (inhibit)

Regional Public Goods (RPGs)

- New regionalism and customs unions can facilitate provision (promote)
- Cultural and spatial propinquity among spillover recipients (promote)
- Fewer countries than TRPGs and GPGs (promote)
- Past and ongoing interactions among regional countries (promote)
- Less donor spillovers owing to regional specificity of benefits (inhibit)
- Regional rivalry (inhibit)
- Absence of a regional leader country (inhibit)
- Collectives must be formed to gain loans and provide collateral (inhibit)

Transregional Public Goods (TRPGs)

- Donor spillovers may arise, especially if there are joint products (promote)
- Multilateral aid agencies have an interest (promote)
- Transaction costs associated with transregional networks (inhibit)
- Large number of countries are involved (inhibit)
- Geographic dispersion of spillover recipients (inhibit)
- Absence of jurisdiction-specific institution (inhibit)

Global Public Goods (GPGs)

- Donor spillovers prevalent (promote)
- Multilateral institutions champion GPGs (promote)
- Large number of countries involved (inhibit)
- May possess unfavorable publicness properties (uncertain)

These customs unions can provide financing and coalesce provision efforts. The regional development banks can also play an important role in providing loans and grants.[4] These banks help countries recognize the benefits from regional collective action, particularly in regards to regional infrastructure. Cultural and spatial propinquity among spillover recipients can bolster RPG provision. At the regional level, countries engage in repeated interactions, which reduce

4. In Latin America, other regional development banks include Corporación Andina de Fomento (CAF), Banco Nacional de Desarrollo Económico de Brasil (BNDES), and Fondo para el Desarrollo de la Cuenca del Plata (FONPLATA) (Sandler, 2013a).

transaction costs and allow countries to establish good working relationships with nearby countries. Realistic expectations are formed among interacting countries that foster a culture of exchange and cooperation (North, 1990).

Reduced spillovers to potential donors can limit RPG provision owing to regional spillover specificity. Many RPGs offer few spillover benefits to many supporters of multilateral organizations. For instance, limiting acid rain in many parts of Latin America may have little benefits to parts of Europe, given prevailing wind patterns. Regional rivalries and past conflicts are apt to curtail cooperation to provide RPGs (Cook and Sachs, 1999). Also, some regions do not have a leader country with the status and resources to champion RPGs locally. These and other factors can inhibit the formation of collectives to provide collateral and obtain loans for RPGs. An individual country does not have the proper incentives to go into debt to provide RPGs for the entire region, especially when its gain is smaller than the costs.

TRPGs represent an interesting class of public goods whose benefit spillover range lies between that of RPGs and GPGs (Sandler, 2013a). Given their greater range of spillovers, TRPGs are more likely to benefit more donor countries than RPGs, thereby offering a greater incentive for these donors to support TRPG provision. At times, donors may gain from TRPGs' jointly produced benefits. The preservation of the rain forest in Brazil not only protects local ecosystems in distinct regions of South America, but also sequesters carbon and preserves species for the benefit of everyone. Multilateral aid agencies have an interest in providing TRPGs, as previously indicated in Table 4.1. Considerations working against TRPG provision include the significant transaction costs associated with transregional networks. These costs are bolstered when a TRPG changes its character between regions (for example, prophylactic measures against malaria and river blindness differ among infected regions). The large number of countries involved and the geographic dispersion of spillovers can also hamper TRPG supply. Another impediment concerns the absence of jurisdiction-specific institutions; this is sometimes rectified by networking regional institutions. The latter action, when feasible, economizes on transaction costs.

Table 4.2 lists some facilitators and impediments to GPGs. A significant boost for GPGs derives from the presence of global spillovers, which offer an incentive for many potential donor countries and institutions to have a GPG interest. In particular, multilaterals have a strong motive to assist in GPG supply. There is now a trust of key multilaterals and their auxiliary organizations (for example, the World Health Organization or the UN Environmental Program) to supply GPGs. Some rich countries and multistakeholder organizations also provide GPGs. The primary inhibitor of GPGs involves the number of benefit recipients, but this concern can be addressed through the actions of multilaterals that can direct action through their collected revenues and their considerable infrastructure. In so doing, transaction costs are economized, because one organization can raise money from many donors and then channel it to worthwhile GPGs. Finally, some GPGs may possess unfavorable publicness properties that block action. In particular, climate change has proven difficult to ameliorate owing to nonrivalry, nonexcludability, and a summation aggregator. GPGs have a better prognosis than RPGs and TRPGs, given a well-established culture to support multilaterals and the ability of GPGs to benefit all countries. Dating back to Olson (1965), a greater number of participants have been viewed as a key inhibitor of collective action. This inhibitor may, however, be counterbalanced by institution-based actions to reduce transaction costs (Libecap, 2014). For example, donor countries have relied on the World Bank to channel their donations into effective development projects, thereby saving monitoring and other transaction costs on the part of the donors. A basic message is that facilitators and inhibitors must be weighed together to ascertain the net proclivity to provide public goods.

TPG CATEGORIES: A FINER TAXONOMY

There are many ways to specify a taxonomy for public goods, so that there is no definitive or best taxonomy for public goods. In Chapter 3, we presented two taxonomies—Table 3.1 categorizes public goods based on the extent of benefit rivalry and excludability, while Table 3.2 pigeonholes these goods based on seven aggregator technologies. As a finer taxonomy, we now combine three public good types—namely, pure public, impure public, and club goods—from Table 3.1 with six of the seven aggregators of Table 3.2. This new taxonomy indicates that *all three characteristics of publicness* must be considered in order to draw a proper prognosis of public good supply. In addition, this new taxonomy shows that public goods come in a rich array of forms, in which even pure public goods may be efficiently supplied under some aggregators. As institutions come to influence the characteristics of the public good, provision can be encouraged by, say, designing institutions to transform the nature of the public good to one that is more amenable to provision.

Recall that pure public goods possess nonrival and nonexcludable benefits; impure public goods display partially rival and partially excludable benefits; and club goods offer partially rival and excludable benefits. Further subdivision of impure public goods is possible—for instance, an impure public good can be partially rival and nonexcludable, nonrival and excludable, or some other combination. For maximum contrast in Table 4.3, we assume a generic impure public good possessing partially rival and partially excludable benefit. When ascertaining the quantity of the public good available for consumption, a summation aggregator merely adds individual contributions together, while a weighted-sum aggregator applies weights to individual contributions. For a weakest-link aggregator, the smallest contribution determines the level of the public good; for a best-shot aggregator, the largest contribution fixes the level of the public good (Hirshleifer,

Table 4.3. Taxonomy based on three dimensions of publicness and aggregators: Supply prognosis

Aggregate technology	Pure public good (nonrival and nonexcludable)	Impure public good (partial rivalry and partial excludability)	Club good (partial rivalry and excludable)
Summation	undersupplied *curbing climate change due to global warming*	overuse/undersupplied *deterrence against terrorism*	efficient supply *transnational canal/waterway*
Weighted sum	undersupply dependent on agent-specific benefits and actions *reducing acid rain*	overuse/undersupplied with agent-specific benefits important *cleansing an oil spill*	efficient supply *INTELSAT*
Weakest link	efficient for a homogeneous group; spending capacity concern *disease containment*	overuse/some undersupply even for homogeneous groups owing to crowding *limiting money laundering*	externality-based undersupply *air transport hub-spoke network*
Weaker link	efficient for a homogeneous group; less spending capacity concern *limiting financial instability*	overuse/some undersupply owing to crowding *maintaining sterilization*	some externality-based undersupply *network with redundancies*
Best shot	undersupply or efficient supply; coordination issue *neutralizing a rogue country*	overuse/some undersupply; coordination issue *intelligence on international crime*	efficient supply *crisis-management teams*
Better shot	undersupply or efficient supply; coordination issue is less worrisome *developing treatment regimes*	overuse/some undersupply; coordination issue is less of a concern *compiling databases*	efficient supply *BSL-4 laboratory*

Note: Examples are in italics

1983). Contributions beyond the smallest add progressively less to the overall level of a weaker-link public good, while contributions below the largest add progressively less to the overall level of a better-shot public good.

By combining three classic types of public goods with six aggregator technologies, we have 18 categories of public goods in Table 4.3, where each type has its own supply prognosis. For each category, we indicate a representative public good. For example, curbing climate change is the quintessential purely public good that abides by a summation aggregator, since climate change due to global warming depends on the aggregate amount of greenhouse gases emitted to the atmosphere. The location or identity of the emitter is not important; rather, the sum of the emissions causes the warming of the earth's atmosphere. A weighted-sum technology applies to reducing acid rain because the transport of sulfur or nitrogen pollutants from a source country in the lower atmosphere depends on wind direction, a polluting country's size, and its location, so that different weights apply to emissions or their reduction (Sandler, 2010a). Infectious disease containment is a weakest-link pure public good, because the smallest containment effort determines the safety of everyone. With some thought, the reader can understand the other examples in light of the detailed discussion of aggregator technologies presented earlier in Chapter 3. For the various impure public goods, some excludability of benefits is present; for example, intelligence on international crime or compiled databases can be partially excluded. Exclusion of these impure public goods is not complete because once someone acquires them, the purchaser may pass them along to others. Moreover, these goods' benefits may diminish with use by others. Intelligence is a best-shot public good because the greatest effort is most apt to discover the required knowledge, while lesser efforts by others generally add nothing to what has already been learned. In contrast, additional data collection of a lower quality may still possess some new information, making it a better-shot public good. The cleansing of an oil spill has a location component owing to sea currents, so that a weighted-sum aggregator applies. Since oil pollutant diminishes with distance from its source, there is partial rivalry. The properties of the other examples of pure and impure public goods can be similarly justified.

In the club good column, each of six goods in Table 4.3 displays some rivalry but is excludable. The International Telecommunication Satellite Organization (INTELSAT) charges users for phone calls, television transmissions, and other utilization of its communication network. The placement of satellites means that coverage and capacity are not the same throughout the globe; hence, a weighted-sum technology applies. Other club goods in Table 4.3 are canals, air transport hub-spoke networks, networks with built-in redundancies, crisis-management teams (for example, Delta Force), and BSL-4 laboratories. BSL-4 denotes the most secure biosafety or biocontainment laboratory, used to isolate and study the most dangerous biological agents. The grade of biosafety laboratories varies from a lowest containment level of 1 to a highest containment level of 4. Air transport hub-spoke networks, such as airports or even air-traffic control systems, are weakest-link public goods because a failure anywhere can disrupt the entire network, which is obvious to European air travelers. In contrast, networks with redundancies allow a less efficient parallel system to take over when the primary network is disrupted, thereby making for a weaker-link club good.[5] Crisis-management teams can be dispatched worldwide to address terrorist events (for example, a ship hijacking). All that is needed is an optimally spaced grid of best-trained teams, giving the public good a best-shot character (Sandler, Tschirhart, and Cauley, 1983). BSL-4 laboratories are better-shot public goods, since lesser-quality laboratories still serve a purpose and can be utilized if a mishap befalls the best laboratory.

When moving away from the summation aggregator, the supply prognosis for a pure public good generally improves in Table 4.3. If, for instance, a weighted-sum aggregator applies and *a large weight is placed on the country's own provision*, then the country is anticipated to contribute a more efficient quantity, because the country's efforts are an imperfect substitute for those of other countries, thus limiting free riding. This explains why such significant progress has been made in reducing sulfur emissions, which largely fall on home soil (see Chapter 12). For a weakest-link TPG, countries that are homogeneous in terms of tastes and endowments will match one another's efficient responses. In a more diverse group, the better-endowed countries may have to raise the contributing capacity of those that cannot meet a desirable provision level (Vicary and Sandler, 2002). The prognoses for the remaining pure public good aggregators follow earlier discussions in Chapter 3. For example, best-shot and better-shot TPGs may be efficiently supplied when there is a leader country with sufficient resources to privilege other countries.

Impure public goods display less drastic changes in their supply prognoses in Table 4.3 as the aggregation technology alters. Overuse is prevalent throughout insofar as partial rivalry implies crowding costs that may not be fully taken into account because exclusion is incomplete. That is, unlike club goods, a crowding-based user fee is not imposed on all users when required. Undersupply is attenuated, but does not disappear, for weakest-link impure goods as provision decisions do not fully account for crowding costs.

In the right-most column of Table 4.3, we distinguish the supply prognosis for club goods associated with the six aggregator technologies. Except for weakest-link and weaker-link club goods, this prognosis is excellent because a club can use tolls to finance the shared good without the need for intervention. Consider, however, a weakest-link club good, such as an air-traffic network in Europe. If, say, France does not maintain its part of the network to the same standards as other European countries and experiences frequent

---

5. A redundant parallel system is a costly safeguard.

disruptions, then reliability of the entire network suffers. Tolls charged to commercial aircraft for using the air corridors adjust for corridor crowding but not for air-traffic control reliability. If a club arrangement is instituted for sharing air corridors, then the same arrangement must be instituted for airport security, air-traffic control, and other aspects jointly consumed with the air corridors (Sandler, 2004, p. 84).

Based on Table 4.3, there are a number of institutional recommendations. First, any supranational intervention in terms of multilateral institutions, treaties, or specialized agencies is mainly required for pure and impure public goods that abide by summation or weighted-sum aggregators. For the latter aggregator, provision and efficiency concerns are particularly worrisome when weights on the countries' own provision are small. Second, as aggregators other than summation are considered, the need for remedial action declines. Third, countries' financial capacity must be addressed for weakest-link and weaker-link public goods. Fourth, club arrangements are especially attractive; however, some remedial action is required for weakest-link and weaker-link club goods owing to maintenance or reliability externalities. Foreign assistance may be necessary for some poor countries if they are to afford clubs' user charges (Kanbur, Sandler, and Morrison, 1999). For club arrangements, private provision is an option as in the case of INTELSAT, which is now in the private sector. Private provision is also an option for infrastructure, where the private provider can recoup its investment over time through toll revenues. As monitoring and exclusion technologies improve with time, more TPGs can be allocated through club arrangements. Fifth, leadership by a dominant country can be essential for best-shot and better-shot TPGs. When this leadership is not possible in a region, efforts for best-shot public goods can be pooled or coordinated by a regional development bank or customs union. Sixth, weaker-link and better-shot TPGs are expected to require less policy intervention than their extreme forms.

ON SUBSIDIARITY

TPGs possess a variety of spillover ranges, which raises the question as to how an institution's jurisdictional range should correspond to its TPGs' spillover range. The principle of *subsidiarity* supports matching, when possible, the allocating institution's jurisdiction and the spillover range of its public good.[6] As such, country-based institutions supply NPGs; region-based institutions provide RPGs; transregional organizations offer TRPGs; and multilaterals oversee GPGs. This ideal is akin to *fiscal equivalence*, first specified by Breton

6. On subsidiarity, see Arce and Sandler (2002), Kanbur (2002), Kanbur, Sandler, and Morrison (1999), and Sandler (2004, 2013a).

(1965) and Olson (1969), which requires that the political jurisdiction of an allocating government coincides with the range of public good spillovers. By matching the decision-making jurisdiction and the good's economic interests, there is a proclivity to aggregate the derived marginal benefits of the public good over the right number of benefit recipients, thereby promoting provision efficiency.[7] If, however, the political jurisdiction is a subset of the good's spill-over range, then too-few benefit recipients will be included in the provision decision and, thus, too little of the public good will be provided. When the Chinese government considers reductions of China-generated sulfur pollution, it will account for harm to Chinese citizens but will not include harm to Los Angeles residents, who experience some of this pollution as it is transported by a trans-Pacific slipstream. Too little cutbacks in sulfur emissions results because the decision-making jurisdiction is too small. If, in contrast, the political juris-diction exceeds the public good's spillover range, then there is a tendency to tax nonrecipients of benefits, thereby resulting in overprovision of the public good (Olson, 1969).

Subsidiarity, like fiscal equivalence, seeks to promote public good efficiency by matching jurisdictional and public good spillover ranges. In addition, subsidiarity stresses the notion that institutions should not reach beyond their jurisdictional mandates, nor should they necessarily serve below their juris-dictional mandates. By not overreaching, subsidiarity aims to limit transac-tion costs by serving those that the institution serves and knows best. Transaction costs are kept in check by reducing the number of participants to just those with a stake in the activity. Moreover, this focus on essential deci-sion makers and those whom they serve fosters repeated interactions, which, in turn, furthers learning and curtails asymmetric information as the two sides come to understand one another. The presence of localized benefits sup-ports the evolution of institutions based on shared culture, norms, and values (North, 1990).

In practice, institutions do not always strictly adhere to subsidiarity—for example, the World Bank promotes public goods below the global level. In Table 4.4, we indicate supporting and detracting influences on subsidiarity. The top half of the table gathers some of the supporting factors mentioned earlier—that is, fostering efficiency by matching recipients' benefits and public goods' costs, limiting tax spillovers, curtailing transaction costs, and promoting institutional evolution. A fifth encouraging consideration is to curb the "mission creep" of multilateral institutions, which continue to em-brace new activities.

As shown in Table 4.4, there are a number of factors that detract from the strict adherence to subsidiarity when choosing a jurisdiction's size. First,

---

7. Provision efficiency requires the sum of marginal benefits, summed over benefit recipients, to equal the marginal cost of the public good.

Table 4.4. Supporting and detracting influences on subsidiarity

- *Supporting factors for subsidiarity*
  - Matching economic and political domains fosters efficiency by equating the good's marginal cost of provision and the recipients' marginal benefits.
  - Fosters efficiency by limiting tax spillovers to nonbeneficiaries.
  - Limits transaction costs by reducing the number of participants, augmenting repeated interactions, curtailing asymmetric information, and capitalizing on propinquity.
  - Supports the evolution of the institution based on shared culture, experiences, concerns, norms, and values.
  - Avoids "mission creep" of global institutions.
- *Detracting factors of subsidiarity*
  - Economies of scale from reduced unit costs favor serving a larger jurisdiction than the spillover range of the public good.
  - Economies of scope from reduced unit cost endorse providing two or more public goods in the same jurisdiction. If these economies of scope are sufficiently large, then subsidiarity may lose its sway when the goods' spillover ranges differ.
  - Economies of learning may require oversized jurisdictions where the cumulative level of the public good is larger.
  - The requisite subsidiarity-based institution may not exist or possess sufficient capacity.
  - Best-shot and better-shot technology may favor pooling beyond the jurisdiction identified by subsidiarity. The same may be true for some threshold aggregators.
  - The requisite financing may require a larger political jurisdiction than the range of benefit spillovers.

economies of scale may justify institutions whose political domain exceeds that of the good's spillover range. Scale economies reduce unit costs as a larger quantity of the public good is produced. Thus, two or more neighboring countries may share a wastewater treatment plant to lower unit costs. These reduced costs may overcome any efficiency losses from sharing production of their NPGs, thereby eliminating the need of subsidiarity. Second, economies of scope from sharing common inputs can reduce unit costs from supplying two or more *different* public goods by the same institution. These common costs may arise from administrative or distribution inputs that can serve multiple public goods. Third, by increasing the cumulative provision of the public good, cost savings from economies of learning may warrant oversized decision-making jurisdictions. Fourth, the requisite sized institution for the public good's spillover range may not exist, thereby mandating that an undersized or oversized jurisdiction takes charge. This is particularly germane for some TRPGs. Fifth, the aggregation technology may favor a jurisdiction larger than that associated with subsidiarity. This is particularly true for some best-shot or better-shot public goods, whose provision is beyond the capacity of an institution with a political domain matching the good's spillover range. Finally, the requisite financing may require a larger political jurisdiction than that associated with the good's spillover range. The U.S. government uses its considerable taxing authority and ability to collect revenues that, at times, are given to the 50 states for them to supply some of their local public goods. This practice is known as revenue sharing.

THE UNITED NATIONS AND THE INTER-AMERICAN DEVELOPMENT BANK

In light of subsidiarity, these two institutions serve as an instructive paired comparison. As a multilateral institution, the United Nations provides GPGs—for example, promoting world peace, reducing global poverty, and curbing global warming. In fact, the United Nations has so many missions that it has created specialized agencies, such as the WHO, to address specific GPGs. Additionally, the UN Environmental Program (UNEP) promotes efforts to curb pollution at the global and regional levels. At the latter level, UNEP assists the provision of RPGs such as reducing acid rain. The United Nations also coordinates actions to supply TRPGs since it is positioned to network distant regions. Finally, UN efforts to curb poverty yield NPGs as they improve education, local infrastructure, population control, sanitation, and healthcare. These NPGs are complementary to public goods with transnational spillovers. Complementary goods enhance one another's usefulness to their consumers (for example, pie crust and filling). Countries have come to depend on the United Nations to facilitate the provision of a wide range of public goods with diverse spillover ranges. The United Nations takes advantage of economies of scale, scope, and learning, as well as other considerations that lessen its adherence to subsidiarity. Over many years, the United Nations established a brand name. What is true for the United Nations is also true of other multilaterals, such as the World Bank, whose mandates and public goods have grown.

The Inter-American Development Bank (IDB) is less an outgrowth of globalization and more a consequence of the new regionalism. IDB does not have the funding resources of the United Nations, and like other development banks, serves a geographically narrower client-state constituency. The IDB only provides GPGs indirectly as a joint product of an RPG—for example, IDB-assisted efforts to protect the Amazon rain forest also sequester carbon and preserve species, which are two GPGs. Most of the IDB's efforts are directed at promoting South-South cooperation, which yields NPGs and RPGs (Shearer and Tres, 2013). In recent years, IDB pushed concerted actions by Latin American countries, donor countries, multilaterals, and other interested institutions to augment regional infrastructure. As such, projects abound to link seaports with interstate highways to improve communication networks, upgrade interoperational rail networks, and facilitate the ease of commerce.

Any transregional actions of the IDB are typically confined to forging linkages between customs unions in two different Latin American regions. Thus, the IDB better displays subsidiarity than the United Nations or the World Bank. There is, however, an interest in linking the North American Free Trade Agreement (NAFTA) to customs unions in Central and South America, where the IDB may come to assume a role in promoting TRPGs with spillovers outside of South America. The growing importance of IDB and other development banks may potentially release the United Nations and the World Bank from some of their regional duties, thereby fostering a somewhat greater adherence to subsidiarity.

SOME DESIGN PRINCIPLES FOR SUPRANATIONAL INSTITUTIONS

In this section, we use some elementary game theory to formulate some useful design principles for supranational institutions joining two or more sovereign states. Our first principle stems from a paired comparison between a Prisoners' Dilemma (PD) game and an assurance game. The latter is associated here with a threshold public good, where a minimal number of units must be contributed before benefits are received. In the top matrix of Figure 4.1, a six-country PD game is depicted, where *each unit* of a public good gives the contributing country and the other five countries nonexcludable benefits, b_i, of 6 at a cost, c_i, of 8 to the contributor. Each country has two possible strategies: contribute no units or contribute one unit. Since similar examples are presented in Chapter 2 (see Figures 2.2 and 2.3), our discussion is understandably brief. When country i does not contribute, it gains 6 in free-rider benefits from each of the contributors, as shown in the top row of matrix a. If country i contributes alone, then it nets $-2 (= 6 - 8)$. When country i and one other country contributes, then it nets $4 (= 2 \times 6 - 8)$, which equals the benefits from two units of the public good, which is 12, less i's costs of 8. Each payoff in the top row of matrix a is 2 greater than the corresponding payoff in the bottom row.[8] Hence, the dominant strategy for country i is not to contribute, so that i and the other five countries do not contribute, resulting in zero all-around contributions as the Nash equilibrium. The social optimum is for every country to contribute for an aggregate gain of $6 \times 28 = 168$.

In matrix b of Figure 4.1, the public good is transformed into a threshold public good where at least three units must be contributed *before* each country receives a benefit of 6 on each contributed unit. Per-unit costs stay at 8. When less than three units are contributed or less than three countries contribute, the threshold is not attained and there are no benefits. In the bottom row of matrix b, country i nets -8 if less than two countries join its efforts; hence, the

8. The shortfall in the bottom row equals $b_i - c_i = 6 - 8$.

	Number of contributors other than country i					
	0	1	2	3	4	5
i Does Not Contribute	Nash 0	6	12	18	24	30
i Contributes	−2	4	10	16	22	28

a. *Prisoners' Dilemma*: everyone receives $b_i = 6$ on each contributed units, while contributors pay $c_i = 8$

	Number of contributors other than country i					
	0	1	2	3	4	5
i Does Not Contribute	Nash 0	0	0	18	24	30
i Contributes	−8	−8	Nash 10	16	22	28

b. *Minimal threshold*: $c_i = 8$ for each unit contributed, but $b_i = 0$ if contributions are less than 3 units and $b_i = 6$ after 3 units

Figure 4.1
Alternative institutional forms based on Prisoners' Dilemma and threshold

first two entries are −8. Past the threshold of three contributors, i's payoffs match those in the bottom row of matrix a. There are now numerous Nash equilibria; the one where no one contributes and those where exactly three countries contribute.[9] Because there are twenty ways that a subset of three countries can be chosen from a set of six countries, there are now 21 Nash equilibria when the no-contribution equilibrium is included. In matrix b, if more than three countries contribute, then the payoffs in the top row again dominate those in the bottom row. For more than three contributors, another unit contributed adds two less in benefits than in costs for a new contributor. A threshold technology improves contribution prognosis because there are now positive contribution equilibria in contrast to the PD representation when there is no threshold.

Environmental treaties often build a threshold membership requirement into their ratification process; that is, unless a set number of countries sign the treaty, it does not go into effect. For UN peacekeeping missions, the UN Security Council waits until a necessary level of force—troops and equipment—is assembled before deploying the troops for the mission. Some charitable organizations wait until a threshold level of contributions is achieved before pursuing a particular goal or activity. In these three examples, the providing institution makes the good a threshold public good. At other times, the nature of the public

9. If r is the threshold number of countries and n is the total number of countries being considered, then the number of different ways that r countries can be chosen from n is $n!/(n-r)!r!$ or 20 when $n = 6$ and $r = 3$.

good, not the nature of some institution, requires a certain level of effort before any benefits are realized. The use of threshold is, however, a common ploy of institutions to induce collective action.

There are a few things to note about threshold public goods. First, as the size of the threshold increases, the social optimum is approached by the Nash equilibrium. When the threshold includes all countries, the Nash equilibrium is the social optimum. Second, there is still a coordination concern, because the right number of contributors must come forward. In matrix b with a threshold of three, three countries do better by being in the noncontributor subset. If countries are heterogeneous, then those countries with the greatest gain will come forward to achieve the threshold. For homogeneous countries, an institution must act to induce the required coordination—for example, letting countries take turns in terms of their contributions. Third, there are other institutional design tricks to promote threshold public goods. Allowing refunds if the threshold is not reached would change the two -8 payments into 0 in matrix b, so that there are no worries about falling short of the thresholds. With refunds, the positive-contribution Nash equilibriums become the focus (Bagnoli and McKee, 1991). Fourth, another institutional design ploy is cost sharing among contributors and noncontributors, which for any group size greater than c_i/b_i makes the contribution strategy dominant, as discussed in Chapter 2 for PD games where $c_i > b_i$.

Next, we investigate institutional design and prospects when countries view their net benefits differently. To do so, we present a stylized, useful example involving two subsets of countries—six of which derive 6 in benefits from each unit of the public good, and four of which derive 12 from each unit

	Number of other contributing countries in group 1					
	0	1	2	3	4	5
i Does Not Contribute	Nash **0**	6	12	18	24	30
i Contributes	−3	3	9	15	21	Social optimum 27

a. Prisoners' Dilemma, $b_i = 6$ and $c_i = 9$

	Number of other contributing countries			
	0	1	2	3
i Does Not Contribute	0	12	24	36
i Contributes	3	15	27	**39**

b. $b_i = 12$ and $c_i = 9$

Figure 4.2
Heterogeneous countries with noncontributors and contributors

of the public good. Each unit costs the provider 9. Every country possesses two strategies: supply nothing or supply a single unit. In matrix a of Figure 4.2, the less-interested countries confront a PD game with a unique Nash equilibrium of no provision. In matrix b of Figure 4.2, each of the other four countries nets 3 from providing a unit of the public good. If country i contributes and is joined by one other contributor, then each earns 15 as costs of 9 are deducted from the gain of 24 on the two contributed units. The other payoffs in the bottom row are computed in a similar fashion. In the top row of matrix b, benefits equal 12 times the number of countries in the second group offering a free ride.[10] This is a harmony game (see Chapter 2) with a dominant strategy to contribute. Hence, the Nash equilibrium for the second group of countries has all four countries contributing for a net gain of 39 apiece. Because the good is purely public, the first group of noncontributors receives a free-rider gain of 24 $(= 4 \times 6)$. If 24 is added to *all payoffs in matrix a*, the dominant strategy for these less interested countries is still not to contribute, because the top row's payoffs still exceed the corresponding bottom row's payoffs by 3. Thus, the Nash equilibrium involves four contributors and six noncontributors.

This bifurcation between contributors and noncontributors is descriptive of many real-world collectives where countries view the public good differently. For example, some countries contribute troops to non-UN-led peacekeeping missions in Afghanistan, the Balkans, and elsewhere while others do not (Gaibulloev, Sandler, and Shimizu, 2009). Some countries have voluntarily curbed greenhouse gas emissions and others have not. Initially, some rich countries signed the Montreal Protocol on Substances That Deplete the Ozone Layer because they valued the ozone layer more than other countries did.[11] In the case of the Montreal Protocol, these ratifiers induced others to join through rewards and punishments. Rewards took the form of grants from the Multilateral Fund (MLF), funded by the rich ratifiers that helped countries to switch from CFCs to other ozone-benign refrigerants. As more countries signed the Montreal Protocol, the burden per rich ratifier of the MLF decreased. Punishment took the form of threatened trade sanctions (Barrett, 2003a; Benedick, 1991; Congleton, 1992; Murdoch and Sandler, 1997).

As contributors increase in number over time, they acquire greater abilities to impose rewards and punishments on noncontributors, so that these noncontributors come to view contributing in a favorable light. The message in institutional design is to start off with a modest number of committed cooperators, whose numbers can be increased over time. Also, the degree of

10. We ignore the countries in the first group since no one in this group will contribute.

11. The Montreal Protocol went into effect after 11 countries, constituting two-thirds of the world consumption of ozone depleters, ratified the treaty (Barrett, 2003a, p. 227).

cooperation can be ratcheted up over time as contributors come to appreciate the net gain from contributing. If a proposed collective aims too high in terms of initial membership size and initial linkage tightness, there may be no countries that view there to be a net benefit.[12] This strongly suggests that a regional collective can evolve into a transregional collective. When warranted, the latter can become a global collective.

CONCLUDING REMARKS

There are some general principles that follow from our analysis. First, all three properties of public goods must be consulted to formulate a proper prognosis for TPG supply. The aggregator technology adds an important dimension beyond benefit nonrivalry and nonexcludability, as shown in Table 4.3. For instance, weakest-link and weaker-link aggregators can inhibit the efficient provision of club goods owing to externalities stemming from maintenance and upgrade decisions. If the aggregator technology is not considered, then club goods have an excellent prognosis. Second, there are various levels of TPGs, based on their range of benefit spillovers, which bring up an institutional decision. The principle of subsidiarity indicates that the jurisdictional range of the institution that supplies the public good should match the good's spillover range. In practice, institutions, such as the United Nations, facilitate the supply of myriad public goods with diverse ranges of spillovers, including those at the regional and country levels. Thus, we analyze considerations that work in favor of and against the application of subsidiarity. Subsidiarity is a useful initial principle that must be relaxed accordingly based on other considerations. Third, we illustrate a large number of TPGs and some of the institutions created or designated to supply these public goods. New institutions have arisen in the last decades that include multistakeholder institutions such as the Global Fund to Fight HIV/AIDS, TB, and Malaria (Sridhar and Woods, 2013).[13] Institutions at the supranational level have grown greatly in number and type. Fourth, institutional design can facilitate the provision of TPGs by aligning agents' net benefits with the motive to contribute. Further design principles could have been discussed such as private inducements or selective incentives to engineer a dominant strategy to contribute. Such institutional engineering is germane to the issue-based chapters. Fifth, an initial formation dilemma for supranational organizations must be addressed. Our analysis suggests that organizations that begin with

12. Downs, Rocke, and Barsoom (1998) established this principle with some formal cooperative game theory. Also see Sandler and Cauley (1977).

13. Stakeholders in the Global Fund include representatives from civil society, the private sector, the Gates Foundation, developing countries, donor countries, and multilaterals (WHO, UNAIDS, and the World Bank).

a limited number of similar-minded countries with a restricted mandate are more apt to form. The organization can later expand its membership and mandate, as has been the case for the EU and NATO.

There are considerations beneath the country level that need to be addressed in ensuing chapters. In particular, how do agents within the country influence decision makers, who negotiate the country's position of TPGs with their counterparts in other countries? The answer involves political concerns that we have thus far avoided. Clearly, public opinion can influence the way that a country formulates or changes its position on TPGs. If, for example, citizens worry greatly about climate change, then country leaders will be forced to take a stronger position on the issue, especially in a liberal democracy, where citizens' well-being is valued.

CHAPTER 5

Sovereignty, Leadership, and U.S. Hegemony

The invasion of Iraq in 2003 focused the world's attention on the power of the United States, its military superiority, and its ability to coerce other states into its preferred policy choices. The U.S. government justified that invasion on the grounds that an untrustworthy leader possessed weapons of mass destruction and *might* use them against his own people. Although these claims were later proven false, the Bush administration clearly believed that its claims justified intervention and the overthrow of Saddam Hussein.

Ten years later, Iraq's neighbor Syria carried out an attack against its own people—rockets carrying sarin gas were fired from a government-controlled neighborhood to a suburb of Damascus that was known to be sympathetic to opposition forces. News reports showed dramatic photos of the dead, which numbered over 1,400 and included more than 400 children. The attack seemed a particularly egregious act that defied President Obama's warnings that such attacks would necessitate a military response. One month later, U.S. officials still debated how to respond, with both the U.S. Congress and American public opinion opposing any military action.[1] Rather than a U.S. invasion, elaborate diplomatic maneuvering allowed a temporary solution in which the Assad regime would voluntarily surrender its chemical weapon stockpiles, which would be destroyed by outside parties authorized by the United Nations (UN).

The incident demonstrated a new unwillingness by the world's great powers—particularly the United States—to enforce their will on rogue states. Some commentators deplored the failure to act, with *The Economist* (2013a) concluding, "it suddenly became clear just how far the influence of the West has ebbed." What happened between 2003 and 2013 to generate such different responses to similar concerns? Was U.S. failure to respond just an expression

---

1. According to Dugan (2013), only 36% of Americans supported a potential strike.

of war weariness after more than a decade of U.S. troops in Afghanistan and Iraq? Or was it a larger omen that U.S. power was declining? And what would the decline of U.S. power mean for future efforts to deter use of chemical weapons and to encourage other forms of transnational cooperation?

This chapter will address the importance of a dominant power, or hegemon, for transnational cooperation. After first setting the context for the continuing importance of power in international relations, we explore the treatment of leadership in game theory, both in the games introduced in previous chapters and in more recent game-theoretic treatments. We then revisit the question of how leadership matters for transnational cooperation in two cases: the U.S. role in post–World War II economic and military institutions, and its role in post–Cold War transnational cooperation.

SOVEREIGNTY AND THE COSTS OF COOPERATION

Thus far, we have treated states as autonomous actors who have the power to make their own decisions, even if the outcomes of those decisions depend on the actions of other states. This is consistent with the modern understanding of states as the primary actors in world politics. Even though other actors, such as multinational corporations (MNCs), nongovernmental organizations (NGOs), and terrorist groups, can now influence international politics, they are rarely recognized as peers to states. Intergovernmental organizations like the UN and the International Monetary Fund (IMF) claim states as their members. These organizations play important roles in facilitating, monitoring, and enforcing cooperation, but their legal authority is granted—and can be removed—by states. So despite the increasing importance of nonstate actors in transnational cooperation, we continue to focus on states as the central actor.

Scholarly attention to states is often traced to the resolution of the Peace of Westphalia that officially ended the 30 Years' War in 1648. One important component of this complex war was a reaction by European monarchs against supranational authorities—in particular, the Catholic Church, the Pope, and the Holy Roman Empire. The peace settlement reached at the war's end revolved around those monarchs' desire to consolidate their power over their own territory. The solution incorporated at Westphalia—sovereignty—became a legal principle that has ordered international relations for the last five centuries.

Sovereignty may have created a sphere of authority for domestic politics in independent states, but it did nothing to order relations between states. As a result, international politics is often portrayed as qualitatively different from domestic politics and, in particular, has been characterized by the realist school as "anarchic." At its extreme, this analogy extends to the state of nature imagined by Thomas Hobbes in which powerful states have their way, while weak states are left with their scraps. Realists are unsurprised when some states cannot defend themselves and are overrun by their powerful neighbors, and when those that survive are preoccupied with national security. De jure sovereignty is guaranteed when states meet the four criteria of the 1929 Montevideo Convention: (1) a clearly defined territory, (2) a clearly defined population, (3) exclusive authority over those two, and (4) international recognition by their fellow states.

In 1648, sovereign states were not a global arrangement—most territories in the world were not recognizable as modern states, and politics often involved actors that transcended empires or territories (such as the Islamic Caliphate or British Empire) or that comprised only pieces of them (such as Lombardy and Prussia). Over time, and especially since the end of World War II, this sovereign state system incorporated more and more members. Much of the Western hemisphere entered as new states in the late eighteenth and early nineteenth centuries, several eastern European and Middle Eastern countries attained statehood after World War I, and many former colonies in Africa and Asia became independent states after World War II. Using data from Hensel (2009), Figure 5.1 depicts the number of new states added to the world system over the last two centuries. While the nineteenth and early twentieth centuries witnessed a steady but small increase, the last four decades of the twentieth century brought forth several waves of new entries, most notably in the 1960s and 1990s.

Sovereignty meant that monarchs recognized each other's political independence and ultimate authority in their own territory; by granting each

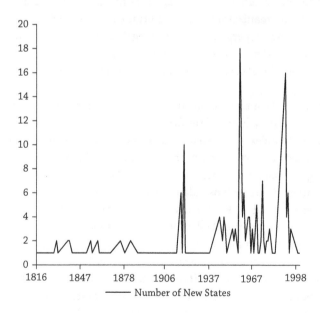

Figure 5.1
Number of newly independent states, 1816–2002

other sovereignty, monarchs promised to respect each other's borders and rights to govern within them. Modern autocrats, like Syria's Bashar al-Assad, still like to trumpet this conceptualization of sovereignty, since the original formulation meant that rulers were free to govern as they wished, free from outside interference. This sovereignty concept suggests that any cooperation with other states might be problematic, because it commits a country to actions that would not be taken otherwise and that limit its independence. This notion of "sovereignty costs" implies that states consider more than just the actual cost of collective action, such as the salaries of peacekeepers or the costs of switching production technologies to reduce pollution. Sovereignty costs involve states accepting limits on their autonomy, and while our example suggests that this is a problem for dictators, even democracies express concern at delegating authority to intergovernmental organizations or other countries. For example, any country that enters a non-aggression pact promises not to attack other members of the agreement, whereas countries that join defense pacts agree to come to the aid of other members. Presumably states use such alliances to achieve higher levels of security, but security cooperation comes with the cost of renouncing some possible action or committing to a new action that would not have been chosen otherwise. Morrow (1995) argues that military alliances involve trading autonomy for security. In contrast, building more weapons or hiring more soldiers could increase security without the same sovereignty costs.

Similar trade-offs exist in non-security forms of transnational cooperation. As noted in Chapter 4, many types of transnational cooperation require financing, which means that national governments prioritize international commitments over domestic ones. However, spending government revenue on national public and private goods is often more politically beneficial to elected officials. Other transnational commitments may not cost money but still reduce a country's ability to use preferred policies. In the European Union (EU), even typically pro-integration states encounter a sizeable backlash against their governments ceding more power to supranational institutions like the European Parliament or Council. Similarly, other multilateral organizations like the World Trade Organization (WTO) or IMF are often criticized for a lack of democratic processes. Historically, national legislatures have been hesitant to delegate much power to international bureaucracies.

Not all states are equally hesitant to empower multilateral organizations. Small states often have worse options without international cooperation, since their legal claim to sovereignty may not translate into nonintervention. Krasner (2009, p. 194) directed attention to frequent sovereignty violations, such as border raids or poaching, in small states, and rightly noted that "weaker states have always been the strongest supporters of the rule of nonintervention." Powerful states, by contrast, regularly ignore the principle of sovereignty when they have interests that transcend borders. Thus, although the modern state system is based on sovereignty, many states regularly experience challenges to their authority, and de facto sovereignty can be much different than the legal norm. If sovereignty is incomplete, then it is more appropriate to examine transnational cooperation with asymmetric players, where some states are more powerful than others.

Given the fragility of survival in such an environment, international relations theorists from the realist school typically attribute great importance to one dimension of international politics: how many great powers—or poles—exist at any given point in time. Periods of unipolarity, such as the United States immediately after World War II, contrast with bipolarity, such as the Cold War, or multipolarity, such as the Concert of Europe in the nineteenth century. Dynamics among the great powers have historically determined systemwide levels of conflict, and have kept weaker states on the defensive. Even when war is not a constant threat, great powers play an important role in international relations due to its most profound difference from domestic politics. Whereas domestic politics is ordered by law or the monopoly of force by the state, international politics often has no obvious enforcer of last resort. Conflicts between private individuals may be settled in domestic courts, by tribal leaders, or by other domestic institutions, but conflicts between states are more difficult to resolve. This is not because there are no international courts or juridical institutions—there are many—but they have little enforcement power compared to their domestic analogs. For example, treaties are difficult to enforce, and international organizations may have difficulty securing compliance on their own from member states.

Powerful states may have an advantage here and may be more likely to enforce cooperation that benefits them disproportionately. If powerful states insist that their weaker neighbors sign a treaty or enact a policy change, they are in a position to enforce it. Early notions of the importance of hegemony in world politics built on the simple observation that, in the last 200 years, the most dramatic periods of transnational economic cooperation overlapped with periods of relative peace and the existence of a unipolar system (Kindleberger, 1974). These include both the expansion of such cooperation under both the British Empire in the nineteenth century and American leadership in the twentieth century. When one state was powerful enough to dominate not just its neighbors but the entire globe, and when that state willingly accepted leadership of the international system, it sometimes provided public goods for all states and, at other times, created conditions for other states to join in the provision of public goods. Both economists (Kindleberger, 1974) and political scientists (Krasner, 1976) have acknowledged the important role that such a hegemon may play for transnational cooperation.

Bolstering the case for the importance of a hegemon for authors like Ruggie (1972) and Kindleberger (1974) was the breakdown of the international economic order both during and between the two World Wars. During the interwar period (1919–1939), countries failed to restore the economic stability that had prevailed under Britain's leadership. The United States, though capable of stepping into the role of hegemon, retreated inward and away from cooperation during this interwar period. This was best demonstrated by U.S. refusal to join the League of Nations. Although initially framed around the expansion of international trade, proponents of "hegemonic stability theory" extended the notion to other global public goods (Gilpin, 1981). Despite its intuitive appeal, both theory and evidence quickly cast doubt on the theory, but it stimulated much research on the importance of power and leadership in solving collective action problems (Keohane, 1997; Krasner, 1976).

GAME THEORY AND HEGEMONY

Our early models in Chapter 2 depicted simultaneous interactions between two symmetric states, which, while simpler, are not in keeping with international relations' focus on size, power, influence, and the like. To incorporate the notion of power into game theory, we must add new features to those games. The easiest one to incorporate is to allow one state to move before another.[2] In Chapter 3, we introduced leader-follower behavior, and this innovation changes the prognosis for collective action in some games, such as assurance, but not others. Leader-follower behavior can also be depicted using a tree diagram, also called the extensive form. Figure 5.2 includes an extensive form of the Prisoners' Dilemma game from Figure 2.1a. By introducing sequencing, or the order of moves, into the game, extensive-form games can help predict more precisely which of multiple Nash equilibria may result. To solve an extensive-form game, we start at the end of the game tree (on the far right in Figure 5.2) and calculate the optimal decision for the player who moves last at each decision node, denoted by the black dot. For an extensive-form game, the payoff for the player who moves first (player A) is listed first at the terminal nodes, followed to the right by the payoff of the player who moves second (player B). Hence, for example, if player A does not contribute and player B contributes, then A receives 7 and B receives −3. In Figure 5.2, player B does not contribute at the top decision node since its payoff of 0 exceeds −3 from contributing. Similarly, player B will not contribute at the bottom decision node since 7 > 4. We boldface these two branches since they denote B's best action at these nodes.

At player A's decision node at the outset of the game, A is better off not contributing because A looks ahead and knows that B will not contribute, no matter what A does. By not contributing, player A receives a payoff of 0 instead of −3 when player B exercises its best strategy at each subsequent

2. Game theory refers to a player who moves first as a Stackelberg leader.

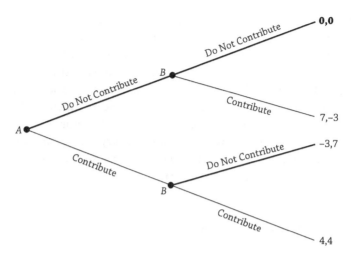

Figure 5.2
Prisoners' Dilemma in extensive form

decision node. Thus A's top branch is boldfaced as well. The "subgame perfect" solution is for A not to contribute and for B not to contribute at each of its decision nodes. For the subgame perfect equilibrium, neither player would change its strategy, if given the chance, at any decision node. Player B exercises its dominant strategy, since $0 > -3$ and $7 > 4$, while player A also exercises its dominant strategy, since $0 > -3$. If we were to reverse who moves first, the subgame perfect equilibrium is still for both players not to contribute at their decision nodes, so that the order of play makes no difference in a Prisoners' Dilemma. Simply changing the placement of the A and B at the decision nodes would reverse the order for this symmetric Prisoners' Dilemma. The predicted outcome in Figure 5.2 is therefore no different than in the original (simultaneous) Prisoners' Dilemma between two symmetric players. In other words, having the players move sequentially makes no difference to the predicted outcome of a Prisoners' Dilemma.

In many other extensive form games, because both players know each other's payoffs and choices, a player gains an advantage by moving first. Figure 5.3 presents the extensive form of the coordination game in 2.4b, but allows player A to move first. The original coordination game has two Nash equilibria, in which one player gives one unit and the other player does not. Again, we solve the game backwards and calculate the optimal move for player B first. At the upper node, player B will contribute and receive a payoff of 4, while at the lower node, player B will not contribute and receive a payoff of 7.

At the initial decision node, player A chooses its best strategy knowing that if it does not contribute that B will contribute, and if it does contribute that B will not contribute. Player A gains 7 from not contributing and gains only 4 from contributing; thus, A will not contribute knowing that it can free ride on

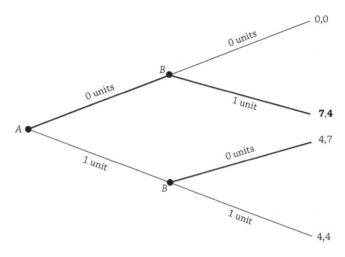

Figure 5.3
Coordination game in extensive form

B's subsequent contribution. In so doing, *A* gains 7 and *B* gains 4. Now that player *A* can move first, he can effectively choose which of the two outcomes will result. Here, player *A* has an incentive to free ride, and will force player *B* to choose to contribute at the upper node, which provides a payoff of 7 to player *A* and 4 to player *B*. Hence, we boldface the upper branch emanating from the initial node. The subgame perfect solution is for *A* not to contribute, and for *B* to do the opposite of what *A* does (for example, *B* contributes when *A* does not contribute). If the reader carefully translates the matrix game in Figure 2.4b into a sequential game with player *B* going first, then *B* will free ride on *A*'s subsequent contribution at the subgame perfect equilibrium. That is, moving first is advantageous in this coordination contribution game. If leadership is interpreted as giving one state the power to move first, which is consistent with the notion of agenda-setting power, that state can constrain others in ways that can benefit the leader. This is particularly true for coordination games.

Table 5.1 displays several of the games from Chapter 2, notes the original outcomes, and the changes—if any—brought about by the introduction of sequencing. In four of the five games, allowing one player to move first changes the game's outcomes. For assurance, coordination, chicken, and benevolent chicken, the leaders are able to narrow the choices of the follower so that only a single equilibrium remains. In each of these games, the leader constrains the follower to choices that result in the leader's preferred outcome. Exact predictions depend on the game structure, but in none of the games in Table 5.1 does moving first translate into a larger burden for the leader. There are other games where moving first is disadvantageous—for example, the game of rock-paper-scissors.

Inserting an order of moves is obviously a narrow definition of leadership, with a leader who is qualitatively different from the follower by having the power to move first. However, the games in Table 5.1 are still played by two symmetric players. More interesting results are obtained when players decide not just *whether* but also *how much* they will contribute to a good. Rather than having just two options, each player has a more complex decision, and one that revolves even more intimately around what the other player will do.

Once players have to decide how much to contribute to a good, their relative resource endowments matter greatly. The larger the aggregate resource of the two players, the greater is the anticipated contribution to a public good. Additionally, many formal models examine what happens as the players' resource levels diverge. These models can be interpreted as having implications for international leadership, especially if hegemony involves disproportionate economic—as opposed to military—power, as did both nineteenth-century British and twentieth-century American dominance.

One classic result in this literature is the exploitation hypothesis, introduced in Chapter 3, which posits that small states pay less than their fair share (as determined by the benefit principle) while large states carry a disproportionate burden. If so, then inequality across states could actually encourage contributions toward public goods. It is also true that when the international system has had enormous concentration of resources, as it did immediately after World

Table 5.1. Game forms with leadership (when player A moves first)

Game	Original Outcome	New Outcome
Prisoners' Dilemma (Figure 2.1a)	One equilibrium, in which neither player contributes	No change
Assurance (Figure 2.4a)	Two equilibria, one of which is better for both players	One equilibrium, in which A contributes; A's leadership is better for both players.
Coordination (Figure 2.4b)	Two equilibria, each of which is preferred by one player	One equilibrium, which is preferred by the leader A, who does not contribute.
Chicken (Figure 2.4c)	Two equilibria, each of which is preferred by one player	One equilibrium, which is preferred by the leader A, who does not contribute.
Benevolent Chicken (Figure 2.5b)	Two equilibria, each of which is preferred by one player	Two equilibria; if A does not act, B acts, and if A acts, B does not act. Leader A prefers to act for an ordinal payoff of 4, and will do so.

War II when the United States held almost half the world's productive capacity, outcomes resembling the original predictions of hegemonic stability may result, and one country may shoulder most of the burden of key transnational public goods (TPGs). Unfortunately, just because a hegemon bears the bulk of the costs, it does not follow that there will also be a greater level of public good provision. Bruce (1990) showed that in addition to forcing followers to pay more, leadership may lower the overall amount contributed to the public good. This result is less robust than the exploitation hypothesis, and Pahre (1999) demonstrated that the concentration of resources may have no effect on the level of public good provision. Thus, in neither of these modified games does leadership necessarily lead to a higher level of public goods.

The game-theoretic models reviewed thus far reveal logical weaknesses in hegemonic stability theory's original assertion that hegemons create higher levels of global public goods. In models where leaders move first, they can shift more costs of the public goods onto followers in some games, while in others, the order of moves has no effect on outcomes. When states have differing levels of endowments, rich countries may contribute disproportionately in regards to the benefits they receive, but the overall level of public good provision is not necessarily higher. From an analytical point of view, we might then question the importance of leadership for providing TPGs. Indeed, the literature has on balance found more evidence against hegemonic stability (Pahre, 1999).

As mentioned in Chapter 2, repeated interactions between players can have dramatic impacts on the likelihood of successful cooperation, because players who expect to play each other again must evaluate the effects of their current behavior on all future rounds. Such games must specify how players value the *Folk* future relative to the present; the more players value their future payoffs, the *Theorem* more likely cooperation is to occur.[3] Repeated games, therefore, are usually interpreted as dramatically enhancing the possibility of cooperation.

Fearon (1998) pointed out that this is not necessarily the case. Even though future payoffs increase the likelihood of a cooperative outcome, they also make reaching an acceptable bargain more difficult. In such scenarios, leadership and asymmetry may play even more important roles (Drezner, 2007, Chapter 2; Snidal, 1985). If a range of acceptable bargains exists, we might expect powerful states to achieve results that are closer to their preferred outcomes, or that maximize their payoffs. Powerful states have some tools or potential choices that others do not possess, including outright coercion, issue linkage, and selective benefits.

---

3. This is the "Folk Theorem" in infinitely repeated games—see Fudenberg and Maskin (1986) for the theorem, and Axelrod (1984) and Sandler (1992) for accessible treatments of its implications.

At the extreme, powerful states may require their weaker partners to cooperate even when the costs exceed the benefits (Krasner, 2009). Such coercion
may bring to mind the threat of violence, such as the gunboat diplomacy of
the nineteenth and early twentieth centuries, when repayment of debts was
often enforced by colonial powers by the takeover of local customs houses.
Coercion can, however, result from nonmilitary means as well. Especially in
the twenty-first century, use of military power may not be a real option, and
countries with large markets possess enormous leverage over smaller states
via their ability to remove economic opportunities from those states. Because
economic opportunities rise with market size, countries with large markets
can use their leverage to link other types of cooperation, as the United States
has since 1979 with its list of countries that sponsor terrorism (U.S. Department of State, 2013). States that are included on the list cannot receive U.S.
foreign aid or preferential trade treatment, and as a result, this becomes an
economic lever to push those states toward cooperating in intelligence gathering and the like. As Drezner (2007, p. 57) noted, "states with the capability to
employ economic coercion can alter the payoff structure of the other player by
tactically linking regulatory coordination to the broader benefits derived from
economic openness."

Linkage across issues can therefore be an important tool for powerful states
to trade leverage in one arena for concessions in another. There may be reciprocal arrangements in which countries cooperate on similar types of issues
where each has some power. Two countries that have control of upstream river
resources might each concede to let sufficient water flow. Linkage can also take
place across issue areas, as in the examples on trade and anti-terrorism. Foreign aid has long had a role for great powers, which is demonstrated recently
by evidence that countries appointed to fill nonpermanent positions on the
UN Security Council receive larger shares of U.S. foreign aid, presumably in
return for their support on crucial votes (Kuziemko and Werker, 2006).

Powerful states often have better alternatives when bargaining fails. Their
contributions to TPGs are usually more crucial than those of small states, because there may be no collective action without the large state's actions. Along
these lines, Stone (2011) portrays any international organization as having
two sets of rules: the negotiated formal outcome that defines rules of cooperation, and the informal understandings that result from powerful states
threatening to stop cooperating. These informal rules maintain the persistent
influence of powerful states in an anarchic international environment. Any
successful effort at transnational cooperation effectively marries two sets of
actors: powerful states who are more tempted to defect, and weak states who
are "willing to tolerate a degree of informal influence in return for receiving a
larger share of formal power, because the participation of important states
makes an international institution more valuable to all of the participants"
(Stone, 2011, p. 14). Although small states technically have the ability to

withdraw from cooperation, they may be less likely to do so precisely because powerful states can effectively foreclose this ability (Snidal, 1985, p. 583). In other words, even though the international legal order equates states of different sizes with sovereignty, this order does not ensure that transnational cooperation occurs on the basis of one country, one vote.

U.S. HEGEMONY AFTER WORLD WAR II

The implications of hegemony for transnational cooperation suggest a natural comparison of U.S. hegemony in 1945–1950 and in the early 1990s. In both cases, the United States emerged as the sole superpower, with the ability to dictate many international outcomes or to shoulder the burden of creating global public goods. Clearly the two time periods share a major similarity—a unipolar system with the United States as hegemon. Of course, these periods also share important differences—during 1945–1950, the United States belonged to few international organizations that served as focal points or administrators for key cooperative activities, while during the 1990s the United States belonged to many such institutions. Additionally, the rise of globalization created demands for even more transnational cooperation in the latter period. Even so, given the identity of the hegemon and the proximity in time of the two periods, they make for a good paired comparison of the contribution of leadership. Although the first period is often portrayed as one in which the United States shouldered the costs of collective action, the reality is more mixed. In the latter period, even as U.S. influence remained broad, its willingness to bear costs of cooperation decreased. Both cases demonstrate that the leadership of one country is not necessary for many forms of cooperation.

In 1945, the United States emerged from the war with unmatched industrial and military power. Thanks to the devastation in Asia and Europe, some 45% of world productive capacity was concentrated in the U.S. economy. Militarily, the United States emerged from the war with new military bases, technological superiority, and, for a short time, the world's only nuclear arsenal. The country's leadership also seemed determined to create a postwar order that avoided the antagonisms that characterized the interwar period, particularly the failed attempts to reestablish the gold standard. Even so, few of those policy makers argued that the United States should selflessly devote itself to the maintenance of a postwar economic order for the good of the world at large. Instead, they generally saw ways in which an international economic recovery could benefit the United States. After all, its military and commercial might were unparalleled and should easily result in disproportionate gains for the United States.

The postwar economic order was created in Bretton Woods, New Hampshire, in 1944, in a conference that was attended by 44 countries, including the Soviet

Union, which was still a U.S. ally. The Bretton Woods system created a basis for international economic exchange based on the U.S. dollar and, in turn, on the dollar's value relative to gold. The International Bank for Reconstruction and Development (IBRD) and IMF became the institutional foundations for that system. The IMF's role was to help stabilize countries undergoing balance-of-payments difficulties, and this role required a significant amount of resources. Member countries of the IMF agreed to hand over some of their own currency as well as some reserve currency—usually U.S. dollars—in the form of *quotas* to provide the IMF with the funding it needed to provide extra reserves to countries in crisis. Those quotas were generally determined on an ability-to-pay principle—the larger the economy, the more it would contribute to IMF reserves. In return, countries received a similar share of influence in the organization via their voting power. The U.S. contribution was the largest at just under $3 billion, but its vote share (27%) was somewhat less than its share of IMF resources. Stone (2011) noted that this was due to concerns about U.S. dominance of the organization: U.S. Assistant Treasury Secretary Harry Dexter White negotiated the United States down to half what its voting share could have been based purely on the contributions. White said that for the United States to have control over the fund "would destroy the truly international character of the Fund, and seriously jeopardize its success" (Stone, 2011, p. 19). The result was an IMF whose formal rules favored the United States, but not to the extent they might have if they were a pure reflection of U.S. power at the time. Of course, since many critical IMF decisions required a supermajority of 85% of votes, the United States still maintained effective veto power over many of the IMF's decisions. Smaller states acquiesced to this disproportionate power in order to secure a larger IMF funding base.

The creation of Bretton Woods's institutions cannot, therefore, be attributed to U.S. benevolence. They were part of a large package of economic commitments, many of which benefited the United States directly, including lower costs of borrowing, more flexibility in adjusting to international macroeconomic conditions, and easier foreign acquisitions for American multinational corporations (Gowa, 1983, pp. 43–44). Promoting the dollar as the world's reserve currency alone was of great private benefit to the United States and was the primary goal for U.S. negotiators at Bretton Woods.[4]

Not all U.S. policies at the time were oriented to the resurrection of the global economy. Unless U.S. trading partners signed new trade treaties, such as the General Agreement on Tariffs and Trade (GATT), they were still subject to high levels of taxes on goods imported into the United States, which was a significant barrier to trade (see Chapter 7). Furthermore, from 1944 to

---

4. The primary goal for Harry Dexter White, the Assistant Secretary of the Treasury, in creating a postwar economic system was to ensure the dollar's role as the world's international reserve currency (Steil, 2013).

1947, European recovery was hampered by U.S. insistence on debt repayment and other transfers that meant a large outflow of gold and dollars from Europe to the United States (Pahre, 1999, Chapter 9). It was not until the emergence of the Soviet Union as a threat to Western Europe that the United States seriously committed itself to Europe's recovery, which came in the form of the Economic Recovery Plan, better known as the Marshall Plan.

The Marshall Plan was not an original component of U.S. plans for the postwar order. Many Americans desired a return to isolationism after the war. The 1946 elections enhanced the power of isolationists in the U.S. Congress, thus worsening the chances for commitments beyond the initial Bretton Woods institutions. A large aid package to war-torn countries was a difficult political sell, until several events following the onset of the Cold War began to change American attitudes toward helping Europe in particular. First, in Greece, fighting continued long after it stopped in most European countries. By 1947, Communist forces in Greece appeared likely to win, and President Truman decided on U.S. aid to Greek anti-Communist forces. In order to justify that policy to the American people, he cast the policy in much broader terms, arguing that Greek Communists took orders from Moscow and declaring that the United States would fight Communism around the world, a policy that became known as the Truman Doctrine. Second, early in 1948, a coup in U.S. ally Czechoslovakia realigned the country with the Soviet Union. Third, Stalin closed land access to West Berlin in June 1948, leading to ten months of supplies dropped by planes. The combined impact of these events, among others, led the United States to reevaluate its relatively harsh economic treatment of its allies. The results were two forms of international cooperation meant to support European allies in the face of the Soviet threat. Importantly from the standpoint of collective action theory, both came at great expense to the United States.

The total Marshall Plan aid of $13.5 billion for Europe and $0.5 billion for Japan approached 5% of U.S. GDP in 1948; a similar number in 2014 would exceed $800 billion (Frieden, 2006, p. 268). The encroaching Cold War was crucial to passing such a gigantic aid package. In fact, the Truman Doctrine convinced the American public of the Soviet threat, thereby promoting a more active foreign policy. While historical counterfactuals are always tenuous, it seems difficult to imagine the Marshall Plan in virtually any other context, and shortly thereafter, the United States enhanced its efforts to rebuild European economies with a commitment to protect them militarily.

The North Atlantic Treaty Organization (NATO), created by 10 Western European countries, Canada, and the United States on April 4, 1949, formed an alliance that bound member states in common hostility toward the Soviet Union. The United States faced a strategic disadvantage in its geographic distance from Europe—the Soviets could easily mount a massive conventional attack without time for the United States to mobilize. NATO thus served to provide the United States with a credible public commitment to defend its allies, and resulted in the establishment of U.S. bases in Western Europe, which reinforced that commitment. Additionally, NATO's Article 5 treated any attack on one member as an attack on all members, thereby committing them in advance to a common defense.

The key deterrent against a Soviet attack was the nuclear umbrella provided primarily by the United States, and the key benefit to NATO members was protection by U.S. nuclear weapons. NATO's doctrine of massive retaliation against any attack meant that both attacker and defender would suffer catastrophic costs, and NATO's nuclear deterrence can be treated as nonexcludable owing to Article 5 and the U.S. commitment to defend allies with a retaliatory strike. This mutually assured destruction (MAD) doctrine remained NATO's primary strategy through 1966, when the initial tensions of the Cold War declined (Hartley and Sandler, 1999).

NATO's nuclear deterrence is the classic example of the exploitation hypothesis (Olson and Zeckhauser, 1966). Small members suffered some sovereignty costs, since they agreed to come to the defense of any ally that was attacked, but NATO's nuclear powers (the United States, the United Kingdom, and France) bore the cost of nuclear deterrence, allowing smaller NATO allies to free ride. As late as 1970, U.S. military spending accounted for almost 75% of total military spending by all NATO allies (Sandler and Hartley, 2001, pp. 869–870). Despite the key role played by the United States, hegemony did not extend to the formal rules of NATO decision making. Instead, NATO allies operated via the "silence procedure," which meant that any action could effectively be vetoed by even the smallest member of the organization (Schimmelfennig, 2007, p. 151). U.S. hegemony was therefore associated with carrying a disproportionate cost of the public good of security with no associated increase in formal power within the organization, and this is similar to the U.S. situation within the IMF.

As the Cold War continued, NATO's military strategy began to rely less on a massive retaliation with nuclear missiles and more on conventional weapons, which could be provided by non-nuclear powers. As a result, burden sharing in NATO grew more equitable, and much research shows that the costs of defense largely aligned with the alliance's benefits from the late 1960s through the end of the Cold War (see Hartley and Sandler, 1999; Sandler and Hartley, 2001).

U.S. HEGEMONY AFTER THE COLD WAR

Given the disappearance of NATO's major threat with the end to the Cold War, many expected the organization to disintegrate—after all, the key benefit of belonging to the organization, deterrence against the Soviet Union, was no longer of any great consequence. Given the increased costs of membership after 1966 and the lower benefits of belonging to an alliance without a major threat, it is perhaps surprising that more countries did not follow France's example. After French appeals for greater power within NATO were denied, France contemplated withdrawing from the alliance, but instead removed its troops from NATO command and then continued to coordinate with NATO when it was beneficial. Not only did no members quit the alliance, but for the first time since Spain's admission in 1982, the alliance also expanded, growing from 16 members in 1999 to 28 in 2014. This expansion included mostly small countries, as well as some medium-sized countries like Poland, and resulted in increased heterogeneity among members. NATO's diversity expanded not only in terms of members' size, but also in their preferences for defense spending. Diversity also characterized members' views on NATO's missions and derived benefits. To ensure that new allies could participate in NATO operations meant that new members faced immediate costs of upgrading or standardizing military equipment, and the organization had to accommodate new members in NATO's decision-making apparatus.

In addition to growing larger, the alliance reoriented its mission, becoming not just a deterrent to interstate war but also a proactive organization with considerably broader definitions of European security. In particular, the organization expanded into peacekeeping in the wars that resulted from the breakup of Yugoslavia. In 1995, NATO forces interceded in Bosnia-Herzegovina in an effort to reduce interethnic conflict, and then again in 1999, they intervened in Kosovo for the same reason.

The alliance's activities during this time included a greater share of nonexcludable benefits; for example, by reducing refugee flows or preventing the spillover of such ethnic conflicts. As a result, we might expect more free riding and greater accuracy for the exploitation hypothesis, and in fact, U.S. leadership was important both in NATO's involvement in those conflicts and in material terms, providing "most of the military equipment" and conducting "most of the military operations by far" (Schimmelfennig, 2007, p. 169). New quantitative research seems to confirm the return of the exploitation hypothesis in recent conflicts (Sandler and Shimizu, 2014). At the same time the organization expanded its missions, it has also begun to treat member obligations as more flexible than during the Cold War, which further fragments cooperation and the provision of public goods.

This pattern of fragmentation is evident after 2001 with the U.S. War on Terror and the protection of NATO's interests outside of Europe, particularly in Afghanistan, where the alliance fought its first war far from European soil. NATO did not lead the invasion of Afghanistan—instead, the United States preferred to wage the war on its own terms until October 2003. Thereafter, NATO assumed command of the International Security Assistance Force

(ISAF) in Afghanistan. Once NATO assumed a larger role, many NATO allies contributed forces, but allies varied widely in how they participated in the war. Saideman and Auerswald (2012) documented differences in Canadian, French, and German participation in ISAF, noting the many restrictions placed on German troops. For example, German troops were stationed in the relatively peaceful northern region, and were not allowed to perform missions elsewhere even if the troops they were training did so. Table 5.2 demonstrates that even though other allies played a role in Afghanistan, the largest share of military expenses by far belonged to the United States, and that U.S. expenses grew even more burdensome after the 2010 surge. Therefore, even though the United States called on its NATO partners, the United States largely shouldered the Afghan war costs.

Why have other NATO members agreed to participate in Afghanistan, and more recently in Libya? In general, new NATO missions are quite different from the Cold War threat around which the alliance formed. In Bosnia, Kosovo, Afghanistan, and Libya, the direct immediate threat to NATO was minimal. Moreover, the alliance's use of force was sanctioned by the international community, particularly the UN Security Council. NATO members who agreed with each mission contributed varying levels of forces, but contributions were voluntary. Coupled with the fact that NATO's operations have strayed farther and farther from Europe, many NATO allies increasingly exercised their ability to free ride on U.S. contributions, similar to the early years of the alliance (Sandler and Shimizu, 2014). Rather than inability to contribute to nuclear deterrence as in the past, free riding in NATO today revolves around flexible commitments—allies wary of particular NATO operations may opt not to participate. Belgium, France, Germany, and other allies expressed outright opposition to the 2003 war in Iraq and NATO's only role was training Iraqi security forces. Increased emphasis on fighting terrorism, which tends to present a greater threat to large states, has further exacerbated the trend toward larger powers shouldering disproportionate costs of security cooperation (Sandler and Shimizu, 2014).

Table 5.2. NATO contributions in Afghanistan

Contributor	Troops in 2009	Troops in 2011
United States	29,950	90,000
United Kingdom	9,000	9,500
Germany	4,050	4,812
France	3,160	3,935
Canada	2,800	2,922
Italy	2,795	3,880

Source: The Guardian (2011).

As the United States has again provided the bulk of NATO's resources, its missions have depended greatly on U.S. foreign policy goals, which, in turn, have often deemphasized legal sovereignty. In Afghanistan, as well as in Libya, NATO effectively overthrew (or contributed to the overthrow of) the sovereign rulers of independent states. They did so in large part due to concerns from the United States and other members of the international community about possible threats from those states, as well as to concerns about the actions of those sovereign authorities toward their own people.

THE DECLINE OF U.S. HEGEMONY: IMPLICATIONS FOR TRANSNATIONAL COOPERATION

We started this chapter with a question: what would the decline of U.S. hegemony mean for transnational cooperation? This question has been asked before. In 1956, after the launch of Sputnik, many Americans feared that the Soviet Union had surpassed the United States, particularly in technology. In the 1970s, American policy makers fretted about OPEC's hold on oil reserves; a few years later, many feared that U.S. leadership was quickly being lost to Japan and West Germany. All of these worries receded with time, and disappeared with the end of the Cold War and the dominance of American economic and military might in the 1990s and beyond.

More recently, the meteoric rise of China has made analysts question whether the United States still retains hegemony. China's economy is now the second largest in the world, and already consumes more energy than the United States. It seems only a matter of time until it is the world's largest economy, perhaps prior to 2020. Additionally, unlike Japan and Germany, China's power is not primarily economic—it is a nuclear power with a large army and is one of the five permanent members of the UN Security Council. China has already turned many of its economic gains into military production, a trend that is apt to continue as China strives for regional, if not global, influence.

The rise of China has been accompanied by other emerging markets such as Brazil, India, Indonesia, and Russia. The 2007 financial crisis deeply impacted the United States and Europe, while emerging markets continued to grow economically and to gain power in international negotiations. This trend is best demonstrated by the expansion of the G-8, a group of countries that attempt to coordinate economic policy, to the G-20.[5] The latter group includes many

5. The G-8 includes Canada, France, Germany, Italy, Japan, Russia, the United Kingdom, and the United States. The G-20 expands that membership to South Africa, Mexico, Brazil, Argentina, China, South Korea, India, Indonesia, Turkey, Saudi Arabia, and Australia. Additionally, in the G-20 the EU is represented as a whole, in addition to those states that were originally members of the G-8.

regional powers and emerging markets like Mexico, Saudi Arabia, South Africa, and Turkey. Many of the emerging markets, especially India and China, are naturally great powers whose economic poverty has until now prevented their exercising a full range of influence on international politics, which now they seem to be poised to do. In short, U.S. hegemony and the unipolar world of the post–Cold War era appear to be giving way to an increasingly multipolar world.

In addition to an increase in the number of great powers, Haass (2008) and others argue that military power is no longer as valuable as it once was due to the rise of nonstate actors as important sources of conflict (for example, terrorist groups or hackers) and power (for example, multinational corporations and social media outlets). Whereas realists tend to argue that military power is fungible and leads to power in other areas, this seems less true in the twenty-first century than before. Germany and Japan have long exercised great influence in economic affairs without threats of military force and, moreover, U.S. military dominance no longer means an ability to dictate decisions in other issue areas. Wars in both Iraq and Afghanistan have been defined by asymmetric warfare with a need to combat insurgent groups. The "battle for hearts and minds" has become as important as military tactics, and as a result, even the U.S. intelligence community expects continued military dominance to be its "least significant asset" in the coming decades (Warrick and Pincus, 2008).

From a collective action perspective, three trends are especially noteworthy. First, a decline in relative power for the United States means a world order in which the United States will have a harder time organizing collective action for its own benefit. Coordination problems and the like are less apt to resolve in U.S. favor as it can no longer dictate outcomes across multiple issue areas. A more likely scenario is that American dominance continues in some areas, while accommodating the greater economic power of China and other emerging markets in others. Second, several of the new emerging powers are likely to view the world differently, with a greater concern about sovereignty costs. China's foreign policy debates revolve around the kind of leadership role it should play in transnational cooperation. While the UN is viewed favorably, many Chinese elites believe that participating in other international organizations would reduce China's ability to win large bargains on a bilateral basis (Shambaugh and Xiao, 2012).

As a result of greater heterogeneity in countries' preferences, some kinds of cooperation will become more difficult. Previous scholarship on hegemonic decline and its effect on transnational cooperation found that as hegemonic contributions to global public goods fall, other rising powers should find it beneficial to shoulder that burden (Keohane, 1984; Pahre, 1999; Snidal, 1985). If so, then existing transnational cooperation should not be threatened, even while new efforts may prove more difficult. Others, notably Norloff (2010), were less sanguine about the provision of existing public goods. When she allowed for partial excludability of TPGs, and incorporated increasing returns to scale, she found that rising powers "will not necessarily have incentives to fully compensate for the leading state's contribution if it declines" (p. 37). Crucial to replacing hegemonic leadership is mutual cooperation among rising powers—one power will contribute only if others also contribute. To the extent that rising powers have similar goals and preferences regarding transnational cooperation, they may be able to sustain existing cooperation.

Such a situation is not unparalleled—U.S. hegemony has in part been easier due to its association with other capitalist democratic allies, primarily Canada, Japan, and the EU. Ikenberry (2011), among others, argued that U.S. hegemony has consistently been restrained by the nature of its association with other democracies. Indeed, it is difficult to imagine Germany and Japan as U.S. allies during the Cold War without their adoption of democracy. Ultimately, this insight is limited in its explanatory power, since both during and after the Cold War, the United States frequently prioritized security or other goals over democratization. The West's tepid response to the Arab Spring (outside Libya) is only the latest example.

Today's emerging powers have less in common than allied democracies emerging from World War II. One commonality across some of today's emerging powers is state capitalism, a form of economic organization in which the state retains significant ownership of business, but even here it is possible to note discrepancies about the proper role of the state in business. The other common factor for today's rising powers is dissatisfaction with the status quo; that is, the dominance of Western countries and Japan that have ordered international cooperation according to their own preferences. To the extent that these factors are creating common interests in China and other emerging powers, they may aid transnational cooperation. If, however, existing great powers continue to matter, these same factors may inhibit cooperation.

CONCLUSION

Olson's (1965) pioneering work on collective action theory argued that leadership could be important in providing public goods; if some group members generated sufficient gains for themselves from public goods, then they will be willing to provide them on their own and tolerate free riding. More recent advances suggested that leadership is not as universally beneficial as Olson originally claimed. If we view a hegemon as qualitatively different from other states, and model its privileged position as moving first, then many games with multiple Nash equilibria resolve to a single equilibrium. However, this resolution comes at a cost—the leader chooses the equilibrium that most benefits its position. Leadership can be helpful, but it depends on the characteristics of the public good in question, and often cooperation will take place on the leader's terms.

As a result, the relative decline of U.S. power does not necessarily translate to a decline in cooperation. U.S. decline may have little effect on the overall level of global public goods, as newly emerging powers may have an incentive to replace U.S. provision of these goods. As Snidal (1985, p. 602) noted, "Not only might cooperation persist after the decline of the hegemonic power, the degree of cooperation might well increase" as states whose power is rising realize new gains in contributing to existing public goods. Finding new contributors may be more likely if emerging powers are similar to the existing hegemon, such as Brazil and India with their robust democracies. Clearly China, in particular, is quite different than the United States and will likely view public goods in a different light than the United States; however, most newly emerging powers are more wary of sacrificing sovereignty and may therefore be hesitant to play the roles we expect.

CHAPTER 6

Foreign Aid and Global Health

As pointed out by Paul Collier (2007) in *The Bottom Billion*, about one in seven people on the planet lives in abject poverty that is increasingly separating them from the living standards in the rest of the world. These bottom-billion countries' economies are lagging further behind other countries owing to one or more traps: enduring ongoing conflict, possessing natural resource wealth, being landlocked, or experiencing bad governance (Collier, 2007). Conflict destroys human and capital resources, breeds diseases, disrupts market transactions, diverts taxes into military spending, and dissuades investment. Resource wealth can result in adverse foreign exchange rates as the country's currency is driven up in value, making imports (including some raw materials) more expensive. In addition, resource wealth can cause opposing interests to battle over this wealth as a way to underwrite conflict (Collier and Hoeffler, 2004). Landlocked countries are at a disadvantage unless their neighbors have good roads, canals, and other transportation infrastructure linking to ports. If such landlocked countries possess neighbors in conflict, then this adds further burdens. Finally, bad governance in a developing country results in a drain on the national treasury and can also lead to unstable macroeconomic policies (for example, corruption or inflation) that drives away foreign and domestic investments. According to Collier (2007, p. 7), 70% of the bottom-billion countries are in Africa, which has been plagued with poor or negative growth, low living standards, and conflict (Easterly and Levine, 1998).

The global community must show concern for these poorest countries, because they can adversely affect world security, resource supplies, financial stability, the environment, and global health. In the latter case, poor countries with insufficient healthcare infrastructure and malnourished populations may allow infectious diseases—both new and old—to gain a foothold that can then threaten rich countries in a globalized world. Air travel can disseminate viruses and bacteria globally in a matter of days, as the world learned from Severe Acute Respiratory Syndrome (SARS) in 2003 (Sandler, 2004, p. 99) and Ebola in 2014.

Because foreign assistance can be an important line of defense in promoting global health, we consider these two topics together even though most of the chapter is focused on global health. Owing to spillovers, rich donor countries understand that the health of poor countries affects the health of donors' citizens, thereby making such assistance an easy political sell at home.

In an ideal world, foreign assistance may help poor countries to develop and grow. Despite hundreds of billions of dollars of foreign aid given to developing countries since the end of World War II, many aid-recipient countries remain poor, with heavy debt burdens and apparently little to show from past loans and grants (Easterly, 2002; Easterly and Levine, 1998).[1] Other developing countries have had a much different experience, becoming developed high-income countries over time. For instance, foreign assistance in the form of the U.S. Marshall Plan was instrumental in helping war-ravaged economies recover rather quickly following World War II. The success of the Marshall Plan is due to these war-torn countries possessing well-educated people, an entrepreneurial class, pent-up demand for consumer goods, a development vision, and appropriate institutions. These institutions included a central banking system, a judicial branch, protection of property rights, rule of law, and well-developed educational and healthcare infrastructures. War-torn European countries already possessed market-promoting institutions that facilitated trade and enforced contracts.

In contrast to many African countries, some Asian economies—for example, China, India, South Korea, Taiwan, and Thailand—prospered from foreign assistance and achieved high growth rates that resulted in viable economies with sustained growth. Why have some countries used foreign assistance to great advantage and others have not? There is no single answer but unsuccessful aid-recipient states likely suffered from one or more of the following: corruption, limited absorptive capacity, an ill-conceived development strategy, bad policies (Burnside and Dollar, 2000), officials' incompetence, or ennui for Western-style development projects. Absorptive capacity refers to a country's ability to channel the aid into worthwhile projects. Such capability hinges on an educated workforce, financial expertise, potential development projects, bureaucratic competence, and technical capacity. Earlier-mentioned traps may also impact unsuccessful aid recipients. The rate of population growth can hold back a country's development because income must grow faster if income per capita or per person is to increase.[2] Income per capita is

---

1. A loan requires repayment, which can result in a debt burden, especially if the money was wasted and did not improve the income-earning abilities of the economy. In contrast, a grant is a gift from a donor country or institution, earmarked for a stated purpose or sector (Mascarenhas and Sandler, 2005).

2. The growth in income per capita is the difference between the growth in income and the growth in population.

the typical standard used to measure the well-being and development of a country.

In the current chapter, we are particularly interested in how foreign assistance can promote health in aid recipients, which is an important aspect behind growth. Countries with healthy populations experience fewer days lost to sickness or premature death, thus augmenting the contribution that countries' labor and human capital make to the economy. We are particularly interested in the collective action aspects of global health. In recent years, rich donor countries and their institutions (for example, the U.S. Centers for Disease Control [CDC]) channeled aid into support for global health, because health exigencies in one part of the world present dangers to other parts of the world (Lele, Ridker, and Upadhyay, 2006; Glassman, Duran, and Sumner, 2013). Globalization creates a health interdependency worldwide that stems from the enhanced transmission pathways for infectious diseases through greater mobility of people and augmented transfrontier exchanges. Even for noninfectious diseases, the Internet and the digital revolution permit new means of training, diagnostic procedures, and knowledge transfers among medical teams in different countries. Globalization opens up unique possibilities for international collaborative efforts in health.

The global community must engineer a holistic approach to promoting global health. As such, countries must put the collective interest of world health ahead of their sovereign interest if socially efficient outcomes are to be obtained. This is a tall order that can, at best, be partially fulfilled as key countries understand that health concerns are interrelated among countries. To date, leadership in fostering global health has come from the World Health Organization (WHO), the United Nations (UN), the World Bank, and some rich countries. More recently, some important multistakeholder organizations and charitable trusts are addressing some global health concerns—for example, the immunization of children, the amelioration of river blindness (Onchocerciasis), and the eradication of malaria (Hwenda, 2013; Kremer, 2006; Murray, 2006; Smith and Woodward, 2002; Sonntag, 2010). Notably, there are great differences between health concerns in rich and poor countries that often limit rich countries' responses to the needs in poor countries. For instance, rich countries are more concerned with noninfectious diseases (heart disease and cancer), while poor countries are more interested in infectious diseases. Such differences make a unified approach difficult to achieve. There may be some convergence as life expectancy increases in poor countries and their population suffers the cancer consequences from increased cigarette smoking (The Economist, 2014a).

Developing countries are more impacted by three twenty-first century plagues: human immunodeficiency virus/acquired immune deficiency syndrome (HIV/AIDS), tuberculosis (TB), and malaria. In 2012, an estimated 35 million people were living with HIV and 1.6 million died from AIDS (UNAIDS,

2013). Although these diseases' trends are in the downward direction in recent years, HIV/AIDS is far from over, with the greatest incidence occurring in Africa. In 2012, malaria killed approximately 627,000 people, primarily in Africa (WHO, 2014). TB killed 1.4 million people in 2011, with about 0.4 million of these casualties being HIV-positive (Global Fund, 2014). The death and incidence rates from both malaria and TB are sharply declining, yet these plagues continue to extract a horrible toll on the developing world. As such, they stifle development and present risks to rich countries, especially in the form of drug-resistant TB strains.

Global health presents myriad challenges to transnational cooperation that are best understood when countries' interests and motives are taken into account, along with those of the pharmaceutical companies, which want to make a profit for their stockholders. As such, these companies are inclined to develop profitable treatment regimes rather than vaccines that can eradicate a disease. Part of the challenge behind developing a unified strategy for global health is to align key interests, such as those of pharmaceutical companies with those of developed and developing countries. Global health is associated with alternative transnational public goods (TPGs), possessing different collective action prognoses. To our knowledge, there is not another global concern that offers such a variety of public goods. These health public goods primarily differ according to the aggregation technology, which indicates how individual contributions determine the overall level of the public good that is available for consumption.

The current chapter has a number of purposes. The initial purpose is to review briefly the way that foreign assistance has changed over the decades following World War II. In performing this review, we are particularly interested in aid's role in bolstering development and ameliorating poverty. Given the nature of our book, we highlight the collective action aspects of aid. This viewpoint explains why aid is increasingly funding myriad kinds of public goods at the national and transnational levels. The second and primary purpose of the chapter is the study of global health, which is bolstered, in part, by foreign aid to developing countries. Global health presents a rich array of public goods, whose properties vary along the three dimensions of publicness. For example, eradicating an infectious disease is a threshold public good, where a certain level of immunity must be reached by the population if future outbreaks are not to be self-sustaining, whereas surveillance is a weakest-link public good, where the poorest vigilance largely determines the effective intelligence gathered on an epidemic. A third purpose is to examine the role of institutions in addressing health-related market failures. Today, there is a rich set of institutions in the public and private sectors that are concerned with fostering transnational health concerns. A fourth purpose is to distinguish health-related market failures with an intergenerational dimension.

FOREIGN ASSISTANCE: A BRIEF RETROSPECTIVE

In 2012, all donors, including multilateral agencies, gave about $133 billion in foreign assistance, which represents a decline from 2011 amounts (Organization for Economic Cooperation and Development, 2014). This aid includes economic and military assistance. Since, World War II, foreign assistance has risen and fallen. For example, the U.S. share of federal spending devoted to foreign aid has fallen from about 9% in the early 1950s to well under 1% in 1997 (U.S. Congressional Budget Office, 1997, p. xii).[3] During 1990–2000, official development assistance (ODA) displayed a general decline. For instance, the share of donor gross national product (GNP) devoted to foreign assistance was 0.24% in 1999, down from 0.33% in 1990 (World Bank, 2001, pp. 87–89, Table 4.2). During the 1990s, nongovernmental organizations (NGOs) and charitable foundations (for example, Wellcome Trust and Gates Foundation) augmented their foreign assistance, which has somewhat offset the decline in ODA. Following the terrorist skyjacking on September 2001 in the United States, the Bush administration increased aid as a means of countering terrorism (Fleck and Kilby, 2010) even though no clear link between poverty and terrorism had been established (Krueger and Maleckova, 2003). Part of this U.S. aid was to assist recipient countries to eliminate terrorist groups from their soil; this was true of aid given to the Philippines to curb Abu Sayyaf's activities. Since 2003, foreign assistance has risen from $98 billion to $141 billion in 2011 U.S. dollars; however, foreign assistance declined in 2006 and 2007 during the start of the financial crisis (Organization for Economic Cooperation and Development, 2014). Foreign assistance is affected by global recessions and booms, declining during the former and rising during the latter. In addition, donors pursue different aid sectors with the health and environmental sectors gaining favor over the last decades (as reflected in the Millennium Development Goals, see Chapter 13), which include curbing child mortality, bolstering maternal health, combating HIV/AIDS, and promoting environmental sustainability (Sandler and Arce, 2007). The giving of foreign assistance changed over the decades with new practices and philosophies coming in and out of favor. Often external events (the rapid industrialization of the Soviet Union, Cold War rivalries, the collapse of the Soviet Union, and the East Asian miracle), new ideologies, and periodic assessments of aid effectiveness exerted tremendous influences on aid practices and recipients.

In the immediate post–World War II era and the 1950s, the focus of aid was on achieving rapid growth in GNP rather than on development. The thinking was that increases in GNP would bolster development by instituting structural

---

3. The United States alone has given $1 trillion in foreign aid (in 1997 dollars) from 1945 to 1997 (Congressional Budget Office, 1997, p. 1).

changes, improving education, promoting health, augmenting social overhead capital (for example, roads, sewage systems, bridges, and communication networks), and developing essential institutions. These include governmental institutions and key firms. If an economy had more income, then the hope was that poverty would be reduced as income per capita rose. Development economists in the 1950s looked to the economic growth models to underscore the importance of savings and investment. These growth paradigms view savings as financing investment, which then fostered economic growth. Foreign assistance could bolster the necessary savings for the growth process. Growth-focused development had a major flaw because higher income or GDP need not reduce poverty if growth favors the rich. In an important contribution, Kuznets (1955) pointed out that income distribution typically worsens before a threshold income per capita level is attained, beyond which industrialization spreads the gains more widely so that inequality falls.[4] Income must grow sufficiently to transform institutions and to provide the infrastructure to sustain growth.

By the 1960s, development economists embraced Rostow's (1960) notion of the precondition for a "takeoff" to sustained growth through an infusion of money for projects, especially those geared to social overhead capital, which lay the foundation for self-perpetuating growth. A viable economy must have roads, schools, security forces, police, bridges, electric grids, waterways, sewage systems, healthcare infrastructure, central banking system, courts, and communication networks to facilitate trade and commerce. Much public and private investment is required before an economy is ready to take off. Economies may initially show little progress until some threshold social overhead capital is in place, along with complementary private investment. The country's citizens must develop entrepreneurial and bureaucratic skills. Today, we realize that this infrastructure must also be linked regionally (see Chapter 4). Landlocked countries without properly linked infrastructure to their neighbors will be growth impaired.

Solow's (1957) seminal work on growth raised another concern about equating development with growth. Solow demonstrated that technological progress, and not investment per se, explained the lion's share of growth. The promotion of technological progress requires more than just an increase in capital because an economy needs the prerequisites to absorb technological progress. This meant investment in human beings—education—so that technological progress could flourish. Growth and economic progress require more

4. The "Kuznets curve" indicates that income inequality increases as income per capita rises until a threshold income per capita level is reached, beyond which income inequality falls. This phenomenon is due to the shift of rural and agricultural population to the cities as income per capita grows. As this shift ensues, a sizeable portion of the population initially suffers.

than savings-financed investment, since educated and trained labor also play an important role. There was also greater interest shown by development economists in distributional concerns and the requirement to provide the "basic needs" of the people of developing countries. Development involved more than capital; it also concerned labor, land, education, and technical change. With this new focus, the social dimension of development grew in importance; that is, there was recognition that social and economic transformations are required for development.

Despite this recognition, development thinking championed new focuses over time that did not always emphasize the social and economic dimension. During the 1970s, development policy was guided by a belief that state-led sectors could promote growth. Certain sectors were viewed as catalysts to the development process—it was just a matter of bolstering the right sector. For example, the export sector was seen as fostering technological transfers and competitiveness. As such, the state should subsidize this sector. By the 1980s, export-led growth lost favor, primarily because the alleged technological spillovers to other sectors were not so evident. Two new ideologies gained favor: the first stressed market-led growth through trade liberalization and privatization, and the second emphasized aid accountability with the help of conditionality. The latter placed requirements on receiving grants and loans for development.

Trade liberalization and greater openness did not necessarily result in high per-capita GDP growth. According to Rodrik (1999), openness only resulted in rapid growth when complementary policies and institutions were present. If an economy does not appear attractive to investors, then privatization of state-owned enterprises need not result in greater development. Moreover, host-country infrastructure and entrepreneurial skills must be adequate to sustain large-scale privatization efforts. Safeguards must be in place to ensure that the proceeds from the sale of state enterprises do not enrich corrupt officials, thereby leaving the public sector more impoverished.

Conditionality resulted in donor countries pushing their own agendas, interests, and ideologies that were not always aligned with those of the aid recipient.[5] Conditionality resulted in joint products that had a strong donor-specific component—for example, the donor could demand that the recipient buy technical expertise from the donor, which was not only costly but also inhibited the recipient country from developing its own expertise. Donor-imposed conditions could extract strategic (a military base on the recipient soil), economic, or political concessions. The latter may require support of the donor's position in UN votes. By pursuing the donor's agenda, conditionality reduced the recipient's "ownership" or interest in the development program

5. Arguments against conditionality are well-stated and supported by Collier (1997, 2007).

being pursued. There are other arguments against the use of conditionality. Since funds are fungible, conditionality does not assure that the conditions will be met. Moreover, conditionality may be time-inconsistent in the sense that the recipient agrees to the conditions that they later choose to ignore (Collier, 1997). The donor's threat to reduce funding in the future if conditions are not followed may not be credible insofar as reducing loans or grants may also damage the donor's interests. Policing conditionality often entails high transaction costs that offset the donor's benefits.

A key concern for development policy in the 1990s was bolstering key institutions that could channel foreign assistance into worthwhile endeavors in recipient developing countries. Properly designed and well-functioning institutions would minimize transaction costs and ensure that aid resulted in the greatest net payback per dollar spent (North, 1990). Tied to building the right institutions was a drive toward the establishment of property rights so that markets could operate without impediments. Institutions to provide the necessary environment for emerging markets (for example, sound financial practices, courts, and central banking system) were essential for development. This concern over institutions extended to regional collectives that promote trade, infrastructure, standardized practices, and public goods.

After 2000, development economists worried about whether aid really alleviated poverty while establishing the foundations for sustainable development. Sound policies in recipient countries became the mantra for 2000 and beyond. Development assistance appears to succeed in recipient countries with stable macroeconomic environments, where governments engage in sensible policies that stabilize prices, protect property rights, establish a development plan, and curtail corruption (World Bank, 1998; Burnside and Dollar, 2000). As such, the recipient country must have transparent governance that accounts for the diverse interests in the country. Good policies and a stable macroeconomic environment attract foreign direct investment, which is an important source of savings to support economic growth. Moreover, recipient countries must become integrally involved in their own development process and direction so that a feeling of ownership is fostered (van de Walle and Johnston, 1996). Aid must harmonize donor-recipient practices and limit aid conditionality. This means that a meaningful partnership must form between the recipient and its key donors, which include donor countries, multilateral organizations, multistakeholder institutions, charitable foundations, and others. A meaningful partnership may be difficult when these different donors are pursuing alternative goals, some of which may be self-serving. At times, multilateral organizations can provide a coherency by coordinating the actions of the many donors. For the recipient to be a true partner, its bureaucratic and technical capabilities must be enhanced. With the Millennium Development Goals and the renewed interests on the part of donors in reducing poverty, aid is being directed into five key sectors—environment, health, knowledge, governance, and security (International Task Force on Global Public Goods, 2006). The associated public goods in these sectors must be provided through recipient and donor actions. In so doing, poverty will be reduced as nutrition, education, health, and peace are pursued.

Table 6.1 provides a ready summary of our aid retrospective.

Table 6.1. Foreign assistance: A retrospective

Goal of aid	Time period	Rationale
Promote growth	Late 1940s 1950s	Economic growth would foster economic development. By providing savings, aid would fund investment and, hence, bolster growth. Institutional and other considerations are ignored.
Precondition for "takeoff"	1960s	For sustained growth, developing countries needed social overhead capital. Substantial levels of private and public investment are needed before nations can sustain their growth.
State-led sectors can foster growth	1970s	Development follows if the right sectors are bolstered by aid. For example, the export sector can foster technological transfers, competitiveness, and growth.
Market-led growth; accountability	1980s	Market-led growth is promoted by trade liberalization and privatization. Aid should flow to countries pursuing these policies. In addition, accountability emphasized the need for aid conditionality, so that grants and loans are used properly.
Bolster institutions	1990s	Aid should flow to countries that establish and extend property rights. Recipient countries need to push sound financial practices, central banking, rule of law, and reduced corruption.
Sound policies	2000s	Development assistance succeeds in recipient countries with stable macroeconomic environments that possess stable prices, transparent governance, and property rights. Good policies also attract foreign direct investment, which is a source of savings.
Ownership and partnership; promote public goods; reduce poverty	2000s and beyond	Recipient countries must be involved in the blueprint for their development. Donor-recipient partnerships are needed to develop these blueprints. Aid needs to help fund public goods in health, security, knowledge, and governance. Poverty needs to be reduced through development goals involving nutrition, education, health, etc.

COLLECTIVE ACTION AND FOREIGN AID

Foreign aid presents collective action concerns for the global community that are analogous to charitable giving within a country. If aid reduces poverty in a developing country, then this reduction results in nonexcludable and nonrival benefits for all countries that have an interest in the recipient's welfare. If, moreover, most derived benefits of this aid-financed reduced poverty are purely public, then potential donor countries have an incentive to free ride on the most generous countries, which are often the wealthiest countries. In this scenario, large, rich countries are exploited by the small. Unlike this prediction, both large and small countries contribute to foreign assistance: the Scandinavian countries give a higher share of their GDP to foreign aid than large, rich countries such as the United States. Of course, Denmark, Sweden, and Norway have high income per capita though their overall GDP is small compared to that of the United States. This outcome suggests that foreign aid is not purely public.

Foreign assistance generally yields both purely public benefits to the world community and donor-specific private benefits that stem from the donors' relative location or relationship to the recipient. That is, foreign assistance gives rise to joint products, whose benefits may be public or private. Countries generally give more foreign aid to past colonies or neighbors (Mascarenhas and Sandler, 2005). Other donor-specific benefits from aid may involve trade, strategic concessions, UN votes, or resource supplies. Conditionality, mentioned previously, is a means for institutionalizing donor-specific benefits, sometimes at the expense of the recipient country. Donors may also gain benefits from enhanced prestige in the world as their generosity is recognized. If a donor has significant foreign direct investment in a recipient country, then, by improving the recipient's economy, the aid also helps its foreign direct investment prospects. Moreover, the donor may gain from its largess if it has citizens living on the recipient's soil.

NGOs also direct their aid to causes and projects that provide the greatest organization-specific benefits; thus, a religion-based NGO may be interested in reducing poverty where religious converts are likely. An environmental NGO contributes to environment-supporting projects, while charitable foundations champion aid projects that further the foundation's agenda. Certainly, a breakthrough in malaria would confer immense prestige on the Gates Foundation and other supporters of these efforts.

Jointly produced donor-specific benefits from aid are both a blessing and a curse. They are a blessing because a sizeable share of such benefits may circumvent the free-rider problem (see Chapter 3); but they are a curse because donors' pursuit of private gains may inhibit poverty reduction. For example, a donor that seeks security gains may create political instabilities in the recipient as certain domestic interests object to furthering the security objectives of the donor. Post-9/11 efforts by the Bush administration to attack the Taliban and al-Qaida in Pakistan and Afghanistan had negative political backlash on these countries' governments.

Multilateral institutions also address the free-rider problem of aid by serving as an intermediary between donors and recipients. For instance, the World Bank identifies worthwhile development projects, channels donors' funds into a specific sector (for example, health), accounts for the disbursement of funds, and evaluates spending outcomes. By collecting and disseminating information, the Bank limits for donors the asymmetric information surrounding recipients, who are better informed than donors on how aid money is being used. Even when depending on the Bank and not giving in a bilateral arrangement, donors can still obtain donor-specific benefits by supporting the countries and sectors of their choice.

In recent years, Brazil, Russia, India, China, and South Africa—collectively known as the BRICS—have played a greater role in giving foreign assistance, especially in Africa (Cooper and Farooq, 2013). BRICS's interests in giving aid are motivated, in part, by their desire to expand their influence in the world. This desire is a donor-specific benefit. As the BRICS's economies grow, they seek foreign direct investment outlets, new trading partners, and new natural resource sources. Foreign assistance is a way to further these goals of the BRICS. What is different is the rapid growth of some of the BRICS, which means that their collective influence on the developing countries may increase at an astounding rate.

PUBLIC GOOD AID — *more free-riding*

"A new form of foreign aid—'free-rider aid'—may come from the provision of transnational public goods and may increasingly replace traditionally tied and untied foreign aid of the post-World War II period. That is, free-riding behavior on the part of the poor may limit even greater worldwide inequality" (Sandler, 1997, p. 183). This form of aid is an easy political sell, especially in terms of the health, governance, environment, and security sectors. This follows because the public goods associated with these sectors in the aid recipient can directly benefit the donor. Consider assistance given to South American countries to preserve their rain forests. This assistance may serve to sequester carbon and maintain biodiversity, which benefit all of humankind. Because rich countries value the environment more than poor countries with more immediate survival needs, there is a proclivity for rich countries to want to support environmental TPGs through aid flows. Next consider governance support given to improve financial regulations in developing countries. This support protects donors' foreign direct investment, stabilizes trade, and promotes financial stability. Peacekeeping efforts keep local conflicts from spilling over to neighboring countries, which, in turn, may sever essential resource supplies. Such efforts also limit refugee flows and curtail the health consequences from conflicts.

The World Bank (2001, pp. 110–113) estimated that foreign assistance directly spent annually on TPGs was $5 billion, with another $11 billion spent on complementary activities, which allowed developing countries to absorb these TPGs.[6] These complementary activities include the provision of national public goods (NPGs) that improve education, health, infrastructure, technical capability, and the environment. Surely this spending figure has grown greatly in recent years with the emphasis on the Millennium Development Goals, with their direct assistance to numerous NPGs and TPGS. A study by Willem te Velde, Morrissey, and Hewitt (2002, Tables 5.1 and 5.2) indicated that the financing of both NPGs and TPGs has risen from just over 16% of foreign assistance in the early 1980s to almost 40% in the late 1990s. Similar increases were documented by Raffer (1999). Of course, the share of foreign assistance earmarked for public goods will vary between researchers since there is no precise means for classifying public good expenditure. Nevertheless, this form of aid will increase especially in light of the recommendation for reforming aid by the UN High-Level Panel (2001), which called for enhanced support of TPGs in health and other key sectors (also see International Task Force on Global Public Goods, 2006). The key concern is that the increased support for TPGs does not divert money from traditional assistance to alleviate poverty.

AGGREGATION TECHNOLOGIES AND PUBLIC GOOD ASSISTANCE

The aggregation technology of TPGs affects the direction of aid flows. For a weakest-link TPG, the issue is one of inadequate capacity for some developing countries to provide an amount of the TPG that is acceptable to the world community since the smallest contribution fixes the level of the TPG that the community consumes. If this level is unacceptable to some rich countries, then they must augment the developing country's capacity to provide the weakest-link TPG. This can be done in at least two ways: augment the developing country's income, or provide the good directly (Vicary and Sandler, 2002). Augmenting income means that foreign aid flows must be directed to those countries without sufficient capacity to supply such goods. In-kind transfers are attractive since the donor then knows that the money will go to the intended purpose. Either method is known as "shoring up the weakest-link."

6. Books on TPGs and their role in development include Arce and Sandler (2002), Ferroni and Mody (2002), Kanbur, Sandler, and Morrison (1999), and Kaul, Grunberg, and Stern (1999).

	B	
	0	1
A 0	Nash 0, 0	0, –4
A 1	–4, 0	Nash 2, 2

a. Weakest-link public good with $c_i = 4$ and matched $b_i = 6$

	B	
	Do Not Act	Shore up
Do Not Act	Nash 0, 0	6, –2
A Shore up	–2, 6	2, 2

b. Shoring up the weakest link

Figure 6.1
Weakest-link public good and shoring up the weakest link

We illustrate the difficulties that shoring up implies with the help of Figure 6.1. Matrix a depicts a weakest-link public good where countries A and B can either provide no units or one unit of the public good at per-unit costs of $c_i = 4$. Matched contributed units give each country a benefit of $b_i = 6$ in matrix a. If no country contributes, then each receives 0. If, however, only one country contributes a unit, then the contributor nets –4 or the cost of the contribution, and the noncontributor receives nothing. There are no benefits because the smallest contribution is zero, so that the effective amount of weakest-link public good consumed is also zero. When both countries contribute a unit, each nets 2 ($= 6 - 4$) as costs are deducted from benefits. The Nash equilibria involve matching behavior along the diagonal of matrix a, in Figure 6.1 (see Chapter 3). Thus far, there is no free-riding incentive since failure to contribute gives no benefits.

Things become interesting when one country tries to provide the public good for the other country in matrix b, where each country has two strategies: do nothing, or pay for both countries' units at combined costs of 8. If one country shores up the other, then the shoring-up country nets −2 (= 6 − 8) and the other gets the free ride worth 6. The payoffs along the main diagonal remain the same as in matrix a. Both countries shoring up means that they share or pay their own costs of 4. The "shoring-up" game is a Prisoners' Dilemma with a single Nash equilibrium of inactivity. Thus, the prognosis for weakest-link TPGs is not so hopeful when one or more countries lack the capacity to supply an acceptable level of the good. Without the use of matrices, let's suppose that there are five countries, where only two have the means to provide the weakest-link TPG. Now, the shoring-up strategy involves funding the good for three other countries. If one of two capable countries did the shoring up, then it must pay its own costs of 4 and the additional costs of 12, or 16 in total, in order to achieve a benefit of 6 before costs are deducted. The "do not act" strategy is now even more dominant over shoring up. In fact, inaction becomes more dominant as the number of countries needing shoring up grows. The only means around the dilemma is if some rich countries achieve asymmetrically large benefits from the provision of the weakest-link TPG. This may well be the case for infectious diseases, where the United States and other rich countries greatly gain from limiting the spread of a disease, which is a weakest-link TPG. Another weakest-link health TPG is surveillance of an outbreak. Gaps in surveillance can be devastating to countries, blindsighted to the spread of an infectious disease. An effective quarantine is another weakest-link TPG.

At the opposite extreme, a best-shot public good requires a single, sufficiently endowed and capable supplier who provides the good and a free ride for everyone. Capacity again becomes a concern because the provider must be able to achieve success in supplying the public good. For a best-shot TPG that enriches rich and poor countries, there is less concern because the incentives are there for the rich to act. When the TPGs only benefit the poor countries—for example, a cure for a disease indigenous to the tropics—the rich may have little incentive to act and the impacted countries may have little capacity to act. In these situations, multilateral institutions, multistakeholder organizations, NGOs, and charitable foundations may have to support the best-shot TPG supply.

Different aggregation technologies may have surprising recommendations for the direction of foreign assistance. As shown earlier, assistance should flow to poor countries when weakest-link or weaker-link TPGs are the concern. This finding is unsurprising. In contrast, assistance should flow to the richer countries in a region where best-shot or better-shot TPGs are needed, since the rich countries possess the best prognosis for providing the TPG. That is, inequality among states is desirable for the supply of best-shot or better-shot TPGs. This recommendation is surprising unless one carefully considers the supply prospects. The supply prognosis for summation TPGs improves when greater inequality is achieved insofar as the rich countries will privilege others with a free ride (Bergstrom, Blume, and Varian, 1986). Threshold TPGs, where the cumulative contribution must surpass a set level before benefits are received, also gain from increased inequality. This follows because there is less need for coordination among contributors if one or a few contributors have the wherewithal to achieve the threshold.

MILLENNIUM DEVELOPMENT GOALS FOR 2015

The establishment of the Millennium Development Goals serves as a coordinating and awareness mechanism to get donor and recipient countries to focus on addressing crucial aspects of extreme poverty. These goals also allow other interested parties—for example, multilateral institutions—to coordinate with these states to achieve certain benchmarks with respect to poverty reduction. As such, the supporters of development have means for gauging their progress. These goals include eradicating poverty and hunger, obtaining universal primary education, fostering gender equality, curbing child mortality, bolstering maternal health, combatting HIV/AIDS, malaria, and other diseases, promoting environmental sustainability, and achieving a global development partnership (Sandler and Arce, 2007).

Specific benchmarks for 2015 include halving hunger, achieving primary education for all children, reducing under-five mortality by two-thirds, lowering maternal mortality ratio by three-quarters, halving the spread of HIV/AIDS and malaria, halving the proportion of people with unsafe drinking water and no basic sanitation, and ameliorating developing countries' debt problems. Greater progress has been made on some goals than on others. The Millennium Development Goals stress the health, knowledge, governance, environment, and security sectors, with the greatest emphasis placed on health. To achieve these goals requires NPGs, regional public goods (RPGs), and TPGs.

A new set of Millennium Development Goals is in the works for post-2015 (see Chapter 13). Health will remain a primary focus, especially because of the spillovers to the rich donor countries. However, with the increased concern about climate change and its impact on health, security, and poverty, the environment is likely to figure more prominently in the next set of benchmark goals. The need for potable water as populations grow will also augment the importance of the environment. Additionally, the recent financial crisis will likely push governance up in importance in the next set of Millennium Development Goals. Increased capital flows to the developing world heighten the importance of sound financial practices.

HEALTHCARE CONCERNS OF THE RICH AND POOR COUNTRIES

An important concern in the development of new medicines, vaccines, and treatments is the "90/10" gap, in which less than 10% of U.S. annual spending on health-related research and development addresses the health concerns of 90% of the planet's population (WHO, 2002, p. 23). Given differences in life expectancy, lifestyles, immunization programs, healthcare infrastructure, education, development, and wealth, people in high-income countries primarily suffer from noncommunicable diseases, whereas people in low-income countries suffer greatly from infectious and parasitic diseases (Kremer, 2002, p. 71; WHO, 2001). Measles, syphilis, and pertussis kill relatively few people in high-income countries but cause hundreds of thousands of deaths in poor countries (WHO, 2001). These differences make it difficult for donor countries to understand the healthcare needs of poor countries, which are compounded by rapid population growth and a proclivity toward conflict. Conflict exposes populations to sexually transmitted diseases, increased poverty, traumatic injuries, and hunger.

Pharmaceutical companies in rich countries are naturally interested in earning profits and, thus, developing medicines to treat cancer and heart disease, which cause more deaths than other diseases in rich countries. During patent periods, new medicines to treat these diseases will garner huge profits. These same companies have little interest in treating diseases in poor countries where effective demand is small because most people cannot afford costly medicines. Moreover, pharmaceutical companies are less concerned with developing vaccines—say to cure HIV/AIDS—than in discovering new antiretroviral regimes to treat diseases, since these regimes provide a steady revenue stream. Because new cases of HIV/AIDS are more prevalent in poor countries, the lack of interest of these companies to develop a vaccine is very troublesome. Pharmaceutical companies pursue drugs where there is a high income responsiveness (elasticity) and low price responsiveness, which is true of drugs that can save lives in rich countries, where insurance can pay much of the medicines' costs. Even when high- and low-income countries share the same healthcare concerns as is becoming true for some kinds of cancers, medical breakthroughs may be ill-suited to low-income countries where medical technology and training are more primitive. Given the low value of life in poor countries, expensive treatment regimes will have a small market except among a few rich individuals.

Another division between rich and poor countries' health concerns involves the Trade-Related Aspects of Intellectual Property Rights Agreement (TRIPS) (see Chapter 7 and the discussion of the World Trade Organization). In the case of medicines, the TRIPS Agreement protects the patents of pharmaceutical companies, thereby making many lifesaving medicines unaffordable to poor countries. In recent years, this concern has been partly addressed by TRIPS Flexibilities, which "permit countries to override patent protection by granting compulsory licenses to third parties to produce patented medical products/processes locally without the consent of the patent owner, at the country's discretion" (Hwenda, 2013, p. 443). This exception to TRIPS protection is considered an extreme measure to be used only after negotiations between the developing countries and the pharmaceutical company fail to produce reasonable commercial terms to sell the medicine in the developing country at a discount. Moreover, a public health exigency must be present to warrant such a commercial concession on the part of the drug company, as has been the case for antiretroviral therapy, used to treat HIV/AIDS in Africa and elsewhere.

The protection of intellectual property rights to new drugs is associated with important considerations. First, there is a trade-off between innovation incentives and saving lives. Patents allow pharmaceutical companies to recoup expensive research and development (R & D) costs. Without such patent protection, these companies would have less incentive to invest in discovering new medicines, which may cost billions and promise no assured success. The high costs of patented medicine provide funds to pursue new medicines and vaccines, and to offset losses from other failures to make breakthroughs. Patents help ensure innovations. Second, TRIPS Flexibilities must protect that licensed third parties do not sell the drug outside of the developed country, which would seriously cut into the pharmaceutical companies' profit and ability to pursue yet newer drugs. Third, patent protection may result in a time inconsistency problem, whereby a developing country promises patent protection or guaranteed sales to entice a pharmaceutical company to discover a needed medicine. Once it is discovered and brought to market, the promising government may renege on its pledges (Kremer, 2002, p. 75). Repeated interactions among the company and government may ameliorate this concern. Such interactions are more likely for large pharmaceutical companies that develop and sell a large range of drugs. Foreign assistance can address this issue by guaranteeing to underwrite a large share of the sales of the drug for the developing country, once the drug is available. Fourth, given the best-shot character of new drug development, the discovering pharmaceutical company will possess monopoly power, at least during the patent period, which will restrict sales in the absence of foreign assistance or negotiated concessions.[7]

MARKET FAILURES AND HEALTH

We have just seen that the TRIPS Agreement may result in market failures as resources do not gravitate to their most-valued use because of monopoly. If, however, property rights to innovations are not protected, then too little investment will go toward discovery of new drugs. Market failures result when

---

7. Monopolies price above their marginal costs. Microeconomics teaches that a monopoly sells where marginal revenue equals marginal costs, but sets a price on the demand curve that exceeds marginal costs.

agents' optimization decisions do not achieve a social optimum. For health decisions, market failures abound and involve externalities, public goods, and asymmetric information (see Chapter 3). Moreover, these market failures may concern present and future generations; for example, eradicating a disease safeguards current and all future generations. Herd immunity, which varies by disease, means that less than 100% of the population needs to be immunized to eradicate the disease—for instance, in the case of smallpox, herd immunity is estimated at around 80%, so that immunization levels as high as 80% can eradicate the disease (Anderson and May, 1991, p. 88). Given the costs and risks of immunization, a person is best off if he or she can free ride on the immunization of others. Such attempts to free ride mean that immunization levels are undersupplied, leaving society at inefficiently high-risk levels. The free-rider incentive is practically insidious for achieving herd immunity because as herd immunity is approached, free-riding benefits rise. This follows because the individual is increasingly less likely to contract the disease as more of the population are immunized. This market failure can be partly addressed if the costs and risks of immunization are reduced with additional vaccination sites and safer vaccines. Concerted efforts by the WHO and member countries achieved herd immunity for smallpox, thereby officially eradicating the disease in 1979, two years after the last reported case.

Another market failure concerns the insufficient efforts devoted to outbreak surveillance and intelligence. The WHO, the National Institute of Health (NIH), and the CDC have sought to redress this underprovision. Underprovision may also involve excludable health public goods that are nonrival since exclusion can limit use by people gaining a positive benefit. Nonrivalry means that extending consumption of the health-related public good involves no marginal costs. Not to exclude nor to charge user fees means that there will be no revenue to fund the good, unless it is provided by a government, multilateral body, charitable foundation, or NGO through donors' contributions. Consider the sharing of healthcare data so that countries can better assess the health risks that their population confronts. An organization, such as the WHO, can make this data freely available or charge an access fee. The latter would limit dissemination to those countries where such fees are burdensome.

GLOBAL HEALTH AND PUBLICNESS

As mentioned earlier, global health activities offer a rich array of public goods, whose publicness character differs according to excludability, rivalry, and aggregation technology. Sandler and Arce (2002) and Smith and Woodward (2002) recognized the plethora of global health public goods (also see Sonntag, 2010). We find this rich variety interesting, but caution the reader that diverse properties of publicness imply that the provision prognoses of alternative global health public goods will differ, where some provision prognoses will be more hopeful than others. Global health public goods can be purely public, impurely public, club goods, or private and marketable. Moreover, some health activities may give rise to joint products, whose outputs vary in their degree of publicness.[8] In this regard, a teaching hospital not only treats patients' illnesses (a private good), but also develops new operative procedures (a global public good). Discovering a cure is purely public, while monitoring disease outbreaks is impurely public. Once found, a cure can be used in a nonrival fashion by anyone who suffers from the disease. Knowledge of the cure will inhibit exclusion. Monitoring is, however, partially nonrival since focusing attention in one area detracts from surveillance elsewhere. Moreover, monitoring is excludable to some extent because monitors can be withheld from some area. When a health-promoting TPG is partly rival in terms of crowding, but nonpayers can be completely excluded at a negligible cost, the activity is a transnational club good. Treatments provided to patients at prestigious hospitals, such as the Mayo Clinic, represent club goods, so that Mayo's oncology unit is a club, whose members pay for a regiment of treatment. Fees collected support the Clinic and its staff and facilities. A technical consultation network via the Internet is a modern-day transnational club good, whose utilization can be monitored and charged accordingly. Augmented utilization can result in slower replies and longer queues, which are manifestations of crowding. Club principles can be applied to determine provision, financing, and membership. Equity concerns arise because some developing countries cannot afford membership fees to health-related club goods. As such, foreign assistance can pay these countries' membership charges.

Rich countries have become increasingly interested in supporting the healthcare infrastructure in poor countries because vulnerable populations in these countries can allow infectious diseases to gain a foothold there before dispersing globally (Lele, Ridker, and Upadhyay, 2006; Sridhar and Woods, 2013). Even noninfectious diseases in poor countries are a concern to rich countries because of compromised immunity systems in the indigenous population that can promote outbreaks of infectious diseases. Diseases are opportunistic, seeking the weakest link or most compromised host population. Rich countries are increasingly aware that they must supply health-related TPGs to developing countries in order to safeguard their own people. Aid given by the United States to West Africa during the 2014 Ebola outbreak is a recent example.

The most interesting dimension of publicness for health activities is the aggregation technology, which possesses important implications for the need and form of the corrective policy. Unlike other sectors, health public goods rarely

8. On the nature of health public goods, also see Chen, Evans, and Cash (1999) and Zacher (1999).

abide by a summation technology, where the level of the good available for consumption equals the sum of the individual contributions. Perhaps the best example of the summation technology is the treatment of diseased patients or the immunization of the population in the case of infectious diseases. In the first case, the public good is the health of the population, while in the second case, the public good is the immunity of the population. For noninfectious diseases, educating the public about screening tests—for example, for HIV/AIDS—adheres to a summation technology. The summation technology is often associated with underprovision and the need for international cooperation.

In Table 6.2, we list seven alternative aggregation technologies for global health public goods. In the left-hand column, each of these aggregators is indicated as a refresher for the reader. They were previously introduced in Chapter 3. In the second and third columns, we provide a public good example of each aggregator technology for infectious and noninfectious diseases, respectively. For instance, maintaining sterilization in hospitals is a weaker-link public good, which is becoming more difficult to achieve in recent years as bacteria have acquired antibiotic resistance. Curbing the spread of a pest is a weaker-link public good in regard to noninfectious diseases. For both examples, the least effort has the greatest marginal influence on the level of the public good supplied. We leave the other examples to the reader insofar as we already devoted much discussion to the aggregation technology for public goods in general.

In the right-hand column of Table 6.2, we indicate some public policy implications. Once again, these follow from our discussion of these aggregators in Chapter 3. By way of illustration, we explicitly consider some of these implications. In a world where countries possess similar tastes and endowments, weakest-link health public goods will be efficiently provided because the smallest effort fixes the level of the public good, thereby removing free-rider incentives. However, in a world with rich and poor countries, the latter will not have the capacity to provide adequate levels of weakest-link or weaker-link health public goods. To address this shortfall, some kind of shoring up of the weakest link is required, and this reintroduces free riding among rich countries, as shown earlier in our discussion of Figure 6.1. Multilateral institutions, charitable foundations, NGOs, and multistakeholder organizations have a real role to play in shoring up weakest and weaker links, especially for infectious diseases. A similar policy conclusion characterizes threshold public goods, where these same organizations can ensure that thresholds for the health public good are met and that the required coordination among contributors is achieved. For best-shot and better-shot health public goods, resources and talent must be concentrated in those countries and institutions most apt to make a breakthrough in developing vaccines, antibiotics, new diagnostic procedures, or best-practice regimes. Coordination is needed so that efforts are not duplicated in a wasteful manner, especial for best-shot health public goods. Some duplication is fine for better-shot

Table 6.2. Alternative aggregation technologies for health-promoting TPGs

Aggregation technology	Infectious diseases	Noninfectious diseases	Public policy implications
Summation: Public good levels equal the sum of individual contributions	Treating diseased patients	Educating the public about screening tests	Need for international cooperation for infectious diseases. Some international assistance is required for noninfectious disease if country is poor.
Weakest link: Only the smallest provision level determines the public good level	Surveillance of an outbreak	Sharing medical information in a network	When the countries have similar income, little intervention is required. If, however, standards for infectious diseases cannot be met by poor countries, rich ones will have to bolster the poor countries' capacities to address the disease. This is more of a concern for infectious than noninfectious diseases.
Weaker link: The smallest provision has the greatest marginal influence, followed by the next smallest, and so on	Maintaining sterilization in hospitals	Curbing the spread of a pest	The need for matching behavior is less pronounced than for weakest-link public goods. Rich countries may assist poor countries if infectious or noninfectious diseases pose a danger. Assistance may be in-kind or monetary.
Best shot: Only the largest provision determines the overall public good level	Developing a vaccine	Developing a diagnostic procedure	Effort must be concentrated where talent is the greatest with discoveries benefiting everyone. Coordination in the form of directing resources to those most likely to succeed is desirable.
Better-shot: The largest provision has the greatest marginal influence, followed by the next largest, and so on	Discovering new antibiotics	Developing best-practice regimes	Less need for concentrated effort, but some coordination still required. Some concentration of resources is still required.
Threshold: Cumulative contribution must surpass a threshold for benefits to be received	Eradicating a disease with herd immunity less than 99%	Assessing health risks from environmental factors	Transnational coordination is needed so that threshold is met. Multistakeholder organizations and charitable trusts can play an important role.
Weighted sum: Each contribution can have a different additive impact	Curbing spread of AIDS	Removing toxins from a shared environment	Need for intervention must be on a case-by-case basis. Localized benefits may limit the need for international policy intervention.

public goods since second-best discoveries can serve a purpose—for example, a less effective new antibiotic may be better tolerated by patients who cannot take the most effective antibiotic. Moreover, the less effective antibiotic may serve as a second line of defense when the bacteria acquire resistance to the better antibiotic. Finally, weighted-sum aggregators must weigh local and more far-reaching benefits when deciding intervention. Since weighted-sum public goods are associated with so many different game forms (see Chapter 3), general conclusions about policy are difficult to draw.

Two general conclusions are, however, still in order. First, given the prevalence of weakest-link health public goods, rich countries must be concerned about bolstering the capacity of developing countries to achieve adequate provision levels of these goods. This, in turn, means that rich countries and other donors must circumvent free riding associated with shoring up these weakest links. Second, the global community must engineer ways for supplying the myriad best-shot and better-shot health public goods to privilege the world. For diseases of little interest to rich countries, such efforts must come from multilateral institutions, charitable foundations, NGOs, and multistakeholder organizations.

KEY INSTITUTIONS IN THE GLOBAL HEALTH SECTOR

Recent years have witnessed a tremendous diversity of institutions addressing global health. To offer a small flavor of this diversity, we list some key institutions in Table 6.3, along with their general purposes and/or functions.

Multilateral institutions include the WHO, the World Bank, and UN Development Program. Among other functions, these organizations pool funds for best-shot, better-shot, and summation health public goods, as well as augmenting the capacity for weakest-link and weaker-link public goods. These institutions also coordinate actions for health public goods so that transnational collectives surpass critical thresholds. Multilaterals also participate in multistakeholder organizations and partnerships, such as the one formed by the World Bank, donor countries, Merck, and others to alleviate river blindness. In addition, these multilaterals coordinate aid inflows into the health sector of developing countries, provide disbursements, collect statistics, coordinate diverse agents, and evaluate mileposts achieved. According to Murray (2006), the WHO is the key multilateral institution in promoting global health. At the regional level, the regional development banks, customs unions, and other regional institutions help promote health-related RPGs.

Over the last couple of decades, multistakeholder institutions and public-private partnerships have emerged as key players in bolstering global health, particularly in developing countries. Prime examples include the Global Fund, Medicines for Malaria Venture (MMV), Onchocerciasis Control Partnership

Table 6.3. Key institutions in the global health sector

Institutional Categories	Purposes/Functions
Multilaterals: WHO, World Bank, UN Development Program	Pool funds for best-shot, better-shot, and summation public goods and bolster capacity for weakest-link and weaker-link public goods. Participate in partnerships and multistakeholder organizations. Coordinate aid inflows to the health sectors of developing countries. Provide knowledge and statistics. Oversee funds disbursement and accounting.
Multistakeholder institutions and partnerships: Global Fund, Medicines for Malaria Venture, Onchocerciasis Control Partnership, Global Alliance for Vaccines and Immunization (GAVI)	Draw on the comparative advantage of diverse participants. Target tropical diseases and other plagues in developing countries. Include diverse participants such as firms, nations, NGOs, multilaterals, and charitable foundations.
Networks: Global Environment Facility (GEF), Consultative Group for International Agricultural Research (CGIAR)	Link together interests within and among regions in providing TPGs. Support sustainable development. Limit air and other forms of pollution. Bolster food supplies for better health. Networks can be used to link places with similar health problems. Contain diverse participants.
Charitable Foundations: Wellcome Trust, Gates Foundation, Open Society Institute, Rockefeller Foundation	Inflow of new funds for supporting orphan drugs and addressing plagues affecting the developing world. Bolster capacity for weakest-link public goods and pool resources for best-shot public goods. Support diseases where there are little commercial interests. Provide leadership.
Nongovernmental Organizations (NGOs): Médecins Sans Frontières (MSF), Red Cross, Save the Children, CARE	Champion specific health public goods and complementary activities (e.g., providing food) including disaster relief, immunization, and charity. Treat the ill.
Nation-Based Institutions: CDC, NIH, Pasteur Institute	Supply health public goods in the form of outbreak surveillance, collecting data, isolating new diseases, and coordinating efforts to develop treatment regimes and vaccines. Address diseases that pose or might present a risk to rich nations. Concerns in host country create a privileged group for poor countries. Provide poor countries with needed capacity to provide weakest-link health public goods.

(OCP), and the Global Alliance for Vaccines and Immunization (GAVI). The beauty of these institutions is that they can draw the comparative advantage of their component agents. The OCP consists of a partnership between Merck, the WHO, host countries to the disease, and donors to control river blindness, endemic to 34 countries in Africa, Latin America, and the Arabian Peninsula. Under OCP, Merck contributes Ivermectin to treat the disease (a single dose is effective for a year), while the other participants facilitate the drug's distribution. MMV arose from the Roll Back Malaria initiative of the WHO and consists of a nonprofit institution that supplies funding incentives for partnerships among pharmaceutical companies, academic entities, and public agencies for the purpose of developing new medicines, treatments, and prevention regimes. In so doing, MMV supplies best-shot and weakest-link public goods for curbing malaria and its consequences. Thanks to MMV, malaria is trending downward. The Global Fund is a partnership with interest in curtailing HIV/AIDS, malaria, and TB, which disproportionately affect poor countries. The Global Fund draws its financial resources from NGOs, charitable foundations, donor countries, and the private sector.

Networks are becoming important institutional participants because health public goods often possess benefit spillovers that transverse regions. As such, institutions and interests in affected regions must be linked, as was done by OCP in the case of river blindness. Examples of these networks include the Global Environment Facility (GEF), whose donors include the World Bank, UN Development Program, UN Environmental Program, NGOs, and others, and the Consultative Group for International Agricultural Research (CGIAR), whose donors include the World Bank, the UN Development Program, and donor countries (World Bank, 2001). GEF is focused on encouraging sustainable development through environmentally friendly program assistance. By improving air and water quality, GEF also supports improved health.

Since air and water pollutants can travel far from their sources, GEF must tie together a network of donor and recipient countries. In some scenarios, donor countries are affected even though they are some distance removed from the pollution source. By preserving species and their habitats, GEF also conserves biodiversity, which benefits everyone. Some species contain chemical compounds—for example, snake venom—that can be used to treat heart disease and some forms of cancer. GEF leverages its funds through some loans to provide additional support to environmental-based programs in diverse regions of the developing world (World Bank, 2001, p. 115). Country-specific benefits motivate client states to borrow from GEF and, in the process, global and regional spillover benefits are received by other countries. The network structure is particularly suited for addressing weakest-link and weaker-link public goods where some acceptable standard of provision is required. Such networks can also pool resources to collectively achieve best-shot, better-shot, summation, and threshold public goods. CGIAR is a network that fosters agricultural-based technological advances to augment food production in developing countries. A well-nourished population is essential for warding off diseases. Like GEF, CGIAR can channel funds and coordinate actions among regions confronted with similar challenges.

Charitable foundations—for example, the Wellcome Trust, Gates Foundation, Open Society Institute, and Rockefeller Foundation—can infuse new sources of funds for addressing orphan drugs provision and the plagues impacting the developing world. Orphan drugs involve situations where the effective demand to develop and produce the drug is insufficient to cover the costs. This occurs for rare diseases in rich countries or diseases confined to poor countries. In the latter case, pharmaceutical companies cannot make a profit unless some donor guarantees a sufficient market or underwrites the costs of developing the drug. These foundations offer funding that does not crowd out other sources of funds because these other sources have been scarce for third-world plagues. In addition, these organizations augment the capacity for weakest-link public goods and pool resources for best-shot public goods. A key function for these charitable organizations is to assume a leadership role to coordinate action and to unite diverse partners with different expertise in health-related causes.

Health NGOs are many in number and include Médecins Sans Frontières (MSF), Red Cross, Save the Children, and CARE. As displayed in Table 6.3, these organizations champion specific health public goods and their complementary activities, such as good nutrition. Other such activities include treating patients, providing disaster relief, helping children, assisting refugees, immunizing populations, and supplying food and other essential needs.

Nation-based institutions—the CDC, NIH, and Pasteur Institute—are prime examples where a rich country offers outbreak surveillance, data collection, new disease isolation, effort coordination, new treatment regimes, or new vaccines. These institutions create a privileged group where a single country (the United States or France) is so concerned about these activities that they alone provide them for all countries. These privileging countries are motivated by altruism and self-interest. The latter arises because of their desire to stop new diseases or outbreaks at their origin before they arrive on their soil. These organizations are primarily providing weakest-link and best-shot health public goods.

PAIRED COMPARISON: POLIO AND SMALLPOX ERADICATION

Even though the herd immunity thresholds are very similar for polio and smallpox (see Table 6.4), polio is still not eradicated, while smallpox was officially eradicated in 1979. Polio remains endemic to Afghanistan, Nigeria, and Pakistan. Eradicating either polio or smallpox yields a global public good. Because global eradication requires ending all cases of the disease in every country in the world, vaccination-induced eradication is a weakest-link public good, whose outcome is solely dependent on the smallest degree of eradication achieved in some country (Sandler, 1992). The only way to overcome this capacity concern is to provide assistance to all weakest-link countries. Since shoring up weakest-link countries is a Prisoners' Dilemma, some multilateral institution must spearhead the eradication action and draw its financing from rich countries and other interested organizations. For both smallpox and polio, the WHO and donor countries have supplied this capacity boost. According to Barrett (2007), the world was lucky in eradicating smallpox when a cease-fire in Sudan allowed the WHO to achieve herd immunity in the last endemic country.

Table 6.4 lists both similarities and differences associated with eradicating the two diseases. The key difference involves the associated vaccines—for polio, a live-attenuated vaccine is administered in developing countries. With this vaccine, the polio virus stays in the environment for some time and can infect others (Barrett, 2003b, 2007, 2010). This live-attenuated polio vaccine is cheap and easy to administer orally in poor countries, unlike the inactive

Table 6.4. Paired comparison: Polio and smallpox eradication

Polio	Smallpox
• 80%–86% Herd immunity threshold	• 83%–85% Herd immunity threshold
• Use of live-attenuated vaccine in developing countries; use of inactive vaccine in rich countries	• Use of live-attenuated vaccine without an environmental threat
• Eradication is an assurance game where weakest-link countries must be shored up.	• Eradication is an assurance game where weakest-link countries must be shored up.
• Shoring up weakest links has free-riding concerns.	• Shoring up weakest links has free-riding concerns.
• Polio is not yet eradicated; it is hoped that it will be eradicated by 2018.	• Smallpox was declared officially eradicated in 1979.
• There is need to stop vaccinating after eradication certified.	• There is less need to stop vaccinating after eradication.
• Vaccination cessation poses an assurance game.	• Vaccination cessation is a harmony game.
• Eradication is funded by charitable trusts, the WHO, UN, and rich countries.	• Eradication was primarily funded by the WHO and rich countries.
• Conflict countries pose a challenge to eradication.	• Conflict countries once posed a challenge to eradication.
• Only about 1 in 2,000 people infected shows symptoms.	• Almost all infected people display symptoms with one third dying.
• Polio does not lend itself to terrorism.	• Smallpox can be used by terrorists.

Sources: Anderson and May (1991) and Barrett (2003b, 2007, 2010)

vaccine used in rich countries. The latter vaccine must be injected by trained individuals using disposable needles. Unfortunately, the live-attenuated vaccine can generate new polio cases. In contrast, the live-attenuated smallpox vaccine does not impose a similar risk. Given the risk posed by the live-attenuated polio vaccine, there is a need to stop vaccinating once eradication is certified (Barrett, 2010). This is not required for smallpox vaccination.

For both diseases, conflict countries posed a challenge to eradication; however, the increased conflict incidence in poor countries since the late 1980s presented a greater challenge for polio eradication. Another key difference is the response of infected people; only 1 in 2000 infected persons display polio symptoms, while almost all infected persons display smallpox symptoms. This means that intelligence on polio exposure is harder than smallpox to ascertain, making polio a difficult disease to track. Moreover, the greater consequences of smallpox motivate countries to take action, which is less true of polio. There is a greater terrorism potential for smallpox because the disease kills a third of its victims and disfigures another third. Fortunately, continued smallpox vaccination, when needed to address a terrorism-based attack, poses no environmental threat. Unlike polio, vaccination cessation is a harmony game. For polio, it is an assurance game since every country must cease vaccinating to keep the virus out of the environment (Barrett, 2003b, 2010). Thus, polio poses more post-eradication challenges than smallpox regarding vaccination. The world is motivated to eradicate both diseases because of the harm that the disease presents and the risk that vaccination presents.

INTERGENERATIONAL AND INTRAGENERATIONAL CONSIDERATIONS

Many global health public goods yield benefit spillovers both spatially among countries and intertemporally over generations (Sandler, 2009). Many aspects of health-related public goods possess intergenerational spillovers, including the overuse of antibiotics and antiretroviral therapies, which reduces their effectiveness for current and future generations. Curing a disease, discovering new antibiotics, or inhibiting microbial resistance yield intergenerational benefit streams, as does eradicating a disease through achieving herd immunity. Other intergenerational market failures tied to healthcare are indicated in the top portion of Table 6.5. For example, inadequate patent protection can limit incentives and, thus, actions to discover new medicines. Insufficient investment in research facilities and hospitals can forestall the development of new treatment regimes that can benefit current and future patients. The other examples are self-explanatory.

In the bottom of Table 6.5, we list health-related actions and public goods, whose spillovers are primarily experienced by the current generation. For example, insufficient outbreak surveillance compromises the efforts of today's

Table 6.5. Intergenerational versus intragenerational market failures

Intergenerational market failures

- Insufficient patent protection
- Overuse of antibiotics or antiretroviral therapies
- Curing a disease or discovering antibiotics
- Eradicating a disease through achievement of herd immunity
- Discovering new vaccines
- Inhibiting microbial resistance
- Insufficient investment in research capacity including research hospitals
- Insufficient control of long-lived pollutants

Intragenerational market failures

- Inadequate healthcare facilities in developing countries
- Monopoly/oligopoly supply of medicines and equipment
- Insufficient outbreak surveillance
- Inadequate quarantines
- Asymmetric information on the part of pharmaceutical companies
- Underprovision of immunization
- Inadequate sterilization

generation to stem an outbreak. Inadequate quarantine and sterilization primarily impact the safety of the current generation. Insufficient healthcare facilities in developing countries place the current generation in other countries in jeopardy.

Spatial spillovers are easier to take into account than temporal spillovers because all recipients are contemporaries and so can make their preferences known and consummate agreements to raise public good provision. For intergenerational spillovers, future generations are not present and so must rely on the far-sighted altruism of the current generation. The sequencing of generations has an important implication for capacity. In the case of weakest-link health public goods, insufficient capacity today spells even greater shortfalls in the future as more people become vulnerable owing to past myopia. Moreover, Collier's (2007) discussion of *The Bottom Billion* emphasized a growing divide between the poor and the rich, which will exacerbate the inadequacy of weakest-link health public goods as the effective level of the public good diminishes. This, in turn, will mean the need for ever greater efforts to shore up weakest-link countries in the health arena. However, capacity concerns for best-shot health public goods can be rectified in the future once a generation acquires the wherewithal to provide the public good now and into the future. Since future generations are ever richer and more capable, the prognosis for best-shot health public goods is hopeful. This is why medical breakthroughs increase over time; healthcare solutions not possible today will become possible tomorrow as future generations' capacity grows. Thus, weakest-link intergenerational public goods pose a greater allocative concern than their best-shot counterparts.

CONCLUDING REMARKS

This chapter began with a retrospective view of foreign assistance. No matter the current thinking about foreign aid, rich countries had to overcome free-riding incentives that encouraged these countries to let others support poor countries. Rich countries came to realize that aid could provide donor-specific benefits along with the global public good of curtailing poverty. Unfortunately, these donor-specific benefits grew with conditions being placed on foreign assistance, which did not typically serve the recipients' interest. More recently, donors realized that their welfare was integrally tied to that of recipient developing countries. Globalization served to unite donor and recipient countries' interests.

Also, a new set of donors—multistakeholder organizations, public-private partnerships, networks, NGOs, and charitable foundations—bolstered multilateral assistance. To ameliorate abject poverty in the developing world, donors began focusing on five sectors: health, governance, security, knowledge, and environment. The key sector is health; hence, the last half of the chapter analyzed global health concerns and their collective action issues. The share of public good funds devoted to supplying health public goods continues to grow because wealthy countries are becoming increasingly aware of the risks that inadequate healthcare in one country means for them. Given the prevalence of weakest-link and best-shot health public goods in developing countries, capacity is a key concern that can be fostered by the many new types of donors. The spatial and temporal mix of benefit spillovers makes these global health public goods particularly interesting to study.

CHAPTER 7

International Trade

Between 1929 and 1932, the world suffered not only a devastating depression, but also a huge decrease in international trade, which fell from almost $3 billion to $1.1 billion a month in that four-year period (Kindleberger, 1974). Countries stopped trading with one another as crisis conditions mounted, and as each country tried to manage the crisis in isolation, the international economic order collapsed. In contrast, although the 2008 global financial crisis was by some counts the worst since the Great Depression, trade did not suffer such a precipitous decline. According to statistics from the World Trade Organization (WTO), merchandise trade fell by less than 25% in 2009, increased in 2010, and exceeded previous levels by 2011. The recent rebound in international trade is not just fortuitous, but results at least in part from successful transnational cooperation on trade. Most countries have now formalized their commitment to keep their markets open to imports, and these commitments have been made credible and long-lasting via a strong intergovernmental organization, the WTO, as well as by a host of other formal agreements.

Given the success of trade cooperation over the last seven decades, it may seem strange to include enhanced trade in a list of needs for transnational cooperation. At the same time, trade politics remain contentious at both the level of domestic politics and that of international relations. Domestic groups often organize to demand protection from the volatile global economy or from unfair competition with foreign producers. WTO meetings often attract throngs of protestors, who decry its influence into their governments' sovereignty. Transnational trade cooperation is consistently challenged, and many argue that states have delegated too much authority to the WTO.

In this chapter, we argue that post–World War II trade cooperation has indeed been quite successful, but that additional trade cooperation offers considerable economic gains, many of which would disproportionately help some of the world's poor countries. As with other transnational problems, potential gains from cooperation are not enough by themselves to guarantee success. All current indications suggest that the considerable gains from continued progress in reducing trade barriers will not be realized as countries haggle over the distribution of these gains. Rather than reducing trade barriers via the multilateral WTO, countries turn to smaller and easier forms of cooperation with regional trade partners and allies. We view this as a negative development for transnational cooperation and therefore treat the revival of multilateral trade liberalization as a key challenge for transnational cooperation.

THE CASE FOR FREE TRADE

Recent surveys show that seven of eight economists agree that countries should reduce barriers to trade, and this idea—known as free trade—has influenced policy makers for two centuries (see, for example, Whaples, 2006). Since its initial articulation by David Ricardo, the theory of comparative advantage has shown that all countries can gain from trade by exporting goods that they can produce more efficiently than other products. The key dynamic supporting this free trade logic is specialization: private goods are produced efficiently when individuals or countries specialize in activities in which they are more skilled. At the country level, this specialization results in trade where consumers in both countries are better off.

This is a country-level argument: free trade creates the most wealth for the country *as a whole*, even though *individuals* in some industries will gain more than others. In other words, even though some industries do worse in the move to free trade, the economy as a whole will gain. Because free trade policies generate more economic gains than losses, societies can always choose to compensate those who did worse under free trade, and still have more wealth on the whole.

A simple example demonstrates the gains from trade. Suppose the United States and Brazil only made two goods, sugar and computers, in a barter economy. A farmer in Brazil makes 40 pounds of sugar a week, and a Brazilian worker makes 2 computers a week. In the United States, a farmer makes 30 pounds of sugar per week, while an equivalent worker makes 10 computers per week (see Figure 7.1). Comparing productivity across the two economies, we see that Brazilian sugar workers are more efficient than their American counterparts, perhaps due to climate or to farming methods, while American computer makers are more efficient than their Brazilian counterparts. Without trade, Brazil's sugar farmer must pay 20 pounds of sugar for a computer, while the American sugar farmer only has to pay 3 pounds of sugar. If the two countries allow these industries to export, then Brazilian sugar workers and American computer workers can both get higher prices for their products. Trade should happen at any price, here defined as the cost of

	Sugar	Computers	Cost of 1 Computer
Brazil	40 pounds	2 computers	20 pounds of sugar
United States	30 pounds	10 computers	3 pounds of sugar

Figure 7.1
Absolute advantage

one good in terms of the other, between the two countries' costs; that is, between 3 and 20 pounds of sugar for each computer.

Of course, with trade, the Brazilian computer makers will suffer a decline in the price of their product, since they will no longer be able to sell as many computers for 20 pounds of sugar. In the United States, sugar producers will suffer as they get fewer computers for the same amount of sugar, but U.S. computer makers will gain as they get more sugar for each computer. So trade creates economic winners and losers, and yet as a whole both countries will do better, since specialization allocates resources—in terms of worker productivity—more efficiently.

To see this, imagine that Brazil's entire workforce consists of 100 laborers, equally divided between the two industries. Brazil's total production consists of 100 computers and 2,000 pounds of sugar. With trade, some workers move from computer manufacturing to sugar farms—suppose 20 workers switch. Brazil's output of sugar increases to 2,800 pounds, while computer production shrinks to 60. But Brazilian sugar farmers can now buy a much larger number of computers with the additional sugar production: if three-quarters of that additional 800 pounds goes toward purchasing American computers at 10 pounds per computer, Brazil can import 60 American computers. The country as a whole can consume more sugar (200 pounds) and more computers (60 in trade plus 60 in domestic production = 120). This demonstrates the principle of absolute advantage: countries can benefit from trade by specializing in goods they produce more efficiently than other countries.

The logic of comparative advantage, however, goes well beyond this case. Even countries that are at an absolute disadvantage in terms of their productivity in both industries can benefit from trade. Figure 7.2 displays a second example. Computer workers in each country have the same output as in the first example (1 worker makes 2 computers in Brazil and 10 computers in the United States). Brazilian cotton farmers produce 40 pounds of cotton per week, while their American counterpart produces 50 pounds of cotton per

	Cotton	Computers	Cost of 1 Computer
Brazil	40 pounds	2 computers	20 pounds of cotton
United States	50 pounds	10 computers	5 pounds of cotton

Figure 7.2
Comparative advantage

week. Workers in the United States have higher productivity in both products so that Brazilian workers seem to be at a disadvantage in both markets. Even so, Brazilians can still benefit from trade!

Figure 7.2 displays the cost of a computer in each country when no trade occurs. Brazil's cotton worker can buy a computer for 20 pounds of cotton, while an American cotton worker can buy a computer for 5 pounds of cotton. This relative price difference indicates that the two countries can still gain from specialization due to the opportunity costs of labor. Brazilian workers can make 40 pounds of cotton or 2 computers in a week, so they are giving up only 1 computer for each 20 pounds of cotton. In the United States, a worker would sacrifice 1 computer to produce only 5 pounds of cotton, so American workers are sacrificing more computers than Brazilian workers to produce the same amount of cotton. As a result, shifting resources (that is, labor) in each country into the industry with the lower opportunity cost results in greater overall productivity, and gains from trade again emerge.

Assume each country has 100 workers, evenly distributed across the two industries. Prior to trade, Brazil would produce 2,000 pounds of cotton and 100 computers. If 25 Brazilian computer workers switch to cotton farming, Brazil will produce $(50 + 25) \times 40 = 3,000$ pounds of cotton, but only 50 computers. Trade should again occur at a price between the two countries' internal exchange rates (how much each good costs in terms of the other). We can assume this external (trade) exchange rate to be 10 pounds of cotton per computer. Brazil could trade all of their increased cotton production (1,000 pounds) for 100 computers, which combined with domestic production (50 computers) would increase their computer consumption to 150.[1] They could also retain some of the increased cotton production for fewer computers. Despite lower overall productivity, Brazil can still benefit from trade, simply because of the relative productivity differences across the two industries in each country.

1. The reverse also holds true: the United States can also consume more of both goods after trade.

Although our two-country case is a simple one, the logic of comparative advantage has been extended to more complex models, including multiple countries, multiple goods, and more than just labor as an input to production. Free trade is beneficial in all such extensions.[2] Despite that fact, trade barriers continue to exist in every country. Free trade may be optimal, but it is rarely observed.

The world has clearly experienced a general trend toward freer trade since World War II, a notable success after the disintegration of the global economy in the first part of the twentieth century. Collective action to reduce the most obvious trade barriers has been quite successful, but even as those trade barriers have been eliminated, others have arisen. Historically, tariffs—taxes on imports—have been the most common trade barriers, but more recently trade barriers have taken more complex forms. For example, countries can negotiate voluntary export restraints, in which the exporting country agrees to limit trade. Barriers may take more subtle forms, such as the European Union's (EU's) hesitation to allow imports of genetically modified foods. Any policy that makes an import more expensive than it would otherwise be is a trade barrier, and this is where international trade politics gets more complicated. WTO-led efforts to reduce those trade barriers have led to what some critics see as overreaching, or as a lack of democratic process. For these and other reasons to be examined, the WTO's efficacy as the primary focus for global trade rules comes into question.

Eliminating trade barriers poses a significant collective action problem and has great potential for not only growing the world economy, but also for disproportionately benefiting poorer countries. This follows because much of the move to free trade—liberalization—has disproportionately affected manufactured goods, while agricultural imports continue to face high trade barriers. Exports from poor countries are typically concentrated in agriculture and raw materials. Unfortunately, these poor countries do not have the same clout as rich countries at the negotiation table. The world's trading rules are therefore biased against the very goods that many developing countries can produce at competitive prices, and this is where some of the remaining gains from trade can be found.

COLLECTIVE ACTION AND TRADE

Despite free trade's ability to generate higher overall standards of living, countries are often tempted to enact protectionist barriers, which reduce imports and increase the price of foreign goods and services. Even countries that have mutually agreed to reduce trade protection may be tempted to raise

2. Some countries with enough market power can benefit from nonzero tariffs, but even under such circumstances, the world as a whole still generates the most wealth with zero trade barriers.

trade barriers because they can enhance revenue to domestic producers at the expense of foreign producers (Bagwell and Staiger, 2002). In other words, protectionist trade policies generate costs that affect other countries, in particular exporters and foreign consumers.[3]

The dynamics of trade cooperation become even more tenuous when we add domestic political concerns to the analysis. Consumers as a whole are potentially one of the biggest beneficiaries of free trade, but, given the sheer size of the group, they face enormous collective action hurdles to organizing. In contrast, industry groups, especially those with few firms, face lower thresholds to organizing, and can often organize, lobby, and achieve trade policy outcomes that benefit them at the expense of consumers. For example, because of trade barriers on sugar imports, U.S. consumers have typically paid twice the world price for sugar (Irwin, 2005, p. 64). Despite the fact that Americans are the largest consumers of sweeteners on a per capita basis, the cost per consumer is relatively small, less than $15 per year (Gokcekus, Knowles, and Tower, 2004). Meanwhile the gains for domestic producers can be quite large, and often accrue to the largest producers. These numbers demonstrate the difficulty of collective action for consumers: the additional benefit to any single individual consumer is so small that lobbying for lower sugar prices is simply not worth the effort.

Because policy makers answer only to constituencies in their own country, they can be tempted to use trade policy as a tool to reward favored industries, thereby sacrificing the general welfare for gains that accrue to only those industries. This constant pull toward protectionism means that international trade can be accurately described by a Prisoners' Dilemma, in which countries' policy makers achieve better outcomes by mutually reducing trade barriers, but in any individual round of the game each state is tempted to increase protection to gain at the expense of its counterpart. In this context, defection can mean either failing to reduce trade barriers or enacting new protectionist barriers.

As outlined in Chapter 2, in a single-play Prisoners' Dilemma between two players, both players defect. This outcome is a Nash equilibrium, and neither player will unilaterally change its strategy; however, there is a better outcome for both players—free trade. Cooperation on reducing trade barriers would be beneficial to both parties, but owing to the incentives to cheat on the cooperative outcome, each player is hesitant to trust the other. Cooperation is not sustainable in a one-time interaction because both countries' dominant strategies are to enact trade barriers.

International trade is easy to imagine as a repeated game in which the players expect to play together again. When interactions are likely to occur

3. Protectionist trade policies also affect domestic consumers, who pay higher prices than under free trade, but are unlikely to mobilize against trade protection owing to their large numbers.

again, players should consider how current choices will impact future payoffs (Axelrod, 1984, Chapter 2). If players place significant weight on the future, it becomes rational to cooperate in any given round despite the possibility that a trade partner may cheat. Even repeated games can pose a cooperation problem if both players know the game will end at some future point. Imagine two countries with increasing hostility toward one another—open trade policies should be difficult to maintain given an increasing probability of war between the parties. Alternatively, during economic crisis, a country may be tempted to cheat on its trade agreements to provide a temporary boost to domestic employers. When a country defects from a trade agreement and enacts new trade protection, its trade partner(s) may be tempted to retaliate. Those retaliations can become a self-perpetuating cycle, leading to a "trade war" or a cycle of increasing protection. Conybeare (1987, Chapter 6) documents one long-lasting trade war between France and England that began in 1664 when Colbert raised tariffs on English textiles; it was not resolved until the Cobden-Chevalier Treaty of 1860.

Rebuilding trust after trade wars can be difficult and is compounded by the lack of a centralized enforcer in international politics. Such trade wars are uncommon, because as long as both parties value the long-term benefits from cooperation, the Prisoners' Dilemma can be solved, and free trade, or at least greater moves toward trade openness, can be sustained. Both the late nineteenth century (1870–1914) and the second half of the twentieth century (1945–present) experienced dramatic expansions of international trade. Despite these successes, trade cooperation did not happen easily. After World War II, international organizations played a key role in helping to overcome the difficulties of unilateral trade liberalization. International institutions had to be designed with adequate incentives to convince the world's largest economies to participate. These selective incentives acted as joint products to make participation a dominant strategy (see Chapter 3).

THE INTERNATIONAL TRADE ORGANIZATION

Toward the end of World War II, the United States and its allies began to plan a collection of international institutions that would serve as the basis for postwar economic cooperation and recovery. As noted in Chapter 5, the 1944 Bretton Woods Conference laid the groundwork for three potential intergovernmental organizations: the International Bank for Reconstruction and Development (IBRD), which is better known now as the World Bank; the International Monetary Fund (IMF); and the International Trade Organization (ITO). Both the IBRD and the IMF reflected the geopolitics of their creation: the United States was given a substantial share of the decision-making power in a weighted-voting scheme. In the Havana Charter of 1947, however, the

ITO was ultimately proposed with a one-country, one-vote scheme. In other words, the world's undisputed economic leader at the time had "far less direct control over the ITO" than it did over the other two Bretton Woods institutions (Barton et al., 2006, p. 37).

The ITO also had an expansive mandate, some of which extended its influence into member-state policies. To promote trade, the ITO was to monitor its members' trade policies and to enforce trade rules through a binding third-party dispute settlement process. In addition, it included many other components in its charter, such as rules on employment, government intervention in industry, and foreign investment. Ultimately, several large business associations in the United States, such as the National Foreign Trade Council, did not stand behind the negotiated outcome and were worried about how the treaty addressed foreign investment (Diebold, 1994). By December 1950, it became clear to President Truman that the ITO did not have the necessary domestic support, and that the Senate would never approve the organization as designed in the Havana Charter. With no support from the world's dominant power, the Havana Charter never came into effect, and the postwar recovery of international trade was initially hampered without a strong institutional foundation.

Instead, the United States shifted its weight behind another international trade institution, the General Agreement on Tariffs and Trade (GATT), in which the United States could exercise greater control. GATT had the added benefit of not requiring a congressional vote, since it could be joined by executive agreement (Barton et al., 2006, p. 38). Despite a weak institutional design, GATT served as the basis for the postwar revival of international trade.

FROM GATT TO THE WTO

Around the time of ITO negotiations, the United States began GATT as a separate, narrower, and more immediate track for trade liberalization among a small set of its allies. GATT effectively implemented elements of bilateral trade treaties that the United States had signed in the decade prior to World War II, including reciprocal tariff reductions and unconditional most favored nation (MFN) clauses (Barton et al., 2006, p. 34; Irwin, 2005). The reciprocity standard required equivalent sets of reductions in tariffs by trade partners, which made trade liberalization more palatable on political grounds because every tariff reduction was tied to opening up a foreign market. Similar to the arms race model in Figure 2.8, GATT negotiations allowed countries to change the game they were playing. Rather than liberalizing trade unilaterally, which mobilizes import-competing industries against policy change, countries used reciprocity to lower trade barriers in foreign markets. This strategy pleased export industries, which were then likely to lobby in favor of liberalizing changes in trade policy. GATT's reciprocity standard in trade negotiations therefore overcame the domestic political hurdle that made trade liberalization a Prisoners' Dilemma. In so doing, reciprocity turned the international interaction into an assurance game, where leadership could achieve the desired outcome of liberalization.

MFN also played a key role, because it expanded tariff reductions to every other partner that had a treaty with such a clause. MFN was particularly important because it simultaneously allowed countries to choose "the terms on which they permitted foreign goods into their country," but did not allow them to differentiate among GATT trade partners (Irwin, 2005, pp. 208–209). These two principles became the core mechanisms for tariff reduction in GATT.

In contrast to the 50 countries that negotiated the Havana Charter, the 15 GATT signatories thought they were signing a short-term agreement aimed at immediate reductions in their wartime tariffs. As a result, it was a relatively weak form of international cooperation. Countries that signed GATT were not "members" but instead were "contracting parties" because the agreement did not require formal ratification and membership (Irwin, 2005, p. 209). Insofar as GATT planned to piggyback on the ITO's institutional capacity, GATT provided for little organizational structure, and had a relatively ambiguous status in terms of members' capabilities from an international legal point of view (Jackson, 1998). GATT did nothing to address longstanding commercial relationships that gave former colonies preferential access to rich-country markets. GATT members could choose partial commitment; no two members had to agree to the same set of rules, a system that became known as "GATT a la carte." Additionally, GATT had no centralized enforcement mechanism, so that countries that violated their promises faced no sanction because any one member could block the organization from authorizing retaliation. Despite these flaws, GATT became a remarkably successful framework for international trade cooperation after World War II.

GATT succeeded in reducing trade protection through frequent negotiations for reductions in trade barriers. Starting in 1947, rounds of negotiations resulted in waves of tariff reduction. Table 7.1 displays the list of GATT bargaining rounds, each of which was named for either the city in which it started or for a prominent person. The Geneva Round (1947) reduced tariffs by around 20% and was followed by Annecy (1949), Torquay (1951), Geneva (1956), and Dillon (1960–61) rounds, all of which resulted in small tariff reductions. The Kennedy Round (1964–67) included major tariff reductions (around 35%) and introduced the restricted use of more complicated nontariff barriers. Tokyo Round negotiations (1973–79) followed suit, establishing a series of codes prohibiting some nontariff barriers, which countries had volition to adopt. The Uruguay Round (1986–1993) dramatically expanded the rules of the organization into nontariff arenas, and succeeded in

Table 7.1. GATT bargaining rounds

Table 7.1. GATT bargaining rounds

Name of Round	Year(s)	Agenda	Number of Countries
Geneva	1947	Tariffs	23
Annecy	1949	Tariffs	13
Torquay	1951	Tariffs	38
Geneva	1956	Tariffs	26
Dillon	1960–1961	Tariffs	26
Kennedy	1964–1967	Tariffs and anti-dumping measures	62
Tokyo	1973–1979	Tariffs, nontariff barriers, and framework agreements	102
Uruguay	1986–1994	Tariffs, nontariff barriers, intellectual property, creation of WTO, and many others	123

Source: WTO, 2013

reforming some of the organization's fundamental flaws. The Uruguay Round also created a new institution—the WTO—to oversee the multilateral trade system's rules and to continue the push toward free trade. Each round progressively increased the commitments by members toward trade liberalization, and ultimately these bargaining rounds were crucial to the postwar growth of international trade.

Subramanian and Wei (2007) and Goldstein, Rivers, and Tomz (2007) documented trade increases among GATT members, particularly the countries that were not admitted to the organization with special preferences as former colonies. Countries that entered GATT with more obligations expanded trade with one another faster, including both early members that accepted most GATT provisions and new developing country members that negotiated their way into the organization.

As trade among members expanded, the benefits to nonmembers for joining the GATT increased. Nonmembers could only depend on their own bargaining power to open foreign markets. Increasingly, exporters in nonmember countries were competing on unfavorable terms with exporters from GATT countries. Additionally, during this time, many former colonies were just gaining independence, and many wanted access to GATT markets. GATT membership rose from 26 in 1960 to over 100 in 1973 (see Figure 7.3). By 1987, GATT's Uruguay Round bargaining included 123 members, many of which had to make significant trade policy concessions before gaining membership into the organization.

The Marrakesh Agreement, which closed GATT's Uruguay Round and created the WTO, was an immensely complicated legal document, more than

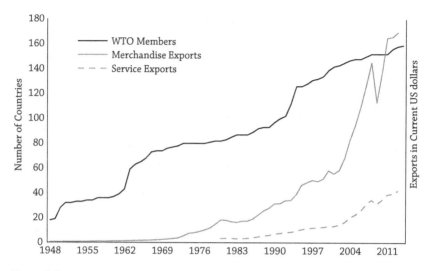

Figure 7.3
GATT/WTO members and the expansion of world trade

26,000 pages in length. Despite this complexity, the agreement corrected many of GATT's weaknesses and the new organization included some—but not all—of the original ITO ideas. The WTO built on GATT's successes, and incorporated many of its legal practices via the "guidance clause." The missing institutional structure was finally provided, and the WTO had a budget, employees, and a headquarters in Geneva. Additionally, WTO members were no longer able to choose which rules they would abide by, and instead had to agree to a "single package" of trade rules.

Perhaps most important, the agreement fixed problems with the dispute settlement procedure (DSP). Previously, any country could effectively veto the final report of the GATT panel of trade experts looking into potential rules violations. The WTO's DSP made panel reports binding, while preventing any one member from blocking those reports. The new agreement also allowed for "compensatory measures"—authorized retaliation against countries that were found to be violating their commitments. This mechanism overcomes the lack of a centralized enforcer, allowing WTO members to enforce the rules on each other and preventing trade wars by capping retaliation. Although it may seem strange to enforce trade liberalization by allowing others to enact protection, smart retaliation can work well, particularly if compensatory measures are enacted in ways that directly affect policy makers' chances of reelection.

For example, in 2002, the Bush administration increased tariffs on imported steel to 30%, a move that advantaged domestic steel producers. The EU quickly challenged the legality of steel tariffs via the WTO DSP; once the EU won the initial dispute ruling, it prepared a list of retaliatory tariffs that it would impose on U.S. imports. These included the American steel industry, whose consumers were already unhappy with the higher price of steel, but also products like Florida oranges, which were chosen due to their political importance for President Bush's reelection chances. Upon losing the appeal, the United States removed steel tariffs rather than subject its exporters to the cost of retaliation.[4]

In addition to these institutional improvements, the Uruguay Round expanded WTO members' commitments to a broader set of trade barriers, including the use of antidumping and countervailing duties as protectionist instruments. Member states also committed to some opening of trade-related investment and of trade in services, and to establish systems for intellectual property rights, such as patents on pharmaceutical drugs. All of these measures were consistently opposed by most developing countries throughout negotiations, and were only included after the United States and EU made a concerted effort to secure their acceptance (Barton et al., 2006, pp. 65–66).

Ultimately, the GATT/WTO system has outgrown its early weaknesses and has greatly promoted trade, but not across the board. Figure 7.3 shows the dramatic expansion of manufacturing trade, and a slower expansion of trade in services. Even within manufacturing, not all goods are fully liberalized. Agricultural goods, clothing, and footwear are all categories in which WTO members do not achieve higher levels of trade with each other due to continued exemptions for trade protection in these areas. Additionally, since the end of the Uruguay Round in 1993 and the creation of the WTO in 1995, the WTO has achieved little additional trade liberalization. Some of the difficulty of moving forward is due to past successes: with 3.5% average tariff on manufactured goods, WTO members have less to gain from additional liberalization than when tariffs were much higher.[5] But the WTO has not stopped trying to reduce tariffs and other forms of trade barriers, and there are still considerable gains from trade liberalization to be had.

THE DOHA ROUND

The WTO has continued GATT's model of multilateral bargaining, but not with the same level of success. The current round of bargaining began in Doha, Qatar, in late 2001, and has been known as the Doha Round. The original agenda for the Doha Round included lowering barriers to trade in services, which would disproportionately benefit more developed economies due to their natural comparative advantage in human capital. The agenda

---

4. For more in-depth treatment of this case, see Mahncke (2004) and Jensen (2007).

5. A 3.5% tariff means that a $100 imported good would cost $103.50 after a tax of $3.50.

also included lowering barriers to agricultural trade, which would disproportionately benefit less developed countries, whose economies are in many cases still primarily agriculture-based. While the potential bargain between rich and poor countries seems straightforward, the agenda also included intellectual property rules, environmental effects of trade, investment rules, competition policy, and many more issues, complicating the bargaining process by creating numerous cross-cutting cleavages of WTO member states.

Further complicating the bargaining was the WTO's portrayal of the round as a "development" round that would disproportionately benefit its poorest members. As a result, rich countries have been expected to surrender more in bargaining than poor countries, a dynamic that has not characterized previous rounds of bargaining. Many of the agenda items disproportionately impact developing countries and can work at odds to foreign aid. For example, the EU's policies that rebate taxes to farmers for their fuel costs provided $24 per hectare on average from 2009–2011, for a total of $4.5 billion (Elliott, 2013). This figure is three times what the EU provided in foreign aid targeted toward agriculture in 2013. It ultimately has the same effect as a subsidy on agricultural goods, which makes European farmers more competitive with their developing world counterparts. At the very least, it prevents some agricultural imports and can also subsidize exports. Such export subsidies are illegal for all nonagricultural goods in the WTO, but they remain in many countries' agricultural policies. At the 2003 Cancun meeting of the Doha Round, developing countries formed a bloc insisting that rich countries cut agricultural subsidies and trade barriers. Prior to the 2005 Hong Kong meeting, the United States proposed steep reductions in those policies, but other countries were not amenable to that proposal (and it is not clear that the U.S. proposal could have gained congressional approval). Since then, little progress has been made in Doha Round negotiations, as deadline after deadline passed for a final agreement.

By 2011, even prominent WTO advocates began to admit publicly that negotiations were unlikely to progress: Susan Schwab (2011), former U.S. Trade Representative, suggested that "it is time to give up on trying to 'save' Doha" and Pascal Lamy, the Secretary-General of the WTO, argued that negotiations had surfaced a "clear political gap" that was "not bridgeable" (*The Economist*, 2011a). Continued progress on multilateral trade liberalization is therefore in serious doubt, despite clear gains for all parties.

Why has international cooperation come to a standstill? Clearly one factor in the failed negotiations is the sheer complexity of simultaneous interactions of more than 155 WTO members across a large number of agenda items. Related to this increased complexity is the decline of the United States and EU relative to emerging powers like China, Brazil, India, and South Africa. Emerging markets experienced dramatic growth in exports during the initial years of the Doha Round, and the need for more access to rich country markets was not pressing. When negotiations were simplified by allowing these countries to represent the developing world, they often negotiated primarily with an eye to their own benefits rather than to their poorer neighbors. Indeed, fast-growing emerging markets will probably have more bargaining power at future negotiations, so their incentives are to wait for a better future outcome than to sign a deal now. While this is not surprising from a strategic perspective, the alternative, which involves simultaneous bargaining by all members, is too unwieldy.

One consequence of Doha Round failed negotiations is the reduced pace of trade liberalization; even though trade continues to expand, existing trade barriers remain. The WTO continues to influence its members' trade policies but only through the DSP, which may encourage some reduced trade barriers as legal proceedings clarify obligations and rule violations. In 2014, WTO members agreed to conclude the Doha Round with a dramatically reduced scope and few of the original agenda items. Such a stripped-down agreement may be portrayed as a success, but it will be a small one and will not be a dramatic advance for multilateral trade cooperation. As a consequence of the long stalemate in multilateral negotiations, countries are turning instead to bilateral and regional trade agreements (RTAs). As the next section will demonstrate, this type of trade cooperation is easier but not as uniformly positive as multilateralism.

REGIONAL TRADE COOPERATION

In the last quarter-century, countries have increasingly attempted trade cooperation on a bilateral or plurilateral basis. Since 2000, countries have signed an average of more than ten new RTAs per year, and the total number of such agreements is now well over 500. And this total does not include other economic agreements, such as nearly 3,000 bilateral investment treaties (BITs), which serve primarily to provide special protection to foreign investors. Most trade and investment treaties are not in fact regional, but are instead comprised of two or three countries that are closely connected either geographically or otherwise.

What should we make of these regional attempts at trade cooperation? Are they equivalent to the multilateral liberalization happening in the WTO? Are they good for free trade? The classic economic answer to the last question is that it depends; bilateral or plurilateral agreements can have contradictory effects (Viner, 1950). They reduce trade barriers among members, thereby increasing trade, but they also discriminate against nonmembers, eroding trading relationships that existed previously. Each trade agreement should therefore be evaluated separately for its unique impact on world trade. In its charter, the WTO has the power to perform this task, and to permit only

RTAs that "substantially" increase trade among their members, but it has generally hesitated to pass judgment on such deals.

As a result, countries have formed both trade-creating and trade-diverting trade agreements as it suits them.[6] Certainly, if RTAs are signed with primarily economic motivations, then they should be trade creating, and much research supports this hypothesis. But such agreements often have other motivations, such as rewarding alliance partners, and so it is quite possible that RTA partners are not always chosen with economic gains as the primary goal. Whatever the motivation, most RTAs fail to consider their impact on countries that are not party to the agreement, thereby imposing trade externalities on other countries. In addition, RTAs have to define which products and services get preferential treatment with "rules of origin." These rules often become new targets for industry groups that are interested in minimizing competition. As a result, there are considerable reasons to be skeptical of the trend toward regionalism in trade liberalization.

At the same time, regional trade cooperation should be expected: our collective action framework suggests several reasons that cooperation on a regional level may be easier than on a global level. First, because regional trade bargaining happens among a small number of states, this should facilitate collective action. Second, states in close proximity should already know each other well and may put more weight on their future relationship, thereby expanding their desire to enhance trade between them. Third, many regional groupings include states that share cultural and/or linguistic ties, as in Latin America, and such homogeneity often promotes collective action.

Not all features of regional bargaining improve the chances of success (see Chapter 4). A regional grouping of relatively similar-sized states will lack an obvious leader to shoulder the costs of collective action. In this way, homogeneity can work positively on one dimension but negatively on another. Some countries that are geographically proximate are also long-time rivals, or have territorial disputes that make trade cooperation less likely. And perhaps the biggest difference from cooperation at the global level, particularly in the twenty-first century, is that regions rarely have the kinds of institutional capacity (that is, the WTO secretariat or World Bank) that we observe at the global level. Despite these barriers, many country groupings have succeeded in negotiating trade agreements that lead to more trade and greater overall economic integration for their members. And in a few cases, trade cooperation has established a foundation for expanded cooperation in other areas as well. An optimistic assessment of RTAs is that they are creating the

---

6. A trade-creating agreement is one that, on balance, generates new trade volumes, whereas a trade-diverting agreement is one that redirects existing trade to new partners. The diversion comes from changes in trade barriers.

conditions for stronger regional institutions, which in turn may enhance the long-term possibilities of regional cooperation.

Given the sheer diversity of regional trade cooperation, it is worthwhile to provide a short overview of its evolution across major geographic areas. Our primary purpose is to investigate whether trade agreements have led to stronger regional institutions, or whether they have remained rather informal and/or restricted to the domain of trade cooperation.

European Union

The EU is easily the farthest-reaching example of trade integration, which has gone well beyond trade liberalization to harmonize the laws of its members and even to create supranational institutions like the European Court of Justice. European cooperation began on a much smaller scale, with the creation in 1952 of the European Coal and Steel Community (ECSC), with its six member states (France, Italy, West Germany, Belgium, the Netherlands, and Luxembourg). This organization was intended as a way to tie together the economies—especially the capacity for military production—of countries that had fought past wars, particularly France and Germany. Economic cooperation continued, with the formation of the European Economic Community (EEC) via the Treaty of Rome in 1957. Importantly, other European countries, not included in the initial EEC, felt threatened by its formation, and joined together in an alternative RTA, the European Free Trade Agreement.

The EEC continued to evolve, and became the EU in 1992. EU members now include 28 countries, including many Eastern European countries like Bulgaria and Romania.[7] This expansion has happened even as economic integration expanded well beyond trade; the Schengen agreement, for example, allows EU passport holders to move to other EU countries in search of work. Although not all EU members chose to participate in the Euro currency zone (notable exceptions include the United Kingdom), most EU countries gave up their domestic currencies and central banks, and handed monetary authority to the European Central Bank. Citizens in each country elect representatives to the European Parliament, and laws are executed in both national governments and the Council of Ministers. The resulting "United States of Europe" is a federated entity that often negotiates as a single block and coordinates policy choices across a variety of areas. Although the EU is still controversial for many Europeans, it has demonstrated to the world how RTAs

7. As of November 2014, EU members include Austria, Belgium, Bulgaria, Croatia (the newest), Cyprus, Czech Republic, Denmark, Estonia, Finland, France, Germany, Greece, Hungary, Ireland, Italy, Latvia, Lithuania, Luxembourg, Malta, the Netherlands, Poland, Portugal, Romania, Slovakia, Slovenia, Spain, Sweden, and the United Kingdom.

and other forms of economic integration can generate economic gains for their members. These economic gains have in turned spurred cooperation among EU countries on other issues, and have effectively generated a new layer of governance above the member states.

The EU's early success can be attributed to the homogeneity of its members: all members were capitalist democracies united in the NATO alliance and sheltered by the United States during the Cold War (see Chapter 5). Expansion has increased cultural and linguistic heterogeneity among members, with considerable consequences that include the recent Euro crisis resulting from revelations about Greek government debt and electoral backlashes against regional integration. Further integration will likely happen at a slower pace given the larger number of countries involved and their greater diversity. Much revolves around the continued economic success of Germany, which is now clearly shouldering much of the burden of integration.

The Americas

Elsewhere regional trade cooperation has not led to the kind of institutional development seen in Europe. The North American Free Trade Agreement (NAFTA) originated as a United States–Canada deal and eventually included Mexico after President Carlos Salinas de Gortari expressed interest in joining. NAFTA was the first agreement between developed states and a developing country that overcame considerable political hurdles. It was intensely debated in the 1992 U.S. elections, which resulted in the Clinton administration's reopening of the finished agreement to incorporate labor and environmental standards. In addition to those side agreements, the treaty went beyond trade issues to include rules on foreign investment, but the treaty has not resulted in extensive noneconomic cooperation. The three NAFTA members are therefore still much less integrated than their European peers.

Many NAFTA components were extended by the United States to six Central American countries in the 2005 Central American Free Trade Agreement (CAFTA). Rather than reducing existing trade barriers, CAFTA largely made permanent existing trade preferences for Central American exporters: over 80% of Central American exports were duty free prior to the RTA, but some of those preferences were due to expire in 2008. The United States gained other concessions in the agreement, including stronger intellectual property protection and fewer barriers to U.S. service industries. Notably, despite the obvious comparative advantage of several CAFTA countries in sugar production, U.S. trade barriers for sugar imports remained in place (Lynch, 2010, p. 106). CAFTA, like NAFTA, has resulted in little additional institutionalization due to the large differences in economic development between the richer and poorer signatories.

South America's RTAs involve less-striking differences across members, who are similar not only in economic development but also in cultural and historical background. The Andean Pact, in particular, has successfully unified its members' trade policies in a common external tariff. Members of the Andean Pact, which formed in 1969, include Bolivia, Colombia, Ecuador, and Peru. The organization also helped to resolve a long-standing territorial dispute between Ecuador and Peru, and attracted other members, including Chile and Venezuela. However, the organization has now reverted to its original membership and does not regularly harmonize nontrade policies.

One of the problems has been rivalry among trade agreements in South America. The other major RTA, MERCOSUR, formed in 1991 with Argentina, Brazil, Paraguay, and Uruguay as members. Trade barriers have fallen among members, and MERCOSUR has institutionalized regular meetings of Ministers of Foreign Affairs and Finance in the Council for the Common Market (Lynch, 2010, p. 113). Additionally, the organization created an executive branch and a judicial institution, the Permanent Review Court. However, the expansion of MERCOSUR to Venezuela in 2006 has potentially jeopardized its members' ability to agree on future advances in integration due to Venezuela's skepticism toward free markets and greater government involvement in the economy.

Asia

Asian trade agreements are fewer in number and less institutionalized than those in other regions. A key reason for the slower pace of RTAs is the continuing geopolitical rivalries, primarily between Japan and China, but also between South Korea and Japan, India and Pakistan, and the two Koreas. In these cases, linguistic and cultural similarities have not advantaged cooperation, while geographic distance and continuing imbalances in economic development have complicated efforts at trade cooperation.

Of the existing RTAs, the Association of Southeast Asian Nations (ASEAN) is the most institutionalized and has gone farthest toward regional trade liberalization. Five Southeast Asian countries (Indonesia, Malaysia, the Philippines, Singapore, and Thailand) created the organization in 1967 for security purposes. Trade talks followed about a decade later, leading to a free trade agreement that entered into force in 2002 for the original members. The organization has expanded to 10 members, and now includes Brunei, Vietnam, Myanmar, Laos, and Cambodia. ASEAN countries plan to liberalize not just trade in goods but also trade in services and investment (Lynch, 2010, p. 139). Although there are economic disparities across the 10 countries, their combined economic weight is substantial enough to garner the attention of the region's biggest powers. For example, China has signed agreements with ASEAN for liberalizing trade in both goods and services, and has proposed a larger agreement with ASEAN and other regional economic powers, known as the Regional Comprehensive Economic Partnership (RCEP).

An alternative to RCEP is now taking shape via the United States' participation in the Trans-Pacific Partnership (TPP), which originally involved only Brunei, Chile, New Zealand, and Singapore. The TPP has emerged as a key part of the Obama administration's "pivot to Asia" and, importantly, only reinforces the geopolitical barriers to intraregional trade by excluding China. Current trends suggest multiple, overlapping trade blocs driven by geopolitical concerns rather than a unified approach to regional trade.

Africa

African states are responsible for the creation of many trade agreements and customs unions, including the Arab Maghreb Union, the Common Market for Eastern and Southern Africa (COMESA), the Economic Community of West African States (ECOWAS), and the Southern African Development Community (SADC). Few of these efforts have been successful in substantially expanding trade among members. In 2002, more than 50 countries joined together to create the African Union (AU). The AU borrows institutional design from both the UN, with a Peace and Security Council, and the EU, with the institution's component parts located throughout the continent. The revamped organization was designed to overcome limitations of its predecessor, the Organization of African Unity (OAU), which primarily opposed colonialism and apartheid but which fostered little economic cooperation. Although the AU has had several successes in preventing nondemocratic transitions of power, the AU's plan for economic integration still revolves around the African Economic Community, which dates back to 1980, and which in turn builds on subregional entities like SADC and COMESA.

The AU's ultimate economic goal, like the EU, is monetary union, but unlike the EU, countries within the organization have low, but increasing, levels of trade. Rather than promote transcontinental integration, the AU has primarily leaned on previous regional trade integration groupings, and thanks to overlapping memberships, it is not clear that integration is happening any faster under the AU than it was previously. There are at least 14 different trade blocs involving some African countries, many of which belong to two or three RTAs (*The Economist*, 2011b). For example, two COMESA members, Namibia and Swaziland, also have membership in the Southern African Customs Union, and the COMESA secretariat is actually located in Lusaka, Zambia, which is a SADC country (Lynch, 2010, pp. 66–67). Some

African countries, such as Tanzania, are still quite dependent on the government revenue they derive from tariffs, which makes trade liberalization much harder.

ECOWAS may be the biggest regional success so far, with clear indications of institutional strengths that reach beyond trade cooperation. ECOWAS's 15 West African states have been at least partially successful in establishing a common external tariff and reducing barriers to trade among members. ECOWAS was also the first RTA to broaden its mandate to peacekeeping with the creation of its cease-fire monitoring group (known as ECOMOG), whose soldiers interceded in civil conflicts in Liberia, Guinea-Bissau, Sierra Leone, and Cote d'Ivoire (Lynch, 2010, p. 73). In addition to its peacekeeping activities, the organization has a functioning regional court and a bureaucracy with the authority to issue regional passports.

Despite some regional successes, a continent-wide African Economic Community faces considerable difficulties in promoting trade. Foremost among these difficulties is the sheer size of the continent, especially given its poor transportation infrastructure across almost half the world's landlocked countries. In addition, trade integration is made more difficult by the diversity among African countries—hundreds of languages, many territorial and ethnic conflicts, and often poor, though improving, political and economic institutions. Although Africa has a long history of RTAs, the treaties have rarely fulfilled their signatories' stated goals of economic integration.

RTA summary

Regional trade cooperation can clearly achieve economic gains for partner countries: if this is the primary motivation, then RTAs should be priorities for big economies that have much to gain from increased levels of trade. However, it should be clear from this overview that RTAs often appear for noneconomic reasons, including broader foreign policy objectives. As such, many of the countries that might benefit most from RTAs are not currently partners in them. The United States has treaties with Bahrain, Israel, and Oman, all of which are small economies that offer few gains to the American economy. The United States does not have an RTA with China, India, or Brazil, economies that would greatly enhance American exports. Arguments that RTAs are simply trade liberalization in another form, or that they will ultimately produce the same result as liberalization via the WTO (for example, Baldwin, 1993) seem far-fetched given these geopolitical realities. From the origin of RTAs, they have circumvented multilateral efforts—the formation of the EEC clearly violated GATT requirements for free trade areas, because West Germany's average tariff on goods from countries outside the community nearly doubled as a consequence of its membership.

U.S.-dominated GATT allowed the EEC to form because it supported other Cold War goals, such as rebuilding Western European countries as capitalist democracies.

From the EEC forward, each new RTA has provoked concerns among non-members about negative repercussions for previously established trading relationships. In response, excluded countries often form another RTA in order to either keep access to the markets in question or to promote alternative opportunities for their exporters. This "domino theory" of RTAs explains the timing of many efforts at regional trade cooperation, including the formation of the EFTA (in response to the EEC), the first U.S. RTA (with Israel, which had just signed a similar deal with the EEC), and enhanced trade liberalization in ASEAN as a response to alternative regional agreements. This primarily defensive proliferation of trade agreements again suggests that trade creation is often a second-order objective and many potential gains from trade cooperation therefore remain unrealized.

RTAs can also impact multilateral negotiations negatively. With the creation of NAFTA (1993) and the EU (1992), the United States and Europe demonstrated that they had solid economic opportunities outside GATT, and they effectively increased their bargaining power in the Uruguay Round (Stone, 2011). As a result, the final agreement not only created the WTO but also included many provisions that disproportionately helped American and European exporters, including the General Agreement on Trade in Services (GATS) and Trade-Related Intellectual Property Rights (TRIPS). If regional trade cooperation aims primarily to strengthen the hand of powerful countries at the WTO, then it is clearly working at odds with multilateral trade liberalization.

CONCLUSION

Trade cooperation provides a model for many other issues that offer significant gains to members if political hurdles can be overcome. International institutions embed trade policy in longer-term relationships in which benefits dominate costs. Through multilateral negotiations, more advanced economies have achieved exceptionally low tariffs on the goods they tend to export, and have increasingly made trade in services easier as well. In the EU, trade cooperation has stimulated cooperation in other issues. Both GATT and the EU started with a small number of similar states, which made initial bargains easier. In turn, each organization has gained more members as it demonstrated the gains to cooperation.

However, the world is still far from free trade, and future liberalization is likely to benefit poorer countries disproportionately due to the fact that a disproportionate number of remaining barriers prevent trade in agricultural products. As a result, developing countries are faced with an unattractive bargain: they must offer concessions in more intrusive policy areas if they want to gain access to rich country markets in agriculture. As a bloc, the developing world has been unwilling to accept such a trade-off, as WTO negotiations in Cancun in 2003 demonstrated. In many cases, the United States and EU have succeeded in achieving these same policy concessions from developing countries via bilateral and regional arrangements. Past trade cooperation has been enormously successful, but unfortunately, its future looks more difficult.

CHAPTER 8

Global Finance

The subprime housing market crisis that began in 2007 affected many countries, perhaps none more so than Iceland. Despite its small size—just over 300,000 people—the country's banks had rapidly integrated into the international financial system after becoming private in the 1980s. They loaned money aggressively, particularly to Icelandic companies seeking to expand into foreign markets, and by the end of 2005, loans exceeded deposits by more than three to one (Carey, 2009). As a result, one bank in particular, Landsbanki, began an aggressive Internet-based campaign (Icesave) to attract British and Dutch depositors. Together with Kaupthing and Glitnir, the three banks comprised 85% of Iceland's financial sector, and all three became heavily dependent on short-term borrowing from other markets to maintain their high ratios of borrowing in relation to their assets (known as leverage).

When Lehman Brothers collapsed in September 2008, the Icelandic banks became part of a vast global credit retraction, and were no longer able to borrow on the short-term markets that they had come to depend on. Glitnir collapsed first, followed by the nationalizations of Landsbanki and Kaupthing, all within 10 days of one another. Government intervention in the banks cost the country approximately 20% to 25% of its entire gross national product, and despite that, British depositors were left with over £1 billion of uncompensated losses, since their deposits were not guaranteed by the Icelandic government. In November 2008, Iceland accepted a loan from the International Monetary Fund (IMF), and thereby became its first Western European customer in 32 years.

The initial success and then downfall of Iceland's banks illustrate the enormous power of global financial markets, which have grown dramatically over the last 50 years, and which can overwhelm even large economies when crisis strikes. The history of financial booms and busts offers many lessons, and domestic regulators have tried to mitigate the worst consequences, but as cross-border lending and borrowing have expanded, banks seized new opportunities and grew internationally. As a consequence, there was a growing need for countries to harmonize their rules and contain crises from spreading globally.

FINANCIAL STABILITY AS A PUBLIC GOOD

When transparent and competitive transactions channel savings to their most-valued uses, a well-functioning financial market can bring enormous benefits to its participants. At the simplest level, a bank (or other financial institution) aggregates the savings of its depositors, lends that money to borrowers, and makes a profit for its owners or shareholders by serving as the intermediary for borrowers and savers. If all participants in the financial transaction have complete information concerning the risks, all receive private benefits from their participation. Unfortunately, information asymmetries often pose problems. Lenders may have good information about their borrowers, but once a loan has been given, the incentives of the borrower to pay it back may change. Alternatively, borrowers may have private information that makes repayment less likely, meaning that the bank underestimated the risk of loan default in the transaction. Asymmetries do not always work in the borrowers' favor; depositors may believe they are putting their savings into safe hands and be unaware of impending troubles on a bank's balance sheet. With better information about the bank's soundness, depositors might demand a higher interest rate or choose another institution.

Banking usually involves taking deposits with short time horizons but making loans with longer time horizons. This "borrowing short and lending long" orientation leaves banks open to a particular type of coordination problem—a bank run—which occurs when a large number of depositors simultaneously decide to withdraw their savings. Because only some portion of those savings is actually on hand at any given time, the bank can quickly reach its liquidity limit, which is the money available to meet the bank's liabilities. Successful financial transactions therefore rely on an element of trust between the parties to a transaction and intrinsically involve uncertainty and imperfect information (Schinasi, 2006).[1] Trust can fail, even when it should not, if parties to financial transactions decide that their counterparty is no longer trustworthy. When depositors lose faith and withdraw savings unexpectedly, banks may not have enough short-term capital to make loans causing a liquidity crunch. When, however, lenders lose faith, they can stop making loans and cause a credit

1. Over the last few decades, game theory has made significant strides in incorporating uncertainty and has demonstrated its ability to gauge rational behavior in the presence of uncertainty. Unfortunately, the requisite toolkit is more mathematically complex than we felt appropriate for this book. For a good introduction to game theory with uncertainty, see Dixit, Skeath, and Reiley (2009).

crunch. In either instance, problems at one bank can be easily transmitted, causing trust issues or contagion at other financial institutions.

Due to uncertainty about credit risks involved in lending to particular individuals, banks may lend less and may charge different prices for loans than they would with better information. In fact, due to risks of nonpayment, some financial markets may never arise. For example, students had difficulty obtaining loans in the United States until those loans were guaranteed by the federal government (Schinasi, 2006, p. 55). Despite the profit potential for lenders, and the demands of potential borrowers, financial markets require solutions to some of these basic information problems prior to their successful operation. These collective action solutions include an acceptable currency and unit of accounting, enforcement of contracts, orderly procedures for bankruptcy, and the like.

Because bank failures and even short-term financial disruptions have potentially contagious effects, governments now protect financial stability through national public goods like bank regulations, designed to reduce the chances of bank failure, and depositors' insurance, such as that provided by the Federal Deposit Insurance Corporation (FDIC) in the United States. Additionally, national governments offer supervision, or the monitoring of banks for compliance with these regulations, coupled with enforcement of the rules against banks that fail to comply. These goods are primarily aimed at correcting market failures that arise due to uncertainty. In the United States, much of this regulatory and supervisory apparatus arose after the Great Depression, with the goal of preventing a collapse of domestic financial institutions like the series of bank runs in 1931 (Broz, 1997).

Despite the clear private good elements of finance, it also has public good properties. Among these, access to finance generates positive externalities by being more flexible than currency as a store of value and by allowing intertemporal exchange (such as student borrowing from their future earnings) (Schinasi, 2006, Chapter 3). Financial systems may also give rise to negative externalities and free riding by agents. Although banks value their own survival and try actively to manage risks, they do not necessarily consider the implications of their own failure for the financial system as a whole. One key safeguard to stave off bank failures revolves around the amount of capital that banks must keep on hand to provide liquidity in times of crisis. Usually expressed as a percentage of overall assets, the *capital-adequacy* ratio is often mandated by national governments to account for potential losses from credit defaults or unexpected deposit withdrawals.[2] While banks should try to ensure their own survival by retaining enough capital to prevent a crisis, doing so decreases their profitability because assets that are held to safeguard financial stability cannot

---

2. The capital-adequacy ratio is defined as the bank's available capital divided by the risk-weighted assets.

be loaned in the same ways as other assets. When banks are left to their own devices, their capital stocks will be less than optimal for reducing the risks of contagion (Singer, 2007, p. 19).[3] Banks generally oppose regulation aimed at establishing a minimum level of capital adequacy. However, when all banks within one country are subject to the same capital-adequacy requirements, they compete on a level playing field. Domestic capital-adequacy requirements thereby shore up a weakest-link problem in which each bank is individually tempted to increase its profitability by keeping less capital on hand, thereby undermining financial stability in the country as a whole.

This system of national bank regulation works reasonably well when finance is largely domestic, but as borrowing and lending become more international, one country's weaker financial regulation of its banks can undermine financial stability in other countries. Finance is no longer confined to national boundaries; it now increasingly flows across borders with potentially transformative effects. Given the stark economic differences across rich and poor countries, it makes great economic sense to channel rich-country savings to poor countries, where the returns on capital investment should be higher. Yet on an international level, there is no multilateral institution that is capable of enforcing international standards or that is designated as an international lender of last resort. The provision of financial stability is still almost completely in the hands of domestic regulators, who struggle to affect the behavior of foreign institutions participating in their domestic financial market. Financial globalization exposes their domestic financial systems to contagion from financial problems that originate elsewhere. The resulting international economic crises can be incredibly costly—the 1982 Debt Crisis started in Mexico, but spread quickly as international banks stopped lending not just to borrowers in Mexico but also in other developing countries. The crisis ultimately affected dozens of Latin American and African countries and trapped many of those countries in debt repayments that exceeded their governments' expenditures on health and education for decades. Likewise, the Asian Financial Crisis started in Thailand, with a crisis over the value of that country's currency, the baht, but it quickly spread to other countries in Southeast Asia and eventually to countries as far away as Russia and Brazil. Given the rapid contagion witnessed in these and other crises, it is not hard to imagine such crises as global public "bads" with negative externalities or to portray financial stability as a global public good. Unfortunately, preventing such crises is an exceedingly difficult task owing to the complexity of international finance and the uncertainties surrounding the origins of financial crises.

Many argue that global financial stability can be treated as a public good (see Kapstein, 1991; Schinasi, 2006; Wyplosz, 1999). While financial markets

---

3. Having liquidity during a crisis is only one reason for banks to reserve a portion of their capital (Wood, 2005, p. 73).

will always exhibit some volatility, Wyplosz (1999) differentiated normal levels, in which changes in information cause changes in asset prices, and excessive volatility, which is easy to identify in theory but difficult in practice. Excessive volatility erodes financial stability and characterizes periods of financial panic, which is a more widespread version of the classic bank run. In a competitive financial sector, financial stability has weakest-link qualities, since no group of banks poses a disproportionate risk to the system. However, as some institutions become dominant, they take on particular importance. The system's financial stability becomes disproportionately dependent on the performance of these institutions, and on their ability to weather any crisis. In noncompetitive financial markets, the aggregation technology for financial stability appears to be that of weighted sum. As a consequence, the derived level of financial stability depends more heavily on some important banks.

This concept extends to the international level—there are systemically important financial institutions for the global economy, and even in the early twenty-first century, they are concentrated in a few financial centers. London and New York have long dominated international finance, and connections between the two meant quick transmission of the subprime crisis to Britain and the rest of Western Europe. Countries that were less densely connected to these financial centers had fewer consequences from the subprime crisis. This pattern of contagion differed from previous crises, which started in the periphery of the global financial system. Both the Debt Crisis and the Asian Financial Crisis affected Western financial institutions, but not to the same extent as the subprime crisis (Oatley et al., 2013). Thus, global financial stability also appears to have weighted-sum properties, which should enhance public good provision. If the countries where financial activities are concentrated enforce capital-adequacy requirements, global financial stability should result, or at least the crises that occur should have limited impact on the system as a whole.

As opposed to the relatively centralized approach of the global rules of trade, international financial coordination remains decentralized. Countries coordinate different efforts in different organizations, including the IMF, the World Bank, the Organization for Economic Cooperation and Development (OECD), and the Bank for International Settlements (BIS). The IMF has formal responsibility for maintaining international financial stability, but its role has evolved over time, and is now disproportionately involved in managing crises once they arise. By contrast, crisis prevention continues to target domestic policy makers as the key actor. Rather than creating a treaty and/or an intergovernmental organization, collaboration among national financial regulators has resulted in broadly subscribed standards with no centralized enforcement mechanism. Instead, markets have often created incentives for countries to adopt these international standards, which in turn have affected cross-border flows of finance. The most important of these efforts have been the three waves of banking standards created by the Basel Committee on Banking Supervision (BCBS), which will be the focus of the rest of this chapter. The next section sets the background for BCBS activities by providing an overview of financial globalization since the demise of the Bretton Woods system. We then compare three different iterations of recommendations from the BCBS and conclude by reflecting on their ability to provide global financial stability.

GLOBALIZATION OF FINANCE

As late as the 1960s, finance still largely existed within the confines of national borders. The Bretton Woods system prioritized the resurrection of international trade, not international finance. In fact, capital controls, which restricted cross-border financial movements to those necessary for international trade, were a key component of Bretton Woods. While capital controls were important for allowing countries to retain policy autonomy in other areas, the goal of minimizing capital flows conflicted with the need to inject credit into war-torn economies. In the 1950s and 1960s, American firms in particular invested greatly in Europe and Japan, and international financial markets grew with the accumulation of dollars in overseas markets (called Eurodollar markets regardless of geography). Large domestic banks became large international banks—from 1964 through 1980, international banking grew by over 30% annually (Singer, 2007, p. 38). After Bretton Woods, international finance grew faster than international trade, particularly in the industrialized countries. The oil crises in 1973 and 1979 played a key role in the dramatic increases in financial flows due to the way that oil-producing countries handled their proceeds. Even as they reaped huge increases in oil prices brought about by the Organization of Petroleum Exporting Countries (OPEC), oil-exporting countries often deposited much of their savings into Western banks, whose assets rose even as their home markets struggled. Given the low profitability of domestic lending, many Western banks sought out foreign borrowers willing to pay higher interest rates.

Rich-country banks had a new tool at their disposal for spreading risk: the syndicated loan, which took one asset, such as a loan, divided it into many parts, and then sold pieces of that asset. Rather than concentrate the default risk associated with the bank holding that loan, as in traditional bank intermediation, syndication spread the risk among the many owners of the new asset. Syndication not only freed banks from having to retain large debts on their books, it also provided banks with new revenue opportunities as they provided syndication services. Syndication has clearly led to greater market efficiency and risk diversification, but it has reduced transparency in financial transactions due to the increased difficulty of tracking counterparties. Rather than one lender, many now have claims on the borrowers. Default on syndicated loans is less likely to imperil the original lending bank, but it could lead to unforeseen problems in other markets. In other words, even while reducing risk, syndication compounds the information problems inherent in financial transactions.

Armed with syndication and awash in petrodollars, during the 1970s, Western banks loaned outside their home economies to the governments of many developing countries. This process hit its high point after the second oil crisis of 1979. As financial globalization proceeded, the risks of contagion across domestic markets increased. In 1974, Bankhaus Herstatt, based in Cologne, West Germany, lost a large amount of money in bad foreign currency trades and became unable to meet its obligations. Its insolvency caused major problems across foreign exchange markets owing to counterparty risk—the danger that other financial institutions could become vulnerable due to their exposure in trades with Bankhaus Herstatt. In the United Kingdom, the British-Israel Bank failed that same year. Also in 1974, different circumstances brought about the bankruptcy of Franklin National, an American bank. In 1975, 13 FDIC-insured banks failed in the United States; in 1976, another 16 FDIC-insured banks failed in the United States. Federal disbursements to FDIC-insured depositors went from tens of millions of dollars in the 1960s to more than half a billion in 1976. It was initially this increasing cost of bank failures for Western governments that led 10 countries to begin discussions on banking supervision via the Basel Committee. Of particular concern was the expansion of banks into foreign markets. Who had supervisory responsibility over banks operating outside their home country? If this authority was shared by regulators in multiple countries, how could they lower risks of contagion in their own country?

The Debt Crisis of 1982 demonstrated the downside of financial globalization and greatly impacted Western banks. In that year alone, there were 34 insured bank failures and 8 government-assisted mergers (Wood, 2005, p. 70). This increase and its cost to taxpayers prompted the U.S. Congress to pass legislation that incorporated new U.S. funding for the IMF along with a requirement to impose capital-adequacy requirements on U.S. banks and to pressure foreign banks to do the same (Singer, 2007, p. 43). Over the course of the 1980s, the FDIC intervened in nearly 1000 bank failures or potential failures due to increasing volatility in asset prices, exchange rates, and interest rates. As a result, the FDIC continued to require higher levels of capital adequacy to prevent more bank failures, but these new regulations did not sit well with American banks, which were unhappy due to a perceived loss in competitiveness. In particular, Japanese banks were subject to no capital-adequacy rules and were attracting increasing numbers of customers in the United States. Figure 8.1 demonstrates the rapid increase in Japanese banks' market share in the 1980s, a trend that, according to American and British banks, was due largely to the frequent and direct intervention of the Japanese Ministry of Finance to prevent the failure of troubled banks

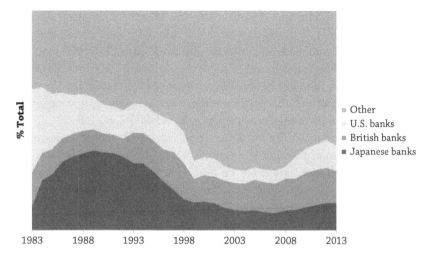

Figure 8.1
Changes in cross-border lending over time (BIS, 2014b)

(Singer, 2007). While these banks did not seek more regulation per se—they continued to lobby against it—they were interested in competing on fairer terms with their Japanese counterparts. The combination of domestic political demands and governments' desire for greater financial stability is crucial to explaining the form and timing of transnational financial cooperation in the form of the Basel Accord.

THE BASEL ACCORD

In response to the financial crises of the 1970s, large bank failures, and the rising importance of foreign banks in their jurisdictions, a group of banking regulators from 10 advanced economies began meeting regularly to discuss banking regulation in a new forum. This forum was originally called the Standing Committee on Banking Regulations and Supervisory Practices, but eventually became known as the Basel Committee for Banking Supervision (BCBS, or the Committee) due to its affiliation with the BIS in Basel, Switzerland. The Committee's self-stated purpose was "to close gaps in the supervisory net and to improve supervisory understanding and the quality of banking supervision worldwide" (Kapstein, 1991, pp. 5–6). BCBS is an early example of transnational cooperation by government bureaucrats, in this case banking regulators, who faced a common problem of how to monitor and supervise foreign banks operating in their jurisdiction.

Although the Basel Committee held its first meeting in February 1975, the Committee had little initial influence, a fact made less surprising by its murky legal status. As an informal organization with no staff or headquarters, the Committee largely functioned as a forum for communication among national bank regulators and had little official authority under international law. Rather than binding its members to particular actions, BCBS allowed banking regulators in its member countries to communicate, study the financial system, share information on cross-border banking activity, and negotiate some harmonization of regulatory practice (Wood, 2005). By 1982, BCBS had turned its attention to the issue of capital adequacy—how much capital should banks retain in order to prevent failures during a crisis? Although BCBS had not reached agreement on desired levels of capital adequacy, the Committee called for national regulators to at least maintain current minimums, which differed across countries. The Committee also wanted to develop a common definition of capital, meaning what kinds of bank assets should count for adequacy calculations (Wood, 2005).

Ultimately, neither the Debt Crisis nor any particular bank failure pushed the Basel Committee's agenda forward, so that the timing of the agreement cannot be attributed to any particular transnational issue. Instead, it was the confluence of domestic politics in great powers, specifically the countries that hosted the vast majority of international finance. In addition to the financial prowess of British and American banks, the two countries' financial markets have historically attracted many foreign institutional investors. In the mid-1990s, the ratio of institutionally held assets to GDP was 170% in the United States, 162% in the United Kingdom, and less than 80% in other major markets like Japan and Germany (Simmons, 2001, p. 593). The dominance of American and British financial centers only grew over the next two decades, and in 2009, 72% of countries maintained assets in U.S. markets, and 35% of countries held assets in British markets (Oatley et al., 2013, pp. 141–142). In short, London and New York are even now dominant financial centers, and their governments' actions have been at the forefront of cooperation on banking regulation.

After the 1984 savings and loan crisis in the United States, both the general public and government officials became increasingly concerned about banking regulation. In examining its peers' practices, a study commissioned by the U.S. Federal Reserve Board found that the U.S. system failed to account for the different kinds of risks in bank assets. In contrast, countries like Belgium, France, and the United Kingdom had created more sophisticated rules that required banks to hold more capital if their asset portfolio grew riskier (Kapstein, 1991). But when the U.S. government announced in January 1986 that it, too, would like to implement such a system, American bankers objected and refused to support such legislation because they worried that higher levels of capital reserves would hurt their ability to compete with foreign banks, particularly Japanese banks, which had no such requirements (Wood, 2005; Singer, 2007).

In part to circumvent congressional opposition to the plan, the chairman of the U.S. Federal Reserve, Paul Volcker, contacted his peer at the Bank of

England, and they facilitated the negotiation of a bilateral agreement between the two governments. This bilateral agreement created a common definition of capital, adopted Britain's risk-weighted approach, and also applied it to bank assets that were previously unsupervised in the United States. This U.S.-UK agreement was announced in January 1987 and provoked complaints from both Japan and from Britain's fellow members of the European Community (as the European Union was known at that time). In particular, countries excluded from the agreement were unhappy at having no say in the negotiations and about potential consequences for their own banks.

As a result, the U.S.-UK deal was followed by negotiations with Japan and, separately, with other European countries, which discussed banking supervision as part of the preparations for the 1992 Maastricht agreement. By September 1987, Japan had agreed to a framework that was similar to the US-UK agreement, but that added new components demanded by the Japanese. Again, the potential loss of markets was a motivating factor: Japanese officials were convinced that, without negotiating, their banks might not be allowed to continue their phenomenal growth in American and British markets. Additionally, according to Wood (2005, p. 77), Japanese negotiators hoped to "fend off criticism from Japanese banks and implement the standards more easily" through an international agreement because it gave "the impression that new, stricter capital standards were being imposed from the outside." Once the three largest markets found an acceptable agreement, other European members and Canada began to fear that their banks, too, would not be allowed to compete in those three large markets unless they also agreed to similar principles of bank supervision.

In that context, the initial Basel Accord (or the Accord) was announced on December 10, 1987, and was finalized over the course of the next year. The final version incorporated elements of the U.S.-UK agreement, by accounting for different types of capital in determining the riskiness of bank assets. However, the Accord was not simply that same agreement with more signatory countries. The Accord's primary innovation was a two-tiered definition of regulatory capital, with Tier One including safer assets, and Tier Two allowing riskier assets that counted for some fraction of their actual worth. Compliant banks, which were intended to be internationally oriented banks only, needed at least 4% of their assets in Tier One, and another 4% in Tier Two by the end of the 1992 fiscal year, for a total 8% capital-adequacy ratio. Within a relatively short time, BCBS members had agreed to implement these common banking regulations across their countries, thereby yielding two benefits. First, by increasing the minimum level of capital that banks were required to reserve, the Accord reduced the risk of contagion across banks experiencing crises. Second, by establishing a common set of rules across those countries, the Accord reduced the competitive advantage accruing to banks in less regulated countries. This second dynamic played a crucial role in the timing of the agreement, and in the motivation of key states—notably Britain and the United States—for leading the effort (Wood, 2005).

The final agreement was signed by all BCBS countries, but created no punishment mechanisms for members that broke the agreement. Importantly, the Accord granted considerable autonomy to individual regulators in implementation, which was necessary since the document had no enforcement power and questionable legal status. Despite this apparent weakness, the BCBS countries achieved compliance well ahead of the original timeline, with the British banks in compliance by the end of 1989 (Wood, 2005, p. 94). Compliance among members is perhaps unsurprising, since those enforcing new banking regulations were also the creators of those regulations. As Simmons (2001, p. 604) notes, "by the end of 1993, international active G-10 banks had capital ratios that exceeded the prescribed minimum, often significantly." The Accord succeeded in establishing a new minimum of capital adequacy across its members.

Perhaps more dramatic was the BCBS's call for other countries to adopt the Accord's 8% capital-adequacy ratios. A 1994 survey found capital-adequacy requirements in all 129 countries surveyed, with a Basel-like risk-weighting approach in 92% of surveyed countries (Simmons, 2001, p. 604). In some cases, such regulations came at great cost—Indonesia's implementation of the 8% capital requirement amounted to 15% of the country's entire GDP (Simmons, 2001, p. 605). Why would other countries import a banking rule that they had no part in negotiating?

Surely part of the explanation, and certainly the one drawn by BCBS itself, revolves around market discipline. No bank would benefit from publicly flouting the Accord's international standards. Even if banks were better off holding less capital, they would not attract customers by being more vulnerable in a crisis. Banks therefore had incentives to meet Basel standards so as to attract more customers. Simmons (2001, p. 605) agrees that "market pressure to meet international financial standards has been far more important . . . than organized political pressure." As such, the Basel I standard became the "seal of approval" for banks all over the world, including in emerging markets (Singer, 2007, p. 62). Banks saw clear advantages to abiding by the Accord's capital-adequacy ratio. In fact, they went beyond the strict 8% minimum, and the average ratio of risk-weighted assets in major banks ranged from 8% to 11.2% by 1996 (Wood, 2005, p. 92). This had the added advantage of making banking markets all over the world more competitively balanced, at least on the surface.

Overall, Basel I had a remarkable impact by harmonizing capital requirements for banks across the globe. It focused bank regulators on minimizing the risk to their financial systems as a whole by requiring a minimum level of stability for individual banks. Banks, in turn, were willing to comply with these new guidelines in order to do business in a rapidly globalizing market, one where finance still concentrated in New York and London. Once the United States and the United Kingdom harmonized their standards, most countries followed, and the Accord was largely the manifestation of market incentives. As long as the United States and Britain complied with Basel standards, other countries had reason to adopt them.

FROM BASEL I TO BASEL II

Soon after the implementation of the original Basel Accord, its weaknesses became apparent. The five categories of risk weights included some rather arbitrary distinctions, especially the fact that all government bonds offered by OECD countries were treated as risk-free Tier 1 assets, which incentivized banks to lend to governments rather than to private firms. As the OECD expanded over the next decade, this classification became increasingly problematic, since it ignored clear differences in risks across member countries. Furthermore, risk differences became more important as the OECD expanded to include emerging markets like Mexico and South Korea.

BCBS addressed some Basel I defects with amendments to the original agreement. Because the original document had no formal legal status, it was easy to change—new rules did not require legislative action, and banking supervisors could rapidly implement revisions to the agreement. In 1996, a particularly crucial amendment allowed banks to use their own in-house risk models instead of the Accord's tiered definitions. The Committee expected only 20 or so globally significant international financial institutions (GSIFIs) to have such capacity, but over time several hundreds of banks claimed the right to use their own in-house risk models (Wood, 2005, p. 136). In theory this made risk assessment more accurate, because such models were typically far more nuanced than the Accord's two-tiered distinction, but the proliferation of different risk models posed new complications for domestic banking regulators. To the extent that these internal risk models allowed their creators to hold less capital, they also advantaged banks who used this method rather than the standard Basel I approach.

Other problems with the original Accord were unable to be addressed by amendments. Perhaps the largest failure was that it only required banks to set aside capital. Increasingly, other financial institutions (investment funds, pension funds, and insurance companies) engaged in cross-border financial activities, competing directly with banks in some markets. Because the Accord applied only to banks, these newer players in global finance bore the same kind of competitive advantage as the Japanese banks in the 1980s. GSIFIs adapted to this new competitive environment, and while they continued to maintain official Basel I requirements, they developed methods of hiding risky assets that were not addressed by Basel I standards. One method that grew in popularity throughout the decade was partnering with nonbank institutions to take advantage of their lighter regulatory burden.

Many of these problems became evident in the wake of a series of crises in the 1990s, starting with the European exchange rate mechanism (a predecessor of the Euro) in 1992, followed by the Mexican Peso crisis in 1994 and then by the Asian Financial Crisis in 1997–1998. The collective impact of these crises persuaded many policy makers that international financial cooperation had not gone far enough, and that the existing "international financial architecture" needed strengthening.[4] Although reformers focused attention on the IMF, the peso and Asian crises in particular drew calls for the BCBS to play a larger role in designing bank supervision for developing countries. BCBS membership remained exclusive to its original 10 countries, but BCBS became an important forum for emerging market banking supervisors to share information on international banks and on best practices. Throughout the 1990s, the Committee became increasingly important as a source for policy innovations.

BCBS responded to these calls with the release in April 1997 of its Core Principles, which essentially brought together 25 key policy recommendations from its work to date. A more detailed set of policy recommendations followed in October 1999. Controversially, the Committee argued that the IMF and the World Bank should incorporate these principles of banking supervision into the conditions required of states seeking their assistance (Wood, 2005, pp. 107–108). BCBS also pushed other initiatives, such as technical assistance and cooperation with regulators of nonbank institutions, which together helped to increase its influence.

Throughout the 1990s, BCBS played a significant role in the policy response to financial crises. The fact that member countries continued to lean so heavily on its policy advice and that this advice was also applied in other countries reflected the "elevated stature" of the organization (Wood, 2005, p. 121). However, the Committee still operated on the belief that the market would reinforce the wisdom of its policy recommendations. Its role in crisis management was limited to intellectual influence on domestic regulators or on other international organizations like the IMF. BCBS did not extend its mandate or capabilities as a formal intergovernmental organization, and so it could not fulfill any role in actually managing international financial crises once they arose.

The process leading to Basel II showed serious flaws in the Basel model of transnational cooperation. Despite widespread compliance with the original Basel Accord, bank capital ratios were decreasing in the late 1990s as banks increasingly created loopholes to "get around the letter and spirit of the Accord" (Wood, 2005, p. 129). Given the decreasing effectiveness of the original Accord, BCBS announced a more comprehensive effort to revise the Accord.

4. Eichengreen (1999) and Kenen (2001) are good examples of the ideas circulating during this time.

From the original invitation for comments on the first draft of Basel II, due in March 2000, negotiations for the new guidelines were much more public and included greater representation of financial actors themselves. The first draft received more than 200 sets of comments, complicating the Committee's task, and its second draft, which ran over 500 pages, received even more comments (Wood, 2005, p. 137). In addition to its original participants (G-10 bank regulators), Basel II negotiations involved regular participation from other government actors, from scholars, from nongovernment organizations, and from the banking industry itself, particularly in the form of the Institute for International Finance, an industry representative of internationally active Western banks (Claessens, Underhill, and Zhang, 2008).

Due to the number of actors involved and the complexity of potential policy recommendations, Basel II negotiations were immensely more complicated than earlier negotiations. Repeatedly, BCBS extended deadlines for the final version. By 2001, it began to lose not just the financial sector but also certain countries that were unhappy with particulars. For example, the German chancellor, Gerhard Schroder, publicly refused for his country to be governed by Basel II's recommendations for small and medium-sized banks. As a result, German negotiators received special permission from the BCBS not to implement this component. In the United States, those same smaller banks organized through the Independent Community Bankers of America to pressure negotiators for a similar exception. U.S. regulators announced their intention to apply Basel II to only its 12 largest banks (Wood, 2005, p. 145). China and India followed this reversal with their own exceptions. Generally, countries were more resistant to Basel II requirements. In contrast, European Union (EU) countries incorporated Basel II into domestic banking laws and complied much more fully with the new Accord.

Ultimately, Basel II was finalized and signed by G-10 representatives in June 2004, and banks were initially given three years to comply. Philosophically, the new agreement emphasized the supervisory role of not just bureaucrats, but also bank owners, bank employees, and market participants. The agreement included revisions to the original capital-adequacy framework, including more differentiation of lending to OECD (and non-OECD) governments. In contrast to Basel I, the new agreement rejected a one-size-fits-all approach and offered not just a standard risk-weighting approach but also allowed banks to use their own internal ratings-based approach to risk management. Additionally, as outlined in Table 8.1, Basel II created an important new role for ratings agencies, such as Standard and Poor's, as arbiters of risk, insofar as their assessments of an asset's riskiness would determine the level of capital that a bank had to set aside.

The first and second Basel Accord negotiations differed dramatically from one another, as did countries' implementation of the Accords. Many critics of

Table 8.1. Comparing the Basel Accords

Agreement	Time period	Key provisions
The Basel Accord	Signed in 1988; implemented by 1992	• Minimum 8% capital-adequacy ratio: half in safer Tier 1 assets (such as government bonds), half in riskier Tier 2 assets (such as subordinated debt)
Basel II	Issued in 2004; effectively implemented through 2009	• Minimum 8% ratio, again half in Tier 1 assets, now expanded to include AAA-rated structured products and collateralized repos, among others • Risk agencies' ratings (for example, Moody's and S&P) became important determinations of the capital adequacy • New options allow wider use of internal risk models
Basel III	Issued in 2009; G-20 endorsement in 2010; implemented through 2019	• Minimum 8% ratio, but shifted toward safer assets • New 2.5% capital conservation buffer and 0%–2.5% countercyclical capital buffer for GSIFIs • New required Liquidity Coverage Ratio (LCR) ensures one-month survival in crisis • New required Leverage Ratio, 3% ratio, but not risk-based • Maximum 13% ratio combined, dramatically increasing capital requirements

Sources: Hannoun, 2010; Singer, 2007; Wood, 2005

the negotiations leading to Basel II maintained that the process was heavily influenced by the very banks the Accord intended to regulate, thereby tainting the legitimacy of the process. The influence of the Institute for International Finance, in particular, provoked charges of "regulatory capture" (Wood, 2005; Claessens, Underhill, and Zhang, 2008). According to these critiques, new regulatory rules favored larger, rich-country banks at the expense of their smaller or developing country counterparts. Wood (2005, p. 150) went so far as to argue that "the current and future ability of the BCBS to produce banking standards at the international level will be determined by the willingness of the Committee to take a stand against calls from international banks to reduce their regulatory burden."

A second criticism has to do with the actual methods by which BCBS attempted to achieve financial stability. By allowing multiple options for banks to calculate capital adequacy, Basel II complicated the task of banking supervision, and this was especially problematic in countries without much bureaucratic capacity, or where banking regulators often lacked the independence of their rich-country peers (Claessens, Underhill, and Zhang, 2008).

In the end, rather than deepening cooperation among bank supervisors, Basel II led to diverse outcomes across even member countries. Some countries, notably the United States and the United Kingdom, chose to apply Basel I capital requirements to all banks, while others followed BCBS's advice to apply it only to internationally active banks (Wood, 2005). This may have prevented contagion but meant that some domestic financial sectors were more stable than others. Basel II resulted in "a decrease in regulatory harmonization, given the wide discretion that [big] banks have to 'game' the system to their own advantage" (Singer, 2007, p. 65).

Even more concerning is a direct attack on the "very concept" of Basel II (Moosa, 2010, p. 96). Questions arose about whether the capital-adequacy ratios, as modified in Basel II, actually prevented financial instability. Many critics contended that contrary to their purposes, the Accords' capital requirements could actually aggravate financial crises. This "procyclical" criticism hinges on what happens to banks' lending practices when a crisis starts. In a crisis, any bank with a required capital ratio must either raise more capital or sell assets, both of which can reduce the amount of credit available in the economy and worsen the overall financial situation. Additionally, new evidence emerged that Basel II's internal risk assessment underestimates risk during boom times, leading banks to a false sense of security (Wood, 2005, p. 137). These questions would receive even greater attention after the subprime crisis and the great recession of 2007–2009.

The Great Recession

THE SUBPRIME CRISIS AND BASEL III

In the wake of the subprime crisis, BCBS and Basel II became the target of much criticism, some of which was just an elaboration of previous complaints and some of which emerged from the housing market crisis itself.[5] Basel II clearly placed too much emphasis on ratings agencies. Basel II's reliance on banks' internal models underestimated the probabilities of the size of financial crisis that actually took place, which, in turn, meant that these models underestimated the amount of capital banks should keep in reserve (Moosa, 2010). In retrospect, it became clear that reducing systemic risk by bank supervision alone is inadequate. Nonbank financial institutions, particularly insurance (such as AIG) and securities firms (such as Lehman Brothers), were a central part of the financial crisis.

5. For a summary of this criticism, see Moosa (2010); for a defense of Basel II and its role in the crisis, see Cannata and Quagliariello (2009).

Even beyond these criticisms, however, new empirical work questioned Basel's key policy focus—capital requirements. Both the British bank Northern Rock and the investment firm Bear Stearns, whose failure heightened concerns about risks of contagion, had adequate capital on hand under the Basel II rules. Each of them, just like the Icelandic banks, was dependent on short-term borrowing to manage high amounts of leverage. Because Basel II failed to address leverage and new financial instruments, it did little to prevent their failure. Rather than focusing only on capital-adequacy ratios, Basel II should have included other measures of bank health. Basel III negotiations were clearly influenced by these lessons and their close proximity in time to the subprime crisis gave the negotiations a new urgency.

What eventually became Basel III was endorsed by G-20 leaders at their November 2010 summit in Seoul. Basel III contained several provisions. First, it modified the previous agreement by further expanding capital buffers for banks during crisis and, for the first time, included explicit arrangements to reduce previous rules' procyclical effects. Second, hoping to avoid expensive government bailouts, Basel III also included extra capital requirements for banks regarded as "too big to fail" for the international financial system. Third, the new agreement harkened back to the success of the original Basel Accord with the inclusion of a leverage ratio—basically, a minimum amount of capital to absorb losses without regard to risk formulas. Fourth, Basel III called for liquidity requirements, which were not initially defined but were to be determined by member countries by 2013. Liquidity was a new target, included due to the reliance of many failed institutions on short-term financing in secondary markets.

Although detailed accounts are still forthcoming, the negotiations leading to Basel III clearly responded to two primary complaints. First, in response to criticisms that BCBS negotiations were not open to emerging markets and developing countries, but that those countries were still expected to implement its recommendations, BCBS extended membership offers to some of the larger emerging markets, thereby increasing the number of individual countries participating to 27. Basel III negotiations thus included a broader variety of countries and allowed emerging market participation for the first time.

The second change is that, at least initially, BCBS negotiators forcefully pushed back against the Institute for International Finance and other industry groups. In a speech outlining the contours of Basel III, BIS Deputy General Manager Hervé Hannoun (2010, p. 1) reflected that "the supervisory community had to fight a fierce battle to require more capital and less leverage in the financial system in the face of significant resistance from some quarters of the banking industry." Thus, it appears that the Committee addressed criticisms that the BCBS had been captured by the very banks its members were charged with regulating.

In short, Basel III both expanded the number of countries participating in the discussion and developed an ambitious agenda for regulators. BCBS called Basel III "a fundamental overhaul for banking regulation" (BIS, 2014a). The new agreement included multiple capital requirements, depending on the type of bank, and directed regulators to expand their attention to other measures of bank stability. Because the BCBS agenda expanded in the new agreement, implementation of the new agreement has been even slower than Basel II. As of the writing of this book, Basel III implementation had been prolonged from its original 2015 deadline to 2019. The Committee extended the implementation period due to the slow recovery from the subprime crisis, and especially its continuing effects in Europe, where banks have had difficulty meeting Basel III's higher capital requirements. In addition to prolonging Basel III's implementation, BCBS reduced stringent leverage ratio requirements in January 2014 due to the difficulties faced by European banks in increasing capital and selling risky assets (*The Financial Times*, 2014). In contrast to the European implementation and to the narrow implementation of Basel II in the United States, American regulators are again complying more broadly with Basel standards, and are enforcing higher-than-Basel-III requirements on international and systemically important banks (*The Financial Times*, 2013). Some countries are already fully compliant with Basel III standards, including new BCBS members India and Saudi Arabia.

While many are optimistic that Basel III dramatically improves on Basel II, it remains to be seen whether most countries will meet the new higher guidelines, and what the agreement's overall impact will be. Early indications are that Basel III may help to lower the chances of another crisis similar in cause to the 2007 subprime crisis, but by addressing those factors, such as reducing the dependence of banks on short-term finance and high leverage, new bank requirements may again push financial activities into nonbank institutions (see *The Economist*, 2014b). Thus, despite innovations in transnational cooperation, familiar patterns of regulatory failure may already be apparent.

Although the original recommendations of Basel III are indeed much stricter, particularly for larger financial institutions, the task of enforcing these tougher rules still falls to domestic regulators and will be determined on a country-by-country basis, where industry groups get a second chance to avoid the new rules. The fact that Basel recommendations are still dependent on domestic regulators for enforcement is clearly a key weakness in the system, and many analysts lament "the lack of any capacity to supervise cross-border institutions and of any clear crisis management (and burden sharing) framework at the international level" (Avgouleas, 2013, p. 77). Even so, BCBS members are unlikely to support a stronger organization with real enforcement power in the near future, and such an innovation might not succeed to the degree the Committee has.

COLLECTIVE ACTION IN INTERNATIONAL FINANCE:
THE BASEL ACCORDS AS SOFT LAW

Given the increasing complexity of BCBS recommendations over time, it becomes easy to lose sight of its key lessons for transnational cooperation. Collective action in finance has differed significantly from its counterpart in trade. While commitments to harmonize trade laws take a binding, legalized form via the World Trade Organization (WTO), commitments to harmonize banking regulations are still largely voluntary, and neither the BCBS nor its members have power to enforce the Basel Accords. Why have the institutional forms chosen for these two areas differed so dramatically?

Lipson (1991) and Abbott and Snidal (2000) distinguish "hard law" like the World Trade Organization from "soft law" like the Basel Accords. States intentionally choose the latter under conditions of high uncertainty, where unforeseen events or rapid change reduce the effectiveness of binding commitments. Had the members insisted on a formal legally binding treaty, it would have been difficult to modify quickly and repeatedly, as the BCBS did between major updates to its core principles. Furthermore, that treaty would have been much more difficult to negotiate than its nonbinding counterpart. Rather than restricting the negotiations to banking supervisors, higher-level diplomats would have had to be involved, and the treaty would have faced dramatically higher hurdles in the form of ratification procedures in member countries (Brummer, 2010). As Abbott and Snidal (2000, p. 444) highlight, soft legal arrangements like the Basel Accords allow "states to capture the 'easy' gains they can recognize with incomplete knowledge, without allowing differences or uncertainties about the situation to impede completion of the bargain." Soft law allows states to learn as they go, adapting commitments as necessary to produce the desired results.

Transnational financial cooperation has continued to revolve around the Basel Committee, where interactions among banking supervisors have allowed them to share best practices and codes of conduct to generate and share data and regulatory reports, and to cooperate in enforcing standards on banks that span multiple jurisdictions. By the 1990s, the Committee had developed considerable expertise and had "built up a body of knowledge about the workings of international finance, through the exchange of information and ideas among regulators, that greatly facilitates the tracking of, and finding solutions to, the problems in that market" (Wood, 2005, p. 49). Additionally, BCBS developed a broad consensus that markets could help reinforce their goals by disciplining firms that failed to implement adequate safeguards. This market discipline, not threats of penalties for noncompliance, motivated countries to adopt BCBS recommendations.

Just as soft law solved some problems, however, it created others. In particular, the flexibility in commitment means that states retain the right to interpret their commitments and to implement agreements as they see fit. Nowhere is this more obvious than the vacillations of the Basel Accord adoption in the United States. American negotiators were a key force behind Basel I, and American regulators applied its recommendations much more widely than originally anticipated. Basel II received a much narrower role in U.S. banking rules, and other large markets followed the U.S. example by not fully implementing the second agreement. With Basel III, the United States appears to have again switched directions, and new banking regulations go even beyond what Basel III recommends. As the single largest financial market, U.S. implementation weighs heavily in determining other countries' responses. Most large economies have followed the U.S. example (Novembre, 2009). In contrast, most small economies adopted BCBS recommendations due to positive market reinforcement, even if they had not been party to negotiations. The EU's strong adherence to Basel II and its difficulty in implementing Basel III without special dispensation stands in dramatic contrast to these other patterns.

Soft law also attempts to deal with perhaps the most difficult and persistent problem for transnational financial cooperation, evident across all three Basel Accords. Although international financial stability may gain from transparent capital requirements, banks and other financial institutions face frequent temptations to cheat on such arrangements. Even as banks worked to comply with Basel I requirements, innovations in the field of finance made it possible to circumvent them. In particular, banks created off-balance-sheet assets whose risks were excluded from the Basel Accord framework. Additionally, even though developing countries agreed in many cases to implement Basel I, developing country regulators were often incapable of enforcing capital-adequacy regulations on their banks.

Basel II was less widely implemented than Basel I, but where it was implemented, the same pattern emerged. The banks to which Basel II rules were applied again developed ways of circumventing the rules—this time by securitizing risky assets and selling them to insurance companies and pension funds, which did not face the same capital requirements as banks (Schinasi, 2006, p. 167). Many international banks again appeared to comply, even while undermining the Accord's goals. Even though Basel III is not yet fully implemented, scholars, regulators, and market watchers expect its continued focus on banks will drive financial activity toward "shadow banking," which consists of the very nonbank financial institutions that have posed problems in previous implementations of Basel.[6] As transnational financial cooperation has evolved, it has continued to struggle with financial innovations and, as a consequence, has lagged behind the banks it tries to regulate.

6. For a timely account of shadow banking, see *The Economist* (2014b).

The pattern of footloose capital outwitting regulation repeats itself, not just in the context of the Basel Accords, but even in purely domestic regulation. Schinasi (2006, pp. 175–176) refers to this repeated interaction as a "bloodhound chasing a greyhound" and fears that the "gap between them may be widening" as financial globalization takes hold. Banks affected by Basel Accord regulations reacted strategically, shifting business activity from traditional activities to new financial instruments like derivatives that would not appear on their balance sheets. The soft law approach to seeking financial stability will only be successful to the extent that domestic regulators are familiar with the current tools of financial institutions, a problem particularly apparent in the difficulties developing countries had implementing the Basel Accords. For domestic regulators to supervise successfully, they must have close connections to financial institutions, which creates a new problem.

Some critics (particularly Wood, 2005, and Claessens, Underhill, and Zhang, 2008) argued that close relationships between bureaucrats and banks are bound to result in regulatory capture, and indeed the negotiations leading to Basel II had extensive participation by representatives of the very banks it sought to regulate. Certainly we agree that BCBS regulators have often prioritized their domestic political goals, some of which coincide with the interests of their banks. The very origins of Basel I have to be attributed to such motivations on the part of American and British regulators. However, the repeated pattern in which Basel Accord requirements attempt to stabilize international finance, only to be undermined by new financial innovations, is the larger problem. This pattern has at its root the uncertainty involved in regulating financial activity and the inability of even expert bureaucrats to develop and quickly modify regulations that constrain financial institutions.

CONCLUDING REMARKS

This chapter has examined transnational financial cooperation, which is both less systematic and more decentralized than trade cooperation. International finance can play a key role in reducing poverty and increasing economic development, but as banks and other financial institutions cross borders, they increase the risk that financial crises in one country can infect others. Financial contagion can be minimized through efforts to harmonize regulations on finance and to minimize incentives for regulatory arbitrage, when financial institutions redirect business operations to take advantage of differences in laws or enforcement. Efforts at harmonization have thus far granted little authority to the IMF and other international organizations with broad membership. Instead, the world's largest economies have generally sought to maintain domestic systems of crisis prevention and to coerce other countries into adopting similar approaches. Through the BCBS, domestic regulators have established new networks to share information and to achieve their policy goals. Regulatory cooperation via BCBS allows banking regulators to adapt constantly to the sheer complexity and rapid innovation in international finance. This soft law approach is ideally suited for sharing information and coordinating responses to financial innovation, but it comes with a cost, the voluntary implementation of its recommendations.

Through three iterations of banking rules, implementation has varied dramatically, and financial stability has not been achieved. The extent to which countries adopt Basel recommendations seems largely determined by whether countries that dominate international finance do so (in recent history, the United States, the United Kingdom, and Japan) (Simmons, 2001; Brummer, 2010; Oatley et al., 2013). Even when broadly adopted, the Basel Accords have thus far failed to prevent crisis, but Basel III goes farther than previous incarnations and clearly addresses its predecessor's mistakes. To the degree key countries implement the new standards, Basel III may be more successful in creating financial stability than previous iterations. Even then, nonbank institutions remain a potential source of instability, so international financial cooperation will need to address insurance and securities firms, or better insulate banks from them, to be successful.

CHAPTER 9

Transnational Crime: Drugs and Money Laundering

Chapters 7 and 8 explored the importance of collective action in maximizing the benefits from globalization. Trade and financial flows offer clear benefits for international cooperation, and generally it is the gains from economic globalization that encourage states to overcome collective action difficulties for those issues. States commit to economic openness through international institutions, and cross-border flows of goods and money follow. Not all such flows are welcomed, though. As globalization makes borders more porous, and as the volume of trade and financial flows increases, illicit goods become more difficult to detect. In this chapter, we explore the implications of transnational crime for collective action, and we pay particular attention to the difficulties of successful cooperation in the illegal trafficking of narcotics and in money laundering. Both of these issues are characterized by incentives for at least one country to renege on international cooperation because the incentives to supply an illegal commodity or service only grow as most other states outlaw it.

FIGHTING ILLICIT MARKETS

Spy movies from James Bond to Austin Powers need a villain to ground their plots. Cold War villains were largely defined by superpower conflict, but the end of the Cold War left both scriptwriters and defense industries with a dilemma—how to justify their continued existence. In the United States, this confusion was largely resolved during the Clinton administration, when transnational organized crime emerged as a coherent villain both for Hollywood and for the Department of Defense. This was perhaps best symbolized domestically by Presidential Directive 42, which defined transnational crime as a national security threat in 1995, and internationally with the signing of the UN Convention against Transnational Organized Crime in 2000 (Andreas and Nadelmann, 2006).

Transnational organized crime may have received greater attention in the 1990s with the rise of the Russian mafia and the dramatic power wielded by Pablo Escobar and other drug lords, but it clearly predates those organizations and will survive current efforts at eradication. This may at first seem surprising since transnational crime networks are nonstate actors. As such, they should surely operate at a disadvantage when compared to the military might and organizational supremacy of the modern state. Indeed, no one criminal organization can withstand the sustained opposition of a great power, as the cases of both Pablo Escobar and the Sicilian mafia demonstrate. A quandary in fighting transnational crime is that as these individual networks are eliminated, others arise to replace them. This process is characterized by the same element that drives efficiency in other markets—the profit motive, which illegality can enhance dramatically.

Criminal activities are defined on a state-by-state basis, according to domestic laws. We consider a crime to be transnational if it meets any of the following four criteria: (1) it is committed in more than one state, (2) it is committed in one state but planned or controlled in another, (3) the responsible party is active across state lines, or (4) the crime itself has substantial effects in another state. Transnational crimes complicate law enforcement for many reasons owing to asymmetries in information and in enforcement. Transnational criminals operate with an advantage if law enforcement efforts are not well coordinated. Because law enforcement often overlaps with the state's security functions, sharing sensitive information about crime or sharing law enforcement resources is likely to impinge on sovereignty. Public officials in countries with rampant corruption may not enforce laws because they personally benefit from lax enforcement. Elsewhere, countries without effective law enforcement may hesitate to invite other states to help fight criminal activity because foreign participation may reduce the domestic government's legitimacy in the eyes of locals. Transnational cooperation on law enforcement occurs, but often faces strict limits. For example, The International Criminal Police Organization (INTERPOL) can issue notices requesting arrests (see Chapter 10), but the organization is completely dependent on the domestic law enforcement agencies of its member states—INTERPOL cannot directly arrest suspects of transnational crimes. Despite this limitation, INTERPOL has found success by focusing on information sharing and other elements of transnational cooperation by its member states.

Cooperation on law enforcement is also complicated because countries vary in their willingness to prohibit particular goods or services. For numerous reasons, states may decide that certain commodities or services possess intolerable social costs and should be unavailable. Where prohibition laws differ across states, enforcement is not a priority for the more permissive state, and a prohibiting state may have great difficulty convincing a permissive state to change its laws. Those laws may have great cultural meaning or historical importance that justifies the permissive state's stance. For example, international efforts to reduce whaling have run into fierce opposition by Japan, and as a result Japanese whalers free ride on the efforts of others to maintain existing populations of whales.

Other criminal activities generate universal agreement among states. For example, murder, theft, and rape are criminally punishable in all countries (Andreas and Nadelmann, 2006, p. 18). Even where laws are perfectly harmonized, enforcement may differ across states; for example, recent high-profile cases of rape in India have called attention to the country's historic tolerance of a legally prohibited act. Trafficking in human beings also continues despite laws prohibiting it across virtually all countries in the world. Harmonization of laws, while important, is not sufficient to generate a successful international prohibition regime (Andreas and Nadelmann, 2006).

For prohibited commodities, different levels of enforcement across countries create incentives for cross-border trade due to different risks of punishment. Since criminalization results in higher risks to producers, they will gravitate toward low enforcement countries to reduce their risks. When the United States made commercial alcohol production illegal in 1920, Canadian production boomed, aimed at the American market. As long as countries differ in the commodities they prohibit, they create incentives for trafficking in illicit goods. Smuggling and trade in illicit goods are long-standing activities, and have often played important roles in the development of the modern world (Andreas, 2013).

Such transnational crimes can have significant effects, undermining laws or the legitimacy of law enforcement institutions. Where the costs of transnational crimes are felt, the demand for cooperation rises as well. Our analysis of collective action in the last two chapters has prioritized its importance in correcting certain market failures, but when states decide to prohibit a market, they work against the laws of supply and demand, and even powerful states often find the task difficult. Making a good or activity illegal may affect the market in complex ways. Once a country has a number of heroin addicts, banning imports of the drug may have little impact on its demand (Caulkins and Reuter, 2010). Likewise, if ivory jewelry is prized by wealthy individuals, the ivory trade may persist long after it has been prohibited in order to safeguard elephant populations.

There are many examples of illicit markets that withstand prohibition efforts by states—trafficking in small arms and other weapons, in illicit drugs, and in human beings. One of the reasons why such markets are so difficult to eradicate is due to their weakest-link nature, which leads to levels of enforcement matching the lowest effort state. Any state that lacks capacity or refuses on other grounds to enforce prohibition undermines the efforts of even the largest efforts to do so. Even when states are successful in their efforts to disrupt illicit markets, they may actually increase the incentives for new providers and supplier networks to arise, thereby undermining their long-term goal of prohibiting the good in question. If there are profits to be made, profit-seeking suppliers will continue to seek out the weakest link in any prohibition regime. As a result, interaction among states can easily result in an enforcement race. Imagine that illicit suppliers are distributed proportionally across states, as they might be for methamphetamine production. If one state increases its enforcement efforts to reduce methamphetamine production in its territory, illicit suppliers will either migrate across borders or new suppliers will emerge in low enforcement states. Such states will then have an incentive to increase their efforts to reduce meth production as well. If all states increase enforcement, then meth production will again be distributed proportionally across states. Whether states gain from the higher level of enforcement depends crucially on how effective enforcement is, and as our comparative cases will suggest, higher levels of enforcement are subject to diminishing returns and may under some conditions result in little overall reduction of criminal activity.

In this chapter, we focus mostly on transnational crimes that do not generally rise to the level of substantial challenges to powerful states. Such issues can still offer benefits to cooperation among states and, in some ways, parallel more important security challenges like terrorism and civil war (see Chapter 10). Under best-shot conditions, states with considerable law enforcement capabilities may take larger roles in fighting a particular form of transnational crime, particularly if they also experience the highest costs from that criminal activity. As we discuss in the next section, the United States has historically been the world's largest consumer market for cocaine, and U.S. law enforcement has played a disproportionate role in disrupting cocaine trafficking networks by working bilaterally with cocaine-producing countries. Where more states are affected by a particular form of transnational crime, as is the case with our second example of money laundering, successful law enforcement requires global cooperation, which is much more difficult to achieve. As we will demonstrate in both cases, despite considerable expenditure and cooperation by countries suffering high costs from existing criminal activity, transnational crime fighting typically falls short. Most "successful" law enforcement efforts displace—rather than eradicate—existing criminal networks, often shifting the costs of transnational crime into neighboring countries. Existing transnational cooperation on law enforcement has only partially addressed this dynamic, which will require higher levels of cooperation on enforcement among a greater number of states before it can succeed.

DRUG TRAFFICKING

The most important illicit market is the trade in illegal drugs, which is estimated to be four times the value of the international arms trade (Dupont, 1999, p. 438). Illegal drugs, like many legal psychoactive substances, affect the brain's systems associated with reward and pleasure (Babor et al., 2010). Some psychoactive substances, such as the class of drugs known as opioids, are licit in some contexts but illicit in others. Heroin, a chemical transformation of opium, is widely prohibited, but morphine is also an opioid, as are other prescription-regulated painkillers. Cannabis can now be legally supplied and consumed in some parts of the United States (Washington and Colorado) as well as some foreign countries (Paraguay and Uruguay). Alcohol and tobacco are widely consumed despite potentially negative health consequences for the user and potential public health concerns. Why are some drugs prohibited while others are not?

Similar to our collective action approach, a public-health approach to drug control would focus on the collective costs of drug use (Babor et al., 2010). Policy choices would be made based on the societal costs of various drugs with prohibition reserved for the most costly drugs in terms of the harm to users, the impact of consumption on others, and societal reactions to drug use. A few systematic attempts to calculate the costs of such use demonstrate that some legal substances—particularly alcohol and tobacco—exceed the costs of some illegal substances (Babor et al., 2010, especially Chapter 4). Room and Reuter (2012, p. 89) reported that "illicit drugs (mainly opioids) accounted for about one fifth as much harm as did alcohol and tobacco" in terms of disability-adjusted life-years lost. Clearly, an additional element of feasibility is part of the decision to prohibit a particular psychoactive substance. Early attempts to prevent alcohol consumption, like American Prohibition, have largely failed, in part because they induced even worse outcomes than legalization.

Drug prohibition must struggle to overcome market incentives to supply a commodity as its price increases. Since a large proportion of imported heroin and cocaine in Western countries goes to heavy users, many of whom are addicts, demand holds relatively steady even as the price of the drug increases. Prohibition is only one of a number of alternative policy choices, and many drugs are not prohibited outright but can be legally used when prescribed by a medical doctor, when obtained from a licensed supplier, or when used by specified consumers. Nonetheless, most international efforts to reduce the drug trade have focused on prohibition, criminalizing the sale and use of particular drugs.

Transnational cooperation on drug prohibition began more than a century ago, with the Shanghai Conference on Opium in 1909. The 13 countries at that conference called for reduction of opium smoking, which was the predominant use at the time. Three years later came the International Opium Convention, which called for signatory states to confine opium use to legitimized medical purposes (Paoli, Greenfield, and Reuter, 2012). The demand for international action emanated from the consequences experienced by the United States and Western Europe in the last decades of the nineteenth century, when opium imports rose significantly. Opium addiction (as a percentage of the population) peaked between 1890 and 1900 in the United States, as it was commonly prescribed by doctors who did not realize the drug's addictive properties.

After World War I, The League of Nations assumed a key role in enforcing the prohibition of opium. Although The League lacked effective enforcement powers, it convinced many pharmaceutical companies to stop diverting opium for heroin production by targeting noncompliant companies with negative publicity (Paoli, Greenfield, and Reuter, 2012, pp. 926–927). Member states agreed to several new treaties in the interwar period. The International Opium Convention of 1925 increased the number of prohibited drugs, instituted import and export limits on those drugs, and established the Permanent Control Board to maintain these regulations. The Limitation Convention of 1931 set limits on domestic manufacturing, and the Convention for the Suppression of the Illicit Traffic in Dangerous Drugs called on signatory states to imprison drug traffickers. Combined, these treaties created a precedent for successive drug control efforts, primarily targeting the supply and trafficking of drugs across international borders.

After World War II, the United Nations largely continued and expanded these efforts, as evidenced by the 1961 Single Convention on Narcotic Drugs, the 1971 Convention on Psychotropic Substances, and the 1988 Convention on Trafficking. This set of treaties constitutes the modern prohibition regime, which targets opioids, cocaine, and cannabis, as well as more than 200 other substances, while legalizing limited use of the substance for scientific and medical purposes as determined by the International Narcotics Control Board. More than 180 countries have ratified the three treaties and, as recently as 1998, the UN General Assembly reiterated its support for international efforts at prohibition (Room and Reuter, 2012). UN efforts are coordinated through the UN Office on Drugs and Crime (UNODC), which publishes an annual report focusing on the success of efforts to reduce and intercept the supply of these and other illicit drugs.[1] The predominant approach to drug policy is thus prohibition.

Complete prohibition of illicit drugs is difficult to achieve, but not impossible. Both the People's Republic of China (in the 1950s) and Myanmar (in 1998–2007) succeeded in virtually eradicating supply and demand for opium

1. Interestingly, the World Health Organization (WHO), another UN agency, has sometimes conflicted with the UNODC due to the WHO's greater focus on public health and harm-reduction policies. In particular, the WHO moved efforts to provide needles for intravenous drug users from the UNODC to UNAIDS in order to achieve better results. See Room and Reuter (2012, pp. 85–86).

despite close proximity to opium-growing regions (Caulkins and Reuter, 2010). Importantly, these two successes occurred in relatively centralized autocracies, and in China's case in particular, drug eradication symbolized the broader fight against colonialism. Elsewhere, prohibition efforts have been less successful due to the resilience both of supply networks and of the demand for drugs (Babor et al., 2010, Chapter 5). Many countries spend (or have previously spent) considerable resources to enforce drug prohibition. Excluding spending that tries to entice drug traffickers into alternative livelihoods, total U.S. spending on counternarcotics exceeded half a billion dollars in 2005 (Glaze, 2007, p. 9). Even countries that are viewed as more tolerant of drug use, such as the Netherlands and Australia, still spend considerable amounts on enforcement (Caulkins and Reuter, 2010).

It is the United States that has taken an increasingly hard line and enhanced enforcement over the last 30 years, particularly in incarceration rates for drug-related offenses. The use of cocaine and heroin is thought to have declined somewhat as a response, particularly since 2000, but neither market is close to eradication, and small decreases in U.S. consumption have been replaced by increasing use in other markets.

These outcomes, in which high levels of enforcement have relatively small effects on consumption of a prohibited product, are consistent with markets for illicit products with few substitutes (Becker, Murphy, and Grossman, 2006).[2] Drug supply networks for cocaine and heroin comprise many growers, and many retail suppliers, each of which is easily replaced. Supply can handle considerable risks of disruption, since only a small portion of the retail cost of drugs accrues to those who grow the original product. As a result, the beginnings and ends of the supply chain are difficult to disrupt, but there tend to be few smugglers and few top-level importers in such supply chains (Babor et al., 2010). Therefore, interdiction, or the interception of drugs in transit from originating to destination markets, has become a favored law enforcement response. Where drug supply networks are already well established, as for heroin and cocaine, efforts to reduce supply typically have small and short-lived effects on street prices (Caulkins and Reuter, 2010). There is some evidence that high levels of enforcement can disrupt or even stall smaller emerging markets for new drugs, because robust networks of producers and consumers have yet to be established and so eliminating one new supplier can prevent others from ever emerging (Caulkins and Reuter, 2010). Established markets in illicit products, however, have proven extremely robust.

Even drugs whose supply is limited geographically can be difficult to prohibit. Coca, the plant from which cocaine is derived, is grown almost entirely

2. In economics parlance, the key factor in determining enforcement success is demand elasticity, or the proportional change in quantity demanded to a proportional change in price.

in the Andean region of South America, particularly in Bolivia, Colombia, and Peru. Given the relatively small geographic area where coca is grown, it might seem straightforward to reduce cocaine trafficking to other countries. Particularly when a hegemonic country exerts a large effort to reduce cocaine trafficking, as the United States has, a best-shot scenario might result in a significant reduction in the market. Instead, the last three decades illustrate myriad difficulties in targeting the international flow of cocaine, which instead exemplifies the weakest-link nature of many transnational crimes.

Coca is an indigenous plant to the Andes, and local consumption of coca—either chewing the leaf or using it to make tea—has been common in indigenous populations for centuries. It was only in the 1970s that international trafficking of cocaine began in earnest, primarily to consumers in the United States (Angrist and Kugler, 2007). U.S. law enforcement responded primarily with interdiction efforts, the primary target of which was trafficking through South Florida, where most cocaine entered the American market. Coordinated through the South Florida Drug Task Force, this initial effort was ultimately quite successful in reducing the amount of cocaine traveling those routes—a cocaine shortage became apparent in 1989 in the United States, during which street prices increased by 50% to 100% (Caulkins and Reuter, 2010, p. 247). However, the shortage lasted only 18 months, as enforcement efforts over the longer term only rerouted cocaine trafficking through Texas, Arizona, and New Mexico. In the literature on drug enforcement, this is called the "balloon effect," since just like squeezing a balloon—where the air shifts to another part of the balloon—focusing enforcement efforts on one area tends to displace existing trafficking into other areas (see Rouse and Arce, 2006). This is a clear illustration of a weakest-link problem for governments trying to prevent drug trafficking. Drug trafficking networks adapt to an initially successful enforcement effort, then law enforcement adapts, and then the cat-and-mouse game continues.

Using data from the U.S. Department of Justice (various years), Figure 9.1 depicts the evolution of cocaine trafficking in response to changing geographic areas of enforcement. Over three distinct time periods, either existing cocaine traffickers shifted their transportation routes, or new traffickers appeared to exploit low enforcement areas. The left panel depicts routes used by Colombian traffickers like the Medellin Cartel to get to Miami. The violence associated with the cocaine trade during that time period led to the nickname "cocaine cowboys" for those associated with the drug trade. The middle panel depicts the traffickers' shift to Mexican routes that led to the southwestern United States, the key point of entry for the next two to three decades. These new routes are associated with increased drug violence in Mexico and, more recently, in Central America. While those routes are still important, Caribbean trafficking routes have now resurfaced as important, as depicted in the right panel of Figure 9.1.

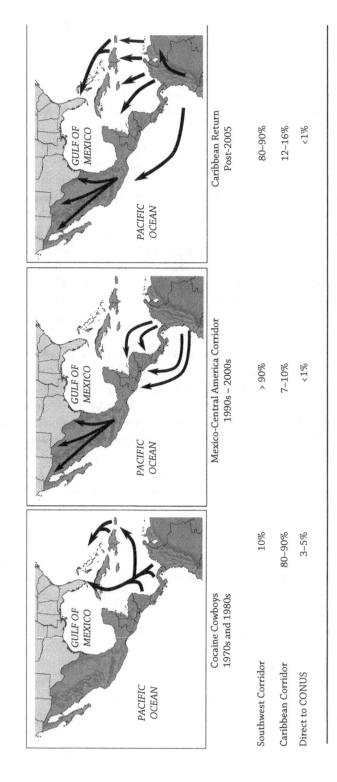

Figure 9.1
The evolution of the cocaine transport corridors

After the limited long-term success of the South Florida Drug Task Force, U.S. law enforcement shifted priorities, focusing more directly on the source of cocaine, the Andean countries. The U.S. Andean Initiative (1989–1993) provided over $2 billion to the three Andean countries to reduce coca cultivation (Rouse and Arce, 2006). The plan provoked controversy in those countries since the plant had an important cultural legacy beyond its designation to foreign consumers. The Colombian and Peruvian governments faced additional difficulties in reducing cocaine trafficking because each faced local insurgencies that funded their operations with money from the cocaine trade (FARC in Colombia and Shining Path in Peru). From 1991, American legislation via the Andean Trade Preferences Act further incentivized Bolivia, Colombia, and Peru, as well as Ecuador, to participate in the U.S. War on Drugs in return for preferential trade access to the American market. When Andean countries stopped cooperating, these trade preferences were withdrawn or threatened to be withdrawn. The United States has frequently linked drug cooperation to benefits in other areas, including foreign aid, in order to persuade other governments to try to reduce drug trafficking.

Prior to 1993, little cocaine was refined in Bolivia and Peru; their coca leaves were turned into more easily transported coca paste, which was then sent by plane to Colombia. Colombia has long served as the primary site for the necessary chemical transformations of coca paste into coca base and then into cocaine hydrochloride (Angrist and Kugler, 2007). Colombia's specialization in the production of cocaine was quite lucrative—some estimates put income from the drug trade anywhere from 4% to 6% of GDP in the early 1990s (Angrist and Kugler, 2007). In 1995 Peru's air force, in cooperation with the U.S. Drug Enforcement Agency, began intercepting planes on their way to Colombia with coca paste. These interdiction efforts dramatically reduced the viability of air transit, which meant that farmers in Bolivia and Peru had difficulty selling their harvested coca and eventually switched to other crops. In response, Colombian farmers expanded coca cultivation every year from 1994 through 2000, and Colombia came to occupy an even more important role in the supply of cocaine to the United States and other consumer markets (Angrist and Kugler, 2007). Because of Colombia's increased role in cocaine trafficking, and because by most estimates the U.S. cocaine market remained largely constant through these increased enforcement efforts, the U.S. government became interested in deeper cooperation with Colombia.

In 2000, Colombian President Andrés Pastrana and U.S. President Bill Clinton formally agreed to enhance bilateral cooperation on drug enforcement. "Plan Colombia," as the agreement became known, called for $13 billion in spending over nine years to improve security and rule of law in Colombia by cutting cocaine production in half and reducing the power of armed rebels and organized crime (Jenner, 2014). While a portion of this money came from the U.S. government, the plan also included enhanced cooperation with European countries and enhanced spending by the Colombian government. Manual and aerial eradication efforts played a central role in the effort to reduce cocaine exports, as did enhanced military capabilities directed to fight drug trafficking.

The result has been a dramatic decrease in Colombian coca cultivation—domestic coca production fell from an estimated 456,000 kilograms in 1999 to 194,000 kilograms in 2008 (Jenner, 2014, p. 78). Plan Colombia clearly achieved its goal of reasserting the central government's authority over the country, and of reducing cocaine exports to the United States. However, the increased focus on Colombia reinvigorated coca production in Bolivia and even more so in Peru. Using data gathered by UNODC (2014), Figure 9.2 demonstrates the dramatic declines in Colombia, with corresponding increases in the other two coca-producing countries.

While Figure 9.2 again illustrates the balloon effect and the weakest-link nature of drug enforcement, the chart fails to reflect other key changes by drug producers and suppliers in response to Plan Colombia. For example, coca cultivation has moved farther away from typically farmed areas, thereby increasing deforestation (Dávalos, Bejarano, and Correa, 2009). Additionally, coca growers have increased their yield by using more productive plants and have reduced the efficacy of aerial spraying by using smaller, disconnected plots of land, and even by spraying their crops with molasses, which reduces the defoliant's efficacy. As a result, the 58% decrease in coca cultivation in Colombia

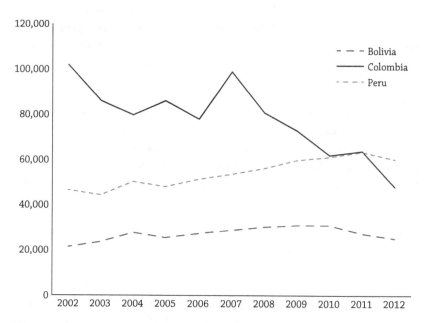

Figure 9.2
Coca bush cultivation (in hectares) in Andean countries

only resulted in a 15% decrease in cocaine production through 2009 (Jenner, 2014, p. 78). Overall, Plan Colombia has successfully reduced coca cultivation, but thanks to strategic responses from coca producers and drug suppliers, it has only marginally reduced the global supply of cocaine. The most recent report by UNODC (2014, pp. x–xi) is more optimistic—it notes "declining usage" due to a "sustained shortage" in the North American cocaine market. Even such optimistic assessments must admit the bilateral effort to reduce cocaine trafficking between Colombia and the United States has come at considerable cost; a numerical simulation by Mejia and Restrepo (2008) finds that a tripling of the current U.S. expenditure toward Plan Colombia would reduce cocaine supply only 17%, and the associated cost for every kilogram of cocaine diverted from U.S. consumers is $15,405. Furthermore, to the extent it has been successful, Plan Colombia has merely displaced cocaine consumption—cocaine suppliers are rapidly establishing new markets in Brazil, as well as in parts of Africa and Asia, and global consumption does not reflect the decline apparent in the United States (UNODC, 2014). Bilateral cooperation on drug enforcement between Colombia and the United States has primarily driven strategic responses from producers that undermine enforcement efforts and supply new markets with their illicit product.

A similar story emerges with respect to heroin production, which has been concentrated historically in the poppy-growing "Golden Triangle" of Burma (Myanmar), Thailand, and Laos. Recently, Afghanistan has emerged as the dominant producer, with more than two-thirds of global supply. In 2013, Afghan poppy production increased for the third consecutive year, and reached 209,000 hectares (UNODC, 2014). This increased cultivation is far more than the legal market in opioids can use and it is almost entirely devoted to heroin production (Glaze, 2007).[3] Individual countries' law enforcement agencies have responded by increasing seizures of the drug, but even as they have succeeded in reducing use of the "northern route" from Afghanistan to European countries through Russia and the Balkans, new routes have emerged through the Middle East and North Africa (UNODC, 2014).

Drug interdiction, even when successful, remains only partially effective at reducing drug consumption. In most cases it simply reroutes the existing supply, and if this is true for coca, which can only be grown in a limited geographic area, then controlling the supply of more widely cultivated plants like cannabis is even more difficult. Reducing supply at the source is even more difficult than interdiction, as is reducing consumption. Eliminating consumption may be impossible in rich, democratic countries where concerns

3. Glaze (2007) estimated that the 2006 Afghan poppy crop would provide five years of the legal supply of morphine, but Babor et al. (2010, Chapter 13) noted that developing country markets in painkillers are often underserved and could handle greater supply.

for human rights and individual liberties make law enforcement tactics more costly. Even the most successful prohibition campaigns in such countries have at best diverted markets elsewhere.

MONEY LAUNDERING

Efforts to reduce drug trafficking lead inevitably to the question of money laundering. Criminals of all stripes face difficulties in trying to reintegrate their illegal revenue into the formal financial system. Money laundering is the process of disassociating money from its illegal origins and, as such, is a necessary complement to any profitable criminal activity. Addressing money laundering is therefore a high priority for law enforcement, because efforts to thwart it can potentially reduce the profitability of multiple criminal activities simultaneously.

Money laundering typically can be broken down into three phases. Illegal proceeds must first be placed in a position for reintegration with the formal economy, after which it must be layered through financial institutions and/or jurisdictions in order to disguise its origins. Lastly, the money must be completely reintegrated into the legal economy (Reuter and Truman, 2004, p. 3). Money laundering can be done by the same criminal networks that earn the money, but the laundering can also be outsourced to financial institutions or other "gatekeepers" to the financial system such as accountants or attorneys. Although laundered money need not cross borders, layering funds through many countries may make it more difficult to trace, and so the expansion of trade and finance via globalization has created both new opportunities and new demand for cross-border money laundering as criminal enterprises tap more foreign markets.

Some of the most common laundering methods include cash smuggling, gambling, insurance policies, and buying and selling securities (Reuter and Truman, 2004, pp. 27–32). Even countries with airtight financial penalties against illegal financial transactions can still be exposed to money laundering via trade. For example, a Mexican drug gang can buy products in the United States and export them to Mexico at a loss. The goods can then be resold in Mexico for their full cost, allowing revenues from drug sales to be transferred as trade profits on legal goods.[4]

Although countries understand many of the methods used to launder money, aggregate estimates of laundering vary widely, and even high-level committees of money-laundering experts who were charged with developing estimates have been unsuccessful at agreeing on the scope of the problem

4. For evidence that such practices are increasingly common as anti-money laundering (AML) policies strengthen, see *The Economist* (2014c).

(Reuter and Truman, 2004, pp. 11–23). In the late 1990s, the International Monetary Fund (IMF) publicly claimed a money-laundering figure from 2% to 5% of global GDP, a large figure for certain, but notable for its wide range (Wechsler, 2001, p. 45). In addition to this uncertainty over the scope of the problem, money laundering poses some unique difficulties for law enforcement. While drug trafficking is associated with increased crime and violence and therefore has direct victims, money laundering is often called a "victimless crime" because no individuals suffer directly from the use of laundering. High volumes of illegal money entering the legal economy can certainly have impacts, such as exchange rate volatility, but those effects are less easily attributed to their cause than are the consequences of drug violence. Money laundering is also the process used by tax evaders and terrorist groups, and law enforcement efforts may therefore encounter social constraints where the same activities are done with different motivations. For example, tax evasion in some countries has long been a national pastime; efforts to enforce money laundering laws may encounter resistance from citizens who want to maintain loose enforcement of tax laws (Unger, 2007). To the extent that efforts to thwart money laundering increase transaction costs on financial institutions or infringe on the privacy of individuals, those affected may oppose strong enforcement (Borlini, 2014).

Efforts to criminalize money laundering have increased dramatically over the last three decades, and have been advocated most forcefully by the United States, France, and other G-7 economies, whose desire to fight money laundering can originate from different motivations. France's primary concern has been tax evasion. For the United States, attention to money laundering followed naturally from its War on Drugs. In 1986, the United States became the first country to criminalize money laundering, which was identified by its association with certain predicate crimes (illegal activities that generate the money to be laundered). The list of predicate crimes has since grown to exceed 150, and can be broadly grouped into drug trafficking, blue-collar crimes, white-collar crimes, bribery and corruption, and, since the USA PATRIOT Act, terrorism (Reuter and Truman, 2004).

To prevent money laundering, U.S. law requires much action by its financial institutions, including careful parsing of applicants for new accounts ("customer due diligence"), and reporting requirements. Prior to 1996, banks had to report any transaction higher than $10,000, and this rule-based system induced the practice of smurfing, in which money launderers switched to more transactions in smaller denominations. In the mid-2000s, banks had to file suspicious activity reports on transactions greater than $5,000 to the Department of Treasury's financial intelligence unit, FINCEN. Additionally, any cash transaction of more than $10,000 had to be reported to the IRS. After 1996 suspicious activity reports became discretionary, which has in turn led to a change in the behavior of banks, whose employees now file many more reports than they need to in order to protect themselves legally from underreporting penalties. This response has been called "crying wolf" (Unger, 2011). In addition to these two reports, the U.S. Customs Agency collected a third type of report, on the international transportation of currency or other monetary instruments, but these are usually filed by individuals (Reuter and Truman, 2004, pp. 54–55). Regulators monitor financial institutions' compliance with these reporting requirements, and those that fail are subject to monetary penalties. A rough estimate of annual U.S. spending (both government and private firms) on the fight against money laundering exceeded $7 billion over a decade ago and has clearly risen since (Reuter and Truman, 2004, p. 5).

Anti-money laundering (henceforth, AML) became an important policy priority for the United States in the late 1980s and early 1990s. Both the United States and France pushed the G-7 to create a new intergovernmental organization, the Financial Action Task Force (FATF), at the Paris summit in 1989. According to Reuter and Truman (2004, p. 81), G-7 countries charged the new organization with reducing "the financial power of drug traffickers and other organized crime groups." However, the FATF had a small staff, housed at the headquarters of the OECD in Paris, and possessed few tools to accomplish its goals. FATF gained more influence at the end of the Clinton administration, when it demonstrated its capabilities for "naming and shaming" countries that it viewed as having inadequate AML protections. Thanks to the small number of member states, just the G-7 countries, and the homogeneity of their preferences to fight money laundering, the FATF became an ideal focal point for establishing high-quality AML standards that would help reduce money laundering across their borders (Wechsler, 2001; Drezner, 2007). At first, cooperation via the FATF had clear club good properties, with member countries agreeing to abide by higher standards for pursuing money launderers (Drezner, 2007). However, the club approach was ultimately undermined by the ability of other countries to shelter money launderers.

Even as G-7 countries expanded AML efforts, globalization was multiplying the possibilities to launder money. Throughout the 1990s, new offshore financial centers (OFCs) emerged to serve the financial needs of nonresidents by offering low tax rates, strict banking secrecy, and close proximity to more regulated markets (Sharman, 2008). Although countries like Switzerland had long offered such services, the 1990s can be differentiated by the sheer number of small island countries that established identities as OFCs in the 1990s. These include Nauru and Vanuatu in the South Pacific, Dominica and Grenada in the Caribbean, the Seychelles in the Indian Ocean, and Bahrain in the Persian Gulf. As Wechsler (2001, p. 44) notes, this "new breed of underregulated financial centers moved from the fringes of the international banking system to full integration into the global economy." As a result, the

G-7 realized that reducing money laundering in their own economies was not enough—as long as foreign jurisdictions offered financial services with few questions asked, AML laws in Western countries became less effective. The G-7 countries therefore expanded their use of the FATF, and developed new mechanisms for expanding its reach.

The Seychelles passed new legislation in 1995 that explicitly offered immunity from prosecution in return for a $10 million investment. FATF reported the new law to its members, and asked them to instruct financial institutions to pay special attention to any transactions with entities in the Seychelles. When G-7 banks and other financial institutions quickly reduced their willingness to deal with Seychelles-based entities, the country repealed its legislation in 2000. This initial demonstration of successful influence emboldened the FATF to expand AML activities, which took the form of a "blacklist" of countries whose laws and/or law enforcement systems made them especially vulnerable to money laundering.

The first FATF blacklist became public in June 2000 and listed 15 countries, including the Bahamas, Israel, and Panama. The blacklist included no formal sanctions, just the same recommendation the FATF had made in the case of the Seychelles—that FATF member states should instruct banks based in their territories to pay special attention to financial transactions that involved the blacklisted economies (Sharman, 2008). Even so, almost half of the blacklisted countries (including the three mentioned above) increased their attention to money laundering. Wechsler (2001, pp. 52–53) claims that within two years, almost half of the blacklisted countries had "completely reinvented" their AML policies. In some cases, this meant quick adoption of boilerplate AML policies—for example, Vanuatu's initial legislative draft was a verbatim copy of UN model laws (Sharman, 2008, p. 642).

OFCs were not the only targets for the FATF. The organization actually suspended Austria from membership in February 2000, and Turkey was frequently targeted for not having strict enough AML policies. In November 2002, the FATF added another eight countries to its blacklist. Interestingly, the FATF rarely had to resort to additional enforcement mechanisms—blacklisting was usually enough because most targeted jurisdictions feared exclusion from the international financial system enough that they were willing to create AML systems (Hülsse, 2008). Once created, domestic financial intelligence units became part of transnational AML networks, which served to reinforce international standards and harmonize policies by educating and socializing government employees charged with enforcing AML policies (Sharman, 2011).

By October 2006, the FATF blacklist had served its initial purpose and had provoked considerable reaction. Myanmar was the last country removed, and the blacklist was shuttered. Although the FATF identified Iran in October 2007 and both Uzbekistan and Cyprus in February 2008 as posing particular AML weaknesses, it abandoned the blacklist approach (Hülsse, 2008). In its place, the FATF now regularly identifies countries that are either high risk for money laundering or that have shown a political commitment to AML policies but demonstrate deficiencies in implementing those policies (Roberge, 2011). These new "graylists" are based on assessments by peer states, and only Iran and North Korea currently receive calls by the FATF for "countermeasures." Other countries are listed as not making enough progress in "addressing deficiencies," including Algeria, Ecuador, Indonesia, and Myanmar (FATF, 2014). In particular, several of these states are noted for failing to criminalize terrorist financing, a focus of the FATF since 9/11.[5] Other countries have passed FATF muster and are now viewed as adequately addressing the use of their economies for money laundering. Recent graduates from the graylist include Kenya, Kyrgyzstan, Mongolia, Nepal, and Tanzania (FATF, 2014).

Despite its limited membership, the FATF has clearly managed to raise the profile of AML and to convince many nonmember states to adopt AML policies. The FATF has gained added influence in recent years as the IMF and World Bank became more willing to add AML to the list of policies they recommend to client states.[6] The FATF plays a key role in setting AML standards with its "40 + 9" recommendations, and it has used naming and shaming methods to great effectiveness. This is striking given its limited toolkit and absence of formal power, but it really has no choice, since the existence of even one OFC undermines greatly the entire effort to thwart money laundering. With AML policies in place in almost all countries of the world, the FATF has come closer to achieving the initial G-7 goals and to shoring up the weakest link. But has it reduced money laundering or at least made it more expensive? Has this sizeable AML effort achieved a cost-effective reduction in transnational crime?

The easiest answer revolves around the difficulty of measuring money laundering. Because the scope of money laundering is unknown both before and after the FATF effort, it is impossible to calculate the benefits of the FATF-led AML campaign. In contrast, the costs are more straightforward. We previously noted a figure of $7 billion per year in public and private costs of AML enforcement in the United States. This is obviously a large number, but even in small countries the cost of implementing AML regulations can be large. Sharman (2008, p. 643) estimates an annual cost of $10 million for

<hr>

5. Initially, the Bush administration was reluctant to continue the Clinton administration's AML practices; particularly the latter's focus on multilateral institutions as a lever for policy change in other countries. That initial hesitation, however, disappeared with the 9/11 terrorist attacks, after which the Bush administration wholeheartedly endorsed AML, but with the new goal of reducing terrorist financing. The fight against money laundering received new legislative authority from Congress, including the ability to prosecute foreign corruption in U.S. courts, and greater authority for American agencies to operate overseas (Reuter and Truman, 2004, p. 74).

6. On this point, see Reuter and Truman (2004) and Hülsse (2008).

Barbados and Mauritius, and $1.5 million annually for Vanuatu. In addition to these direct costs, leaders of developing countries who implement AML policies also lose the ability to use government finance for their preferred purposes, as government activities respond to international demands as opposed to chief executives or legislatures. Additionally, even relatively poor countries must shift valuable human capital into the bureaucracy for regulatory needs (Drezner, 2007, pp. 128–129). OFCs that implement AML policies also lose some of their financial sectors' competitive advantage relative to their rich-country peers.

The U.S. number includes the costs to financial institutions, which can be considerable. *The Economist* (2014d) reports that many international banks are retreating from jurisdictions where they have been asked to pay increased attention to transactions. Costs also accrue at the level of the individual customer, who faces higher time costs in establishing accounts and, possibly, fewer privacy protections. These costs are not measured in any of these estimates.

Assessments of the AML regime vary. More than a decade ago, Levi (2002) found that even rich-country AML policies have a limited effect on criminal activity. Reuter and Truman (2004, p. 67) argued that despite significant costs, the FATF-led system "will do little more than marginally inconvenience" money launderers. They reported that average laundering costs range from 4% to 8% of the aggregate amount to be laundered and that, similar to drug trafficking, enforcement efforts are subject to diminishing returns. Sharman (2011, p. 5) agreed that AML policies are of "dubious worth" and were not adopted on the basis of their own benefits and costs but due to fears of being locked out of the international financial system. As a result, he expected and found that developing country AML policies have even less success in thwarting money laundering than in more financially developed countries.

Given the victimless nature of money laundering, it is surprising that governments around the world have imposed such costs on the financial sector and on voters. This is especially true of small countries that are not key cogs in international financial networks; but such efforts demonstrate the extent to which the weakest-link nature of the money laundering has mobilized the G-7 states to exercise their power in the fight against money laundering. Some other countries that have shown their AML commitments have joined the organization, as have two regional organizations (the European Commission and the Gulf Cooperation Council). In 2012, the FATF's 34 member states extended its mandate for another eight years and seem committed to continuing the AML agenda. As a result, other scholars assess the FATF as broadly successful in spreading AML (Roberge, 2011), or a successful exercise in club standards enforcement (Drezner, 2007).

However, new research suggests that equating successful harmonization of AML laws is not the same as preventing money laundering. Findley,

Nielson, and Sharman (2013) overcame the lack of data on money launder-ing by attempting to create shell corporations that explicitly violate FATF requirements, which mandate that financial institutions must verify the identity of the person requesting incorporation. Across 182 different coun-tries, they found that slightly less than half of corporate service providers that respond to their query are willing to violate FATF rules. They concluded that there is a "substantial level of noncompliance" with standards aimed to prevent money laundering (p. 681). Despite a considerable push from the G-7 and FATF, money laundering continues—and due to its weakest-link proper-ties, eradicating it seems virtually unattainable.

CONCLUSION

Efforts to reduce transnational crime have been extensive but have ulti-mately met with only temporary successes. Drug trafficking and money laun-dering continue on a large scale, and even cooperation backed with the coer-cive tools of the great powers has not greatly reduced their impact. The logic of weakest-link games and our case studies suggest that efforts to fight transnational crime are bound to fail without a greater commitment on the part of all states to international prohibition.

For this to happen in the case of illicit drugs, many more countries would have to suffer the social ills associated with large-scale drug use. While the list of countries with such costs has increased, it is still largely confined to rich and middle-income countries. Low-income countries are mostly unin-volved in the drug trade, with the exception of those that supply necessary agricultural products, like coca and poppies. For poor countries that are in-volved in the drug trade, cultivation of illicit crops is often more lucrative than other options, thereby offering jobs and economic development. Pro-hibiting such opportunities can mean a difficult and unpopular choice for governments even when drug enforcement is compensated with greater trade concessions or more foreign aid. Supplying illicit drugs, particularly cocaine and heroin, is largely confined to a few poor countries, and if the social costs of drug use are more widespread, a concerted effort by wealthier countries to reduce supply simultaneously in all source countries might be more successful. For drugs that can be supplied from a greater number of countries, such as cannabis or many synthetic drugs, successful prohibition will require global cooperation, and even one state's refusal to join in that prohibition regime is enough to largely undermine it.

This same dynamic holds true for money laundering. The fight against money laundering has all the trappings of successful cooperation—the G-7 countries have used their ability to reduce access to international finance to coerce offshore financial centers to implement legislation against money laundering. The enforcement of those rules seems partial at best, however, and countries that can successfully market their offshore financial services still have much to gain by allowing those activities. As the FATF cracks down on some, the incentives for new players to enter the market only grows, and OFCs can appear virtually anywhere—even online, as the growing popularity of virtual currencies like Bitcoin suggests. The global nature of international finance means that AML requires cooperation among all states, making success extremely unlikely.

In both cases, then, countries that bear little cost from transnational problems have incentives to defect on international cooperation, thereby undermining enforcement efforts. Some economists and policy analysts advocate legalization as the best response to reducing the negative costs of illicit drugs (Becker, Murphy, and Grossman, 2006). Admittedly, legalization with taxation can generate resources to counter the negative social effects of drug use or other illegal activities, but if those costs are high, the amount of revenue needed from taxation may be enough to keep those markets underground. Furthermore, tax revenue in consumer countries is unlikely to be shared with producer countries, thereby creating an additional problem for transnational cooperation. The world's historical focus on prohibiting illicit drugs has made experimentation on drug policy more difficult, but several experiments with legalization are currently underway and could have enormous influence on future drug policies. To the extent that such efforts succeed, the importance of—and attention to—money laundering may also decline.

CHAPTER 10

Political Violence: Civil Wars and Terrorism

Political violence assumes myriad forms that include civil wars, interstate wars, terrorism, and genocide. Since 1970, the world has experienced these and other forms of political violence (for example, coups) that have cost thousands of lives each year. In 2010, there were nearly 20,000 people killed in battles (Stockholm International Peace Research Institute (SIPRI), 2012, p. 67). The Syrian civil war has claimed tens of thousands of lives in recent years. All forms of political violence may threaten peace and security by generating destabilizing influences that can transcend the borders of the host country. To address these transnational externalities, countries must, at times, consider regional or even global collective action.

A civil or intrastate war is an armed conflict between a sovereign government and organized domestic groups, the latter of which can engage government forces in combat (Sambanis, 2004, 2008). In Colombia, the Revolutionary Armed Forces of Colombia or Fuerzas Armada Revolucionaries de Colombia (FARC) is a paramilitary group numbering in the thousands. FARC controls territory and engages the Colombian military on occasion. Generally, a civil war must surpass some cumulative threshold of battle-related deaths before being recorded in datasets (Uppsala Conflict Data Program [UCDP], 2014). This threshold often requires cumulative deaths of 1,000, in which at least 25 battle-related deaths must occur annually for the war to be considered as ongoing. Interstate wars are conflicts involving two or more sovereign states. Unlike intrastate wars, no battle-related death threshold is imposed on such conflicts to be recorded in conflict datasets. A genocide involves actions by some entity to exterminate some well-defined group, based upon its race, religion, culture, or national identity.

Terrorism is the premeditated use or threat to use violence by a subnational group to gain a political or social objective through intimidation of a large audience beyond that of the immediate victim (Enders and Sandler,

2012). To be considered terrorism, the act must be politically motivated. Kidnappings or skyjackings for ransom with no political or social motive are extortion but not terrorism. Other acts of terrorism—bombings, assassinations, and armed attacks—must be intended to induce political change. By requiring the terrorist group to be subnational, we rule out state terror where a government terrorizes its own citizens to maintain control, as was the case of the Stalin or Saddam Hussein regimes. We do not, however, rule out state-sponsored terrorism where a government aids a terrorist group or its actions, as the Iranian government supported those who took hostages at the U.S. embassy in Tehran on November 4, 1979. Terrorists broaden their audience beyond their immediate victims by making their actions appear to be random, so that everyone feels anxiety. In contrast to a drive-by shooting on a freeway, terrorist acts are not random but well-planned and typically well-executed attacks where terrorists account for risks and associated costs, as well as possible gain. Terrorist groups may be small (for example, the Combatant Communist Cells in Belgium) or large (al-Qaida or Palestine Liberation Organization). These groups may possess diverse goals (for example, ending economic discrimination, protecting animal rights, promoting Marxist ideology, or ending a war) that do not necessarily involve the overthrow of the government.

The primary purpose of this chapter is to investigate collective action associated with civil wars and terrorism. We focus on these two forms of political violence because they are more prevalent than interstate wars or genocides in recent time. Moreover, civil wars and terrorism are anticipated to remain important in the decades to come. Although civil wars are localized to the conflict-ridden country or its immediate neighbors, these wars pose a concern for the global community, worthy of collective action in the form of peacekeeping, diplomacy, or military intervention. Civil wars disproportionately influence developing countries, where they limit development and the effectiveness of foreign assistance (Collier, 2007; Collier and Sambanis, 2002; Elbadawi and Ndung'u, 2000). Adverse economic consequences from these wars may disperse up to 800 kilometers from the conflict country's borders (Murdoch and Sandler, 2002, 2004). A peaceful state in the vicinity of multiple conflicts, as has been true for some states in Africa, may experience significant negative economic impacts from surrounding intrastate wars, thereby impeding its growth and development. These impacts may arise from refugee flows, increased military expenditures, severed resource flows, lost trade, negative health spillovers, and/or reduced foreign direct investment (FDI). There is also a risk that the conflict may spread to neighboring states as border skirmishes embroil a neighbor country in the conflict (Siverson and Starr, 1990; Starr and Most, 1983). In other instances, the rebel force may take safe haven in a neighboring country (Menkhaus, 2003), thereby tangentially involving the peaceful neighbor in the affairs of its at-war neighbor. This involvement may be less tangential when the government in the civil-war state conducts a cross-border raid on the rebel's safe-haven encampment (Salehyan, 2009). At times, the intrastate war may lead to terrorist attacks in a foreign capital to publicize the rebel's cause, which is known as "spillover terrorism."

With the formation of global and regional terrorist networks, terrorism also presents security worries for the world community. On occasion, terrorism may give rise to attacks with significant loss of life as was true of the four hijackings on September 11, 2001 (henceforth, 9/11); the Madrid commuter train bombings on March 11, 2004 (henceforth, 3/11); the seizure of the Beslan middle school on September 1, 2004; and the downing of Air India Flight 182 on June 23, 1985. The death tolls in these terrorist incidents were 2,871, 191, 329, and 385, respectively (Enders and Sandler, 2012). More recently, Boko Haram's kidnapping of almost 300 schoolgirls in northern Nigeria has made the world acutely aware of how even localized terrorism can have implications globally, as the United States sent advisers to Nigeria to help recover the girls.[1] There is the fear that future death tolls in chemical, biological, radiological, or nuclear attacks by terrorists will be higher (Institute of Medicine, 2002; Ivanova and Sandler, 2006, 2007; Levi, 2007). Such attacks could potentially kill tens of thousands. The first major chemical terrorist attack was Aum Shinrikyo's sarin attack on the Tokyo subway on the morning of March 20, 1995, which killed 12 and sickened 1,000 (Enders and Sandler, 2012). This attack could have easily killed thousands during the peak morning rush hour had the sarin not been diluted.

In the course of this chapter, we investigate the nature of civil wars and terrorism, while assessing the current and future threat that each poses for the global community. We commence by distinguishing between civil wars and terrorism. Next, we present a short overview of civil wars and identify some collective action issues associated with these wars. In so doing, we highlight the role and prospects for diplomacy and peacekeeping. We then turn to terrorism and address its nature, trends, and causes, before investigating counterterrorism and its effectiveness. After distinguishing between proactive and defensive measures to counter transnational terrorism, we indicate some collective action prognoses for these measures with the use of simple game theory. We conclude with an evaluation of the feasibility of various forms of transnational cooperation in the "War on Terror." Given that we are covering a lot of ground, we have to be rather selective in our discussion and analysis.

---

1. Boko Haram's political motive is to end Western education of Nigerian children. The group also seeks an independent state. Any ransoms that the group receives from its kidnappings are used to support the group's political aims.

CIVIL WARS VERSUS TERRORISM

Terrorism is at times a tactic employed by opposing sides in a civil war (Findley and Young, 2012). However terrorism need not be associated with a civil war and can often be employed in the absence of a civil war—that is, the European leftist terrorist groups (for example, Italian Red Brigades, Red Army Faction, 17 November, and Direct Action) in the late 1960s, the 1970s, and the 1980s sought political goals that did not result in an intrastate conflict. These groups were seeking some issue-specific goals or political change that did not resonate with a large segment of the population, so that widespread unrest never resulted. Some of these leftist terrorists wanted an anarchic state, which threatened most citizens' well-being and livelihood. Thus, the group's ability to attract only a small cadre is easy to fathom. By limiting its Draconian measures to the terrorists and not to the population at large, the government did not ignite a greater amount of violence (Rosendorff and Sandler, 2004). Moreover, civil wars do not necessarily imply terrorist attacks even though terrorism may precede, coincide with, or follow *some* civil wars (Findley and Young, 2012). A civil war is more frequently associated with a subnational opposition group that resorts to terrorism when it is weak and has its limits in confronting government forces directly (Sambanis, 2008). In these instances, the rebel group will set ambushes against a small number of government troops or use improvised explosive devices (IED) to manage the group's exposure.

We favor treating terrorism as a distinct form of political violence that differs along many dimensions from civil wars.[2] First, unlike civil wars, which require a threshold of casualties, terrorism can affect a single individual who is killed, injured, or threatened by a subnational group in its pursuit of a political motive. As such, terrorism is a much milder form of political violence than civil war even in a terrorism-plagued country. Second, one of the combatants in a civil war must be a sovereign state, which is not necessarily the case for terrorism. In fact, terrorists often attack unprotected private parties in order to create an atmosphere of fear so that citizens pressure their government to concede to terrorists' demands (Brandt and Sandler, 2010). In other instances, terrorism may involve internecine violence—e.g., the Abu Nidal Organization (ANO) terrorist campaign against Fatah—where governments were content to sit on the sideline and watch the adversaries butcher one another after their split. Third, rebel armies in civil wars are better equipped and organized than terrorist groups so that rebel forces pose a greater danger to society. Terrorists purposely avoid engagements with the country's military (Sambanis, 2008). Fourth, terrorist groups may survive much longer than rebel groups fighting civil wars. A few major terrorist groups, such as Euskadi ta Askatasuna (ETA)

2. This paragraph draws, in part, from the useful analysis of Sambanis (2004, 2008).

and the Palestine Liberation Organization (PLO), have been around for over 40 years (Blomberg, Engel, and Sawyer, 2010; Blomberg, Gaibulloev, and Sandler, 2011; Gaibulloev and Sandler, 2013, 2014). Civil wars usually end more quickly than long-term terrorist campaigns, which last for decades. Fifth, terrorism is typically supported by a smaller power base than insurgent rebels in a civil war. Sixth, civil wars are associated with rebel groups controlling territory, which often is not the case for terrorist groups. Seventh, by presenting a greater level of violence, civil wars generate greater economic ramifications than terrorism (Blomberg, Hess, and Orphanides, 2004; Gaibulloev and Sandler, 2008, 2009, 2011). Eighth, unlike terrorism, civil wars may create a refugee problem. Finally, civil wars give rise to more transnational externalities than terrorism.

ON CIVIL WARS

Table 10.1 indicates armed conflicts during 2001–2010 for Africa, the Americas, Asia and Oceania, Europe, and the Middle East, based on data from SIPRI (2012). Since 2001, the overwhelming majority of these conflicts have been intrastate wars, which include internal conflicts between the host government and one or more internal rebel groups with or without intervention from other states. If there is intervention from abroad, then it is termed an *internationalized* internal armed conflict (UCDP, 2014). During this recent sample period, interstate wars between two or more states only included wars between India and Pakistan (2001–2003), Iraq and the U.S.-led coalition (2003), and Djibouti and Eritrea (2008). On average, there were just over 33 wars per year, with 32.5 of them being intrastate wars, primarily in developing countries. Asia and Oceania, followed by Africa, had the greatest incidence of intrastate wars since 2001. This table supports our earlier statement that civil wars are far more prevalent than interstate wars in recent years. In Table 10.1 and later in Figure 10.1, intrastate wars require a cumulative threshold of 1,000 battle-related deaths, with at least 25 such deaths per year for the war to be considered ongoing.[3] No threshold is imposed by the data on interstate wars involving two or more states.

Figure 10.1 provides a longer-term view of intrastate and interstate wars based on UCDP (2014) data for 1970–2012.[4] Civil wars increased greatly in number from around 1975 until 1991, marking the end of the Cold War. During 1975–1991, many intrastate wars were supported by the two

3. See Sambanis (2008) for an interesting discussion of these thresholds.
4. Figure 10.1 excludes extrasystemic armed, or colonial, conflicts from intrastate wars. These extrasystemic conflicts involve battles between a sovereign state and a nonstate group over territory controlled by the state.

Table 10.1. Armed conflicts, 2001–2010

Region	2001	2002	2003	2004	2005	2006	2007	2008	2009	2010
Africa	15	15	10	10	7	10	12	13	12	9
The Americas	2	2	1	3	2	2	3	3	3	3
Asia and Oceania	14	12	15	14	16	15	14	15	15	12
Europe	2	1	1	2	2	1	2	2	1	1
Middle East	3	2	3	3	5	5	4	4	5	5
Total	36	32	30	32	32	33	35	37	36	30
Intrastate	35	31	28	32	32	33	35	36	36	30
Interstate[a]	1	1	2	0	0	0	0	1	0	0

[a] Interstate wars include those between India and Pakistan (2001–2003), Iraq and U.S.-led allies (2003), and Djibouti and Eritrea (2008).
Source: Stockholm International Peace Research Institute (2012, Table 2.7, pp. 66–79).

superpowers in an attempt to maintain or expand their sphere of influence using proxy adversaries. Civil wars since the end of 2001 are primarily fueled by ethnic differences (Denny and Walter, 2014). Intrastate wars fell in number between 2001 and 2004; thereafter, the number of these wars maintained a sawtooth pattern from 2005 on, similar to that between 1998 and 2000.

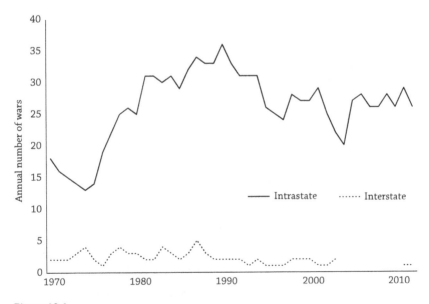

Figure 10.1
Annual number of intrastate and interstate wars

Interstate wars are somewhat less prevalent than in the late 1980s, but have been relatively few in number throughout the sample period. Intrastate wars far outnumber interstate wars during 1970–2012.

Causes of civil wars

In a recent article, Denny and Walter (2014) showed that ethnic-based civil wars outnumbered non-ethnic civil wars by two to one, so that two-thirds of all civil wars have been generated by ethnic grievances since 1945. Ethnicity is tied to culture through language, race, appearance, religion, or traditions. Non-ethnic conflict is not based on cultural, racial, or religious grounds. The U.S. Civil War, fought over slavery and states' rights, was not ethnic-based. Civil wars solely founded on territorial disagreement or autonomy are not ethnic-based (Toft, 2014). Additionally, civil wars solely motivated by ideological differences—Marxists versus capitalists—are not ethnic-based.[5] Wars between two religious sects (for example, the Shias and Sunnis) are ethnic-based. Denny and Walter (2014) argued that ethnic civil wars are especially difficult to extinguish owing to deep-seated grievances, greater mobilization, and greater sources of funding than non-ethnic civil wars. These grievances can stem from economic discrimination that the ethnic group in power visits on other ethnic groups not in power. At times, the group in power may be the minority—for example, Sunni rule under Saddam Hussein over a Shia majority in Iraq—which can make for extreme measures to maintain its grip on power. If a civil war later erupts, the ensuing violence can be particularly brutal to "rectify" past wrongs. According to Denny and Walter (2014), ethnic-based civil wars last a long time due to the three factors mentioned earlier.

In his empirical study of civil wars, Sambanis (2008) found a robust negative relationship between income per capita and the onset of civil wars regardless of casualty thresholds and other defining features of civil war. This result implies that countries with a poorer standard of living, as captured by their income per capita, are more inclined to experience the onset of a civil war. Similarly, Sambanis found that countries with high rates of income per capita growth were less inclined to experience a civil war.[6] Another empirical regularity concerned democracy—less democratic countries were more prone to civil

5. Non-ethnic civil wars may involve the ouster of a tyrant ruler, who has created sufficient economic grievances and hardships that citizens unite.
6. In a study of Africa, Collier and Hoeffler (2002) showed that low income per capita increased the likelihood of civil war, while high income per capita growth lowered this risk. These authors also found that the level of primary commodities had a nonmonotonic influence on the risk of civil war. As this dependency of primary commodities increased, the risk of civil war increased until a peak level of dependency, beyond which the risk of civil war decreased.

wars. However, income per capita was a more important determinant than democracy on the onset of civil wars. Surprisingly, there was no clear evidence that income inequality per se was a cause of civil wars. Collier and Hoeffler (2004) showed that greed could bolster the risk of civil war. Up to a threshold level of natural resources, countries with abundant natural resources were more at risk for civil wars. These resources may create rivalries for the lootable wealth that can finance government and/or rebel forces. Past civil conflicts may ignite new conflicts, particularly when the previous conflict was in the recent past (Collier and Hoeffler, 2004). A higher education level of the population lessens the possibility of civil war.

CONSEQUENCES OF CIVIL WARS

The most obvious consequence of civil wars is the human toll in lost lives and injuries. In particularly long-lived and intense conflicts, the toll may result in a population imbalance when a large number of young men perish or are disabled in conflict. In more recent times, civil wars are more indiscriminate in their carnage, resulting in the deaths of all ages, as the ongoing civil war in Syria sadly demonstrates. By destroying physical and human capital, an intrastate war can reduce income per capita and its growth at home. Such reductions are two essential factors that lengthen civil wars, so that negative consequences of these wars can become an engine that perpetrates the conflicts (Collier, Hoeffler, and Soderbom, 2004). Civil wars may also result in a flight of human capital as skilled and educated workers emigrate for better opportunities abroad in a safer environment. The same exodus has been noted for capital (Collier et al., 2003). Adverse economic impacts from civil wars may also arise from disruption to trade flows and day-to-day market activities. Given the high risk associated with conflict, civil wars will divert FDI, a crucial source of savings for developing countries, to countries without civil conflict. A decline in FDI may reduce investment and, hence, income growth, thus perpetrating the conflict. Civil wars also redirect government expenditure from growth-promoting social overhead capital to less productive defense spending. Migration of people from rebel-controlled and conflict-plagued areas adversely impact income and its growth through economic disruption and relocation costs. Pitched battles also destroy a country's infrastructure, which further hampers economic activity. Murdoch and Sandler (2002, 2004) found that these negative consequences in the war-torn country harm the economy of neighboring countries up to 500 miles away. Adverse economic influences in these neighboring countries would have further harmful economic backlash on the war-plagued country, stemming from a regional multiplier effect.

As crop production is often impacted by civil wars, famines may ensue. These famines are particularly devastating when war compromises the country's healthcare system; thus, it is not surprising that civil wars and diseases are correlated. Ghobarah, Huth, and Russett (2003) established that diseases kill long after the civil war is over. By compromising the conflict country's healthcare system and by weakening its population, civil wars can jeopardize world health as opportunistic diseases take advantage of a compromised host population living with an inadequate healthcare system. In addition, civil war countries have kept the world from achieving herd immunity in the case of polio, thereby having a negative global spillover.[7]

The duration of civil wars is influenced by the ratio of primary commodity exports to GDP, ethnic dominance, the growth of income per capita, the level of income per capita, and the frequency of past conflicts (Elbadawi and Sambanis, 2001, 2002; Fearon and Laitin, 2003). A country heavily dependent (say 30%) on primary commodity exports would on average experience a 12% shortening of its civil war if collective action could reduce these exports' prices by 10% (Collier, Hoeffler, and Soderbom, 2004; Collier, 2007). Efforts to curtail trade in, say, diamonds from a conflict-torn country, such as Sierra Leone, lowered diamond prices and shortened the conflict. Past battles can fuel future grievances so that intense civil wars may become particularly difficult to extinguish. Outside support also lengthens the war. This support may come in the form of remittances or foreign earnings that are sent home by the country's diaspora to support one of the warring sides. Foreign intervention can also extend the civil war owing to the influx of weapons and/or manpower.

CIVIL WAR AND INTERNATIONAL COLLECTIVE ACTION

Given civil wars' transnational externalities (for example, refugee flows, trade disruption, resource supply interruptions, economic spillovers, conflict contagion, lost investments, and negative health consequences), there are ample grounds for the international community to mount some type of collective action to conclude the conflict. When most of these externalities are confined to the region, the principle of subsidiarity (see Chapter 4) dictates that countries in the region should intervene to settle the conflict. This then raises some important considerations. Is there a sufficiently strong regional country to take a leadership role in a peacekeeping mission? There are some regions of Africa or elsewhere where such leadership is unavailable. If a regional country is to assume leadership in ending the conflict, then it is essential that this country is neutral or else its intervention may fuel the conflict. Leadership by Australia in East Timor worked, as did leadership by the United States in Haiti. In contrast, Nigeria-dominated Economic Community of West African States

7. Herd immunity for smallpox was achieved following a cease-fire in Sudan that allowed for vaccination (see Chapter 6).

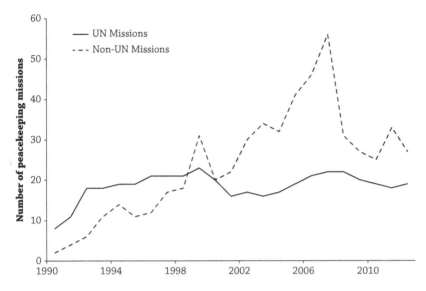

Figure 10.2
Number of peacekeeping missions, 1990–2012

(ECOWAS) intervention in Sierra Leone resulted in ECOWAS troops looting the country (Dorn, 1998). In the absence of neutral and capable regional power, the world must rely on the United Nations for peacekeeping or diplomacy.

Until the era of peacekeeping and peacemaking in the 1990s, the world community had turned to the United Nations to intervene in civil wars following a cease-fire; however, the large increase in civil wars over the last decades has stretched the UN's logistical and financial capabilities. As a consequence, NATO has taken over some important peacekeeping roles in Bosnia, Kosovo, Macedonia, Albania, Iraq, and Afghanistan (Gaibulloev, Sandler, and Shimizu, 2009; Gaibulloev et al., 2015). The Commonwealth of Independent States (CIS), Economic Community of West African States Monitoring (ECOMOG), ECOWAS, European Union Forces (EUFOR), and African Union (AU) have conducted non-UN-led peacekeeping operations in recent years. In Figure 10.2, we depict the number of UN and non-UN peacekeeping missions during 1990–2012 (Gaibulloev et al., 2015). Since 2000, non-UN missions outnumber UN peacekeeping missions. More important, the costs and manpower of these non-UN operations are far greater than those of UN operations during the last 12 years (Gaibulloev, Sandler, and Shimizu, 2009; Gaibulloev et al., 2015).

DIPLOMACY OR PEACEKEEPING

To end a civil conflict, the world community possesses limited options. If the two sides are willing to negotiate, the community can bring together the two sides and serve as an impartial mediator. This often occurs after the two sides have fought to a stalemate, where neither is gaining any ground so that the status quo is not attractive. The United Nations is the logical party to assume the mediator when the countries are ready to negotiate, but at times the mediation has been conducted by a state—for example, the American efforts in the Dayton peace agreement in 1995 ending the Bosnian war, or the Norwegian actions to broker an Israeli-Palestinian accord. At other times, a regional institution may try to facilitate a peace agreement to "privilege" the rest of the world with less conflict and more stability. When diplomacy is not an option, the world community may have to apply pressure through trade boycotts or other sanctions to get the sides to agree to diplomacy. As mentioned earlier, countries that boycott trade in looted natural resources can reduce their prices and limit the length of the conflict. Another possible avenue is to sever arms supplies to warring factions. This latter action faces collective action difficulties as a country or firm that profits in this arms trade may clandestinely or openly continue to sell weapons. Russian sales of weapons to the Assad government during the ongoing Syrian civil war is an example. As the global community acts in unison to end arms supplies, a supplier's profit opportunities rise and these enhanced gains motivate greater defection.

Arms embargoes are the quintessential weakest-link public good, where even one defecting country can undo the collective efforts of everyone else. This makes effective collective action difficult to achieve. The same type of weakest-link concern applies to trade boycotts; this is why targeted countries can survive such boycotts almost indefinitely when the world community is not completely united. Even when the community is fairly united, private firms can surreptitiously smuggle in goods, thereby weakening the boycott.

Once diplomacy finally works and the two sides agree to separate, then peacekeeping becomes an option. In its traditional form, peacekeeping involves the deployment of lightly armed military personnel to monitor or observe a ceasefire between hostile forces when the opposing sides agree to accept the monitors. Traditional peacekeepers serve as a buffer between hostile factions. If hostilities were to erupt, these lightly armed peacekeepers can do little to maintain the peace. In such scenarios, these peacekeepers retreated or took cover. In the post–Cold War era, peacekeeping assumed a more active role in promoting peace during some operations. At times, peacekeeping has assisted in the transition to democracy by training police, establishing legislative and other democratic institutions, and providing humanitarian relief (for example, Bosnia since 1995, Haiti since 1996, and East Timor since 2002). The fuller role is known as peacebuilding and, at times, involves country building, as in the cases of Iraq and Afghanistan. The most logistically demanding form of mission is peace enforcement where invited forces are deployed to separate warring sides in order to impose peace on at least one combatant. Obviously, in a peace-enforcement operation, peacekeepers need heavy weaponry and sufficient forces to neutralize or separate hostile forces. In recent years, these more complex peacebuilding and peace-enforcement operations have been assumed by non-UN missions. In contrast, UN missions have been more traditional in nature.

By eliminating negative spillovers to other countries stemming from a civil war, peacekeeping has been characterized as either a pure public good or a joint product activity.[8] If peacekeeping ends a conflict and brings peace and stability to a region, then this stability provides nonrival and nonexcludable benefits to all countries that are negatively affected by the conflict. Countries may also gain public benefits from the knowledge that people are not suffering in a conflict-torn country. These public benefits may also arise from reduced health risks emanating from the country receiving peacekeepers. For the joint product characterization, peacekeeping yields multiple benefits that vary in their degree of publicness. In particular, peacekeeping supplies purely public benefits for the world community and contributor-specific benefits. The latter benefits may include improved trade with the conflict-plagued country, enhanced FDI returns from a contributor's investments, and reduced conflict risks and refugee flows for the contributor. Smaller conflict risks and refugee flows are especially germane to countries within the same region as the conflict country. In the past, Bosnia and Kosovo posed these risks to nearby NATO allies (Gompert and Larrabee, 1997), while Haiti presented refugee concerns to the United States. With the current Syrian civil war, conflict spillovers and refugees are issues for Lebanon, Jordan, and other nearby countries. If Ukraine erupts into civil war, then parts of Eastern and Western Europe will be at risk.

Based on our analysis in Chapter 3, joint product activities have a more favorable collective action prognosis than pure public goods when the share of contributor-specific benefits is large. Thus, in the case of peacekeeping, countries are more willing to be peacekeepers, particularly for non-UN-led peacekeeping operations, when these peacekeeping countries gain substantial country-specific benefits.

Recent analyses have distinguished between UN and non-UN peacekeeping operations regarding public benefits (Bove and Elia, 2011; Gaibulloev, Sandler, and Shimizu, 2009). Not surprisingly, UN-led peacekeeping has been concentrated in Africa and Asia, where the share of public benefits tend to be high.[9] Since the ratification of UN General Assembly Resolution 3101 on December 11, 1973, the United Nations escaped the free-rider problem by assigning assessment shares to member states to finance UN peacekeeping. The bulk of the payment comes from the five permanent members of the UN Security Council (who decide peacekeeping missions) and rich industrial countries (for example, Japan, Germany, Canada, Italy, and Spain). In contrast, financial

8. This distinction is discussed in greater detail in Gaibulloev et al. (2015), Khanna and Sandler (1997), Khanna, Sandler, and Shimizu (1998, 1999), and Sandler and Hartley (1999, Chapter 4).
9. This is established in Gaibulloev, Sandler, and Shimizu (2009).

support for non-UN-led missions in Bosnia, Kosovo, Afghanistan, Iraq, and elsewhere is solely voluntary—there are no assessments. Research showed that these non-UN missions are supported by countries deriving trade, FDI, and other private gains from the restoration of peace (Gaibulloev, Sandler, and Shimizu, 2009; Gaibulloev et al., 2015). UN peacekeeping operations require assessment accounts owing to the higher share of public benefits, while non-UN peacekeeping operations do not require such accounts owing to the higher share of contributor-specific benefits. As previously seen in Figure 10.1, non-UN peacekeeping operations outnumber UN peacekeeping operations. The former are more complex and more expensive than UN missions.

UN and non-UN peacekeeping offer another interesting paired comparison. In recent years, UN peacekeepers are disproportionately drawn from India, Bangladesh, Pakistan, Ethiopia, Ghana, and Nigeria (United Nations, 2014a). This is because these countries can make a net gain from supplying their troops at a UN compensation rate of $1,028 per month for each peacekeeper. Troops from countries with volunteer UN forces are many times less expensive than those from rich countries (Shimizu and Sandler, 2002); hence, in recent years these rich countries have not supplied many troops for UN peacekeeping operations that they have minor immediate interests in. Since the end of the Cold War, the international community has addressed its collective action concerns associated with peacekeeping through a separation of mission types.

TERRORISM: DOMESTIC VERSUS TRANSNATIONAL TERRORISM

We now turn to the study of terrorism, which was earlier defined as premeditated violence by a subnational entity to induce political change through intimidation of a targeted audience beyond the immediate victim. Terrorism comes in two varieties—domestic and transnational—that have vastly different collective action implications for the world community. Domestic terrorism is homegrown and home-directed with consequences for only the host or venue country, its institutions, people, property, and policies. In a domestic terrorist incident, the perpetrators and targets (victims) are from the venue country. Through its victims, targets, institutions, supporters, or terrorists, transnational terrorism involves more than a single country. If a terrorist attack begins in one country but terminates in another, then it is transnational terrorism, which would be the case of a letter bomb mailed from France to Italy for political purposes, or a printer cartridge bomb shipped from Yemen to the United States to extract political concessions. The toppling of the World Trade Center towers was transnational because victims hailed from many different countries, the mission was planned abroad, and the perpetrators were foreigners. An incident may also be transnational if its implications or demands transcend the host nation's borders. The kidnappings of foreigners following the Abu Ghraib prisoner abuse revelations in April 2004 constitute transnational terrorist incidents. In contrast, the Beslan middle school barricade and hostage seizure on September 1, 2004 by Chechen separatists was domestic terrorism, as was the bombing of the Alfred P. Murrah Federal Building in Oklahoma City on April 19, 1995. Transnational terrorist incidents represent transboundary externalities because actions of the terrorists or authorities in one country may result in uncompensated costs or benefits on the interests of another country. The so-called War on Terror is intended to assuage some of these transboundary externalities, but may create new ones if its conduct causes new grievances (Rosendorff and Sandler, 2004).

Terrorists apply various modes of attack, including bombings, kidnappings, skyjackings, nonaerial hijackings (of buses, trains, and ships), barricade and hostage taking, assassinations, armed attacks, and suicide missions. These and other modes of attacks are directed at four primary targets: officials, military targets, business targets, and private parties. Bombings are terrorists' preferred mode of attack, comprising just over half of all terrorist attacks.[10] Figure 10.3 displays annual totals of all transnational terrorist attacks for 1968–2012 based on *International Terrorism: Attributes of Terrorist Events* (ITERATE), which was developed by Mickolus et al. (2013). Transnational terrorist incidents grew more common from 1968 to 1974 and then peaked in the early 1990s. Since 1994, these terrorist attacks have become less frequent. The 1980s was the era of state-sponsored terrorism, where some states, such as Iran and Syria, clandestinely supported terrorist groups and some of their attacks (Hoffman, 2006). Annual bombings are depicted by the dashed line in Figure 10.3 and constitute about half of all attacks. The shape of the bombing series generally mimics that of the total attack series, which is understandable since bombings are the most common method of terrorist attack. Also, notice how both series display cycles with peaks and troughs.

Figure 10.4 displays the annual number of domestic terrorist incidents based on the Global Terrorism Database (GTD), compiled by the National Consortium for the Study of Terrorism and Responses to Terrorism (START) (2014) for 1970–2012. We again distinguish bombings with a dashed line. To discern domestic terrorist incidents, we used a division of GTD terrorist incidents into domestic, transnational, and unknown event types, engineered by Enders, Sandler, and Gaibulloev (2011). For Figures 10.4 and 10.5, we rely on these authors' identification of domestic terrorist events.[11] There are a few things to highlight about domestic terrorism, as displayed in Figure 10.4. First, like transnational terrorism, the amount of domestic terrorism rose from 1973

10. Bombings include explosive bombings, letter bombs, missiles, mortars, rocket-propelled grenades, incendiary bombings, and car bombings.
11. GTD recorded both domestic and transnational terrorist incidents, but until 2014 did not distinguish the two types of incidents. Enders, Sandler, and Gaibulloev's division is more complete than that of GTD.

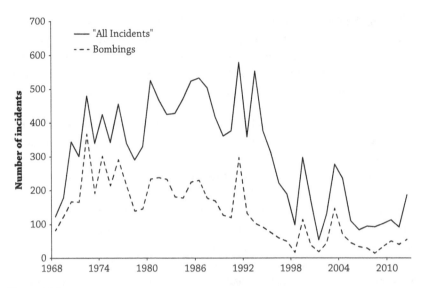

Figure 10.3
Number of transnational terrorist incidents (ITERATE), 1968–2012

to 1992. Second, the left-hand scale on the vertical axis shows that domestic terrorist events far outnumber transnational terrorist events. For every transnational terrorist incident, there are six to eight domestic terrorist incidents. Third, since 2007, domestic terrorist incidents are on the rise in number. The downturn in 1993 is an anomaly, caused because GTD data for 1993 fell off a

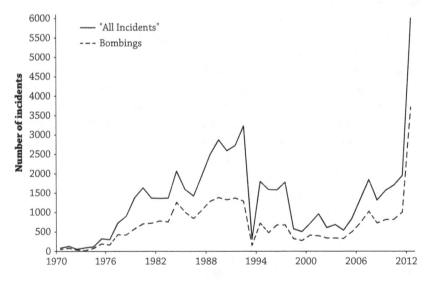

Figure 10.4
Number of domestic terrorist incidents (GTD), 1968–2012

truck in transit between offices (START, 2014). The peak number of incidents in 2012 results, in part, from START changing its coding convention.

Next, we turn to the changing carnage of these two types of terrorism over time. In Figure 10.5, we display the proportion of transnational and domestic incidents that resulted in casualties with one or more people killed or injured. Figure 10.5 uses ITERATE data for transnational terrorist attacks and GTD data for domestic terrorist attacks. We see that the proportion of transnational terrorist incidents ending in casualties generally rose since 1974. This is particularly true after 1999. In recent years, over half of transnational terrorist incidents involved casualties. This casualty trend is due to the changing nature of terrorism. Up until 1993 or so, leftist terrorist groups were the dominant influence (Rapoport, 2004; Enders, Hoover, and Sandler, 2015). Leftist terrorists are more interested in publicity, while religious fundamentalist terrorists are more interested in carnage (Hoffman, 2006). Leftist terrorist groups, such as the Italian Red Brigades, ETA, and Direct Action, did not want to kill indiscriminately since they wanted to maintain a constituency. These groups engaged in assassinations and highly directed bombings. In contrast, religious fundamentalist terrorists, such as Hamas, Jemaah Islamiyah, and al-Qaida, viewed unbelievers as a target to be annihilated (Enders and Sandler, 2012; Hoffman, 2006). Unlike leftist terrorist groups, religious fundamentalist terrorist groups employed suicide bombings, which kill and maim indiscriminately. Each suicide bombing kills, on average, 12 times as many people as a conventional terrorist incident (Pape, 2003). In Figure 10.5, the proportion of domestic incidents with casualties outnumbers that for transnational

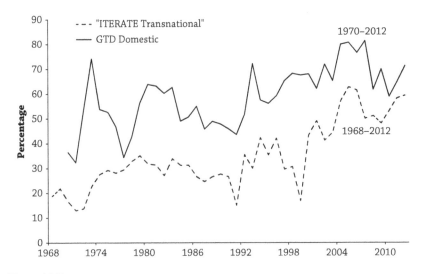

Figure 10.5
Proportion of transnational and domestic terrorist events with casualties

terrorist incidents throughout the entire sample period (Gaibulloev, Sandler, and Santifort, 2012). Given their larger numbers and their greater carnage proportion, domestic terrorist incidents pose a larger threat for the global community; yet, the War on Terror is only aimed at transnational terrorism. This is quite ironic since Blomberg, Gaibulloev, and Sandler (2011) showed that domestic terrorist groups resort to transnational terrorism over time when these groups make no headway with their demands (also see Enders, Sandler, and Gaibulloev, 2011).

The rising carnage of religious fundamentalist terrorists is reflected in Figure 10.6, where the left-hand axis measures the annual number of transnational terrorist incidents for 1968–2012 and the right-hand axis indicates the number of casualties (deaths or injuries) per incident. The solid line denotes the number of incidents, while the dashed line indicates the average number of casualties per incident in a given year. Since 1992, the carnage per transnational terrorist incident has risen, while the number of these incidents has fallen. This is consistent with religious fundamentalist terrorists gaining dominance and going for more casualties. The largest increase in casualties per attack came after 1999. This was after Osama bin Laden issued a *fatwa* against the United States in 1998. The rise in casualties is due, in part, to the greater use of suicide terrorism, where the perpetrator sacrifices his or her life in committing the act.

In Figures 10.3 through 10.6, the plots of terrorism indicate the presence of cycles; that is, transnational and domestic terrorism do not rise or fall in a linear fashion. In fact, research showed that each type of terrorist attack has

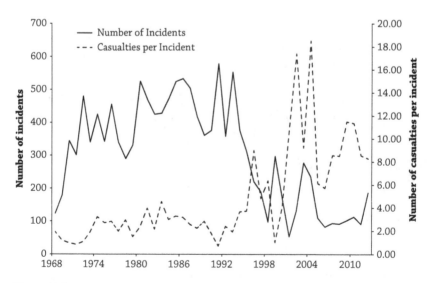

Figure 10.6
Number of transnational terrorist incidents and number of casualties per incident, 1968–2012

its own unique cycle. Logistically complex incidents display long cycles, while logistically simple events display short cycles (Enders and Sandler, 2012, pp. 77–81). The length of cycles is determined, in part, by the amount of time that it takes for the authorities to devise effective countermeasures, followed by the time that it takes for the terrorists to circumvent these countermeasures. The authorities required time to develop and deploy metal detectors to inhibit hijackings, while terrorists subsequently needed time to bypass these detectors. Plastic guns and bottles filled with flammable liquids circumvented metal detectors. For overall terrorism, peaks in attacks may stem from common grievances being expressed by various terrorist groups worldwide. This clumping of events may be bolstered by a demonstration phenomenon, where terrorist attacks in one part of the world induce terrorists elsewhere to follow suit.[12] The eventual downturn in terrorism may ensue when terrorists must replenish their resources or when governments institute significant countermeasures to protect their citizens. The sharing of counterterrorism innovations by governments and the sharing of attack innovations by terrorists may also foster troughs and peaks in terrorism.

CAUSES OF TERRORISM

There is no single cause of terrorism. Terrorist groups fall into four primary categories: leftists, nationalists/separatists, religious fundamentalists, and right wing (Jones and Libicki, 2008). Leftist terrorist groups often espouse Marxist/Leninist doctrines and are anticapitalists. Some leftist groups champion a specific cause, such as promoting animal rights, ending their country's NATO membership, or concluding some war. At times, leftist groups are in favor of anarchy with no formal government. Nationalist/separatist terrorists want their own state and have been more successful than the other three ideologies (Jones and Libicki, 2008). Ethnic grievances and discrimination motivate some forms of nationalist/separatist terrorism. Religious fundamentalist groups want to impose their religious beliefs on others. Some Islamic terrorists, such as Jemaah Islamiyah, want a pan-Islamic state in Asia. Other fundamentalist groups want to remove U.S. troops from parts of the Middle East.

Terrorism empowers the weak. With few resources, a terrorist group may be taken seriously after a few well-planned attacks that grab headlines. Terrorist groups will come and go, but terrorism as a tactic of political violence is here to stay. The real fear is that terrorists will develop new forms of mass-casualty attacks along the lines of 9/11. This may involve chemical, biological, radiological, or nuclear (CBRN) terrorist attacks. On the morning of March

12. Gaibulloev, Sandler, and Sul (2013) showed that transnational terrorist incidents in Lebanon explained two-thirds of the pattern of such incidents worldwide.

20, 1995, Aum Shinrikyo engaged in a sarin gas attack on the Tokyo subway during rush hour; fortunately, there were relatively few deaths.

COUNTERTERRORISM AND TRANSFERENCE

An important concept is transference, which is a policy-induced change in behavior. In the case of terrorism, transference highlights how effective counterterrorism measures may have unintended harmful consequences. Enders and Sandler (1993) showed that metal detectors induced a huge decrease in skyjackings; however, the installation of these detectors in January 1973 also increased other forms of hostage taking and terrorism not prevented by these metal detectors. Thus, kidnappings and barricade and hostage-taking incidents increased greatly in number. In fact, the installation of metal detectors was associated with an increase in casualties as terrorists substituted out of skyjackings, which during the 1960s and 1970s rarely resulted in deaths, into other forms of terrorism which did result in deaths (Enders and Sandler, 2012, pp. 90–91). To fully evaluate metal detectors, a researcher must look for still other impacts that stem from the application of these barriers. Enders and Sandler (1993) found that metal detectors reduced threats and hoaxes involving air travel.[13] When metal detectors were later installed in embassies, attempted takeovers of and attacks against embassies decreased.

Thus, to evaluate defensive barriers and fortifications, policy makers must account for impacts (both good and bad) on other modes of attack, along with the future innovations by terrorists to circumvent these defensive measures. By affecting select modes of attack, defensive countermeasures create substitutions by the terrorists that may not improve things. Effective defensive measures must raise the costs of a large number of attack modes so that terrorists are forced to choose more benign attack modes. Offensive counterterrorism measures that reduce terrorists' assets or resources, which are known as proactive measures, decrease all forms of attack and do not result in substitutions or transference among attack modes.

Among offensive countermeasures, retaliatory raids have been used against a suspected state-sponsor or the terrorist groups. These raids are politically motivated *ephemeral* lashing out for the government to show its citizens that it punished the perpetrators or their supporters. Such raids are not like the long-lasting U.S.-led War on Terror that killed many top leaders in al-Qaida and its affiliate groups, thereby weakening their capabilities. On April 15, 1986, the United States launched a one-time retaliatory raid against Libya for

13. A threat is a promise of a future attack, such as a hijacking, while a hoax is a false claim of a past attack, such as a bomb on a plane in flight.

its involvement in the bombing of the La Belle discotheque in West Berlin on 5 April 1986, which killed a Turkish woman and two U.S. servicemen.[14] Enders and Sandler (1993) showed that the raid on Libya caused the number of terrorist attacks to jump sharply before falling back to these attacks' pre-intervention mean. The terrorists merely moved planned attacks into the present to voice their displeasure, which is a policy-induced intertemporal transference. This one-time action had no lasting effect.

Another study examined the impact of Israeli retaliatory raids that followed significant terrorist incidents (Brophy-Baermann and Conybeare, 1994). Investigated Israeli retaliations included the raid on PLO bases in Syria following the Black September massacre of Israeli athletes during the 1972 Olympic Games; the attack on Palestinian guerrilla bases in Lebanon following a March 1978 Haifa bus hijacking; and the bombing of Palestinian bases in Lebanon following a June 1982 assassination attempt against the Israeli ambassador in London. This study found that such raids only temporarily suppressed terrorism: within nine months, terrorism had returned to its old average. To have a lasting influence, proactive retaliatory actions must be sustained to curtail the terrorists' assets.

Transference among targets

Another interesting transference is associated with the terrorists' choice among the four kinds of targets: officials, military, business, and private parties. As shown in Figure 10.7 (based on ITERATE),[15] transnational terrorists rationally responded to security measures in their targeting decisions. As officials were afforded protection by the state, transnational terrorists increasingly attacked softer business targets in the 1970s. As businesses protected their assets, terrorists switched to attacking private parties, and in 1980 the number of attacks of this type surpassed the number of business attacks (Brandt and Sandler, 2010). By 1999, terrorist attacks against private parties even surpassed those directed at officials. Domestic terrorism showed an analogous but faster progression among target types, where attacks on private parties overtook those against officials by 1981, with an ever-growing gap thereafter (Gaibulloev, Sandler, and Santifort, 2012, p. 141). Another disturbing trend is that terrorists directed more of their attacks against people than against property after the early 1990s (Brandt and Sandler, 2010).

14. The bombing injured 230 people (Enders and Sandler, 2012, p. 164).
15. Figure 10.7 is an update of a graph in Sandler (2014), which is an open access article in the creative commons.

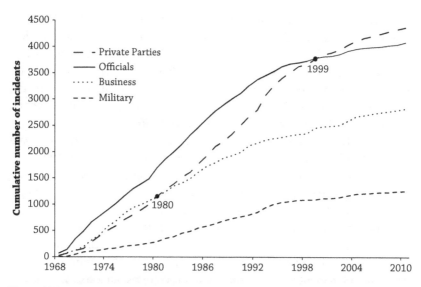

Figure 10.7
Cumulative number of transnational terrorist incidents by target type, 1968–2010

PROACTIVE AND DEFENSIVE COUNTERMEASURES AGAINST TRANSNATIONAL TERRORISM

We next investigate the strategic dilemmas confronting countries that employ proactive and/or defensive measures when facing a common transnational terrorist group. This situation would apply to countries targeted by al-Qaida, al-Qaida in the Arabian Peninsula (AQAP), Hezbollah, and other terrorist groups. In so doing, we highlight that both types of counterterrorism measures are plagued by collective action problems. Moreover, we can apply game-theoretic principles presented in earlier chapters to elucidate the problems. For simplicity, we consider the case of two targeted countries, but our analysis can be extended to more countries.

In matrix *a* of Figure 10.8, a canonical proactive game is displayed, in which each of two targeted countries—*A* and *B*—must decide whether to launch a proactive strike against a common terrorist threat. The strike is, of course, intended to reduce the threat by weakening the terrorist group or its sponsors. This reduction is a pure public good for both targeted countries. If a sole country applies such measures, then it confers a public benefit of 5 to itself and the other country at a cost of 7 to just itself. In the off-diagonal cells in matrix *a*, the country doing the proaction nets -2 $(=5-7)$, while the free rider receives 5. When neither country acts, each receives 0, whereas mutual action gives 10 $(=2 \times 5)$ in benefits at a cost of 7 for a net payoff of 3, as listed, for both countries. The dominant strategy is not to proact (that is, status quo), since $0 > -2$ and $5 > 3$. Mutual inaction results in a Nash equilibrium, whose payoffs of 0 are in boldface, for this Prisoners' Dilemma game.

For this paired comparison, we now turn to the defensive game counterpart where countries *A* and *B* must decide whether or not to harden targets to protect against the common terrorist threat. Suppose that increased defensive measures provide a private, country-specific gain of 7 to the defending country at a cost of 5 to *both* countries. For the defending country, the cost arises from the expense associated with enhanced defensive measures, which may involve greater border surveillance. For the other country, the cost stems from the increased likelihood of sustaining damages from an attack deflected to its soil if it does not increase its defense (Enders and Sandler, 2006). The terrorists will respond to an asymmetric change in defense and redirect their attack to the now relatively less-defended country. For simplicity, we assume that the two alternative costs are the same. The analysis would carry through if they are not identical.

Based on a country-specific gain of 7 and the public costs of 5 for each country's defensive measures, the payoffs in matrix *b* of Figure 10.8 can be computed as before. If, for example, only one country increases its defense, then it receives 2 $(=7-5)$, while the non-acting country incurs a loss of -5 by becoming the target of opportunity by not augmenting its defenses. The payoffs from mutual defense and mutual inaction are computed in the standard way.

		B	
		Status quo	Proactive
A	Status quo	**0, 0**	5, –2
	Proactive	–2, 5	3, 3

a. Two-target proactive game, $b_i = 5$, $c_i = 7$

		B	
		Defense	Status quo
A	Defense	**–3, –3**	2, –5
	Status quo	–5, 2	0, 0

b. Two-target defensive game, $b_i = 7$, $c_i = 5$

Figure 10.8
Two counterterrorism games

The defense game has a dominant strategy of mutual defense. Each country exercises its dominant strategy and augments its defense, thereby ending up at the Nash equilibrium where payoffs are less desirable than any of the other payoff combinations! This defensive scenario is again a Prisoners' Dilemma, analogous to an arms race, where countries spend more but do not necessarily become more secure if the terrorists are bent on attacking some country.

Even though in their most basic form the defensive and proactive games result in a Prisoners' Dilemma, there are essential collective action differences in these two problems. First, the Nash equilibrium for the defensive game requires mutual action, while the Nash equilibrium for the proactive game requires mutual inaction. Second, the matrix games are negative transposes of one another, in which the Nash payoffs are more damaging for the defensive game. Third, the proactive game is associated with public benefits and private costs; the defensive game is associated with public costs and private benefits (Sandler and Arce, 2003). Fourth, defense efforts are complementary, while proactive measures are substitutable. As such, increased defense by one country should augment these efforts by the other country, whereas proactive measures by one country should limit these efforts by the other country.

In matrix *a* of Figure 10.9, we allow each country to possess three strategies—defend, status quo (do nothing), and proact. For the boldfaced northwest 2 × 2

		B Defense	B Status quo	B Proactive
A	Defense	Nash **-3, -3**	2, -5	7, -7
A	Status quo	-5, 2	0, 0	5, -2
A	Proactive	-7, 7	-2, 5	3, 3

a. Defensive versus proactive – symmetric case

		B Defense	B Status quo	B Proactive
A	Defense	-3, -3	2, -5	7, -7
A	Status quo	-5, 2	0, 0	5, -2
A	Proactive	Nash **-2, 7**	3, 5	8, 3

b. Defensive versus proactive – asymmetric case

Figure 10.9
Two defensive-proactive games

defensive game within matrix a, the payoffs are identical to those of matrix b in Figure 10.8; for the boldfaced southeast 2×2 proactive game within matrix a, the payoffs are identical to those of matrix a of Figure 10.8. If country A defends and country B proacts, then A nets 7 $(=7-5+5)$, while B nets -7 $(=5-7-5)$. These payoffs are reversed in the bottom left-hand corner of matrix a in Figure 10.9. For both countries, defense is the dominant strategy with corresponding payoffs greater than those for the status quo and proactive strategies. As both countries choose their dominant strategy, mutual defense is the Nash equilibrium, whose cumulative payoff is less than that in the other eight cells (Arce and Sandler, 2005). Pursuit of a country's self-interest by playing its dominant strategy leads to the worst social outcome in terms of total payoffs. Ironically, the countries are led to the more undesirable of the two Nash equilibria in this embedded Prisoners' Dilemma situation. This example demonstrates that compound Prisoners' Dilemmas can worsen situations compared to single Prisoners' Dilemma scenarios. Our stylized game also shows that, when symmetric countries confront the same transnational terrorist group, there is a pronounced tendency to rely on defense and to eschew offense against the terrorists. This leads to an overly defended world where the terrorist threat is not alleviated through proactive measures.

Next, suppose that the two countries are asymmetric. In particular, country A is favored as a target by terrorists owing to its foreign policy decisions, so that its own proactive measures provide 10 in benefits at a cost of 7. The other benefits and costs remain as before, including that both countries gain 5 from B's proactive response. Country A receives an extra 5 from its own proactive measures owing to the political favor that its government wins with citizens by acting to punish the terrorists. This follows because the terrorist group poses a greater threat to country A than to country B, given the terrorists' targeting proclivity. We term A a "prime-target country" like the United States, whose interests sustain 40% of all annual transnational terrorist attacks (Enders and Sandler, 2012). The payoffs in matrix b of Figure 10.9 differ from those in matrix a by adding 5 to A's payoffs (on the left) in the bottom proactive row. Now, the proactive strategy is dominant for country A, while defense is still dominant for country B. As such, the Nash equilibrium is for the prime-target country to take proactive measures and the other country to defend. In an n-country scenario, there will be a group of prime-target countries going after the terrorists with most countries tightening up their defenses. This is reflective of which countries have taken an active role in the War on Terror. In the October 2001 invasion of Afghanistan, the United States and the United Kingdom sent the most troops and weapons to battle the Taliban and al-Qaida. These two countries lost the most people on 9/11.

Finally, we consider defensive and proactive responses for domestic terrorism. Countries plagued with domestic terrorism have better incentives to root out the terrorists since they cannot rely or free ride on other countries to lessen their domestic terrorism threat (Sandler, 2010b). This follows because domestic terrorism in, say, country *A* does not pose a threat to other countries. Moreover, the central government of *A* is charged with internalizing externalities within the country. Thus, we anticipate that the proper mix of defensive and proactive measures against the resident terrorists will be applied if the government has the capacity to do so. Thus, the Italian government destroyed the Italian Red Brigades; the French government annihilated Direct Action; and the Belgium government neutralized the Combatant Communist Cells. Many other examples exist.

TERRORISTS VERSUS THE GOVERNMENT

There is a fascinating collective action conundrum: why are terrorists relatively successful in forging networks to confront governments, while governments are generally less successful in creating these links except during times of dire threat (such as after 9/11). Terrorist groups have displayed a tendency to cooperate in loose networks since the onset of modern-day terrorism in 1968 (Enders and Sandler, 2012; Hoffman, 2006). Early terrorist networks cooperated on many levels, including training, intelligence, safe haven, financial support, logistical help, weapon acquisition, and the exchange of personnel (Alexander and Pluchinsky, 1992). In more recent years, the al-Qaida network operates in upward of 60 countries and stages its attacks worldwide. This network includes such groups as AQAP (Yemen), Abu Sayyaf (the Philippines), al-Jihad (Egypt), Harakat ul-Mujahidin (Pakistan), Islamic Movement (Uzbekistan), Jemaah Islamiyah (Southwest Asia), al-Qaida of Iraq, and al-Qaida (Afghanistan and Pakistan).

Why do governments have greater difficulty addressing their collective action concerns than their terrorist adversaries? There are at least three underlying reasons. First, governments' strength lulls them into a false sense of security, thereby inhibiting them from fully appreciating the need for coordinated action against a common terrorist threat. Moreover, such cooperation means sacrificing some autonomy over security matters, which governments are loath to do. By contrast, terrorist groups are weak in relation to their government adversaries, thereby leaving them little choice but to forge linkages with other terrorist groups with similar grievances against targeted governments. These linkages bolster the component groups' strength by pooling resources, know-how, and other assets. Terrorist groups put more emphasis on being effective than in maintaining their full autonomy. Second, governments do not agree on which groups are terrorists—for example, until recently, the EU did not view Hamas, despite its suicide bombing campaign, as a terrorist organization. Even though terrorist groups pursue alternative agendas and aims, these groups often share similar opponents—for example, the United States, the United Kingdom, and Israel—that offer a unity of purpose. Third, terrorists take a long-term view of their struggle and consider their interactions with other groups as continual; in contrast, governments are prone to a short-term view (limited by the election period) of the terrorist threat and do not necessarily consider their interaction with other governments as continual. As a consequence, terrorists view the underlying game as infinitely repeated while the governments do not, so that cooperation becomes a potential solution for terrorists but not for governments.

In Chapter 2, we saw that repeated Prisoners' Dilemmas with no endpoint had a good prognosis for cooperation, provided that the agents sufficiently valued the future. Cooperation among governments, or alternatively cooperation among terrorist groups, often involves overcoming Prisoners' Dilemmas. Terrorist leaders are tenured for life, unlike elected government leaders. Consequently, terrorist leaders will place more value on the future than their government counterparts, thereby enabling terrorist groups to cooperate with one another. Given these tenure differences, terrorist leaders place a high value on their reputation. Breaking a promise to another terrorist group will result in long-run redistribution by other groups in terms of withholding their cooperation. This loss of future cooperative gains may outweigh any short-run gain from reneging on a pact. In contrast, government leaders view that their actions do not promote or tarnish their successor's reputation; thus, current government leaders are more predisposed than terrorist leaders to break pacts. For example, Spanish Prime Minister Zapatero pulled the country's troops out of the U.S.-led coalition in Iraq following his victory in the 2004 national elections.

This cooperation asymmetry gives terrorists a clear advantage over their government adversaries. Uncoordinated responses on the part of governments mean that there is a weakest-link vulnerability for the terrorists to exploit. Moreover, terrorist groups' networks allow the linked organizations to assemble its most formidable attack team. In a globalized world, where a country's citizens can be targeted almost anywhere, the implication of terrorist cooperation coupled with government noncooperation is that the real level of protection of targets is quite small. The external cost imposed by the most inadequate prophylaxis is further exacerbated because the terrorist network dispatches its best-shot response in the form of its best placed and trained squad.

TRANSNATIONAL COOPERATION OF GOVERNMENTS: FURTHER CONSIDERATIONS

In regards to transnational terrorism, we begin with two additional failures with respect to government cooperation and then end with one successful example of such cooperation. Over the years, countries have ratified international conventions and resolutions to thwart transnational terrorist acts.

Early instances include the 1971 Montreal Convention on the Suppression of Unlawful Acts against the Safety of Civil Aviation (Sabotage) and the 1977 UN General Assembly Resolution 32/8 on the Safety of International Aviation.[16] Although well intended, neither of these treaties appeared to have had much effect on aviation's safety from terrorism.[17] Other significant UN antiterrorist treaties protected diplomats, forbidden hostage taking, outlawed skyjackings, and banned explosive bombings. These UN conventions and resolutions required countries to rely on their own judicial systems to implement and enforce the treaty. There is, however, no central enforcement agency that can force countries to comply; hence, signatories will do what is convenient. As such, a Prisoners' Dilemma game generally characterizes the pattern of payoffs, not unlike the proactive or defensive games.

When the average number of attacks is examined both before and after the adoption of these conventions and resolutions, there is *no* statistically significant reduction in the post-treaty number of attacks for the relevant outlawed mode of attack (Enders and Sandler, 2012, Chapter 4). Thus, we view these efforts as ineffective. A more effective treaty-making action involves neighboring states agreeing to control a common terrorism problem. This was true of an antihijacking treaty between the United States and Cuba in the 1980s, where Cuba arrested the hijacker when he landed on Cuban soil and sentenced him immediately to a 40-year prison term. After the first such arrest, these hijackings virtually ended (Enders, Sandler, and Cauley, 1990b).

Another potential area of transnational counterterrorism cooperation involves countries pledging never to concede to hostage takers' demands.[18] The logic of this pledge is that if a state adheres to this stated no-concession policy, then would-be hostage takers have little to gain. For the policy to work, the state must preserve its reputation and *never give in*, no matter the hostage(s). Virtually every country that confronts hostage taking has, at times, violated its pledge to never negotiate with or to concede to hostage takers. The Reagan administration's barter of arms for the release of Rev. Benjamin Weir, Rev. Lawrence Jenco, and David Jacobsen during 1985–86 was a violation of this pledge that resulted in the "Irangate" scandal (Mickolus, Sandler, and Murdock, 1989, vol. 2). Even Israel, the staunchest supporter of the no-concession policy, has made notable exceptions, such as in the case of the hijacking of TWA Flight 847 in June 1985. The terrorists attempt to abduct sufficiently valuable hostages so that the government reneges on its pledge. In the case of Israel, schoolchildren and soldiers served this purpose. For the government's pledge to deter hostage takers, it must be completely credible to the terrorists.

16. See Alexander, Browne, and Nanes (1979) for the text of the treaties on the suppression of terrorist acts.
17. The statistical analysis is presented in Enders, Sandler, and Cauley (1990a, 1990b).
18. This paragraph derives from the analysis found in Lapan and Sandler (1988).

Past concessions drastically erode this credibility. Moreover, the terrorists' gain from hostage taking must only derive from ransoms received. If the terrorists highly value publicity and/or martyrdom, then, even in the absence of concessions, hostage taking may be worthwhile.

There is a transnational externality that is associated with the effectiveness of the no-concession pledge. When one country caves in to hostage takers' demand, its inconsistent pledge reduces the credibility of all other countries' pledges. As such, this is an intertemporal externality since one country's action today imposes costs on other countries in the future. Brandt and Sandler (2009) showed that every successful kidnapping negotiation results in 2.6 new kidnappings. Terrorists may also abduct private individuals and businesspeople, thereby extorting ransoms from families and businesses to support their campaigns. Thus, governments must enact laws to punish families and businesses from paying ransoms. The United Nations is considering a convention that outlaws the paying of ransoms or concessions to terrorists. If this treaty is framed and ratified, there is the usual enforcement problem.

One bright spot of transnational cooperation has been efforts by the International Criminal Police Organization (INTERPOL) since 9/11 to tie countries' law enforcement agents together in the War on Terror.[19] INTERPOL supplies the assistance through its secure communication system (I-24/7), its extensive database, its investigative resources, its dissemination of best practices, its bioterrorism program, its workshops, and its weapons and explosive tracking system. Its most effective counterterrorism assistance comes from the use of I-24/7 to issue notices for the arrest of suspected terrorists. Moreover, member countries can install portals at ports of entry that permit passports and other documents to be scanned instantly and compared to a database on stolen and lost travel documents. The latter are frequently used by terrorists and fugitives to transit international borders. For example, INTERPOL-assisted efforts resulted in 74 terrorist-related arrests in 2006 and 104 such arrests in 2007 (Sandler, Arce, and Enders, 2011). Gardeazabal and Sandler (2015) showed that countries adopting *and using* INTERPOL surveillance system experienced a 30% reduction in transnational terrorism compared to similar countries not using the system. There is, however, a weakest-link problem that can only be addressed by more universal use of INTERPOL-supplied assets. This will come as countries see the benefits of the system and as terrorist attacks are deflected to the soil of nonusers.

19. The discussion in this paragraph depends on Sandler, Arce, and Sandler (2011) and Gardeazabal and Sandler (2015).

CONCLUDING REMARKS

This chapter is full of paired comparisons: for example, civil wars and terrorism, domestic and transnational terrorism, and defensive and proactive counterterrorism measures. Each of these comparisons presents its own challenges and collective action concerns. In the case of civil wars and terrorism, civil wars represent a much stronger form of violence with much greater economic consequences than terrorism (Gaibulloev and Sandler, 2008, 2009, 2011). Terrorism is a tactic that, at times, is applied with other tactics before, during, or after a civil war. Both forms of violence generate transnational externalities, requiring collective action at the regional or global level. For civil wars, these externalities involve capital flight, reduced trade, refugee flows, and conflict contagion; for transnational terrorism, these externalities concern terrorists' safe havens, money laundering, spillover terrorism, and concession-induced hostage incidents. Transnational terrorism implies greater collective action challenges than domestic terrorism. For the latter, a country's central government is properly incentivized to account for policy benefits and costs, so that a judicious mix of proactive and defensive measures is taken. Transnational terrorism requires cooperation among sovereign governments, which is often difficult to achieve. For transnational terrorism, both defensive and proactive counterterrorism policies are often associated with Prisoners' Dilemmas. Defensive measures generate private benefits and public costs, while proactive measures yield public benefits and private costs. The collective action failure of defensive measures can be more dire than that of proactive measures. Both civil wars and terrorism will pose collective action challenges now and into the future.

CHAPTER 11
Rogue and Failed States

Not all countries are created equal: some are tremendously wealthy, while others are desperately impoverished; some are governed with ease, while others are ungovernable; and some display altruism and benevolence, while others practice avarice and malevolence. At times, the global community must act collectively to address abject poverty, ungovernable states, and rogue behavior. Globalization ties the prospects of countries together, while exaggerating some differences among them. For example, by the late 1990s, the richest 20% of countries earned 86% of world gross domestic product (GDP), leaving the poorest 20% of countries to earn a mere 1% of GDP (United Nations Development Program, 1999). Milanovic (2009) showed that inequality of global GDP rose throughout the twentieth century, peaking in 2002. The recent reversal in this inequality is due, in large part, to rapid economic growth in Brazil, Russia, India, and China; nevertheless, the world remains a very unequal place.

Attitude and income differences among some states have beset the world with collective action problems stemming from rogue and failed states. Rogue states operate outside of accepted norms by invading other states, sponsoring transnational terrorism, using weapons of mass destruction (WMD), threatening other states, or proliferating WMD. In contrast, failed states possess dysfunctional central governance that results in economic, political, or security inadequacies, which greatly limit their integration in the global community. According to Piazza (2008, p. 470), "Failed and failing states are states that, due to severe challenges, cannot monopolize the use of force vis-à-vis other non-state actors in society and are therefore incapable of fully projecting power within their national boundaries." Helman and Ratner (1992), who coined the term "failed states," characterized them as incapable of functioning in the world community owing to legal, welfare, and security impairments. In addition, failed states have poor civil and political rights, along with limited rule of law, so that citizens do not necessarily observe and adhere to laws.

Rogue and failed states present different exigencies to the international community. Rogue states primarily pose a security challenge that a powerful state or coalition of states (for example, the NATO alliance) must counter in order to provide safety for all other countries. Curbing the risks stemming from a rogue country is analogous to the children's fable about a colony of imperiled mice needing a brave volunteer to bell a cat as an early-warning device. Any brave volunteer would assume tremendous risk for the safety of others, which is a pure public good if his efforts are successful. Obviously, each mouse is inclined to step aside to allow another to supply the public good. A particularly clever and agile mouse or one that seeks the admiration of the colony might take up the challenge. The admiration may be the selective incentive or joint product (see Chapter 3) that motivates the courageous act. By contrast, failed states present a host of challenges that may include disease outbreaks, refugee flows, transnational crime, drug trafficking, piracy, and others. Some failed states may be plagued by guerrilla warfare, civil wars, and corruption. Hence, assisting a failed state may supply a host of public goods that transcend security concerns. Such assistance may be akin to foreign aid (see Chapter 6). At times, this assistance may involve getting one or more failed states to meet minimally acceptable contributions to a weakest-link public good—for example, bolstering inoculation efforts to achieve herd immunity against an infectious disease.

The purpose of this chapter is to investigate collective action means for dealing with rogue and failed states at the transnational level. In so doing, we draw some essential contrasts and comparisons between these two concerns. For rogue states, best-shot and better-shot public goods come into play as one or more countries must annihilate the impending threat. Asymmetric capabilities and/or payoffs among threatened countries are especially efficacious in finding a country to take on the rogue state. The presence of selective incentives for the acting country is conducive to its willingness to confront the rogue. These incentives allow the acting country to perceive a net gain despite the grave risks that it must assume. Effective action against a rogue state is generally more difficult to achieve among more equally matched at-risk countries, because the logical best shooter or coalition organizer is harder to identify. Consider U.S.-led action against Afghanistan in 2001, or against the Islamic State of Iraq and Syria (ISIS) in 2014. The United States' overwhelming might and its losses prior to action—9/11 in the case of Afghanistan and the beheadings of two U.S. journalists in the case of ISIS—made it the logical country to confront the Taliban and ISIS. For failed states, a weakest-link public good is often present, where all countries must perform up to an acceptable standard. In weakest-link scenarios, failed states inhibit the good's provision—for instance, transnational terrorism or piracy cannot be greatly curtailed when failed states provide sanctuary to terrorist groups or pirate enterprises. Such weakest-link contingencies are particularly problematic when there are many failed states requiring shoring up and there is more than one capable country to assist. Rogue and failed states have cropped up in past chapters on global health (Chapter 6), global finance (Chapter 8), transnational crime (Chapter 9), and political violence (Chapter 10).

We first take up the study of rogue states, followed by an analysis of failed states. In the conclusion, we highlight differences and similarities between the two types of states.

ROGUE STATES: BEST-SHOT AND BETTER-SHOT PUBLIC GOODS

In its starkest form, mounting a sufficient offensive against a rogue state is a best-shot public good in the sense that the greatest effort fixes the overall level of damage to the adversary, and thereby determines the amelioration of the associated threat. This amelioration offers nonrival and nonexcludable benefits to all at-risk countries. Smaller responses provide no benefit in the presence of the largest effort. For example, once a brave knight slays the dragon, lesser effort accomplishes nothing. The best-equipped research team is likely to make the research breakthrough with lesser-equipped teams falling short of making the discovery.

In Figure 3.5 of Chapter 3, the Nash equilibria for a best-shot public good for two like agents are where a single agent contributes. This then requires coordination so that efforts are not wasted. If, however, there is a sole capable country, the collective action dilemma is solved provided that this country derives a positive net payoff even after footing the entire cost. Asymmetric payoffs with the most capable savior country getting the greatest payoffs offer the greatest hope for action. If the only capable country receives a negative net payoff from acting alone, then others have to bolster this country's efforts or share the costs so that a positive net payoff is perceived by the best-shot country. During the Gulf War of 1990–91, which started as Desert Shield and ended as Desert Storm, U.S. efforts were bolstered by the United Kingdom and France, with Saudi Arabia, Kuwait, Japan, and others underwriting some the costs of the war against Iraq, a rogue country at the time that invaded Kuwait (Sandler and Hartley, 1999).

In some rogue-country scenarios, the consequences of inaction become so dire that countries will coalesce forces, as was the case in World War II against Nazi Germany. Prior to the start of the war, European countries engaged in unsuccessful appeasement. Germany's invasion of Poland left little choice but for Europe and, eventually, the United States to take on the rogue. Following World War II, NATO was formed by countries in North America and Europe to halt the aggression of the Soviet Union, which was expanding its sphere of influence in Europe. From March through August 2011, NATO forces used airstrikes to assist rebel forces to topple the Gaddafi regime in Libya. Under

Gaddafi, Libya had been classified by some countries as a rogue state that sponsored terrorism. Moreover, Libya had chemical weapons and had tried to develop nuclear weapons.[1]

Globalization-induced asymmetries among countries assist in the provision of best-shot public goods by eliminating the need for coordinating who must take action. The growing inequality in income and technology associated with modern-day globalization promotes the asymmetry favorable for tackling rogue-like threats. This asymmetry and subsequent reliance on one or two countries to confront rogues come with costs to the rest of the world as the best-shot country or countries control the agenda and may gain disproportionately in the spoils. For instance, the defeat of Nazi Germany allowed the allies to partition Berlin such that the more essential participants received the best portions. The defeat of a rogue state may yield natural resource wealth (for example, oil), rebuilding contracts, strategic opportunities, or trading opportunities for the best-shot country or coalition. These selective incentives or agent-specific benefits may be crucial in motivating a best-shot country to put its soldiers in harm's way to eliminate or weaken a rogue state. This is particularly true if the state does not present an imminent danger to the best-shot state. There are situations where the rogue is more of a regional than a global threat and there is no capable state in the region to confront the rogue.

During the Cold War, the United States protected Western Europe against Soviet Union expansion (see Chapter 5). This example illustrates how the most capable country—the United States—confronted the rogue state to deter aggression in a region where the United States had vested interests. U.S., and later French and British, deployment of strategic nuclear weapons threatened the Soviets with unacceptable destruction if they expanded further westward.[2] Later, the United States deployed theater nuclear weapons (low-yield nuclear weapons designed for battlefield use) to counter Soviet tank numbers in Europe. For these weapons, the United States required that only it, and not the host countries, maintained launch control—an agent-specific benefit. By controlling the launch button, the United States could not only threaten the Soviets, but also extract political concessions from its European allies. Selective incentives or agent-specific benefits are generally a prime motivator for the provider of a best-shot public good. Throughout NATO's history, the United States set the agenda and the alliance's strategic doctrine, which gave selective incentives to the United States. This doctrine determined what weapon platforms and systems were needed, many of which were supplied by U.S. defense firms. Later Europe developed its own defense industrial sector to provide weapons to Europe and the United States (Hartley, 2007).

1. Gaddafi announced in 2003 that he was voluntarily giving up the pursuit of nuclear weapons.
2. On NATO's role during and after the Cold War, see Sandler and Hartley (1999).

Less coordination is required when confronting the rogue state is a *better-shot public good*. The latter is a less extreme example of a best-shot public good, insofar as contribution levels less than the greatest also add to aggregate benefits (Arce and Sandler, 2001; Cornes, 1993). For a better-shot public good, the greatest marginal or incremental gain arises from enhanced efforts by the provider already making the largest overall contribution. Contribution levels below the greatest also add smaller incremental benefits for those consuming the better-shot public good. For example, efforts below the largest to monitor a rogue state may still provide some intelligence gains, but at a smaller level than the best effort level. In the search for new antibiotics, less effective ones may still provide benefits, particularly when bacteria become resistant to the most effective antibiotics. Actions against a rogue state can be a better-shot public good with smaller efforts also bolstering gains. Examples include supportive efforts by Germany, Japan, and other countries in the U.S.-led coalition against the Taliban and al-Qaida in October 2001, or lesser actions to U.S.-directed attacks against ISIS in 2014.

To illustrate the implications of a better-shot public good, we turn to an instructive stylized example, where two identical countries confront a rogue state.[3] Each confronted country can supply 0, 1, or 2 units of the offensive action against the rogue. This action constitutes the better-shot public good. In Table 11.1, possible payoffs for a better-shot public good are displayed, where payoff amounts are indicated in the left-hand column and agent (country) contribution levels are given under q_i (q_j) in the right-hand columns. If, for example, country i contributes one unit of offensive action and country j contributes nothing, then each country gets benefits of 4 *before the costs of contributing is deducted*. When a second unit comes from the same contributing state as the first unit, then each receives 7; when, however, the second unit comes from a different contributor (that is, each country contributes a unit), then each receives just 6. Additional contributions by others add less to aggregate benefits than additions to the largest single effort. This reflects marginal benefit behavior associated with better-shot public goods. The remaining payoffs in Table 7.1 have a similar interpretation and are self-explanatory. Unlike best-shot public goods, contribution levels smaller than the largest help the effort and even duplicate effort levels add to the gain, but at a much diminished rate.

The gross benefits of alternative contribution level can be translated into a 3×3 normal-form game, displayed in Figure 11.1. Country 1 is the row player, while country 2 is the column player. To derive these net payoffs, unit costs of provision are assumed to be 2. If country 1 provides two units and country 2 provides one unit of this better-shot public good, each country gains 9 in

3. This example draws greatly from work with Daniel Arce; see Arce and Sandler (2001) for further details. This previous analysis is also extended here.

Table 11.1. Payoffs for better-shot

Payoffs	q_i	q_j
0	0	0
4	1	0
4	0	1
6	1	1
7	2	0
7	0	2
9	2	1
9	1	2
10	2	2

benefits prior to costs being covered. Country 1 must cover 4 in costs, leaving it with a net gain of 5; country 2 must cover 2 in costs, leaving it with a net gain of 7. If both countries supply two units, then both net 6 as benefits of 10 are reduced by the costs of two units, which is 4. The other entries are computed similarly. As indicated, four Nash equilibria result: two involve a single country contributing two units, and two others have one country contributing two units and the other country giving one unit. The latter two equilibria constitute welfare-superior outcomes compared to the standard best-shot (associated) equilibria of a single country contributing all of the units. Better-shot public goods allow for a diffusion of activities, which promotes the usefulness of coalitions where actions are differentiated among contributors.

		q_2		
		0	1	2
q_1	0	0, 0	4, 2	Nash 7, 3
	1	2, 4	4, 4	Nash 7, 5
	2	Nash 3, 7	Nash 5, 7	6, 6

Figure 11.1
Better-shot game derived from Table 7.1, $c_i = 2$

There is a curse of symmetry[4] since these countries must engineer a means for coordinating their actions in order to decide who gives the larger contribution. Without the requisite coordination, lower payoffs will be hit—for example, where both countries contribute a single unit. To achieve the desired asymmetry, a coordination mechanism is required. This mechanism can be provided by a supranational structure such as an alliance, where allies' roles in neutralizing a rogue state are assigned. Small effort levels may correspond to providing logistical support and maintaining supply lines, while the large efforts are tied to the bombing missions and deploying ground troops. Such differentiation was the case in the first Gulf War, during the U.S.-led invasion of Afghanistan, in NATO's air campaign on Serbia in 1999, and during U.S.-led attacks against ISIS in 2014. Many institutions in better-shot scenarios correlate actions by agreeing to simple rules of thumb. When confronting a rogue state or hostile subnational group, a correlation mechanism can achieve the proper asymmetric response by signaling whose turn it is to expend the greater effort—this correlation may be based on relative location to the threat (for example, the United States quelling unrest in Haiti or Australia leading peacekeeping efforts in East Timor) or some scheme for taking turns.

In Figure 11.2, we reduce the costs of a unit to $c_i = 1$ and again apply the better-shot gross payments in Table 11.1. The payoffs in the normal-form game are calculated as before with these reduced per-unit costs. Reduced costs result in an even greater diffusion of Nash equilibria, since there are now five of them. The new equilibrium is associated with both countries contributing

		q_2		
		0	1	2
				Nash
	0	0, 0	4, 3	7, 5
				Nash
q_1	1	3, 4	5, 5	8, 7
		Nash	Nash	Nash
	2	5, 7	7, 8	8, 8

Figure 11.2
Better-shot game derived from Table 7.1, $c_i = 1$

4. Skyrms (1996) coined the phrase "curse of symmetry." Also see the extensive discussion in Arce and Sandler (2001).

equal effort. In this example, the maximum equal-effort equilibrium is the social optimum with the greatest payoff sum. Now, symmetry is desired, which is a most unusual outcome for such games. If, instead, unit costs are 3, then four equilibria (not shown) result that have a single country supplying either one or two units, with the latter outcome being the more desirable equilibrium. The associated better-shot game is like that of best-shot with the need for unilateral action. Asymmetry is again desirable.

Successfully confronting rogue states generally requires asymmetric effort owing to the better-shot or best-shot nature of the underlying public good. Thus far, we have assumed symmetric countries. When some countries have greater capabilities, reduced costs of action, or receive greater payoffs, the necessary action becomes more assured as the better-shot or best-shot country is motivated to assume the lion's share of the provision. This follows because these asymmetries are apt to result in a positive net benefit from taking action.

MORE ON ROGUE STATES

One huge concern about rogue states is that they will acquire WMD and the means (for example, ballistic missiles) to deliver them. In some instances, rogue states have sponsored transnational terrorism—for instance, Syria supported Hezbollah in Lebanon and Libya supported the downing of Pan Am Flight 103 in December 1988.[5] The U.S. Department of State (2003) branded Iran, North Korea, and Syria as state sponsors of terrorism.

The number of rogue states has fallen in recent years. In the past, five states had been characterized as rogues: Iran, Iraq, Libya, North Korea, and Syria (Klare, 1995). Obviously, Iraq and Libya are no longer on this list given the toppling of the Saddam Hussein regime in Iraq and the defeat of the Muammar Gaddafi regime in Libya. In both instances, the better-shot public good was provided by U.S.-led or NATO-coordinated action, thereby illustrating that a rogue threat can be handled. There are now three remaining alleged rogue countries. There are another three "possible rogues"—China, Russia, and Pakistan. China is on the list given its aggressive actions in nearby seas; Russia is included because of its expansionary actions (into Ukraine and elsewhere) in recent years; and Pakistan is listed because of nuclear proliferation concerns and its hosting of terrorist groups. A Pakistani scientist, A. Q. Khan, sold sensitive components and materials to countries seeking nuclear weapons (Gartzke and Kroenig, 2009, 2014).

---

5. On state sponsorship of the downing of Pan Am Flight 103, see Enders and Sandler (2012). Libya agreed in 2003 to compensate the victims' families.

Table 11.2. Rogue and possible rogue states: Selective military indicators, 2013

Country	Nuclear weapons[a]	Chemical weapons[a]	Biological weapons[b]	Ballistic missiles	Active armed forces[c]	Heavy tanks	Combat aircraft	Def/GDP (%)
"Rogues"								
Iran	u.d.	yes	prob	Yes	523	1,663	334	4.1
North Korea	yes	yes	yes	yes	1,190	3,500	603	n.a.
Syria	no	yes	prob	yes	178	4,950	295	n.a.
"Possible Rogues"								
China	yes	prob	prob	yes	2,333	6,840	2,193	8.3
Russia	yes	yes	yes	yes	845	2,550	1,389	2.6
Pakistan	yes	prob	poss	yes	644	2,501	422	2.5

[a] From Stockholm International Peace Research Institute (2012, Chapters 7–8).
[b] From Dando (1994, p. 181) and Stockholm International Peace Research Institute (SIPRI) (2012).
[c] In thousands. Does not include reserves or paramilitary.
u.d. = under development
prob = probably
poss = possibly
n.a. = not available
Source: International Institute for Strategic Studies (2014) for active armed forces, heavy tanks, combat aircraft, and Def/GDP for 2013.

In Table 11.2, we indicate each of three rogues and potential rogues and their likely status with respect to nuclear, chemical, and biological weapons. For Iran, nuclear weapons are under development (u.d.). North Korea conducted a successful nuclear weapon test in 2009, and Syria does not have nuclear weapons (Stockholm International Peace Research Institute, 2012). It is well known that all three possible rogues possess nuclear weapon arsenals and ballistic missiles. The three rogue states have chemical weapons. Syria agreed to destroy its chemical weapons in September 2013 and started doing so in October 2013. The current state of the Syrian chemical weapon arsenal is not known with certainty. North Korea never signed the Chemical Weapons Convention. Iran used battlefield chemical weapons on Iraqi troops during the 1980–88 Iran-Iraq War, which prompted the 1993 Chemical Weapons Convention. As of October 2013, this Convention has been signed by 190 states (Arms Control Association, 2014). As shown in Table 11.2, the possession of biological weapons is more speculative (Dando, 1994; Stockholm International Peace Research Institute, 2012). Possession of these weapons is not as important as a country's ability to "weaponize these assets," so that they can be used against opponent troops or population centers.

Table 11.2 also indicates these countries' active armed forces (not including reserves or paramilitary), their heavy tanks, their combat aircrafts, and their defense spending as a share of GDP, denoted by Def/GDP. The true size of Syrian forces is rather speculative given the ongoing civil war and Russia's resupply of Syrian weapons. There is no available information on Def/GDP for North Korea or Syria (International Institute for Strategic Studies, 2014). It is not uncommon that the true capabilities of a rogue state are uncertain. The invasion of Iraq led by the United States was motivated, in part, by Iraq's alleged WMD, which never materialized.

For 2014, Table 11.3 rank orders countries according to the size of their active armed forces. Only the top 16 armies are displayed. Among the three rogues, North Korea possesses the fourth-largest army; Iran has the eighth largest; and Syria is not listed. China possesses the largest army, with Russia and Pakistan occupying the fifth and seventh positions, respectively. The size of a country's army may not reveal very much about its true military prowess, because large armies may be poorly equipped, poorly trained, and no match to superior technology. This is particularly telling when comparing China with the United States. China's army ranks first in size, but its military expenditure is about one-fifth that of the United States, so that Chinese spending per soldier is dwarfed by that of the United States. Thus, Chinese forces must be seriously discounted when compared to U.S. forces. China is putting more money into its military and intends to become a formidable power in Asia and the world.

A real concern for the world is that rogues' nuclear or chemical weapons will get into the hands of substate groups, particularly terrorists, that

Table 11.3. Sixteen largest armies in the world, 2014

Country	Rank	Numbers in armed forces (000)[a]	Military expenditures[b] in millions of U.S. dollars
China	1	2,333	112,173
United States	2	1,492	600,400
India	3	1,325	36,297
North Korea	4	1,190	Not known
Russia	5	845	68,163
South Korea	6	655	31,846
Pakistan	7	644	5,890
Iran	8	523	17,749
Turkey	9	511	10,742
Vietnam	10	482	3,800
Egypt	11	439	5,278
Myanmar	12	406	2,400
Indonesia	13	396	8,366
Thailand	14	361	6,213
Brazil	15	318	34,730
Colombia	16	281	7,016

[a] Does not include reserves or paramilitary.
[b] In 2013 current prices.
Source: International Institute for Strategic Studies (2014, Table 13, pp. 486–492).

then extort money from other countries. This is certainly worrisome in Syria if ISIS were to acquire any of Syria's remaining chemical weapons. To keep rogues in check, the world must know the true threat posed by these countries. Acquiring this intelligence is a best-shot public good, which is apt to be undersupplied as countries rely on U.S. efforts. As at-risk countries take a wait-and-see attitude hoping that the United States will always come forward, rogue states and agents are able to build up their capabilities. This buildup makes future action riskier as the rogue becomes more formidable.

FAILED STATES

Failed states are politically, economically, and security-wise challenged. In general, such states lack sufficient central governance and observance of laws. Moreover, the government is too weak to look after the needs of its citizens so that key sectors, such as health, are severely compromised. As indicated earlier, failed states are unable to exercise control within their borders, which can then provide opportunities for terrorist groups to take refuge (Coggins,

Table 11.4. List of weakest 25 countries according to the Center for Systemic Peace's 2014 State Fragility Index

1	Central African Republic
2	Democratic Republic of Congo
3	Afghanistan
4	Sudan (North)
5	South Sudan
6	Ethiopia
7	Somalia
8	Chad
9	Iraq
10	Myanmar (Burma)
11	Yemen
12	Burundi
13	Guinea
14	Guinea-Bissau
15	Mali
16	Niger
17	Uganda
18	Nigeria
19	Rwanda
20	Zimbabwe
21	Angola
22	Burkina Faso
23	Cameroon
24	Cote d'Ivoire
25	Liberia

Source: Center for Systemic Peace (2014), *Annual Global Report 2014 on Conflict, Governance, and State Fragility.* Available at http://www.systemicpeace.org/globalreport.html

2015; Piazza, 2006, 2007, 2008). In other failed states, civil wars or guerrilla wars can erupt leading to refugee flows into neighboring countries.

In Table 11.4, we display the weakest 25 countries from the weakest (Central African Republic) to the 25th weakest (Liberia), based on the Center for Systemic Peace's 2014 report on state failure. These ranks are based on an aggregation of ranks given to a country's economic, political, social welfare, and security well-being. In examining these rankings over time, we find that they are very fluid in terms of composition and order. For example, Somalia had been ranked as the weakest in recent years, but is now seventh. Given recent lawlessness, Libya will surely make the list next year. Despite NATO's efforts at nation building in Afghanistan and Iraq, both countries are high on the list

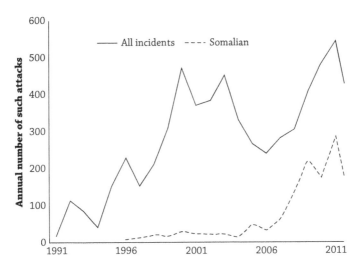

Figure 11.3
Piracy and armed robbery against ships

of failed states. There are other noteworthy things. First, Africa contains most of the failed states. Second, some failed states—Afghanistan, Mali, Nigeria, Somalia, and Yemen—host noteworthy transnational terrorist groups. Third, piracy characterizes two weak states—Somalia and Nigeria. Fourth, the recent Ebola outbreak involves Nigeria and Liberia, which reflects disease vulnerability of failed states.

Failed states may be tied to many concerns: transnational terrorism, piracy, disease outbreaks, civil unrest, criminal activities, and refugee outflows. These concerns give rise to negative transnational externalities that can yield far-reaching consequences. As such, the world community needs to take action against some of these challenges. Consider the case of piracy, which raises the cost of shipping.

Figure 11.3 indicates all incidents of piracy and armed robbery against ships for 1991–2011, recorded by the quarterly reports of the International Maritime Organization (2014). The solid line indicates all piracy incidents, while the dashed line denotes Somalian piracy incidents. Since 1991, piracy has been on the rise. Somalia has been a focal point of piracy after 2007 (Percy and Shortland, 2013; Shortland and Vothknecht, 2011). Piracy occurs off the coasts of East and West Africa. It also takes place in the Java Sea, the East China Sea, the Indian Ocean, the Malacca Straits, and myriad other places.

To stem the rising Somalian piracy problem, the European Union (EU), NATO, the United States, and other interested countries have escorted ships in a designated shipping channel (Percy and Shortland, 2013). Some ships have installed simple defenses (for example, barbed wire on deck or armed crews). Many shipping companies weigh the risks and costs of piracy against those of defensive measures, and then choose to negotiate a ransom when a ship and crew are abducted. This passive decision is due, in large part, to Somalian pirates rarely harming the crew. Although ransoms may be sizeable, they are small relative to the value of the cargo, ship, and crew. Percy and Shortland (2013) showed that naval interdiction efforts at sea have not significantly limited Somalian piracy. They argued that piracy is a mixture of an international security concern and domestic organized crimes. According to Percy and Shortland (2013), piracy is a land-based problem that cannot be effectively eliminated at sea. Piracy requires an infrastructure to thrive, so that as a failed state increases its well-being, the extent of its piracy will likely grow. This follows because the supportive infrastructure will improve in the base country. Their argument is reminiscent of a recent study concerning the relationship between income per capita of perpetrators' countries and the level of transnational terrorism. Enders, Hoover, and Sandler (2015) showed that transnational terrorist attacks increase as income per capita in the perpetrators' countries rises to some intermediate level, then these attacks decline for yet higher income per capita. This then suggests that the most failed states are usually not the source of transnational terrorism; rather, moderately weak states are the source of such terrorism. Patrick (2011) also makes the point that the most failed states may be less worrisome compared to somewhat better-off states that make an attractive home to criminals, terrorists, drug traffickers, and pirates owing to the supporting infrastructure. Returning to Table 11.4, we see that this is the case for Somalia, Iraq, Mali, Nigeria, and Yemen. Based on Percy and Shortland's (2013) characterization, there seems to be a "sweet spot" in terms of per capita income for illicit activities.

SHORING UP FAILED STATES

Failed and failing states often require shoring up, particularly in the case of weakest-link public goods, where the level of consumption equals that of the smallest contribution. For example, disease eradication requires that all countries achieve herd immunity (see Chapter 6). As such, failed or failing states may inhibit eradication, as is currently true for polio in Afghanistan, Nigeria, and Pakistan. Patrick (2011) characterized failed or failing states as weak links, which they may be for addressing many weakest-link public goods associated with reducing transnational terrorism, piracy, counterfeiting, and money laundering.

To show how shoring up weakest links applies to failed states on many occasions, we remind the reader about a concern associated with shoring up weakest links that we first encountered in Chapter 6. In matrix a in Figure 11.4, we display the assurance game associated with a weakest-link public good, where each country can contribute zero or one unit (see Chapter 3). A matched

	B	
	0 units	1 unit
A 0 units	Nash 0, 0	0, –5
A 1 unit	–5, 0	Nash 3, 3

a. Weakest-link public good with $c_i = 5$ and $b = 8$ for matched units

	B	
	Does not act	Shore up
A Does not act	Nash 0, 0	8, –2
A Shore up	–2, 8	3, 3

b. Shoring up the weakest link

Figure 11.4
Weakest-link public good and shoring up the weakest link

contribution gives 8 in benefits to both countries, while an unmatched contribution provides no benefits, since the smallest contribution is zero. If per-unit costs are 5, then the payoffs displayed in Figure 11.4a result.[6] There are two Nash equilibria in matrix a along its diagonal for matching behavior; contributing more than the smallest contribution would waste resources. Leadership by either country to contribute would result in the other country also contributing *provided* that it possessed the requisite means. For failed or failing states, these means may not exist.

For this two-country example, shoring up is displayed in matrix b, where each country can shore up—that is, contribute for itself *and* for the other country—or do nothing and gain nothing. Unilateral shoring-up efforts give the assisted country 8 in benefits and leave the assisting country with −2 as it must pay 10 in costs for a benefit of 8. If each country shores up, then it is akin to each covering its own provision costs, insofar as each pays half of the

---

6. There is also a mixed-strategy Nash equilibrium where the countries play their strategies probabilistically, choosing each strategy a certain proportion of the time.

	B	
	Does not shore up	Shore up
Does not shore up	Nash 0, 0	3, –12
A		
Shore up	–12, 3	–4.5, –4.5

Figure 11.5
Two capable shoring-up countries, three needing help

total costs of 10. The resulting game in matrix b is a Prisoners' Dilemma with no country acting. This two-country outcome would not arise if payoffs were asymmetric so that the rich country gets greater payoffs from its action, inducing it to do the shoring up.

The situation becomes more interesting in Figure 11.5, where there are three countries requiring shoring up and two capable countries. We assume that when all five countries' contributions are covered that every country receives 8 at a per-unit cost of 5. If neither country A nor B shores up the three failed states' efforts, then countries A and B receive no gain, If, say, A does the shoring up, then it gains −12 as it covers its own costs and that of the three failed states, or 20 in costs for a benefit of 8. For unilateral action by A, we assume that country B will cover its own costs for a net gain of 3, since B is capable. When both capable countries act in unison to shore up the three failed states, each nets −4.5 as it assumes half of the total costs of 25 (or −12.5) for a gain of 8. The dominant strategy in Figure 11.5, providing a larger benefit regardless of the other country's action, is to *not* shore up the weak states. As each capable country exercises its dominant strategy, the Nash equilibrium results in no action, which is the social optimum (highest summed payoffs) for just these two capable countries. However, this inaction equilibrium is not the highest overall summed payoff for the *five* countries. The true social optimum corresponds to the other three cells, for which the summed payoff is $15 \left[=-9+(3\times8)\right]$ when the gains to the three assisted states are taken into account.

In a recent article, Sandler (2015) extended this analysis to a greater number of assisted *and* capable countries. As the number of assisted (weakest-link) or failed countries increases, the social dilemma captured by Figure 11.5 grows in severity. This follows because capable countries have less incentives to lend a hand given the larger costs of doing so. A larger number of capable countries makes mutual shoring up more desirable but creates a coordination problem as capable countries prefer that others come forward, thereby giving rise to a chicken or Prisoners' Dilemma. Pernicious drivers for shoring up failed states now involve the large number of these states *and* the large number of capable states. The former is the bigger concern. If, in regards to capable countries, there is sufficient asymmetry in terms of payoffs, then one or more of these countries will come forward, as was true in Afghanistan in 2001 or in Iraq in 2003 (Sandler, 2015). The coordination problem for multiple capable states can be addressed through a supranational organization as the World Health Organization did in eradicating smallpox and in its ongoing campaign against polio. In many instances of weakest-link public goods and failed states, asymmetry can be a key to muster the considerable effort to shore up many failed states.

Failed states tax capable states in ways that transcend the mere number of weak states. Weak or failing states are involved with multiple weakest-link public goods that require shoring up—for example, financial instability, terrorist safe havens, and criminal activities. Thus, the demands placed on capable countries may be very great.

PAIRED COMPARISON—ROGUE VERSUS FAILED STATES

There are some noteworthy differences between rogue and failed states. First, there are many more failed and failing states than there are rogue states. This means that remedial efforts are concentrated for rogue states, but these efforts are diffused for failed states. Second, rogue states primarily present security concerns, while failed states raise more than security worries. Failed states may be associated with disease outbreaks, refugee outflows, financial instability, guerrilla wars, transnational crime, and other problems. Security concerns posed by rogue states serve to coalesce efforts, while the plethora of problems posed by failed states work against transnational assistance. For failed states, action may arise if a single exigency places sufficient risks on the world at large. This could involve an infectious disease outbreak or a resident transnational terrorist threat. Third, failed states display more changes in their composition over time than is the case for rogue states. Fourth, strategic aspects differ between the two kinds of states.

Rogue states are generally associated with the provision of a best-shot or better-shot public good as efforts are mounted to neutralize a security threat. Asymmetric payoffs and abilities among challenged countries fostered action. Selective incentives to the acting country or countries can engineer the necessary asymmetry of benefits. Over time, the most capable country may, however, become fatigued from having to respond too often. For example, the Obama administration is asking other countries to supply ground forces in the military campaign against ISIS. Coalition leadership by a strong country against a rogue state is particularly useful and allows for a better-shot public good as small efforts augment the good's supply. In contrast, addressing many issues tied to failed states involves provision of a weakest-link public good. As such, the failed state is unable to make its own contribution, and other countries must make its contribution for this state. Now symmetry, in terms of the number of capable countries, may be a help or hindrance. Symmetry assists if the capable countries' efforts can be coordinated by some supranational structure as the costs of shoring up are spread over more countries. Without such a coordination device, symmetry inhibits shoring up the failed states as capable countries wait for others to volunteer. If, however, a capable country possesses asymmetric payoffs, then a savior may materialize when the costs of shoring up weak countries are not too onerous—that is, derived benefits are larger than such costs.

CHAPTER 12

Environmental Cooperation

Earth's population grew from 3 billion in 1960 to 7 billion in 2012, with a leveling off at 10 billion anticipated by 2100 (UN Environment Program, 2013; UN Population Fund, 1994). Human population strains the soils, oceans, water supplies, forests, fisheries, rivers, airsheds, resource pools, and the atmosphere. Increased population puts pressures on ecosystems[1] to surpass their "carrying capacity." Prior to this capacity being reached, an ecosystem can withstand pollutants and utilization without measurable impairment. However, once the carrying capacity is surpassed, further demands on the ecosystem result in permanent degradation. Post-capacity degradation limits the system's offerings to all future generations, thereby resulting in an intergenerational negative externality.

Many ecosystems—for example, airsheds, the atmosphere, and rivers—transverse multiple countries. The stratospheric ozone layer is a global ecosystem, while a watershed may be a regional ecosystem. The degradation of these ecosystems does not respect political borders since pollutants can flow or fly among countries, thereby causing temporary or permanent damage. In the case of sulfur emissions, atmospheric rains cleanse the pollutants, which transfer them from the troposphere to the ground. For stock pollutants, such as heavy metals (for example, cadmium, mercury, and lead) in lakes, no such cleansing occurs and the ecosystem degrades with long-term consequences. Given the international character of many ecosystems, effective protection of such ecosystems necessarily involves global and regional agreements or treaties. Satellites, atmospheric observations on Mauna Loa (Hawaii), and other modern monitoring stations have shown that transboundary pollutants are

---

1. An ecosystem is a community of living organisms and their environment. Ecosystems involve exchanges (for example, nutrients and energy) between its living and nonliving components. Such systems vary in size and type from a coral reef or forest to the entire planet.

ubiquitous and on the rise. The Mauna Loa observatory tracks carbon dioxide in the atmosphere on a continuous basis at an altitude of just over 11,000 feet. Traditional military defenses and border controls cannot protect countries from being invaded continuously by pollution from economic activities abroad.

This chapter focuses on two paired comparisons—one at the global level and one at the regional level—to underscore how seemingly similar pollution (public good) problems have vastly different collective action or cooperation prognoses. At the global level, we contrast failed action to date to stem climate change with successful actions to curb ozone shield depletion. Despite the Kyoto Protocol's mandated cutbacks in greenhouse gases (GHGs) that warm the planet's atmosphere, GHG emissions have increased by about 50% since 1990 (Harvey, 2012). The Kyoto Protocol, which entered into force on February 16, 2005, requires Annex I countries to curb their GHG emissions by about 5% from their 1990 level by 2012 (UN Framework Convention on Climate Change, 2014). The disappointing outcome of the Kyoto Protocol is easy to understand because the treaty-mandated reductions in GHGs only affected 15% of the world's emissions (UN Environment Program, 2013, p. 10). Major GHG emitters—the United States, China, the Russian Federation,[2] and India—are currently not bound by the treaty to reduce emissions.[3] A much better outcome is associated with the Montreal Protocol and its amendments to curb the consumption and production of ozone shield depleters, with the intent to increase the density of the stratospheric ozone layer. Today, there is universal adoption of the Montreal Protocol. Moreover, countries are adhering to the protocol's cutbacks. As a consequence, the ozone layer should return to its pre-1980 density within the next 35 to 60

2. The Russian Federation was mandated by the Kyoto Protocol to reduce its GHG emissions to their 1990 level. When Russia signed the Kyoto Protocol in 2005, its GHG emissions were much less than those in 1990 owing to the economic downturns following the collapse of the Soviet Union. Hence, Russia earned GHG credits to sell to other countries, which made its signing of the Kyoto Protocol quite lucrative. Russia had no requirement to reduce its emissions during the first commitment period of the Kyoto Protocol. At the start of the second commitment period in 2013, Russia withdrew from the treaty allegedly because the United States, China, and India had not consented to reduce their GHG emissions.

3. In Lima in December 2014, the Conference of Parties considered proposals for updating GHG emission cutbacks for the next commitment period of the Kyoto Protocol. A few small countries accepted the Doha amendment to the protocol, bringing to 21 the 144 signers required to adopt the amendment. Pledges of over $10 billion were made by some developed countries to fund a new Green Climate Fund. Some pledges were made by tropical countries to limit deforestation (UN Framework Convention on Climate Change, 2015). Although the Lima meeting seemed hopeful, the true dimensions of new GHG reduction are far from known at this time. Moreover, there is no certainty that countries will fulfill their new pledged cutbacks. Many old roadblocks remain.

years (UN Environmental Program, 2013). Ironically, stemming climate change and increasing the density of the ozone layer are quintessential global public goods (GPGs) that possess the same degree of nonrivalry and nonexcludability. Hence, why has the world failed to address climate change, but has successfully confronted ozone shield depletion? The answer hinges on myriad considerations that transcend the three properties of publicness; the answer involves collective action notions at the local, country, regional, and global levels.

At the regional level, our paired regional public goods (RPGs) comparison concerns sulfur-based and nitrogen-based acid rain. Curbing the emissions of these two acid rain inducers constitutes the public good. Although regional treaties have made headway on both concerns, more rapid and better progress characterizes reducing sulfur emissions. For this paired comparison, we show that the properties of the two RPGs are partly behind the different successes achieved. However, other factors—for example, the nature of the polluters and monitoring capabilities—also figure into the contrasting outcomes.

By making the reader aware of the favorable and unfavorable drivers associated with supplying GPGs and RPGs in key situations, we educate the reader about considerations that either foster or inhibit collective action. By understanding such drivers, the reader can better fathom the prognosis of other GPGs and RPGs. For policy makers, our analysis can help them to design better treaty instruments that account not only for the nature of the underlying public good, but also for the motives and actions of the polluters. The ability to identify key differences between seemingly identical problems is important for effective policy making. Generalization is good up to a point when ascertaining the prognosis and required response to promote collective action. By distilling essential (simple) maxims, Mancur Olson's seminal 1965 study of collective action generalized too much. For example, the number of participants may not be such a crucial determinant of collective action failure or success. There are collective action problems involving the entire global community—for example, conventions to avoid accidents at sea—that were solved effectively. The ability to identify essential differentiating features is important for collective action concerns.

OZONE SHIELD DEPLETION

Living organisms are greatly protected by the stratospheric ozone layer, which ranges from 10 to 25 miles above the earth (de Gruijl, 1995). If fully concentrated, the ozone layer is just three millimeters thick and represents less than one part per million of the atmosphere. The ozone layer absorbs much of the harmful ultraviolet-B radiation from the sun.[4] A thinned ozone layer can result in the extinction of species, the disruption of the food chain, inducement of skin cancers, the incidence of cataracts, and the impairment of the immune system. For instance, food supplies can be harmed through reduced phytoplankton at the base of the marine food chain.

By the early 1970s, Mario Moline and Sherwood Rowland hypothesized that released chlorofluorocarbons (CFCs) migrated to the stratosphere, where they could be decomposed during frigid winter conditions by sunlight, thus releasing chlorine that combines with ozone. The resulting chemical action would lead to the capture of ozone which, in turn, would deplete the ozone layer (Toon and Turco, 1991). The thinning of this layer could also result from the release of other halocarbons (known as halons) and bromide-based substances (for example, methyl bromide and bromochloromethane). The real wake-up call came in 1985 when the British Antarctic Survey discovered that the springtime concentration of the ozone layer over Halley Bay, Antarctica, had declined by 40% from measured levels in 1964. This finding motivated major consuming and producing countries to act to stem the release of ozone-destroying substances. This motivation was greatly enhanced by an Environmental Protection Agency (EPA) (1987a, 1987b) report that estimated that a 50% reduction in CFC emissions from 1986 levels could save the United States $64 trillion by 2075 in reduced health costs associated with skin cancers. Without these reductions, skin cancer incidence was based on an annual growth of CFC use at 2.5% through 2050. The long-term costs from cutting CFC use were estimated to be between $20 and $40 billion during the 1989–2075 period, based on the projected growth rates in CFC use; thus, U.S. benefits from individual actions far outweighed the costs. In fact, the benefit-cost ratios were over 1,000 to 1, so that the United States had little choice in terms of cutting back on CFCs and in assuming a leadership role in getting other major consumer and producer countries to curb CFC use and production.

Curbing ozone depleters is a purely public GPG. A thicker ozone layer shields everyone and all species, so that the benefits are nonexcludable. Moreover, benefits are nonrival insofar as the protection that a denser ozone layer affords to one country does not detract from the protection experienced by other countries. Efforts at curbing ozone-depleting substances are cumulative, thereby abiding by a summation aggregator technology in which global reduced emissions correspond to the sum of all countries' cutbacks. From a supply viewpoint, curbing ozone depleters is a classic public good. However, from a demand standpoint, its effect may differ based on geographic location because countries at high latitudes receive greater ultraviolet exposure during

---

4. On the beneficial effects of the ozone layer, see de Gruijl (1995). A scientific description of the process of ozone depletion can be found in Stolarski (1988) and Toon and Turco (1991).

the springtime before a uniform mixing of the layer has occurred. Additionally, countries in the Southern Hemisphere are at greater exposure risk in the
springtime than those in the Northern Hemisphere, because ozone shield
thinning is greater in the Southern Hemisphere. This occurs because the win-
ters at the South Pole are slightly colder than those at the North Pole owing to
the earth's tilt and its orbit. Coldness in the stratosphere is more conducive to
the breakdown of halons and the subsequent destruction of ozone as ozone
combines with chlorine, bromine, and other elements.

Even though ozone shield thickening is a pure public good, the world has
taken decisive action to improve the shield, as shown in Table 12.1. In March
1985, the Vienna Convention was framed, which merely mandated that the
world community study the possible harmful effects of CFC emissions on the
ozone shield. This convention was subsequently ratified in September 1988
after the findings of the British Antarctic Survey and the EPA reports. Given

Table 12.1. Treaties controlling ozone-depleting substances

Treaty/Number of ratifiers	Dates[a]	Notable Accomplishments
Vienna Convention/197 ratifiers	March 1985 September 1988	Mandated ratifiers to study the harmful effects of CFC emissions on ozone layer.
Montreal Protocol/197 ratifiers	September 1987 January 1989	Progressive cuts, rising to 50% of 1986 levels, in the consumption and production of five CFCs. The production and consumption of three halons frozen.
London Amendment/197 ratifiers	June 1990 August 1992	Cuts for 15 CFCs increased to 85% of 1986 levels and eventually eliminated. Increasing cuts imposed on three halons, carbon tetrachloride, and methyl chloroform. Nonbinding cuts on HCFCs.
Copenhagen Amendment/197 ratifiers	November 1992 June 1994	Accelerated the phasing out of 15 CFCs (by 1996), 3 halons, carbon tetrachloride, and methyl chloroform. Explicit cuts to HCFCs. HBFCs and methyl bromide added to list of controlled substances
Montreal Amendment/197 ratifiers	September 1997 November 1999	Phase out of methyl bromide. List of controlled depleters increased to 94.
Beijing Amendment/195 ratifiers	December 1999 February 2002	Bromochloromethane controlled. Better controls developed for ozone depleters.

[a] The first date is when the treaty was enacted, while the second date is when it was ratified.
Sources: Barrett (2003a), Fridtjof Nansen Institute (1996), and United Nations Environment Program (2014) at http://ozone.unep.org/new_site/en/treaty_ratification_status.php.

the mounting evidence that CFCs and other substances depleted the ozone layer, the world community started framing a treaty to mandate cuts in ozone-depleting substances. The resulting Montreal Protocol, framed in September 1987 and ratified in January 1989, required progressive reductions in the consumption and production of five CFCs rising to 50% of 1986 levels. Moreover, the production and consumption of three halons were frozen by the treaty. Subsequent amendments—London, Copenhagen, Montreal, and Beijing—augmented the levels of cutbacks, increased the number of controlled substances, and accelerated the timetable for the cutbacks. Eventually all CFCs were scheduled for complete elimination, and the number of controlled substances increased from 8 to 95 with the ratification of the Beijing Amendment in February 2002. Noteworthy additions included hydrochlorofluorocarbons (HCFCs) and hydrobromochlorofluorocarbons (HBFCs), which were added to the list of controlled substances by the Copenhagen Amendment. These substances were the initial substitutes for CFCs. However, since these substitutes still contained chlorine and bromine, HCFCs and HBFCs depleted the ozone layer but to a much smaller extent than CFCs. Eventually, hydrofluorocarbons (HFCs) that contain no ozone depleters replaced HCFCs and HBFCs for air conditioning, refrigerators, aerosols, insulating foam, the cleansing of circuit boards, and other applications. Unfortunately, HFCs constitute a GHG, which raises other concerns. Table 12.1 indicates the now-universal ratification of the Vienna Convention and its four subsequent amendments, where the EU is counted as a single ratifier. The Beijing Amendment is close to universal ratification (UN Environment Program, 2014).

Many factors supported this unprecedented global collective action despite the global implications (see Benedick, 1991; Morrisette et al., 1990). In 1986, just three countries—the United States, Japan, and the former Soviet Union—accounted for about half of CFC emissions. At the time of ratification of the Montreal Protocol, just 12 countries caused over 78% of the emissions (World Resources Institute, 1992, Table 24.2). If these 12 countries were to limit production and consumption of CFCs, significant reduction in ozone shield depleters would occur. This follows because the other countries did not have the collective means in the near term to undercut their efforts.

Another facilitator of this international collective action was that no country could gain from ozone layer thinning. Although some countries were more harmed than others during the springtime, none were helped by a thinning ozone layer. Even those countries with commercial interests in manufacturing CFCs were positioned to profit from their reduced use owing to the discovery of substitutes, produced by the same chemical companies. Faced with the mounting case against CFCs in the destruction of ozone, the primary producers quickly found substitutes and could exhaust current CFC supplies during the phase-out period. Commercial interests in CFCs were concentrated in just 16 companies in 1987. Just five firms accounted for all U.S. production: DuPont,

49%, Allied Signal, 25%; Pennwalt Corporation, 13%; Kaiser Chemicals, 9%; and Racon, 4% (Morrisette et al., 1990, p. 57). These firms were well diversified with CFC production representing a small fraction of sales—less than 2% for DuPont (Morrisette et al., 1990, p. 15). Thus, producing firms did not lobby the U.S. Congress to vote against the Montreal Protocol.

Everything seemed to line up to promote the protocol. The scientific evidence showed that CFCs were not benign to the ozone layer. The EPA report indicated to the main polluting and producing countries that the benefits from their individual action to curb consumption far exceed the costs—that is, $b_i - c_i > 0$. Moreover, other countries could not undo the collective action of those doing the cutbacks. For many consuming and producing CFC countries, these considerations meant that the dominant strategy was to cutback on CFCs. Later, the same factors promoted action to curb other ozone-depleting substances. Action was fostered by the leadership of the United States, which in 1980s was the largest producer and consumer of CFCs. The resolution of the scientific uncertainty concerning how CFCs and other substances destroyed the ozone layer also bolsters international cooperation. Intertemporal considerations regarding when action today is able to improve the ozone shield in the future also promoted cooperation. That is, treaty-mandated reduction in CFCs would allow the ozone shield in the next 50 years or so to recover its pre-1980 concentration (World Meteorological Organization, 1998). Since improvement to the ozone layer's density would begin some time after 2000, the current generation would reap some benefits from its action. Collective action is much more difficult when benefits are experienced only by the next generation or even more distant generations.

At least three other considerations bolstered efforts to replenish the ozone layer by curbing ozone depleters and allowing natural forming ozone to thicken the layer. First, decision makers were more informed about the benefits than the costs. The news media also focused on these benefits and did not mention much about taxes on consumers as CFCs and other ozone depleters would be phased out over time. Other costs involved replacing refrigerators and air conditioning units with those that could use the substitute coolants. Gradual replacement would limit these costs. Second, despite their varied applications, ozone-depleting activities were relatively few in number, especially compared to activities resulting in climate change. Third, at the time of the Montreal Protocol, developing countries were not large emitters of ozone depleters. The Montreal Protocol actually allowed developing countries, whose annual consumption was less than 0.3 kilograms per capita on their entry to the treaty, a 10-year grace period before cutbacks had to be made (Sandler, 1997, p. 110). A Multilateral Fund was established to provide technical and financial assistance to developing countries once they had to adopt more ozone-friendly technologies. This fund served to shore up weakest links and was financed by rich countries.

Table 12.2. Atmospheric concentration of ozone-depleting gases (in parts per trillion)

Years	Carbon Tetra-chloride	Methyl Chloroform	CFC-11	CFC-12	CFC-13	Total Gaseous Chlorine
1982	92	81	175	325	26	1,865
1983	93	85	182	341	28	1,939
1984	94	88	190	355	31	2,016
1985	96	92	200	376	36	2,121
1986	97	96	210	394	40	2,216
1987	99	98	221	413	48	2,322
1988	100	103	231	433	53	2,425
1989	100	107	240	452	59	2,524
1990	101	110	249	470	66	2,620
1991	101	113	254	484	71	2,685
1992	101	116	259	496	77	2,751
1993	101	112	260	503	80	2,764
1994	100	106	261	512	81	2,769
1995	99	97	261	518	82	2,753
1996	98	85	261	523	82	2,725
1997	97	73	260	528	83	2,693
1998	96	64	259	530	82	2,664

Source: World Resources Institute (2000, Table AC.3, p. 285)

Based on historical statistics from the World Resources Institute (2000), Table 12.2 indicates the atmospheric concentration in parts per trillion of select ozone-depleting gases for 1982–1998, prior to and after the ratification of the Montreal Protocol. By the start of the 1990s, most key ozone-depleting compounds were falling in their atmospheric concentration or their increases were leveling off owing to a significant drop in consumption. Total gaseous chlorine in the atmosphere fell after 1994. Major emitters—the United States, Japan, and the EU—had reduced their CFC consumption by greater than 50% between 1986 and 1992 (Fridtjof Nansen Institute, 1996, p. 24). This strongly suggests that ratifiers were adhering to their Montreal Protocol pledges. The willingness of ratifiers to later phase out CFCs and curb other ozone depleters in subsequent amendments also indicates treaty adherence. As stated earlier, the ozone layer will return to its pre-1980 concentration some time between 2050 and 2075 (UN Environment Program, 2013, p. 10), so successful global collective action was achieved with respect to replenishing the protective ozone layer.

CLIMATE CHANGE

Our contrasting case involves curbing climate change, which stems from a greenhouse effect as sunlight heats the earth releasing infrared radiation that gets partly trapped in the earth's atmosphere, thereby raising the mean temperature. Carbon dioxide and other GHGs comprise less than 1% of the atmosphere, but can warm the planet like an insulating blanket (World Meteorological Organization, 2013). According to the World Meteorological Organization (2013, p. 3), GHGs continue to rise: "the period 1990 to 2011 saw a 30% increase in radiative forcing – a measure of the warming effect on climate – because of increased atmospheric concentrations of GHGs." GHGs include carbon dioxide, CFCs, HCFCs, HFCs, methane (CH_4), and nitrous oxide (N_2O). Carbon dioxide is a byproduct of the burning of fossil fuels and deforestation, while methane is primarily the result of solid wastes, coal mining, oil and gas production, wet rice agriculture, and livestock. Nitrous oxide comes from biomass burning, fertilizers, myriad industrial processes, and energy production.

Unabated accumulation of GHGs can raise the mean temperature on earth by as much as 2°C to 5°C during the twenty-first century; estimates differ and much uncertainty remains. There is, however, growing certainty that man-made GHGs contribute to climate change. "A 2010 paper in the Proceedings of the National Academy of Sciences of the United States . . . concluded that 97%–98% of the most active climate researchers support the reality of human-induced climate change" (World Meteorological Organization, 2013, p. 1). In past years, there had been a debate whether climate change was taking place and, if it was, whether it was due to man-made or natural (for example, volcanoes) sources. These debates have mostly been settled. Nevertheless, the precise relationship between the accumulation of GHGs in the atmosphere and the extent and timing of climate change is still not quantified with precision, though improved models are being developed. A rise in mean temperature is not the only harmful consequence of climate change, there is also the rise in sea levels as polar and Greenland ice melts. Additionally, climate-change-induced droughts and devastating storms are expected to increase in number and severity. For example, stronger hurricanes may come from warmer seas. Climate change may affect rainfall distribution, ocean currents, and food-producing regions.

Unlike ozone shield depletion where all countries are harmed, climate change may actually benefit some countries in high latitudes with longer and even wetter growing seasons. Understandably, countries that may gain from such agreeable changes are reluctant to institute carbon taxes and other measures that would slow down their economic activities before their climate-change-induced fate is known. It is then not surprising that Canada pulled out of the Kyoto Protocol in 2011 (Harvey, 2012).

Like limiting ozone depletion, curbing climate change is an example of a purely public GPG that abides by a summation aggregator. Such GHG cutbacks yield benefits that are not only nonrival but also nonexcludable globally.[5] Efforts by any countries to emit fewer GHGs limit the atmospheric concentration of GHGs globally as mixing occurs in the atmosphere; therefore, all countries are affected. A summation aggregator applies since the cumulative atmospheric emissions or reductions are the sum of all countries' emissions or reductions.

Following the Earth Summit in 1992, the United Nations Framework Convention on Climate Change was framed and entered into force in 1994.[6] This convention mandated scientific study of the problem with a protocol, if necessary, to follow that would reduce GHG emissions. On December 11, 1997, the Kyoto Protocol was framed and opened for signatures. This treaty called for ratifiers to reduce GHG emissions by about 5% of their 1990 levels between 2008 to 2012. The Kyoto Protocol entered into force on February 16, 2005. Developing countries were exempted from cutbacks because most of atmospheric stock of GHGs in 1997 was due to activities in developed countries. Although this exemption is equitable, it is nonetheless myopic, since some exempted countries (for example, China, Brazil, and India) have the fastest-growing GHG emissions (Sandler, 2004, Table 10.3). Although the Kyoto Protocol had some effect on reducing emissions by the EU and some other countries, the overall impact is disappointing since many of the main GHG emitters—China, the United States, India, the Russian Federation, and Canada—are currently not bound by the treaty to limit emissions. The Conference of Parties (COP) meets periodically to promote adaptation (engineered resilience to climate change such as sea barriers for major coastal cities), mitigation of emissions, Reducing Emissions from Deforestation and forest Degradation (REDD), and financing of green societies. The sixteenth meeting of the COP in Cancun, Mexico, recognized the need for significant cuts in GHG emission to keep temperature increases to 2°C by 2100. More recent COP meetings in Durban, South Africa (in 2011) and in Doha, Qatar (in 2012) acknowledged the need to require GHG cuts from developing countries. A new commitment in GHG reductions is needed for a resurrected Kyoto Protocol by 2015 for 2015–2020. Some progress was seen in the twentieth meeting of the COP in Lima, Peru; however, much more progress is needed (UN Framework Convention on Climate Change, 2015).

The initial commitment period of the Kyoto Protocol ended in 2012, with many ratifiers not achieving their pledged reductions (Harvey, 2012). How the new commitments will treat (punish) these cutback shortages is another

5. Nonrivalry does not necessitate that recipient countries benefit from the public good; it only requires that consumption opportunities are unaffected by the consumption of the other recipients.
6. Facts from this paragraph are drawn from UN Environment Program (2013) and UN Framework Convention on Climate Change (2014).

awkward issue to be negotiated. There is also the concern about long-term financing to support mitigation and adaptation in developing countries, which will cost hundreds of billions in U.S. dollars (UN Environment Program, 2013). This shoring-up effort, unlike ozone depletion, is hugely expensive. Unless the new commitment involves a much greater cutback of GHG emissions, climate change will continue on its disastrous path. This ominous path is reflected in the annual rise in sea levels of about 3.2 millimeters between 1993 and 2011, which is twice that observed during the twentieth century (World Meteorological Organization, 2013, p. 7). The projected 2°C to 5°C anticipated rise in mean temperature must be compared to the mere 0.6°C increase over the entire twentieth century (World Meteorological Organization, 2013, p. 4).

Table 12.3 provides essential contrasts between factors that support collective action for protecting the ozone shield and those that inhibit collective action for reducing climate change. Since the favorable influences for ozone depletion have already been discussed, we will concentrate on the unfavorable ones for controlling GHGs. As displayed in the table, the two problems possess almost opposite drivers where facilitators are replaced by inhibitors. For climate change, virtually every country adds to GHG emissions, some through manufacturing, others through deforestation, others through heating and cooling, and still others through agricultural activities. In 2006, the United States, the EU, the Russian Federation, China, India, and Japan accounted for 70% of all GHG emissions. This concentration sounds promising for collective action (Hannesson, 2010); however, only the EU and Japan have cutback commitments under the Kyoto Protocol. Unlike ozone depletion, there are some potential gainers from climate change that are understandably reluctant to assume costly abatement commitments. The rising sea level may, however, make for more losers insofar as many major cities are on ocean coasts, putting them at risk from flooding and storm surges. When the Kyoto Protocol was first signed, there did not appear to be many commercial gains from developing substitutes to GHG emission activities. This is now changing somewhat with greater utilization of solar, wind-generated, and wave-generated energy. We are still many years away from these green sources of energy becoming a sizeable share of energy production. There is still much unresolved uncertainty with respect to the process of climate change and its consequences, even though there is now virtually no doubt that man-made GHG emissions are a major contributor to climate change. For many countries, the benefit per unit of abatement is less than the associated cost, so that not abating is a dominant strategy.[7] This is changing as new technologies are developed and countries better assess the cost of not abating their GHGs. For example, the costs of coastal flooding and moving cities inland are huge if seas continue to rise.

7. Nordhaus (1991) showed this to be the case for the United States.

Table 12.3. Different collective action factors affecting ozone shield depletion and climate change

Ozone-shield depletion	Climate change
• Emissions concentrated in relatively few countries	• Virtually every country adds to GHGs with some developing countries being the source of the greatest increases, but these countries are excluded from making cutbacks
• Every country loses from a thinning ozone layer	• There are gainers and losers from climate change
• Commercial gains from substitutes	• No commercial gains from substitutes initially, but this is now changing
• Resolved uncertainty in terms of process and consequences	• Unresolved uncertainty in terms of processes and consequences
• Dominant strategy for some key polluters is to curb pollutants since $b_i - c_i > 0$	• Dominant strategy for most key polluters is not to curb pollutants since $b_i - c_i < 0$, but this is changing
• Leadership by key polluters	• Lack of leadership by key polluters
• Some intertemporal reversibility within 50 years	• No intertemporal reversibility within 50 years
• Decision makers were more informed about benefits than costs	• Decision makers were more informed about costs than benefits
• Relatively few activities add to ozone shield depletion	• Many activities add to the accumulation of GHGs
• Not so costly to help developing countries adjust to ozone-friendly technologies	• Very costly to help developing countries to reduce their carbon footprint

In contrast to ozone depletion, the primary GHG emitters are not leading the efforts to curb GHGs. Currently, China is the largest GHG emitter; yet China has never committed to reducing its emissions. Additionally, the time profile for action today to have noticeable future effects is much longer for climate change because carbon dioxide resides within the atmosphere for a much longer period than ozone depleters (Nordhaus, 1991). The current generation must be quite altruistic to future generations if much progress is to be accomplished. Decision makers appear more informed about abatement costs than abatement benefits for climate change owing to unresolved uncertainties. Additionally, myriad activities add to climate change; even taking a breath or warming a meal gives off carbon dioxide. In addition, actions to help developing countries mitigate their GHG emissions or adapt to the consequences of climate change are much more costly than in the case of ozone shield depletion. Even rich countries will find that curbing their GHG emissions will be hugely expensive.

There is another key difference involving leakages, where emission activities can be displaced from one country to another (Busnell, Peterman, and Wolfram, 2008). For climate change, Kyoto Protocol ratifiers can limit their GHG emissions by transferring manufacturing activities from home to developing countries that are not committed to cutbacks. Leakages may also involve the growth of emissions in countries with no reduction obligations more than offsetting efforts in countries with Kyoto commitments. This concern is behind the continued growth of atmospheric GHG despite the Kyoto Protocol. Unless these leakages are addressed, more countries, like Canada, will abandon the treaty. Such leakages were not a problem with the Montreal Protocol, which imposed penalties on trade in CFC-using products. Moreover, noncommitted developing countries did not contribute much ozone-depleting substances to the atmosphere.

These contrasting factors mean that collective action with respect to climate change is unlikely to mimic that for controlling ozone-depleting substances. Current realities bear this out: atmospheric GHGs are accumulating at alarming rates, while the ozone shield's concentration is gradually improving. The Kyoto Protocol must be renegotiated, whereas the Montreal Protocol has universal adherence. In our estimation, the use of the Montreal Protocol as a template for the Kyoto Protocol (see the recommendation of Benedick [1991]) was inadvisable. A treaty instrument for climate change must account for its unique aspects. Too generous provisions for developing countries, while effective for the Montreal Protocol because these countries were minor CFC polluters, kept major polluters, such as the United States, from ratifying the Kyoto Protocol. In addition, the leakage problem must be addressed in the renegotiated Kyoto Protocol.

There is some hope on the horizon as countries are slowly accepting that climate change is real and its consequences are dire. Commercial alternatives

ing activities are also being developed. If extreme weather
se and are unequivocably traced to climate change, then there will
ner countries to assume a wait-and-see attitude. As pointed out by
n (2010), a large number of activist countries are not needed if the
ht largest GHG emitters agreed to act collectively. The problem is that
f these large emitters are not bound to act; however, their collective
action, if it were to occur, would be hard to undo by other countries. Unfortunately, this dream coalition is unlikely to materialize in the near term. If, however, countries like China were pressured by its people to address its growing
city pollution problem, then the prognosis for action would improve.

CONTRASTING ACID RAIN PROBLEMS

We now consider a more localized regional contrast between sulfur-based and
nitrogen-based acid rain. We want to explain why greater and faster progress
characterized addressing sulfur-based acid rain. When sulfur and nitrogen
oxide (NO_x) emissions from various pollution sources combine in the lower
atmosphere with water vapor and tropospheric ozone, sulfuric acid and nitric
acid form, respectively. These acids later fall with the rain and degrade lakes,
rivers, coastal waters, forests, and man-made structures. This degradation can
also stem from dry depositions of sulfur and NO_x that lead to increased acidity
of soils and watersheds. In 1980, prior to any collective action, sources of
sulfur emissions were 47.8%, power plants; 37.4%, industry; 10%, residential
and commercial; 3.7%, cars and trucks; and 1%, miscellaneous. In 1980,
sources of NO_x emissions were 53.6%, cars and trucks; 23.5%, power plants;
15.4%, industry; 6.1%, residential and commercial; and 1.3%, miscellaneous
(Organization for Economic Cooperation and Development, 1990).

There are alternative strategies for controlling both types of emissions. Obviously, these emissions can be reduced through efficiency in terms of transportation vehicles, residential and commercial uses, and energy generation.
The primary means for controlling sulfur emissions are the burning of low-
sulfur coal and oil and the use of flue-gas desulfurization for power plants
(Wolfson, 2008). For NO_x, emissions can be reduced in power plants by installing low-NO_x burners. Vehicle emissions can be curtailed through
improved control technologies (for example, better catalytic converters),
turnover of vehicle fleets, more stringent emission standards, and improved
gasoline efficiency. Once emitted into the air, sulfur and NO_x emissions can
remain aloft for days and travel from their emission sources to be deposited
on downwind countries, thereby causing a transnational pollution externality
within a region. Since NO_x particles are lighter than sulfur particles, the
former remain aloft for longer and travel further from their emission source.
NO_x particles remain airborne for two to eight days, while sulfur particles stay

airborne for from less than an hour to up to seven days (Alcamo and Runca, 1986, p. 3). Although the publicness properties of these two regional pollutants are quite similar, they differ greatly from the two previously considered GPGs. Once airborne, sulfur and NO_x are deposited downwind in a rival fashion; a ton of these emissions deposited on France is a ton that cannot be deposited elsewhere. In aggregate, all such airborne pollutants must eventually fall somewhere: on the emitting country, on another country, or at sea. Larger countries will receive more of their own emissions as dry or wet deposits, which provides such countries a strong incentive to reduce their emissions. Actions to control acid-rain-inducing emissions are thus rival based on where emissions will be deposited. However, control efforts provide nonexcludable benefits; that is, countries, destined for deposition, gain from these control efforts whether or not they support such efforts.

For "flow" air pollutant problems where emissions stay in the atmosphere for a relatively short time frame, spatial considerations become important. As a consequence, a weighted-sum aggregator technology characterizes these control efforts. This is illustrated in Figure 12.1, which displays a transport matrix, where countries are numbered or ordered from west to east in the direction of the prevailing winds. In the matrix, country 1 is the western-most country and country n is the eastern-most country. Emitter countries are indicated along the matrix's columns, while recipient countries are displayed along the rows. Each country must be assigned a column and a row placement because each is both an emitter and a recipient to some sulfur or NO_x pollution deposits. We use an arbitrary number of countries, denoted by n. The matrix entries A_{ij}s indicate the percentage of country j's emissions deposited on

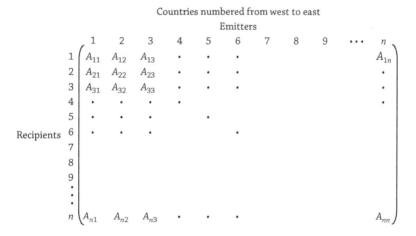

Figure 12.1
Transport matrix in share terms

country i. As is the convention, the first subscript indicates the row (recipient) country, while the second subscript denotes the column (emitting) country. If all emissions fall within the designated set of countries, then column totals must add to 100%. If, however, some emissions fall at sea or beyond the matrix-displayed region, then column totals would add to less than 100%. For Europe, the column totals for sulfur are close to 100%, while the column totals for NO_x are less than 100% (Eliassen and Saltbones, 1983). This follows because more nitrogen oxide falls at sea or drifts beyond the confines of Europe. The diagonal entries—the A_{ii}s—represent self-pollution and capture an essential localized benefit from reducing the acid rain problem, since less emissions translate into less self-pollution.[8] The A_{ji}s entries are the weights in the weighted-sum technology, so that the reduction in country i's pollution deposits is the sum of the emitting countries' cutbacks weighted by the appropriate A_{ij}s—for instance, country k's reduction in emissions is multiplied by A_{ik} to identify how its efforts limit depositions in country i during the relevant time period. Suppose that A_{ik} equals 40% and country k reduces its sulfur discharges by 1,000 tons, country i then receives 400 fewer tons of sulfur deposits as public good spillovers (Murdoch, Sandler, and Sargent, 1997).

With the west to east ordering in Figure 12.1, the entries above the diagonal indicate the import of pollution depositions from Eastern countries, while the entries below the diagonal represent the import of pollution depositions from Western countries. In Europe, the prevailing winds are from the west, so that the below-the-diagonal entries will in general greatly exceed those above the diagonal. Despite prevailing winds, entries above the diagonal are not zero because the configuration of high- and low-pressure systems can push some pollution from the east to the west. The generally larger values of the entries below the diagonal mean that Eastern European countries endure more imported sulfur or NO_x depositions than their Western counterparts. This, in turn, motivates Eastern countries to ratify treaties curbing acid rain once the flow of pollutants was documented.

In 1977, the Cooperative Program for Monitoring and Evaluation of the Long-Range Transmission of Air Pollutants in Europe (henceforth, EMEP) was established to calculate these transport matrices for sulfur, NO_x, and volatile organic compounds (VOCs). VOCs are hydrocarbons emissions that cause surface ozone or smog. EMEP-measured transport matrices were a crucial precursor to acid rain and associated air pollution treaties in Europe, since countries learned how they were adversely affected by their neighbor's pollutants.

---

8. If all A_{ij}s were 100, then the good would be purely public with every country in the matrix receiving all of a producer's output (emissions). If instead, all A_{ii}s were 100 and all off-diagonal entries were zero, then the good would be a private good with just the provider (emitter) receiving the good's benefits (emission deposition).

The EMEP matrices removed uncertainty which then paved the way for pollution-reducing protocols in Europe.

On November 13, 1979, the Long-Range Transboundary Air Pollution (LRTAP) Convention was adopted at a high-level meeting of the UN Economic Commission for Europe on the Protection of the Environment (UN Environment Program, 1991). Like other conventions, LRTAP called for the study of air pollution in Europe with subsequent protocols mandating action if deemed necessary. This evaluation was highly dependent on EMEP-measured transport matrices for sulfur, NO_x, and VOCs. The LRTAP Convention was ratified on March 16, 1983 by most European countries (UN Environment Program, 1991). A fascinating aspect of the ratification was the participation by the then-Communist countries—Bulgaria, Czechoslovakia, East Germany, Romania, the Soviet Union, and Yugoslavia—which generally did not participate in such treaties with Western Europe. On July 8, 1985, the Helsinki Protocol to the LRTAP Convention was framed and committed eventual ratifiers to curtail sulfur emissions by 30%, based on 1980 levels, as soon as possible or by 1993. On September 2, 1987, the Helsinki Protocol entered into force. Eastern European countries were generally quick to ratify this treaty—early ratifiers in 1986 included Belarus, Bulgaria, and the Soviet Union. Their behavior is easy to fathom insofar as the EMEP transport matrix for sulfur showed that these countries imported large quantities of sulfur depositions. As of 2014, the five westernmost European countries—Iceland, Ireland, Portugal, Spain, and the United Kingdom—still have not ratified the Helsinki Protocol (UN Economic Commission for Europe, 2014). This ratification reticence is understandable since these Western countries import little or no sulfur so that ratification places constraints on their behavior with little benefit except from reduced self-pollution.[9]

For NO_x emissions, protocols have been much slower and less stringent. On October 31, 1988, the Sofia Protocol was framed, requiring reductions in NO_x to return emissions to 1987 levels by December 31, 1994 (UN Environment Program, 1991). The Sofia Protocol entered into force on February 14, 1991. On June 14, 1994, the just-framed Oslo Protocol mandated further reductions in sulfur emissions beyond that of the Helsinki Protocol for most countries. The Oslo Protocol, which entered into force on 5 August 1998, tailors emission reductions for signing parties based on their marginal costs of abatement, thus ending the practice of across-the-board percentage cuts (Finus and Tjøtta, 2003). By tailoring these reductions to a country's marginal abatement costs, the Oslo Protocol promotes cost minimization;[10] that is,

9. The height of smokestacks in England meant less self-pollution of sulfur from power plants; however, some sulfur depositions affect Scotland to the north.

10. Cost minimization requires the equality of all participating countries' marginal abatement costs. In the absence of this equality, abatement levels can be adjusted to bring down abatement costs by making high marginal-cost countries abate less and low marginal-cost countries abate more.

Table 12.4. Select treaties on acid rain

Treaty	Date Ratified	Provision
• Long-Range Transboundary Air Pollution Convention (LRTAP)	March 16, 1983	Mandated scientific investigation and evaluation.
• Helsinki Protocol	September 2, 1987	Reduce sulfur emission by 30% of 1980 level by 1993 or as soon as possible.
• Sofia Protocol	February 14, 1991	Reduction in NO_x to 1987 levels by December 31, 1994.
• Oslo Protocol	August 5, 1998	Further sulfur reductions. Tailors emission reductions based on the signers' costs of abatement.
• Geneva Protocol	September 29, 1997	Reduce VOCs by at least 30% by 1999.
• Gothenburg Protocol[a]	May 15, 2005 May 4, 2012	Reduce sulfur dioxide, NO_x, ammonia, VOCs, and fine particulates in 2020 from 2005 levels. Assigned reductions vary by country according to costs of abatement and health consequences.

[a] Framed on November 30, 1999, and revised on May 4, 2012.
Source: UN Economic Commission for Europe (2014) at http://unece.org/env/lrtap/status/lrtap_s.html

countries with small marginal abatement costs are assigned greater mandated cutbacks than those with larger marginal abatement costs. With its nuclear energy dependence, France has a lower marginal abatement cost for sulfur than countries like Poland that relied on coal-fired power plants. This tailoring practice gives the treaty instrument greater flexibility in ensuring that each party perceives a net gain from its participation, despite different dependencies on fossil fuels and diverse abilities to curb emissions. As a consequence, treaty participation is wider.

For VOCs, the Geneva Protocol of November 18, 1991 required ratifiers to reduce annual emissions of select VOCs by at least 30% by 1999, using a chosen year between 1984 and 1990 for calculating the baseline emissions. A few ratifiers—Bulgaria, Greece, and Hungary—were allowed to choose 1999 for the baseline level (UN Economic Commission for Europe, 2014). This protocol entered into force on September 29, 1997, just over 10 years after the Helsinki Protocol. As in the case of the Oslo Protocol, there was some tailoring to countries (according to their baseline level) even though a set percentage reduction was mandated. The Geneva Protocol did not achieve cost minimization.

There is still fine tuning of the LRTAP in progress with the framing of the Gothenburg Protocol on November 30, 1999.[11] The most recent LRTAP Protocol continues to increase mandated reductions of sulfur, NO_x, ammonia, VOCs, and fine particulates (for example, black carbon or soot). The new protocol was ratified on May 15, 2005 and then made more stringent on May 4, 2012 for slated reductions for 2020. Countries' assigned reductions account for marginal abatement costs to promote minimization of abatement costs.

Table 12.4 summarizes the LRTAP Convention and its five primary protocols with their ratification dates and primary provisions. LRTAP agreements and actions underscore that there has been transnational cooperation within Europe regarding air pollution. When milestones in pollution reduction are obtained, new protocols increase mandated cutbacks.

Our current task is to explain why efforts to curtail sulfur emissions outpaced those to reduce NO_x. That is, why did the Helsinki Protocol have stricter mandatory reductions than the Sofia Protocol, and why was the Helsinki Protocol framed and ratified before the Sofia Protocol when both were addressing acid rain problems that possessed nearly identical nonrivalry and nonexcludability of benefits? A number of factors answer these two questions. First, sulfur causes more self-pollution than NO_x as shown in Figure 12.2,

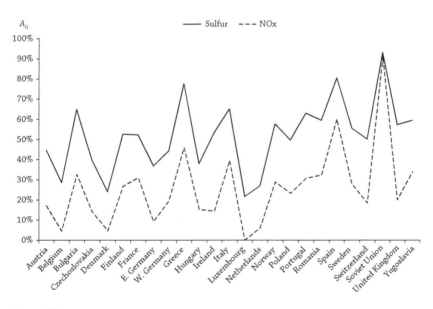

Figure 12.2
Self-pollution percentages for 1990

11. This paragraph is based on facts about the Gothenburg Protocol gleaned from UN Economic Commission for Europe (2014).

which displays the A_{ii}s for sulfur and NO_x during 1990.[12] With the exception of the former Soviet Union, sulfur self-pollution percentages are larger than those of NO_x, thereby giving countries a stronger incentive to curtail sulfur emissions.[13] The two plots in Figure 12.2 have nearly identical shapes because the countries' size is the prime determinant of self-pollution from emission depositions. Second, sulfur travels a shorter distance than NO_x from their sources; hence, more sulfur deposition is within the LRTAP Convention countries' territory (Sandnes, 1993). This gave these countries a stronger interest in consummating agreements with respect to sulfur. Third, for sulfur, major polluters are easy-to-control public utilities or large companies; for nitrogen, major polluters are more-difficult-to-control vehicle owners. The use of these vehicles varies directly with economic activity, rising during booms and declining during recessions. Thus, once countries signed pollution-reducing agreements, sulfur control was easier to accomplish within each ratifying country. Fourth, information on NO_x transport matrix took longer to develop than for sulfur, so that uncertainty was resolved more slowly in the case of NO_x. Fifth, rather substantial sulfur cutbacks from 1980 levels were achieved by 1985 before framing, as shown in Table 12.5, which indicates the percentage reduction in sulfur in 1985 from a 1980 benchmark (%SUL85) *prior to the* formulation of the Helsinki Protocol. Average reductions in sulfur from 1980 levels were already 20.59% in 1985. Projections for the next few years indicated that most potential ratifiers would exceed reductions of 30% prior to the treaty's date of ratification in 1987 (Murdoch, Sandler, and Sargent, 1997).

In Table 12.5, average sulfur cutbacks were almost 4% over the treaty-mandated cutbacks by 1990 (see %SUL90). Recall that countries had until 1993 to attain the 30% reduction. Apparently, the Helsinki Protocol essentially encoded cutbacks that most ratifiers would have achieved even without the treaty (Murdoch, Sandler, and Sargent, 1997; Murdoch, Sandler, and Vijverberg, 2003). So did the treaty achieve any real reduction in sulfur emissions? We believe that it had two important accomplishments: (1) it served to bring along some stragglers through peer pressure, and (2) it provided an institutional framework for future treaties. The latter characterizes the Oslo and Gothenburg protocols, where greater sulfur reductions were mandated.

We now turn to the Sofia Protocol on NO_x, where Table 12.5 tells a somewhat different story. The $\%NO_x87$ column shows that there was virtually no

---

12. The A_{ii}s values do not change annually since they involve percentages (Eliassen and Saltbones, 1983). Statistical tests show these transport matrices to be stable over time (Murdoch, Sandler, and Sargent, 1997). We chose 1990 because it corresponds to when NO_x cutbacks, mandated by the Sofia Protocol, were about to go into effect.

13. Our contrasts follow, in part, those provided in Murdoch, Sandler, and Sargent (1997).

Table 12.5. Percentage reductions in voluntary sulfur and NO_x emissions by country

Country		%SUL85	%SUL90	%NO_x87	%NO_x90
1.	Austria	50.75	47.39	4.88	5.13
2.	Belgium	45.41	16.38	32.81	−12.46
3.	Bulgaria	−12.88	−28.54	0.00	9.62
4.	Czechoslovakia	10.32	−8.79	16.28	2.08
5.	Denmark	23.89	30.18	−11.72	7.21
6.	Finland	34.59	25.48	−2.27	−7.41
7.	France	55.96	32.25	10.59	−7.36
8.	East Germany	−25.58	−41.63	−13.56	5.97
9.	West Germany	24.98	40.57	1.78	11.17
10.	Greece	−25.00	−55.00	0.00	0.00
11.	Hungary	13.97	8.11	−1.10	13.77
12.	Ireland	36.94	−5.68	−57.53	−17.39
13.	Italy	34.11	12.63	−14.86	−3.59
14.	Luxembourg	33.33	3.33	17.39	0.00
15.	Netherlands	40.77	25.36	−2.01	1.27
16.	Norway	28.57	31.43	−25.14	−1.75
17.	Poland	−4.88	−8.29	−2.00	16.34
18.	Portugal	25.56	−6.69	30.12	−5.17
19.	Romania	0.00	−30.00	0.00	0.00
20.	Spain	34.04	0.24	11.68	0.00
21.	Sweden	43.85	37.31	−2.86	6.26
22.	Switzerland	23.81	20.79	−2.04	8.00
23.	Soviet Union	13.05	3.12	−23.44	−7.84
24.	United Kingdom	23.97	−7.05	−10.03	−7.27
25.	Yugoslavia	−14.88	−43.34	−25.71	4.55
Average		20.59	3.98	−2.75	0.84

%SUL85 = % reduction in total sulfur emissions from 1980 to 1985 as a percent of 1980 emissions.
%SUL90 = % reduction in sulfur emissions, *beyond the 30% target reduction*, from 1980 to 1990 as a percentage of 1980 emissions.
%NO_x87 = % reduction in total NO_x emissions from 1980 to 1987 as a percentage of 1980 emissions.
%NO_x90 = % reduction in total NO_x emissions from 1987 to 1990 as a percentage of 1987 emissions.
Source: Data in Sandnes (1993)

average cutback in NO_x from 1980 levels in 1987, around the time when the Sofia Protocol was framed. Near the time of this treaty's ratification, the average reduction of NO_x emissions were less than 1%—specifically, 0.84%—of 1987 emissions, as shown by the %NO_x 90 column. This modest drop obviously influenced the rather small mandated cut in NO_x emission based on 1987 levels, encoded in the Sofia Protocol. Once again, noncooperative Nash behavior affected the treaty's provision.

Table 12.6. Different collective action factors affecting sulfur- and nitrogen-based acid rain

Sulfur-based acid rain	Nitrogen-based acid rain
• There is a great deal of self-pollution.	• There is much less self-pollution.
• Sulfur travels a shorter distance due to its weight.	• Nitrogen travels a longer distance due to its weight.
• Most of sulfur pollution falls within the treaty region—columns of transport matrix add to near 100%.	• Some NO_x falls on countries outside of the treaty region or at sea—columns of transport matrix add to less than 100%.
• Major polluters are easy-to-control public utilities or large corporations.	• Major polluters are difficult-to-control vehicle and truck owners.
• Information on sulfur transport matrix was known sooner.	• Information on NO_x transport matrix took longer to develop.
• Rather substantial sulfur cutbacks from 1980 levels achieved by 1985 before framing.	• Very modest cutbacks from 1980 to 1987 as a percentage of 1987 levels preceded framing.

Table 12.6 indicates the underlying differences that did more to facilitate sulfur than nitrogen cutbacks. In this regional paired comparison, spatial factors, embodied in the transport matrices, were partly behind the greater success with sulfur-based acid rain. Thus, the weighted-sum aggregators (or the third property of publicness) affected the contrasting success achieved by these two region-based acid rain problems. Remember that the aggregator technology did not influence the collective action outcomes for ozone shield depletion and climate change. Other regional pollution problems—for example, river and lake pollution—are influenced by their transport matrices. This is also true for disease and pest dispersion.

Finally, we turn to the Geneva Protocol on curbing VOCs. This protocol's contrast to the Helsinki Protocol depends on some of the same considerations that distinguished the Helsinki and Sofia Protocols. The delay in the Geneva Protocol was because VOCs transport was not monitored until years after sulfur and NO_x. VOC polluters include a large and diverse set of hard-to-control emitters, similar to those associated with NO_x emissions. VOCs can travel long distances, particularly the fine particles. A collective action inhibitor unique to VOCs was the large number of hydrocarbon compounds that required evaluation and control. Prior to any treaty, potential participants had to agree upon which VOC compounds' emissions to limit.[14] This necessitated potential treaty ratifiers to learn about more than one pollutant: in particular, how much progress they had made in curbing emissions to date, and how

14. This pollutant choice is still unfolding with the adoption of the Gothenburg Protocol and the recent inclusion of black carbon.

much progress they anticipated in the near term. When more than one pollutant is included in the same treaty, a bundling problem may arise where the toughest pollutant to control becomes the weakest link that holds up progress on the entire treaty.

CONCLUDING REMARKS

Our two paired comparisons provide some interesting insights. First, the three publicness properties of GPGs or RPGs are not sufficient to draw adequate prognoses of collective action. Other defining institutional characteristics—for example, the availability of substitutes, the extent of uncertainty, temporal aspects, and the nature of vested interests—may be more important determinants of collective action. As the ozone depletion and climate change contrast demonstrates, two GPG problems with virtually identical public good properties had much different success outcomes. Second, many regional challenges possess a spatial dimension that must be identified to gauge the prospects for successful collective action. Third, the Helsinki Protocol was smart not to include cutbacks in NO_x and VOCs, where less was known and collective action considerations were less conducive. Rather than providing greater grounds for negotiation as hypothesized by Barrett (2003a), bundling different pollutants into the same treaty instrument can delay progress to that for the pollutant where the least is known or which is the hardest to control. In the absence of bundling, any added-in transaction costs are likely to be countered by the increased efficiency stemming from faster and more decisive action on the easier-to-address pollutants. Fourth, the resolution of uncertainty with respect to any GPG or RPG environmental concern promotes effective and quick collective action. Fifth, flow pollutants (for example, sulfur emissions) are generally easier to handle than stock pollutants (for example, atmospheric stocks of GHGs), because action with respect to flow pollutants can result in immediate paybacks, thus motivating the current generation to act. Sixth, the sequence of amendments for the Montreal Protocol or the LRTAP Convention underscores that successful treaties can begin modestly so that countries become committed and an institutional framework for collective action is established. From this initial platform, greater degrees of commitments can be achieved as milestones are passed.

CHAPTER 13

Conclusion

As we conclude this book, a variety of global problems are vying for the attention of the international community. Greenhouse gas concentrations have risen to ever-increasing levels in the atmosphere. A controversial trade agreement between the Ukraine and the European Union (EU) has provoked a conflict with Russia over Ukraine's territorial integrity. The Ebola virus has overwhelmed the healthcare systems in some West African states, and has spread to Europe and North America. The terrorist group Islamic State of Iraq and Syria (ISIS) has captured territory in Iraq and Syria and has executed Western journalists and aid workers. And these prominent concerns overlook a host of other issues that affect multiple states and that can be solved only with political attention and economic resources. Our world frequently appears on the brink of disaster and, as a result, it is easy to disengage and become pessimistic about the future. In this book, our approach responds to these concerns differently. By examining issues one or two at a time through the framework of collective action theory, we detect common elements in what first seemed like quite different problems. Through further exploration, we find myriad grounds for optimism.

Despite countries' zealous protection of their sovereignty, the international community has a number of impressive achievements that are the result of successful cooperation. These successes include the post-war recovery in international trade, the eradication of smallpox, the thickening of the ozone layer, and dramatic decreases in sulfur-based acid rain. Other cooperative achievements—the eradication of polio, the elimination of agricultural trade barriers, and the destruction of chemical weapons—appear within easy reach. Thus, a longer-term and more systematic analysis of global problems offers much evidence that the barriers to transnational cooperation can be overcome in many circumstances.

Even when transnational problems dominate headlines for days or weeks at a time, the international community rarely has the resources and/or political will to deal simultaneously with them all. The most pressing problems often receive the most attention, whether or not they are likely to be solved. In this chapter, we compare efforts to prioritize different transnational collective actions. To simplify our task, we ask the reader to imagine himself or herself in the shoes of Microsoft Chairman Bill Gates in January 2000, when he began a new career as a philanthropist. Gates faced criticism over the marketing tactics of the company he founded, Microsoft, but his company's success provided him a plethora of resources to distribute via the Bill and Melinda Gates Foundation. How should this foundation spend resources in an efficient way to maximize their benefits for the planet? If you were Mr. Gates, how would you decide which of the world's compelling problems deserved your attention and resources? How can we even begin to compare such drastically different global issues as failed states and climate change? In this chapter we examine some answers to these difficult questions, highlight their strengths and weaknesses, and argue that collective action theory provides a set of tools that are suitable for this purpose.

One possibility is to simply ask people what the biggest problems are. In some ways, this is the mechanism behind responding to "most pressing" conflicts. Over the last decade, the Pew Research Global Attitudes Project established a reasonable list of priorities based upon such surveys. In 2007, for example, Pew found HIV/AIDS to be the biggest concern in sub-Saharan Africa and Asia. Pew also found that hunger and malnutrition were more important in Latin America and the Middle East, while access to medical care was the biggest priority in Central/Eastern Europe (Pew Research, 2007). Unfortunately, public opinion can change quickly, along with variations in media focus on particular problems. Moreover, survey responses may not accurately reflect choices when respondents must consider budget constraints or feasibility concerns. Thus, setting priorities according to the popularity of particular global issues may not generate the most efficient use of resources or even favorable political responses for policy makers. Furthermore, sustained responses to global problems on the basis of public support may not be possible.

Ideally, Bill Gates would be able to compare several potential solutions to global problems in terms of their aggregate benefits, anticipated costs, and political feasibility. At least two recent efforts have attempted to set a list of priorities for the world, with particular attention to the pervasiveness of poverty and development. One of these efforts occurred at the highest levels of international diplomacy, while the other was a largely academic exercise. Neither effort offers a perfect solution for sorting through the vast array of transnational problems, but together they help point a way forward.

Since the early 1960s, the United Nations (UN) has repeatedly created nu-merical goals to reflect its commitment to developing states. For several decades, the primary focus of these goals was raising economic growth to some minimally acceptable level—in the 1960s, it was 4% annually—in as many poor countries as possible (Anstee, 2012). Over time, the goals have expanded to include broader development concerns, such as child mortal-ity and the status of women. The latest—and arguably most important—iteration of the UN's development goals emerged from the "Millennium Summit" in September 2000, when representatives from 189 countries signed the Millennium Declaration. This Declaration created the Millen-nium Development Goals (MDGs), a list of eight brief goals with subcompo-nents that would be measured, tracked, and hopefully achieved over the next 15 years (United Nations, 2014b). The document reflected a crucial bargain struck between rich and poor countries. Rich countries would in-crease and better coordinate foreign aid toward these goals, while poor states agreed to improve governance and to take greater ownership of the goals (Bourguignon et al., 2010). Indeed, 18 months later in Monterrey, Mexico, rich countries agreed to greatly enhance their foreign aid contribu-tions to support the MDGs.

The MDGs specify eight general goals, each of which is a simply-stated aspiration like "ensure environmental sustainability" (for a complete list, see Table 13.1). These eight goals are elaborated in 18 specific targets, which are in turn measured by 60 specific quantitative indicators. For example, the general goal of ensuring environmental sustainability (the seventh MDG) includes a specific goal of cutting in half the proportion of the population without sustainable access to safe drinking water and basic sanitation.[1] As a whole, the MDGs reflect a broad and important set of priorities, and they have served as focal points for development and poverty reduction for rich and poor countries, for multilateral development agencies, and for nongov-ernmental organizations (NGOs).

As the original window for achieving the MDGs closes, some of the goals have already been achieved, and others are not far from their targets. For example, it was apparent by 2010 that the world had already cut extreme poverty in half. The United Nations (2014b) also claimed success in other

---

1. While these specific goals included exacting targets, some of the task of defining how to measure the targets was left to others. In the case of the goal for safe drinking water, that measurement was left to the Millennium Projects Task Force for Water and Sanitation. Even then, the measures used to assess progress toward the goal in question could differ across countries. Poor countries were more likely to have data that reflected surveys performed in five-year increments, while middle income coun-tries were more likely to have annual data collected directly by their bureaucrats.

Table 13.1. The Millennium Development Goals

Goal 1: Eradicate extreme poverty and hunger.	**Target 1a**: Halve the proportion of people whose income is less than one dollar per day.[a] **Target 1b**: Achieve full and productive employment and decent work for all, including women and young people. **Target 1c**: Halve the proportion of people who suffer from hunger.
Goal 2: Achieve universal primary education.	**Target 2a**: Ensure that children everywhere, boys and girls alike, will be able to complete a full course of primary schooling.
Goal 3: Promote gender equality and empower women.	**Target 3a**: Eliminate gender disparity in primary and secondary education, preferably by 2005, and in all levels of education no later than 2015.
Goal 4: Reduce child mortality.	**Target 4a**: Reduce by two-thirds the under-five mortality rate.
Goal 5: Improve maternal health.	**Target 5a**: Reduce by three-fourths the maternal mortality ratio. **Target 5b**: Achieve universal access to reproductive health.
Goal 6: Combat HIV/AIDS, malaria, and other diseases.	**Target 6a**: Halt and begin to reverse the spread of HIV/AIDS. **Target 6b**: Achieve, by 2010, universal access to treatment for HIV/AIDS for those who need it. **Target 6c**: Halt and begin to reverse the incidence of malaria and other major diseases.
Goal 7: Ensure environmental sustainability.	**Target 7a**: Integrate the principles of sustainable development into country policies and programs and reverse the loss of environmental resources. **Target 7b**: Reduce biodiversity loss and, achieving, by 2010, a significant reduction in the rate of loss. **Target 7c**: Halve the proportion of people without sustainable access to safe drinking water and basic sanitation.
Goal 8: Develop a global partnership for development.	**Target 8a**: Develop further an open, rule-based, predictable, nondiscriminatory trading and financial system. Include a commitment to good governance, development, and poverty reduction, both nationally and internationally. **Target 8b**: Address the special needs of landlocked developing countries and small island developing states.

[a]All targets explicitly set 2015 as a deadline, unless otherwise noted.

goals: reducing malaria and tuberculosis, improving drinking water, equalizing primary school enrollment for boys and girls, and increasing the political participation of women. These are impressive accomplishments, and indeed the prominence of the MDGs has not only increased overall levels of foreign aid, but has also raised awareness of mass poverty and its associated deprivations. Importantly, the push for measurable targets for the MDGs has greatly improved data collection on poverty and deprivation (Wilkinson and Hulme, 2012).

In other ways, the MDGs' process is less impressive. Inevitably, some critics quibble with the list of goals and argue that MDGs miss or overemphasize certain aspects of development, such as political violence and reducing inequality. Others argue that even the successful achievement of MDGs reflects concentrated efforts in just a few countries. For example, China and other East Asian countries have been disproportionately responsible for the decrease in extreme poverty. In contrast, India still retains a large concentration of the world's poor—32.9% of those living on less than $1.25 per day (United Nations, 2014b, p. 9). Despite the MDGs' focus on sub-Saharan Africa, those states are still some of the worst performing in some categories, including poverty reduction. Even in sub-Saharan Africa, countries can still vary widely in their performance on particular MDGs. For example, Bourguignon et al. (2010, p. 22) pointed out that the nine best performers in primary education enrollment have increased their enrollments by more than 5% per year, while in the same region, the five worst performers suffered declines in enrollment. The most persuasive critics argued that even successfully achieved MDGs mask great country heterogeneity, and that the process endangers good policy analysis by focusing the world's attention on a few indicators (Bourguignon et al., 2010; Clasen, 2012; Oestergaard, Alkema, and Lawn, 2013). Many of these measures are still not collected annually, and so year-to-year changes can really only be assessed for a limited number of countries.[2]

From our perspective, a bigger problem is the lack of prioritization across the goals. How important is women's education compared to maternal prenatal care? Should access to clean water take precedence over the fight against hunger? How should funding be allocated across goals? Are there synergies in tackling particular problems together? We contrast the MDGs with a different approach, the Copenhagen Consensus, which has prioritized the kind of cost-benefit analysis we have undertaken in places in this book.

2. Bourguignon et al. (2010, p. 20) reported that the capacity for producing the high quality information needed to assess annual progress toward MDGs is only held by "a limited number of countries in Latin America, together with China, India, Indonesia, South Africa, and Thailand."

In contrast to the MDGs, the Copenhagen Consensus was a relatively small-scale and academic operation. In May 2004, Danish academic Bjørn Lomborg, together with *The Economist* magazine, organized the first Copenhagen Consensus conference. For each of 10 broad global issues, the conference invited three leading scholars to focus on specific solutions. In a first stage, those academics would present their best case for why that problem deserved consideration by the global community. Importantly, presenters were asked to evaluate the benefits of spending each dollar on measurable solutions, and this provided a common framework for evaluation. In a second stage, a separate panel of eight highly reputed economists would each rank the 10 global issues, and the median value of their ranking would determine overall rankings.

In the first round of the conference in 2004, the issues included climate change, communicable diseases, civil wars, education, hunger and malnutrition, population and migration, trade barriers, water quality, and poor governance and corruption (Lomborg, 2006). Control of HIV/AIDS was ranked at the very top, along with the provision of micronutrients, trade liberalization via the World Trade Organization's (WTO's) Doha Round, and control of malaria. At the very bottom of the list were two different types of carbon taxes, the Kyoto Protocol, and guest worker programs for unskilled migrant laborers.

In 2008, the exercise was repeated with a modified list of 10 global challenges, including air pollution, conflicts, diseases, education, global warming, malnutrition, sanitation and water, subsidies and trade barriers, terrorism, and women in development. Different experts were asked to present their research,[3] and again a separate panel ranked potential solutions based on cost-benefit analysis. At the top of the panel's rankings was vitamin A and zinc for children, finishing the Doha round of trade liberalization, iron and iodization, immunization, bio fortification, deworming and nutrition, reducing the price of primary school and improving access to school for girls.

In 2012, the Copenhagen Consensus was no longer sponsored by *The Economist*, and the nonrenewal of additional funding by the Danish government meant that the third round of the conference was the final one. Again, categories were refined, and both trade barriers and corruption were dropped due to the political hurdles involved in overcoming those goals. Additionally, terrorism was dropped as a category, primarily due to the low benefit-cost ratios associated with most counterterrorism policies found in the second

---

3. For full disclosure, co-author Sandler presented research on terrorism at this conference. The paper is available at http://www.copenhagenconsensus.com/publication/second-copenhagen-consensus-terrorism.

Table 13.2. Challenges and solutions from the 2012 Copenhagen Consensus

Hunger and education	Bundled interventions to reduce undernutrition in pre-schoolers ($3 billion)
Infectious disease	Subsidy for malaria combination treatment ($300 million)
Infectious disease	Expanded childhood immunization coverage ($1 billion)
Infectious disease	Deworming of schoolchildren ($300 million)
Infectious disease	Expanding tuberculosis treatment ($1.5 billion)
Hunger and biodiversity and climate change	Research and development on crop yields ($2 billion)
Natural disasters	Effective early-warning systems ($1 billion)
Infectious disease	Strengthening surgical capacity ($3 billion)
Chronic disease	Hepatitis B immunization ($120 million)
Chronic disease	Acute heart attack low-cost drugs ($200 million)

Copenhagen Consensus. New categories were added, including biodiversity, natural disasters, and population growth.[4] In addition to ranking the solutions, the panel was also given a hypothetical budget to spend for this third round of the Copenhagen Consensus. The 2012 rankings were again determined by benefit-cost ratio, and are shown in Table 13.2. At the top of the list was $3 billion to be spent on bundled micronutrients for children, followed by $300 million on malaria treatment, $1 billion on childhood immunization, $300 million on child deworming, and $1.5 billion on tuberculosis treatment. Next on the list, agricultural research and development received $2 billion, an early-warning system for natural disasters received $1 billion, increased surgical capacity in developing countries received $3 billion, hepatitis B immunization received $120 million, and low-cost drugs for heart attacks received $200 million.

Across the three rounds, it is striking that several public health items, particularly focused on children in the developing world, rise to the top of the list. Partly as a result, public health has received real-world support from the Gates Foundation, the Global Polio Eradication Initiative, the Global Fund to Fight HIV/AIDS, and others. Likewise, some solutions consistently appear at the bottom of the list, including various carbon taxes and efforts to control total emissions of greenhouse gases (GHGs). This is not by chance—we have already pointed out the time profile of costs and benefits, which do

---

4. Research papers are still online, and can be accessed at http://www.copenhagenconsensus.com/Projects/CC12/Research.aspx.

not yield positive net benefits in the short term (see Chapter 12 on the environment).

A key criticism of both MDGs and the Copenhagen Consensus revolves around the treatment of global problems as separable or distinct. Consider, for example, that reducing agricultural trade barriers would lessen malnutrition by making food cheaper. Reduced barriers could also generate new resources for consuming other important services like education. In fact, many of these challenges are interrelated. Lomborg (2006, p. 111) recognized this: "programs have a low chance of success unless the country targeted is peaceful and not corrupt, and sustained long-term improvement will not occur without substantial progress being made in poverty reduction." In general, more thought needs to go into not just the net benefits of these solutions, but also the sequence in which they should be tackled.

Another criticism concerns the reasons for dropping trade liberalization and corruption. Some solutions are more politically thorny than others, but political costs are not included in these calculations. To the extent that political costs mirror estimations of economic costs, this is not a concern, but where collective action solutions with low economic costs have high political costs, the Copenhagen Consensus overestimates the return on investment by ignoring these political costs.

The Copenhagen Consensus served an important purpose. Utilizing an economic approach, it attempted to understand how the international community can best spend resources today to maximize benefits over the near term. As a result, it encouraged researchers to speak more directly to policy makers in a common framework that allows comparisons across pressing issues. The approach has real strengths, particularly in its ability to find consistent policy priorities, but like the MDGs, it is ultimately an imperfect attempt to sort global issues by importance. While it may influence policy makers, the absence of any institutional connection to international organizations or national policy makers reduces the chances of its findings being implemented.

The MDGs' prioritization is more difficult to understand, since the process by which MDGs were chosen was largely closed. It includes many important goals, but separates those from other issues entirely. Issues such as civil wars that do not appear on the list of MDGs are unaddressed by those focused on measuring and accomplishing the items on the list. This is particularly problematic because civil wars and other forms of political violence plague developing countries and hamper their development (see Chapter 10). MDGs also prioritize states and the United Nations as actors. By contrast, the Copenhagen Consensus has a transparent process and uses a common methodology that allows for direct comparisons across issues. Because the Copenhagen Consensus is largely an academic exercise, it does not privilege any particular actors as driving solutions, and this approach clearly reduces its impact. What both of these efforts miss is an effort to gauge the viability of solutions to global issues. Here collective action theory shows its strengths.

COLLECTIVE ACTION THEORY

Our approach in this book is built on collective action theory, which has influenced scholars for 50 years, ever since the publication of Olson (1965). Its applications to international politics have been appreciated since at least Sandler and Cauley (1975), and it was particularly important for scholarly debates in the 1980s and early 1990s (Axelrod, 1984; Keohane, 1984). Collective action theory offers a unique perspective to the problem of prioritizing global issues because it organizes problems according to their strategic similarity and offers insights regarding which may be most easily solved (see Chapters 2 through 4). Combined with the principle of subsidiarity, it also identifies the level at which each problem could be solved most efficiently— bilateral, multilateral, regional, or global. As an added bonus, basing the analysis on game theory means that the exercise is transparent and open to debate like the Copenhagen Consensus.

Our book repeatedly demonstrates the analytical capabilities of collective action theory. Chapters 1 through 4 review basic collective action theory, its connection to market imperfections, and the rules of thumb that result. Transnational problems can be characterized across a number of dimensions, including the number of actors affected, the presence of a leader country, the distribution of those effects across the actors, the knowledge of the costs and benefits of potential solutions, (non)excludability and (non)rivalry of potential solutions, and the aggregation technology associated with public good problems. Different constellations of these attributes lead to different prognoses for successful transnational cooperation. Table 13.3 offers a summary of collective action theory's factors that are conducive to effective transnational cooperation. Some factors are relatively straightforward—for example, having fewer actors generally makes cooperation easier—but in many cases factors interact in complex ways. Many of collective action theory's predictions are contingent on the characteristics of the problem and the interaction of those characteristics. For example, high levels of resource inequality across a group of states can hinder efforts to address weakest-link problems, but can promote solutions to best-shot problems. The lowest hurdles to collective action involve scenarios with a smaller number of countries in close proximity, and those whose costs and benefits are well understood. Additionally, solutions that provide near-term benefits are more likely than those whose benefits accrue only to future generations.

Our issues-based chapters use paired comparisons to demonstrate collective action theory's insights, and in many cases this theory makes clear

Table 13.3. Factors that enhance the likelihood of cooperation

- The presence of fewer relevant actors assists the achievement of cooperation.
- Positive net benefits for all affected countries promote cooperative action.
- Having more winners than losers bolsters cooperative action.
- Little uncertainty about costs and benefits fosters cooperative action.
- A favorable time profile in which benefits are felt quickly relative to costs increases action.
- Group homogeneity (i.e., similar tastes and endowments) helps provision for weaker/weakest-link public goods.
- Leadership by a key country that is willing to expend resources is particularly useful for providing better/best-shot goods.
- Partial rivalry and excludability (club goods) are conducive to collective action.
- Use of selective incentives to enhance net benefits fosters cooperative action.

predictions of individual countries' behaviors. In Chapter 9 on transnational crime, we present evidence that global weakest-link problems like money laundering are unlikely ever to be completely solved due to the enormous incentives for a single country to cheat. In Chapter 10, we compare counter-terrorism policies and find that defensive policies are more likely to be provided than offensive ones, leading to wasteful overspending on defense and underspending on proactive measures that can make all potential targeted countries safer.

Collective action theory not only generalizes the benefit-cost framework of the Copenhagen Consensus to a larger set of issues, but it also adds the dimension of strategic interactions. Strategic thinking is crucial in the arena of transnational politics because states and other actors can rarely achieve their goals alone. Each actor in international politics is constrained by its ability to influence other actors, but outcomes are determined by their joint actions. Game theory addresses precisely these essential interdependencies. By capturing the most important features of international interactions, game theorists can offer explanations for unsatisfactory but persistent outcomes, such as inaction on a pressing international problem. Similarly, game theory explains successful cooperation as following from individual actions that result in positive net benefits for participants. Game theory is a particularly useful tool for analyzing the behavior of sovereign states, which cannot rely on supranational actors to reward cooperation and punish defection. Without credible enforcement mechanisms, states work together most readily when facing a particularly dire outcome in the absence of collective action—such chicken games can explain many alliances and other forms of cooperation. As states successfully resolve some collective action problems, they may be able to build on those successes to work together on other problems.

Collective action theory also provides insights about the limits of cooperation. Some global issues are particularly difficult to solve due to their underlying strategic properties. Of all the problems analyzed in this book, reducing GHG emissions is perhaps the most difficult for multiple reasons (see Chapter 12). These include the uncertain benefits to acting now; the time profile of those benefits; the presence of gainer and loser countries; and the current unavailability of cheap substitutes for fossil fuels. Other issues that require truly global cooperation, such as establishing global standards for financial stability, face difficult hurdles due to the very incentives created by their success—the more countries agree to harmonize banking regulations, the greater are the economic incentives for other countries to cheat or never to cooperate.

The form of cooperation matters as well. In some cases, collective action theory offers ideas for customizing international negotiations and/or institutions in ways that can maximize the likelihood of continued cooperation. This is perhaps most easily demonstrated in the WTO example from Chapter 7— the WTO allows states to renege temporarily on commitments to free trade when those commitments become too onerous, usually due to their domestic political cost. When rich states receive disproportionately large benefits from subsidizing the efforts of poor states, weakest links can be strengthened. Chapter 6 describes several mechanisms through which international institutions—not just formal organizations but also treaties—can be designed to enhance benefits for cooperation. These include threshold membership requirements, refunds, and cost-sharing (see Chapters 2 through 4).

For truly global problems, significant capacity exists in the form of the many organs of the United Nations, as well as the international financial institutions (the International Monetary Fund, World Bank, and the WTO). However, these organizations are often tasked with addressing problems that are less than global in scope (see Chapter 10's discussion of the United Nations' role in many civil wars). The principle of subsidiarity suggests that many of these problems would be better addressed by regional organizations instead (see Chapter 4). Other key elements of global governance are still not well funded, including peacekeeping and the World Health Organization (WHO). As such, they continue to depend on powerful states, nonstate actors, and other international organizations to accomplish their missions (see Chapter 6). This scenario is unlikely to change in the near future, since states are extremely unlikely to delegate the power to raise taxes to international bodies or to substantially increase their direct funding of those organizations. As a result, much transnational cooperation is funded via ad hoc and short-term methods that leave organizations without permanent capabilities. The WHO's campaign against smallpox, for example, did not leave the organization with a significantly enhanced capability over the long term. The resources that WHO devoted to that project did not simply shift into eradicating another disease, but were dismantled once its goal was achieved.

Enhancing regional institutions can encourage solutions to problems whose effects are confined to that geographic area. Regional approaches reduce the number of actors involved—enhancing the collective action prognosis—and typically involve the states that are most affected (Chapter 4). Unfortunately, few regional organizations possess significant budgets or staff to coordinate information gathering, much less sustained diplomacy toward regional issues. Even small capabilities can translate into success in transnational cooperation, however. In the case of the Convention on Long-Range Transboundary Air Pollution (LRTAP), measuring pollution levels and sharing that information was enough to reduce sulfur pollution in most European states, as shown in Chapter 12.

Our approach shows that these institutional gaps may not hinder the resolution of some global problems that can be addressed by existing institutions or via ad hoc transnational cooperation. Problems that disproportionately affect powerful states are more likely to be addressed if they increase those states' willingness to lead. Resource inequality can likewise enhance the probability of successful cooperation for best-shot public goods. "Coalitions of the willing" and other loose collectives will continue to play an important role in addressing short-term threats with undesirable consequences. Existing institutions like the United Nations play important roles in legitimizing such groupings, but need not serve as the key actor in all cases.

In fact, rather than expecting more and more of existing institutions, new structures of international cooperation may be better suited to address existing and new problems. Although each new treaty or international organization poses transaction costs, those costs have surely declined in recent years as communication costs have declined and as networks of related government officials and NGOs have grown more robust (Slaughter, 2004). Even relatively weak organizations like the Financial Action Task Force and the Basel Committee have had some successes in coordinating states' actions due to their narrow focus. Clubs or organizations that start with a few likeminded states are likely to establish higher standards, which can then be adopted by others (or foisted on them) as their benefits become clear (Chapters 4 and 8). Such clubs also facilitate regular interactions among bureaucrats or other relevant individuals, which help to harmonize standard operating procedures and regulatory understandings. The EU is a good example of cooperation that has grown over time as its benefits to members have become apparent, but Euro-skepticism has arisen in virtually all member states. As a result, expanding transnational cooperation via Brussels is likely to become more difficult, and countries are unlikely to surrender much more sovereignty in sensitive areas like fiscal policy and national security. Even as some elements of cooperation have become cheaper, others—particularly sovereignty costs—remain high. We therefore conclude that the EU's federated model is not one that will be widely emulated.

Collective action theory draws our attention to a specific set of variables that identifies common strategic elements across different problems—for example, the three properties of public goods. We are the first to admit that those variables are not always sufficient to explain why some problems get solved and others do not. In a few of our cases, we have highlighted additional considerations that may be relevant. Domestic political benefits may be difficult to measure (for example, President Clinton's targeting narcoterrorism as a national security threat). Likewise, NGOs may have preferences that promote nonmonetary objectives (the willingness of Doctors without Borders to provide first responder services for many disease outbreaks). In principle, these motivations can be considered in the cost-benefit framework with ranges of appropriate estimates, just as with other data that are measured with error.

In scholarly circles, approaches similar to ours have been criticized for a number of reasons, including ignoring power in international relations (Mearsheimer, 1994), failing to consider domestic politics and the rising importance of nonstate actors, and requiring too much self-interest on the part of states. We incorporate some of these elements into our analysis. In Chapter 5, we show that some consideration of power is possible by allowing a more powerful state to move first. This is clearly a limited notion of power, but allowing agenda control or other special powers to a small number of states is within the capabilities of more advanced game-theoretic models (see Powell, 1999; Stone, 2011). Power is particularly relevant as the United States declines relative to newly emerging great powers, especially China. Many global public goods cannot be provided without the participation of such rapidly growing states. China's and India's participation is crucial in revising the Kyoto Protocol if it is to slow GHG accumulations. Likewise, multilateral trade liberalization will only proceed with China's and India's support as long as other developing countries look to them for leadership.

Our analysis focuses primarily on states, which we treat in most cases as unitary actors, but throughout the text, we note the importance of domestic politics in structuring the incentives to the leaders of countries. Understanding trade liberalization as a Prisoners' Dilemma revolves around the preferences and power of domestic groups, particularly import-competitors and exporters. Many game-theoretic models of international cooperation incorporate domestic actors (Dai, 2005; Bueno de Mesquita et al., 2003), so that game theory is not confined to treating states as the predominant actor. We confine our game-theoretic analysis to state interactions for tractability—adding nested players would complicate games considerably.

Modeling nonstate actors that create or worsen transnational problems has a long history in the literature on terrorism. Where nonstate actors, like terrorist groups or pirates, are likely to be part of collective action problems for states, they are more likely to be included in formal models. Where non-state actors like Doctors without Borders or the Bill and Melinda Gates Foundation attempt to help resolve challenges for the international community, they deserve greater consideration as strategic actors. This is beginning to change (see Murdie, 2014) but incorporating the unique capabilities of NGOs as a force for transnational collective action is an area that needs improved scholarship. Throughout this book, we endeavor to highlight the potential and existing roles for nonstate actors.

The most frequent criticisms of using game theory for applied analysis center on the underlying assumptions of the models. For example, game theory usually presumes no credible communication on the part of the actors (i.e., the players are in separate rooms in a Prisoners' Dilemma). Obviously this is a strong assumption, and through communication, players can establish considerable trust over time. In international politics, for example, conventions set expectations for states to then sign a treaty that constrains their future actions in some way (Sandler, 2008). Often, successive treaties then expand the constraints on their member states—witness the Montreal Protocol, the EU, and the multilateral bargaining successes in GATT. The no-communication assumption can be broken with sequential-play games when one agent moves first as in a leadership model, pre-play communication corresponding to cheap talk, or institutional rules correlating actions among countries. Such situations are discussed throughout the book.

Results of individuals participating in laboratory-based games have shown that face-to-face interactions result in more cooperation than predicted in some game-theoretic models. It is, however, unclear how such results transfer to international diplomacy. Because international relations still involves intercultural communication in a high-stakes atmosphere of mutual distrust, noncooperative game theory provides an excellent first approximation of the interactions, and it will continue to do so for the foreseeable future because states remain reluctant to yield sovereignty to supranational institutions.

CONCLUDING REMARKS

The world can overcome collective action problems—for example, the MDGs and the Copenhagen Consensus direct considerable attention toward addressing some current transnational issues. Our analysis suggests that best-shot problems will be overcome most easily, often without the need for new institutions or prolonged diplomatic negotiations. Likewise, assurance problems often lend themselves naturally to solutions, particularly if one state has agenda-setting power. Prisoners' Dilemmas are more difficult, but when addressed with institutional mechanisms that penalize defection, such as the WTO's retaliation mechanism, they can also be overcome. Weakest-link problems, especially those that are truly global in scope, are particularly difficult to address given countries' different abilities to meet an acceptable level of action. For the hardest problems, the international community—states, intergovernmental organizations, and NGOs—must strive to find solutions that overcome these basic strategic dilemmas as well as the unique characteristics of each issue.

We repeatedly emphasize the importance of understanding the costs and benefits of cooperation, which points to a particularly important role for scientific understanding. As such, MDGs, Copenhagen Consensus, and the collective action approach all agree that reducing uncertainty about the costs and benefits of particular policy choices is enormously important. Scientific discoveries can enhance cooperation in their own right if they improve the perceived benefit-cost ratio for states; such discoveries have played an important role in previous successes. For example, the bifurcated needle and freeze-dried vaccines improved the success rate of smallpox vaccines, reducing the overall cost of WHO's campaign to eradicate the disease. Having substitute production processes, not dependent on chlorofluorocarbons or other ozone-shield depleters, was crucial for the success of the Montreal Protocol (Chapter 12). Developing alternative energy sources that produce fewer GHGs may be the single most important step in combating climate change, because these alternative sources could dramatically reduce the present-day costs of action. Interaction between scientists and policy makers is thus more crucial than ever in addressing the biggest challenges of the next century.

Globalization will continue to expand the number of issues that require transnational cooperation, and new efforts will be needed. Novel disease outbreaks, new security threats (both physical and virtual), and innovative criminal activities will emerge. Fortunately, existing transnational networks should help to identify the relevant actors capable of effecting change. In many cases, these may be existing multilateral organizations or government agencies with requisite capabilities and past experience. To the extent that future transnational problems resemble prior problems, cooperation through existing institutions can speed responses and facilitate solutions. As such, prior cooperation will enhance the world's ability to address future problems. In other cases, new institutions or novel forms of cooperation may need to be created to address unique properties of emerging problems. As the world identifies transnational problems, collective action theory still offers key insights into customizing responses for each.

REFERENCES

Abbott, Kenneth W., and Duncan Snidal (2000), "Hard and Soft Law in International Governance," *International Organization*, 54(3), 421–456.

Akerlof, George A. (1970), "The Market for 'Lemons': Quality Uncertainty and the Market Mechanism," *Quarterly Journal of Economics*, 84(3), 488–500.

Alcamo, Joseph M., and Eliodora Runca (1986), "Some Technical Dimensions of Transboundary Air Pollution," in Cees Flinterman, Barbara Kwiatkowska, and Johan G. Lammers (eds.), *Transboundary Air Pollution: International Legal Aspects of the Cooperation of States* (Dordecht: Martinus Nijhoff), 1–17.

Alexander, Yonah, Marjorie Anne Browne, and Allan S. Nanes (1979), *Control of Terrorism: International Documents* (New York: Crane Russak).

Alexander, Yonah, and Dennis Pluchinsky (1992), *Europe's Red Terrorists: The Fighting Communist Organizations* (London: Frank Cass).

Anderson, Roy M., and Robert M. May (1991), *Infectious Diseases of Humans: Dynamics and Control* (Oxford: Oxford University Press).

Andreas, Peter (2013), "Gangster's Paradise," *Foreign Affairs*, 92(2), 22–28.

Andreas, Peter, and Ethan Nadelmann (2006), *Policing the Globe: Criminalization and Crime Control in International Relations* (Oxford: Oxford University Press).

Andreoni, James (1988), "Privately Provided Public Goods in a Large Economy: The Limits of Altruism," *Journal of Public Economics*, 35(1), 57–73.

Angrist, Joshua D., and Adriana D. Kugler (2007), "Rural Windfall or a New Resource Curse? Coca, Income, and Civil Conflict in Colombia," IZA Discussion Paper 2790, Institute for the Study of Labor, Bonn, Germany.

Anstee, Margaret Joan (2012), "Millennium Development Goals: Milestones on a Long Road," in Rorden Wilkinson and David Hulme (eds.), *The Millennium Development Goals and Beyond: Global Development after 2015* (New York: Routledge), 17–34.

Arce, Daniel G., and Todd Sandler (2001), "Transnational Public Goods: Strategies and Institutions," *European Journal of Political Economy*, 17(3), 493–516.

Arce, Daniel G., and Todd Sandler (2002), *Regional Public Goods: Typologies, Provision, Financing, and Development Assistance* (Stockholm: Almquist and Wiksell International for Expert Group on Development Assistance, Swedish Ministry for Foreign Affairs).

Arce, Daniel G., and Todd Sandler (2005), "Counterterrorism: A Game-Theoretic Analysis," *Journal of Conflict Resolution*, 49(2), 183–200.

Arms Control Association (2014), "Chemical Weapons Convention Signatories." Available at https://www.armscontrol.org/factsheets/cwcsig. Accessed September 19, 2014.

Avgouleas, Emilios (2013), "Effective Governance of Global Financial Markets: An Evolutionary Plan for Reform," *Global Policy*, 4(Supplement 1), 74–84.

Axelrod, Robert (1984), *The Evolution of Cooperation* (New York: Basic Books).

Babor, Thomas, Jonathan Caulkins, Griffith Edwards, and Benedikt Fischer (2010), *Drug Policy and the Public Good* (Oxford: Oxford University Press).

Bagnoli, Mark, and Michael McKee (1991), "Voluntary Contribution Games: Efficient Private Provision of Public Goods," *Economic Inquiry*, 29(2), 351–366.

Bagwell, Kyle, and Robert W. Staiger (2002), *The Economics of the World Trading System* (Cambridge: MIT Press).

Baldwin, Richard (1993), "A Domino Theory of Regionalism," NBER Working Paper 4465, National Bureau of Economic Research, Cambridge, MA.

Bank for International Settlements (BIS) (2014a), "History of the Basel Committee." Available at http://www.bis.org/about/history.htm. Accessed May 5, 2014.

Bank for International Settlements (BIS) (2014b), "Consolidated Banking Statistics." Available at http://www.bis.org/statistics/consstats.htm. Accessed May 5, 2014.

Barrett, Scott A. (1994), "Self-Enforcing International Environmental Agreements," *Oxford Economic Papers*, 46(4), 878–894.

Barrett, Scott A. (1999), "Montreal versus Kyoto: International Cooperation and the Global Environment," in Inge Kaul, Isabelle Grunberg, and Marc A. Stern (eds.), *Global Public Goods: International Cooperation in the 21st Century* (New York: Oxford University Press), 192–213.

Barrett, Scott A. (2003a), *Environment and Statecraft: The Strategy of Environmental Treaty-Making* (New York: Oxford University Press).

Barrett, Scott A. (2003b), "Global Disease Eradication," *Journal of European Economic Association*, 1(2–3), 591–600.

Barrett, Scott A. (2007), "The Smallpox Eradication Game," *Public Choice*, 130(1–2), 179–207.

Barrett, Scott A. (2010), "Stop! The Polio Vaccination Cessation Game," *The World Bank Economic Review*, 24(3), 361–385.

Barton, John H., Judith L. Goldstein, Timothy E. Josling, and Richard H. Steinberg (2006), *The Evolution of the Trade Regime: Politics, Law, and Economics of the GATT and the WTO* (Princeton, NJ: Princeton University Press).

Becker, Gary S., Kevin M. Murphy, and Michael Grossman (2006), "The Market for Illegal Goods: The Case of Drugs," *Journal of Political Economy*, 114(1), 38–60.

Benedick, Richard E. (1991), *Ozone Diplomacy* (Cambridge, MA: Harvard University Press).

Berglas, Eitan (1976), "On the Theory of Clubs," *American Economic Review*, 66(2), 116–121.

Bergstrom, Theodore C., Lawrence Blume, and Hal Varian (1986), "On the Private Provision of Public Goods," *Journal of Public Economics*, 29(1), 25–49.

Berrettoni, Daniel, and Jorge Lucángeli (2012), "MERCOSUR: Asymmetries and the MERCOSUR Structural Convergence Fund (FOCEM)," *Integration & Trade Journal*, 16(1), 33–43.

Biello, David (2013), "Greenhouse Goo," *Scientific American*, 309(1), 56–61.

Binmore, Ken (1992), *Fun and Games* (Lexington, MA: D. C. Heath).

Blomberg, S. Brock, Rozlyn C. Engel, and Reid Sawyer (2010), "On the Duration and Sustainability of Transnational Terrorist Organizations," *Journal of Conflict Resolution*, 54(2), 303–310.

Blomberg, S. Brock, Khusrav Gaibulloev, and Todd Sandler (2011), "Terrorist Group Survival: Ideology, Tactics, and Base of Operations," *Public Choice*, 149(3–4), 441–463.

Blomberg, S. Brock, Gregory D. Hess, and Athanasios Orphanides (2004), "The Macroeconomic Consequences of Terrorism," *Journal of Monetary Economics*, 51(5), 1007–1032.

Borlini, Leonardo (2014), "The Economics of Money Laundering," in Philip Reichel and Jay Albanes (eds.), *Handbook of Transnational Crime and Justice* (Thousand Oaks, CA: Sage), 227–242.

Bourguignon, François, Agnès Bénassy-Quéré, Stefan Dercon, Antonio Estache, Jan Willem Gunning, Ravi Kanbur, Stephan Klasen, Simon Maxwell, Jean-Philippe Platteau, and Amedo Spadaro (2010), "The Millennium Development Goals: An Assessment," in Michael Spence and Ravi Kanbur (eds.), *Equity and Growth in a Globalizing World* (Washington, DC: Commission on Growth and Development), 17–39.

Bove, Vincenzo, and Leandro Elia (2011), "Supplying Peace: Participation in and Troop Contribution to Peacekeeping Missions," *Journal of Peace Research*, 48(6), 699–714.

Brandt, Patrick T., and Todd Sandler (2009), "Hostage Taking: Understanding Terrorism Event Dynamics," *Journal of Policy Modeling*, 31(5), 758–778.

Brandt, Patrick T., and Todd Sandler (2010), "What Do Transnational Terrorists Target? Has It Changed? Are We Safer?" *Journal of Conflict Resolution*, 52(2), 214–236.

Breton, Albert (1965), "A Theory of Government Grants," *Canadian Journal of Economics and Political Science*, 31(2), 147–157.

Britannica (2009), "The Financial Crisis of 2008." Available at http://www.britannica.com/EBchecked/topic/1484264/The-Financial-Crisis-of-2008-Year-In-Review-2008/. Accessed July 11, 2013.

Brophy-Baermann, Bryan, and John A. C. Conybeare (1994), "Retaliating against Terrorism: Rational Expectations and the Optimality of Rules versus Discretion," *American Journal of Political Science*, 38(1), 196–210.

Broz, J. Lawrence (1997), *The International Origins of the Federal Reserve System* (Ithaca, NY: Cornell University Press).

Bruce, Neil (1990), "Defence Expenditures by Countries in Allied and Adversarial Relationships," *Defence and Peace Economics*, 1(3), 179–195.

Brummer, Chris (2010), "Why Soft Law Dominates International Finance—And Not International Trade," *Journal of International Economic Law*, 13(3), 623–643.

Buchanan, James M. (1965), "An Economic Theory of Clubs," *Economica*, 32(1), 1–14.

Bueno de Mesquita, Bruce, James D. Morrow, Randolph Siverson, and Alastair Smith (2003), *The Logic of Political Survival* (Boston: MIT Press).

Burnside, Craig, and David Dollar (2000), "Aid, Policies, and Growth," *American Economic Review*, 90(4), 847–868.

Busnell, James, Carla Peterman, and Catherine Wolfram (2008), "Local Solutions to Global Problems: Climate Change Policies and Regulatory Jurisdiction," *Review of Environment Economics and Policy*, 2(2), 175–193.

Cannata, Francesco, and Mario Quagliariello (2009), "The Role of Basel II in the Subprime Financial Crisis: Guilty or Not Guilty?," CAREFIN Working Paper 3/09, Milan, Italy.

Carey, David (2009), "Iceland: The Financial and Economic Crisis," OECD Economics Department Working Paper 725, Paris, France.

Caulkins Jonathan B., and Peter Reuter (2010), "How Drug Enforcement Affects Drug Prices," *Crime and Justice*, 39(1), 213–271.

Center for Systemic Peace (2014), *Annual Global Report 2014 on Conflict, Governance, and State Fragility*. Available at http://www.systemicpeace.org/globalreport. html. Accessed September 19, 2014.

Chen, Lincoln C., Tim G. Evans, and Richard A. Cash (1999), "Health as a Global Public Good," in Inge Kaul, Isabelle Grunberg, and Marc A. Stern (eds.), *Global Public Goods: International Cooperation in the 21st Century* (New York: Oxford University Press), 284–304.

Claessens, Stijn, Geoffrey R. D. Underhill, and Xiaoke Zhang (2008), "The Political Economy of Basle II: The Costs for Poor Countries," *The World Economy*, 31(3), 313–344.

Clasen, Thomas F. (2012), "Millennium Development Goals Water Target Exaggerates Achievement," *Tropical Medicine and International Health*, 17(10), 1178–1180.

Coase, Ronald H. (1960), "The Problem of Social Cost," *Journal of Law and Economics*, 3(1), 1–44.

Coggins, Bridget L. (2015), "Does State Failure Cause Terrorism? An Empirical Analysis (1999–2008)," *Journal of Conflict Resolution*, 59(3), 455–483.

Collier, Paul (1997), "The Failure of Conditionality," in Catherine Gwin and Joan M. Nelson (eds.), *Perspectives on Aid and Development*, Policy Essay No. 22 (Washington, DC: Overseas Development Council), 51–77.

Collier, Paul (2007), *The Bottom Billion: Why the Poorest Countries Are Failing and What Can Be Done About It* (Oxford: Oxford University Press).

Collier, Paul, V. L. Elliot, Håvard Hegre, Anke Hoeffler, Marta Reynal-Querol, and Nicholas Sambanis (2003), *Breaking the Conflict Trap: Civil War and Development Policy* (Washington, DC: The World Bank and Oxford University Press).

Collier, Paul, and Anke Hoeffler (2002), "On the Incidence of Civil Wars in Africa," *Journal of Conflict Resolution*, 46(1), 13–28.

Collier, Paul, and Anke Hoeffler (2004), "Greed and Grievance in Civil Wars," *Oxford Economic Papers*, 56(4), 563–595.

Collier, Paul, Anke Hoeffler, and Måns Soderbom (2004), "On the Duration of Civil War," *Journal of Peace Research*, 41(3), 253–273.

Collier, Paul. and Nicholas Sambanis (2002), "Understanding Civil War: A New Agenda," *Journal of Conflict Resolution*, 46(1), 3–12.

Congleton, Roger D. (1992), "Political Institutions and Pollution Control," *Review of Economics and Statistics*, 74(3), 412–442.

Conybeare, John A. C. (1987), *Trade Wars: The Theory and Practice of International Commercial Rivalry* (New York: Columbia University Press).

Conybeare, John A. C., James C. Murdoch, and Todd Sandler (1994), "Alternative Collective-Goods Models of Military Alliances: Theory and Empirics," *Economic Inquiry*, 32(4), 525–542.

Conybeare, John A. C., and Todd Sandler (1990), "The Triple Entente and the Triple Alliance 1880–1914: A Collective Goods Approach," *American Political Science Review*, 84(4), 1197–1206.

Cook, Lisa D., and Jeffrey Sachs (1999), "Regional Public Goods in International Assistance," in Inge Kaul, Isabelle Grunberg, and Marc C. Stein (eds.), *Global Public Goods: International Cooperation in the 21st Century* (New York: Oxford University Press), 436–449.

Cooper, Andrew F., and Asif B. Farooq (2013), "BRICS and the Privileging of Informality in Global Governance," *Global Policy*, 4(4), 428–433.

Cornes, Richard (1993), "Dyke Maintenance and Other Stories: Some Neglected Types of Public Goods," *Quarterly Journal of Economics*, 108(1), 259–271.

Cornes, Richard, and Todd Sandler (1984), "Easy Riders, Joint Production, and Public Goods," *Economic Journal*, 94(3), 580–598.

Cornes, Richard, and Todd Sandler (1985), "The Simple Analytics of Pure Public Good Provision," *Economica*, 52(1), 103–116.

Cornes, Richard, and Todd Sandler (1994), "The Comparative Static Properties of the Impure Public Good Model," *Journal of Public Economics*, 54(3), 403–421.

Cornes, Richard, and Todd Sandler (1996), *The Theory of Externalities, Public Goods, and Club Goods*, 2nd ed. (Cambridge: Cambridge University Press).

Costa, Sérgio Paulo Muniz (2012), "South American Regional Integration by Land Transport: A Historical Perspective," *Integration & Trade Journal*, 16(1), 7–15.

Dai, Xinjuan (2005), "Why Comply? The Domestic Constituency Mechanism," *International Organization*, 59(2), 363–398.

Dando, Malcolm (1994), *Biological Warfare in the 21st Century* (London: Brassey's).

Dávalos, Liliana M., Adriana C. Bejarano, and H. Leonardo Correa (2009), "Disabusing Cocaine: Pervasive Myths and Enduring Realities of a Globalized Commodity," *International Journal of Drug Policy*, 20(5), 381–386.

Denny, Elaine K., and Barbara F. Walter (2014), "Ethnicity and Civil War," *Journal of Peace Research*, 51(2), 199–212.

de Gruijl, Frank R. (1995), "Impacts of a Projected Depletion of the Ozone Layer," *Consequences: The Nature & Implications of Environmental Change*, 1(2), 13–21.

Diebold, William (1994), "International Trade after the Cold War: Revisiting the Allies' Idealistic Vision of the Post-World War II International Economic Order," *Northern Illinois University Law Review*, 14(Spring), 335–346.

Dixit, Avinash, Susan Skeath, and David H. Reiley, Jr. (2009), *Games of Strategy*, 3rd ed. (New York: W. W. Norton & Co.)

Dodds, Klaus (1998), "The Geopolitics of Regionalism: The Valdivia Group and Southern Hemisphere Environmental Co-Operation," *Third World Quarterly*, 19(4), 725–743.

Dorn, William (1998), "Regional Peacekeeping Is Not the Way," in William J. Durch (ed.), *The Evolution of UN Peacekeeping: Case Studies and Cooperative Analysis* (New York: St. Martin's Press), 39–55.

Downs, George W., David M. Rocke, and Peter N. Barsoom (1998), "Managing the Evolution of Multilateralism," *International Organization*, 52(2), 397–419.

Drezner, Daniel W. (2007), *All Politics Is Global: Explaining International Regulatory Regimes* (Princeton, NJ: Princeton University Press).

Dugan, Andrew (2013), "US Support for Action in Syria is Low vs. Past Conflicts." Available at http://www.gallup.com/poll/164282/support-syria-action-lower-past-conflicts.aspx. Accessed March 9, 2014.

Dupont, Alan (1999), "Transnational Crime, Drugs, and Security in East Asia," *Asian Survey*, 39(3), 433–455.

Durch, William J. (1993), "Paying the Tab: Financial Crisis," in William J. Durch (ed.), *The Evolution of UN Peacekeeping: Case Studies and Cooperative Analysis* (New York: St. Martin Press), 39–55.

Easterly, William (2002), *The Elusive Quest for Growth: Economists' Adventures and Misadventures in the Tropics* (Cambridge, MA: The MIT Press).

Easterly, William, and Ross Levine (1998), "Troubles with the Neighbors: Africa's Problem, Africa's Opportunity," *Journal of African Economies*, 7(1), 120–142.

The Economist (2011a), "Dead Man Talking; The Doha Round," *The Economist*, 399(8731), 81.

The Economist (2011b), "Intra-African Trade: The Road Less Travelled," *The Economist*, April 17, 2011. Available at http://www.economist.com/node/21576346. Accessed October 6, 2013.

The Economist (2013a), "The Weakened West," *The Economist*, 408(8854), 11.

The Economist (2014a), "Cancer in the Developing World: Worse than AIDS," *The Economist*, 410(8876), 61.

The Economist (2014b), "Shadow and Substance: Special Report on International Banking," *The Economist*, 411(8886), S1–S16.

The Economist (2014c), "Uncontained: Trade and Money Laundering," *The Economist*, 411(8885), 53.

The Economist (2014d), "Poor Correspondents: International Banking," *The Economist*, 411(8891), 65.

Eichengreen, Barry J. (1999), *Toward a New International Financial Architecture: A Practical Post-Asia Agenda*. (Washington, DC: Peterson Institute).

Elbadawi, Ibrahim A., and Njuguna Ndung'u (2000), "External Indebtedness, Growth, and Investment in Conflict and Post-Conflict African Countries." Unpublished manuscript, The World Bank, Washington, DC.

Elbadawi, Ibrahim A., and Nicholas Sambanis (2001), "External Interventions and the Duration of Civil Wars." Unpublished manuscript, The World Bank, Washington, DC.

Elbadawi, Ibrahim A., and Nicholas Sambanis (2002), "How Much War Will We See? Explaining the Prevalence of Civil War," *Journal of Conflict Resolution*, 46(3), 307–334.

Eliassen, Anton, and Jørgen Saltbones (1983), "Modelling of Long-Range Transport of Sulphur over Europe: A Two-Year Model Run and Some Model Experiments," *Atmospheric Environment*, 17(8), 1457–1473.

Elliot, Kimberly (2013), "Subsidizing Farmers and Biofuels in Rich Countries: An Incoherent Agenda for Food Security," CGD Policy Paper, Center for Global Development, Washington, DC.

Enders, Walter, Gary A. Hoover, and Todd Sandler (2015), "The Changing Nonlinear Relationships between Income and Terrorism," *Journal of Conflict Resolution*, 59, DOI: 10.1177/0022002714535252, forthcoming.

Enders, Walter, and Todd Sandler (1993), "The Effectiveness of Antiterrorism Policies: A Vector-Autoregression-Intervention Analysis," *American Political Science Review*, 87(4), 829–844.

Enders, Walter, and Todd Sandler (2006), "Distribution of Transnational Terrorism among Countries by Income Classes and Geography after 9/11," *International Studies Quarterly*, 50(2), 367–393.

Enders, Walter, and Todd Sandler (2012), *The Political Economy of Terrorism*, 2nd ed. (Cambridge: Cambridge University Press).

Enders, Walter, Todd Sandler, and Jon Cauley (1990a), "UN Conventions, Technology, and Retaliation in the Fight against Terrorism: An Econometric Evaluation," *Terrorism and Political Violence*, 2(1), 83–105.

Enders, Walter, Todd Sandler, and Jon Cauley (1990b), "Assessing the Impact of Terrorist-Thwarting Policies: An Intervention Time Series Approach," *Defence Economics*, 2(1), 1–18.

Enders, Walter, Todd Sandler, and Khusrav Gaibulloev (2011), "Domestic versus Transnational Terrorism: Data, Decomposition, and Dynamics," *Journal of Peace Research*, 48(3), 319–337.

Environmental Protection Agency (EPA) (1987a), *Assessing the Risks of Trace Gases That Can Modify the Stratosphere*, 7 vols. (Washington, DC: EPA).

Environmental Protection Agency (EPA) (1987b), *Regulatory Impact Analysis: Protection of Stratospheric Ozone*, 3 vols. (Washington, DC: EPA).

Estevadeordal, Antoni, Brian Frantz, and Tam Robert Nguyen (eds.) (2004), *Regional Public Goods: From Theory to Practice* (Washington, DC: Inter-American Development Bank and Asian Development Bank).

Fearon, James (1998), "Bargaining, Enforcement, and International Cooperation," *International Organization*, 52(2), 269–306.

Fearon, James D., and David D. Laitin (2003), "Ethnicity, Insurgency, and Civil War," *American Political Science Review*, 97(1), 75–90.

Ferroni, Marco, and Ashoka Mody (eds.) (2002), *International Public Goods: Incentives, Measurement, and Financing* (Boston: Kluwer Academic Publishers).

Financial Action Task Force (2014), "Improving Global AML/CFT Compliance: On-going Process." Available at http://www.fatf-gafi.org/documents/news/fatf-compliance-june-2014.html. Accessed July 2, 2014.

The Financial Times (2013), "Fed Goes Further than Basel III with Fresh Bank Liquidity Rules," *The Financial Times*, October 25, 2013, 2.

The Financial Times (2014), "Investment Banks Hail Victories in Basel Battle," *The Financial Times*, January 14, 2014, 16.

Findley, Michael G., Daniel L. Nielson, and J. C. Sharman, (2013), "Using Field Experiments in International Relations: A Randomized Study of Anonymous Incorporation," *International Organization*, 67(4), 657–693.

Findley, Michael G., and Joseph K. Young (2012), "Terrorism and Civil War: A Spatial and Temporal Approach to a Conceptual Problem," *Perspectives on Politics*, 10(2), 285–305.

Finus, Michael, and Sigre Tjøtta (2003), "The Oslo Protocol and Sulfur Reduction: The Great Leap Forward?" *Journal of Public Economics*, 87(9–10), 2031–2048.

Fleck, Robert K., and Christopher Kilby (2010), "Changing Aid Regimes? US Foreign Aid from the Cold War to the War on Terror," *Journal of Development Economics*, 91(1), 185–197.

Fridtjof Nansen Institute (1996), *Green Globe Yearbook of International Cooperation on Environment and Development 1996* (New York: Oxford University Press).

Frieden, Jeffry A. (2006), *Global Capitalism: Its Fall and Rise in the Twentieth Century* (New York: Norton).

Fudenberg, Drew, and Eric Maskin (1986), "The Folk Theorem in Repeated Games with Discounting or with Incomplete Information," *Econometrica*, 54(3), 533–554.

Gaibulloev, Khusrav, Justin George, Todd Sandler, and Hirofumi Shimizu (2015), "Troop Contributions to UN and Non-UN Peacekeeping Missions: A Public Good Approach," *Journal of Peace Research*, 52, forthcoming.

Gaibulloev, Khusrav, and Todd Sandler (2008), "Growth Consequences of Terrorism in Western Europe," *Kyklos*, 61(3), 411–424.

Gaibulloev, Khusrav, and Todd Sandler (2009), "The Impact of Terrorism and Conflicts on Growth in Asia," *Economics & Politics*, 21(3), 359–383.

Gaibulloev, Khusrav, and Todd Sandler (2011), "The Adverse Effect of Transnational and Domestic Terrorism Growth in Africa," *Journal of Peace Research*, 48(3), 355–371.

Gaibulloev, Khusrav, and Todd Sandler (2013), "Determinants of the Demise of Terrorist Organizations," *Southern Economic Journal*, 79(4), 774–792.

Gaibulloev, Khusrav, and Todd Sandler (2014), "An Empirical Analysis of Alternative Ways that Terrorist Groups End," *Public Choice*, 160(1–2), 25–44.

Gaibulloev, Khusrav, Todd Sandler, and Charlinda Santifort (2012), "Assessing the Evolving Threat of Terrorism," *Global Policy*, 3(2), 135–144.

Gaibulloev, Khusrav, Todd Sandler, and Hirofumi Shimizu (2009), "Demands for UN and Non-UN Peacekeeping: Nonvoluntary versus Voluntary Contributions to a Public Good," *Journal of Conflict Resolution*, 53(6), 827–852.

Gaibulloev, Khusrav, Todd Sandler, and Donggyu Sul (2013), "Common Drivers of Transnational Terrorism: Principal Component Analysis," *Economic Inquiry*, 51(1), 707–721.

Gardeazabal, Javier, and Todd Sandler (2015), "INTERPOL's Surveillance Network in Curbing Transnational Terrorism," *Journal of Policy Analysis and Management*, 34, forthcoming.

Gartzke, Erik, and Matthew Kroenig (2009), "Strategic Approach to Nuclear Proliferation," *Journal of Conflict Resolution*, 53(2), 151–160.

Gartzke, Erik, and Matthew Kroenig (2014), "Nuclear Posture, Nonproliferation Policy, and the Spread of Nuclear Weapons," *Journal of Conflict Resolution*, 58(3), 395–401.

Ghobarah, Hazem A., Paul Huth, and Bruce M. Russett (2003), "Civil Wars Kill and Maim People—Long After the Shooting Stops," *American Political Science Review*, 97(2), 189–202.

Gilpin, Robert (1981), *War and Change in World Politics* (New York: Cambridge University Press).

Glassman, Amanda, Denizhan Duran, and Andy Sumner (2013), "Global Health and the New Bottom Billion: What Do Shifts in Global Poverty and Disease Burden Mean for Donor Agencies," *Global Policy*, 4(1), 1–14.

Glaze, John A. (2007), "Opium and Afghanistan: Reassessing US Counternarcotics Strategy," Working Paper, Strategic Studies Institute, Carlisle, PA.

Global Fund (2014), "Fighting Tuberculosis: The Global Tuberculosis Epidemic." Available at http://www.theglobalfund.org/en/about/diseases/tuberculosis/. Accessed February 22, 2014.

Gokcekus, Omer, Justin Knowles, and Edward Tower (2004), "Sweetening the Pot: How American Sugar Buys Protection," in Devashish Mitra and Arvind Panagariya (eds.), *The Political Economy of Trade, Aid and Foreign Investment Policies* (New York: Elsevier), 177–196.

Goldstein, Judith, Douglas Rivers, and Michael Tomz (2007), "Institutions in International Relations: Understanding the Effects of GATT and the WTO on World Trade," *International Organization*, 61(1), 37–67.

Gompert, David C., and E. Stephen Larrabee (eds.) (1997), *America and Europe: A Partnership for a New Era* (Cambridge: Cambridge University Press).

Gowa, Joanne (1983), *Closing the Gold Window* (Ithaca, NY: Cornell University Press).

The Guardian (2011), "Afghanistan Troop Numbers Data: How Many Does Each Country Send to the NATO Mission There?" Available at http://www.theguardian.com/news/datablog/2009/sep/21/afghanistan-troop-numbers-nato-data. Accessed January 10, 2014.

Haass, Richard N. (2008), "The Age of Nonpolarity: What Will Follow U.S. Dominance," *Foreign Affairs*, 87(3), 44–56.

Hannesson, Rögnvaldur (2010), "The Coalition of the Willing: Effect of Country Diversity in an Environmental Treaty Game," *Review of International Organizations*, 5(4), 461–474.

Hannoun, Hervé (2010), "The Basel III Capital Framework: A Decisive Breakthrough," Bank for International Settlements, Basel, Switzerland. Available at http://www.bis.org/speeches/sp101125a.htm. Accessed April 16, 2014.

Hardin, Russell (1982), *Collective Action* (Baltimore, MD: Johns Hopkins University).

Hartley, Keith (2007), "The Arms Industry, Procurement and Industrial Policies," in Todd Sandler and Keith Hartley (eds.), *Handbook of Defense Economics: Defense in a Globalized World* (Amsterdam: North-Holland), 1139–1176.

Hartley, Keith, and Todd Sandler (1999), "NATO Burden-Sharing: Past and Future," *Journal of Peace Research*, 36(6), 665–680.

Harvey, Fiona (2012), "The Kyoto Protocol is not Quite Dead." Available at http://www.theguardian.com/environment/2012/nov/26/kyoto-protocol-not-dead. Accessed July 28, 2014.

Held, David, and Anthony McGrew (2003), "Political Globalization: Trends and Choices," in Inge Kaul, Pedro Conceição, Katell Le Goulven, and Ronald U. Mendoza (eds.), *Providing Global Public Goods: Managing Globalization* (New York: Oxford University Press), 185–199.

Helman, Gerald B., and Steven R. Ratner (1992), "Saving Failed States," *Foreign Policy*, 89(2), 3–20.

Hensel, Paul (2009), "ICOW Colonial History Data Set, version 0.4." Available at http://www.icow.org/colhist.html. Accessed January 30, 2014.

Hirshleifer, Jack (1983), "From Weakest-Link to Best-Shot: The Voluntary Provision of Public Goods," *Public Choice*, 41(3), 371–386.

Hoffman, Bruce (2006), *Inside Terrorism*, revised and expanded edition (New York: Columbia University Press).

Hülsse, Rainer (2008), "Even Clubs Can't Do without Legitimacy: Why the Anti-Money Laundering Blacklist Was Suspended," *Regulation & Governance*, 2(4), 459–479.

Hwenda, Lenias (2013), "Towards a Balanced and Sustainable Global Health Innovation and Access Policy," *Global Policy*, 4(4), 442–444.

Ikenberry, G. John (2011), *Liberal Leviathan: The Origins, Crisis, and Transformation of the American World Order* (Princeton, NJ: Princeton University Press).

Institute of Medicine (2002), *Biological Threats and Terrorism: Assessing the Science and Response Capabilities* (Washington, DC: National Academy Press).

International Institute for Strategic Studies (2014), *The Military Balance 2014* (London: Routledge).

International Maritime Organization (2014), "Piracy Reports." Available at http://www.imo.org/knowledgecentre/shipsandshippingfactsandfigures/statisticalresources/piracy/. Accessed September 19, 2014.

International Task Force on Global Public Goods (ed.) (2006), *Summary: Meeting Global Challenges* (Stockholm: Erlanders Infologistics Väst AB).

Irwin, Douglas A. (2005), *Free Trade under Fire* (Princeton, NJ: Princeton University Press).

Ivanova, Kate, and Todd Sandler (2006), "CBRN Incidents: Political Regimes, Perpetrators, and Targets," *Terrorism and Political Violence*, 18(3), 423–448.

Ivanova, Kate, and Todd Sandler (2007), "CBRN Attack Perpetrators: An Empirical Study," *Foreign Policy Analysis*, 3(4), 273–294.

Jackson, John H. (1998), "Designing and Implementing Effective Dispute Settlement Procedures: WTO Dispute Settlement, Appraisal and Prospects," in Anne O. Krueger (ed.), *The WTO as an International Institution* (Chicago: University of Chicago Press), 161–179.

Jenner, Matthew S. (2014), "Drug Trafficking as a Transnational Crime," in Philip Reichel and Jay Albanese (eds.), *Handbook of Transnational Crime and Justice*, 2nd ed. (Thousand Oaks, CA: Sage), 65–84.

Jensen, Nathan M. (2007), "International Institutions and Market Expectations: Stock Price Responses to the WTO Ruling on the 2002 U.S. Steel Tariffs," *Review of International Organizations*, 2(3), 261–280.

Jones, Seth G., and Martin C. Libicki (2008), *How Terrorist Groups End: Lessons for Countering al Qa'ida*, Monograph MG-741-1 (Santa Monica, CA: RAND).

Kanbur, Ravi (2002), "IFIs and IPGs: Operational Implications for the World Bank," Working Paper WP2002-17, Department of Applied Economics and Management, Cornell University, Ithaca, NY.

Kanbur, Ravi, Todd Sandler, and Kevin Morrison (1999), *The Future of Development Assistance: Common Pools and International Public Goods*, Policy Essay No. 25 (Washington, DC: Overseas Development Council).

Kapstein, Ethan B. (1991), *Supervising International Banks: Origins and Implications of the Basle Accord* (Princeton, NJ: Princeton University Press).

Kaul, Inge, and Pedro Conceição (eds.) (2006), *The New Public Finance: Responding to Global Challenges* (New York: Oxford University Press).

Kaul, Inge, Pedro Conceição, Katell Le Goulven, and Ronald U. Mendoza (eds.) (2003), *Providing Global Public Goods: Managing Globalization* (New York: Oxford University Press).

Kaul, Inge, Isabelle Grunberg, and Marc A. Stern (eds.) (1999), *Global Public Goods: International Cooperation in the 21st Century* (New York: Oxford University Press).

Kenen, Peter B. (2001), *The International Financial Architecture: What's New? What's Missing?* (Washington, DC: Peterson Institute).

Keohane, Robert (1984), *After Hegemony* (Princeton, NJ: Princeton University Press).

Keohane, Robert (1997), "Problematic Lucidity," *World Politics*, 50(1), 150–170.

Khanna, Jyoti, and Todd Sandler (1997), "Conscription, Peacekeeping and Foreign Assistance: NATO Burden Sharing in the Post-Cold War Era," *Defence and Peace Economics*, 8(1), 101–122.

Khanna, Jyoti, Todd Sandler, and Hirofumi Shimizu (1998), "Sharing the Financial Burden for UN and NATO Peacekeeping: 1976–1996," *Journal of Conflict Resolution*, 42(2), 176–195.

Khanna, Jyoti, Todd Sandler, and Hirofumi Shimizu (1999), "Demand for UN Peacekeeping, 1975–1996," *Kyklos*, 52(3), 345–368.

Kindleberger, Charles P. (1974), *The World in Depression, 1929–1939* (Berkeley, CA: University of California Press).

Klare, Michael T. (1995), *Rogue States and Nuclear Outlaws: America's Search for a New Foreign Policy* (New York: Hill and Wang).

Krasner, Stephen D. (1976), "State Power and the Structure of International Trade," *World Politics*, 28(3), 317–347.

Krasner, Stephen D. (2009), *Power, the State, and Sovereignty: Essays on International Relations* (New York: Routledge).

Kremer, Michael (2002), "Pharmaceuticals and the Developing World," *Journal of Economic Perspectives*, 16(4), 67–90.

Kremer, Michael (2006), "Global Public Goods in Communicable Disease Control," in International Task Force on Global Public Goods (ed.), *Expert Paper Series One: Infectious Diseases* (Stockholm: Erlanders Infologistics Väst AB), 25–45.

Krueger, Alan B., and Jitka Maleckova (2003), "Education, Poverty, and Terrorism: Is There a Causal Connection?," *Journal of Economic Perspectives*, 17(4), 119–144.

Kuziemko, Ilyana, and Eric Werker (2006), "How Much Is a Seat on the Security Coun-cil Worth? Foreign Aid and Bribery at the United Nations," *Journal of Political Economy*, 114(5), 905–930.

Kuznets, Simon (1955), "Economic Growth and Income Inequality," *American Economic Review*, 45(1), 1–28.

Lapan, Harvey E., and Todd Sandler (1988), "To Bargain or Not to Bargain: That Is the Question," *American Economic Association Papers and Proceedings*, 78(2), 16–20.

Lapan, Harvey E., and Todd Sandler (1993), "Terrorism and Signalling," *European Jour-nal of Political Economy*, 9(3), 383–397.

Lee, Dwight R. (1988), "Free Riding and Paid Riding in the Fight against Terrorism," *American Economic Review*, 78(2), 22–26.

Lele, Uma, Ronald Ridker, and Jagadish Upadhyay (2006), " Health System Capacities in Developing Countries and Global Health Initiatives on Communicable Dis-eases," in International Task Force on Global Public Goods (ed.), *Expert Paper Series One: Infectious Diseases* (Stockholm: Erlanders Infologistics Väst AB), 119–194.

Levi, Michael (2002), "Money Laundering and Its Regulations," *Annals of the American Academy of Political and Social Science*, 582(1), 181–184.

Levi, Michael (2007), *On Nuclear Terrorism* (Cambridge, MA: Harvard University Press).

Libecap, Gary D. (2014), "Addressing Global Environmental Externalities: Transaction Costs Considerations," *Journal of Economic Literature*, 52(2), 424–479.

Lipson, Charles (1991), "Why Are Some International Agreements Informal?," *Interna-tional Organization*, 45(4), 495–538.

Lomborg, Bjørn, ed. (2006), *How to Spend $50 Billion to Make the World a Better Place* (New York: Cambridge University Press).

Lomborg, Bjørn, ed. (2009), *Global Crises, Global Solutions*, 2nd ed. (Cambridge: Cam-bridge University Press).

Lynch, David A. (2010), *Trade and Globalization: An Introduction to Regional Trade Agree-ments* (Lanham, UK: Rowman & Littlefield Publishers).

Mahncke, Hans (2004), "U.S. Steel Tariffs and the WTO Dispute Resolution Mechan-ism," *Leiden Journal of International Law*, 17(3), 615–624.

Marwell, Gerald, and Pamela Oliver (1993), *The Critical Mass in Collective Action: A Mi-cro-Social Theory* (New York: Cambridge University Press).

Mascarenhas, Raechelle, and Todd Sandler (2005), "Donors' Mechanisms for Financing International and National Public Goods: Loans or Grants?," *The World Economy*, 28(8), 1095–1117.

Mearsheimer, John (1994), "The False Promise of International Institutions," *Interna-tional Security*, 19(3), 5–49.

Mejia, Daniel, and Pascual Restrepo (2008), "The War on Illegal Drug Production and Trafficking: An Economic Evaluation of Plan Colombia," Working Paper, Docu-mento CEDE No. 2008–19, Bogotá, Colombia.

Menkhaus, Ken (2003), "Quasi-States, Nation-Building, and Terrorist Safe Havens," *Journal of Conflict Studies*, 23(2), 1–9. Available at http://journals.hil.unb.ca/index.php/JCS/article/view/216/444. Accessed September 5, 2014.

Mickolus, Edward F., Todd Sandler, and Jean M. Murdock (1989), *International Terror-ism in 1980s: A Chronology of Events*, 2 vols. (Ames, IA: Iowa State University Press).

Mickolus, Edward F., Todd Sandler, Jean M. Murdock, and Peter Flemming (2013), *International Terrorism: Attributes of Terrorist Events, 1968–2012* (Ponte Vedra, FL: Vinyard Software).

Milanovic, Branko (2009), "Global Inequality and the Global Inequality Extraction Ratio: The Story of the Past Two Centuries," Policy Research Working Paper 5044, The World Bank, Washington, DC

Mills, Susan R. (1990), "The Financing of UN Peacekeeping Operations: The Need for a Sound Financial Basis," in Indar Jit Rikhye and Kjell Skjelsback (eds.), *The United Nations and Peacekeeping: Results, Limitations and Prospects: The Lessons of 40 Years of Experience* (Houndmills, UK: Macmillan), 91–110.

Moosa, Imad A. (2010), "Basel II as a Casualty of the Global Financial Crisis," *Journal of Banking Regulation*, 11(2), 95–114.

Morrisette, Peter M., Joel Darmstadter, Andrew J. Plantiga, and Michael A. Toman (1990), "Lessons from Other International Agreements for a Global CO2 Accord," Discussion Paper ENR91–02, Resources for the Future, Washington, DC.

Morrow, James D. (1995), "Arms versus Allies," *International Organization*, 47(2), 207–234.

Murdie, Amanda (2014), *Help or Harm: The Human Security Effects of International NGOs* (Stanford, CA: Stanford University Press).

Murdoch, James C., and Todd Sandler (1997), "The Voluntary Provision of a Pure Public Good: The Case of Reduced CFC Emissions and the Montreal Protocol," *Journal of Public Economics*, 63(2), 331–349.

Murdoch, James C., and Todd Sandler (2002), "Economic Growth, Civil Wars, and Spatial Spillovers," *Journal of Conflict Resolution*, 46(1), 91–110.

Murdoch, James C., and Todd Sandler (2004), "Civil Wars and Economic Growth: Spatial Dispersion," *American Journal of Political Science*, 48(1), 137–150.

Murdoch, James C., Todd Sandler, and Keith Sargent (1997), "A Tale of Two Collectives: Sulphur versus Nitrogen Oxides Emission Reduction in Europe," *Economica*, 64(2), 281–301.

Murdoch, James C., Todd Sandler, and Wim P. M. Vijverberg (2003), "The Participation Decision versus the Level of Participation in an Environmental Treaty: A Spatial Probit Analysis," *Journal of Public Economics*, 87(2), 337–362.

Murray, J. L. Christopher (2006), "The Role of the World Health Organization in the Control of Communicable Diseases," in International Task Force on Global Public Goods (ed.), *Expert Paper Series One: Infectious Diseases* (Stockholm: Erlanders Infologistic Väst AB), 87–118.

National Consortium for the Study of Terrorism and Responses to Terrorism (START) (2014), *Global Terrorism Database*, CD-ROM (College Park, MD: University of Maryland).

Nordhaus, William D. (1991), "The Cost of Slowing Climate Change: A Survey," Cowles Foundation Paper No. 775, Yale University, New Haven, CT.

Norloff, Carla (2010), *America's Global Advantage* (Cambridge: Cambridge University Press).

North, Douglass C. (1990), *Institutions, Institutional Change and Economic Performance* (Cambridge: Cambridge University Press).

Novembre, Valerio (2009), "The Bargaining Process as a Variable to Explain Implementation Choices of International Soft-Law Agreements: The Basel Case Study," *Journal of Banking Regulation*, 10(2), 129–152.

Oatley, Thomas, W. Kindred Winecoff, Andrew Pennock, and Sarah Bauerle Danzman (2013), "The Political Economy of Global Finance: A Network Model," *Perspectives on Politics*, 11(1), 133–153.

Oestergaard, Mikkel Z., Leontine Alkema, and Joy E. Lawn (2013), "Millennium Development Goals National Targets Are Moving Targets and the Results Will Not Be

Known Until Well after the Deadline of 2015," *International Journal of Epidemiology*, 42(3): 645–647.

Olson, Mancur (1965), *The Logic of Collective Action* (Cambridge, MA: Harvard University Press).

Olson, Mancur (1969), "The Principle of 'Fiscal Equivalence': The Division of Responsibilities among Different Levels of Government," *American Economic Review*, 59(2), 479–487.

Olson, Mancur, and Richard Zeckhauser (1966), "An Economic Theory of Alliances," *Review of Economics and Statistics*, 48(3), 266–279.

Organization for Economic Cooperation and Development (OECD) (1990), *Control Strategies for Photochemical Oxidants across Europe* (Paris: OECD).

Organization for Economic Cooperation and Development (OECD) (2014), "Donors' Statistics." Available at http://stats.oecd.org/qwids/#?x=1&y=6&f=3:51,4:1,5:3, 7:1,2:262&q=3:51+4:1+5:3+7:1+2:262+1:1,2,25,26+6:2003,2004,2005, 2006,2007,2008,2009,2010,2011,2012. Accessed March 17, 2014.

Ostrom, Elinor (1990), *Governing the Commons: The Evolution of Institutions for Collective Action* (Cambridge: Cambridge University Press).

Ostrom, Elinor, Roy Gardner, and James Walker (1994), *Rules, Games, and Common-Pool Resources* (Ann Arbor, MI: University of Michigan Press).

Pahre, Robert (1999), *Leading Questions* (Ann Arbor, MI: University of Michigan Press).

Paoli, Letizia, Victoria A. Greenfield, and Peter Reuter (2012), "Change Is Possible: The History of the International Drug Control Regime and Implications for Future Policymaking," *Substance Use and Misuse*, 47(40), 923–935.

Pape, Robert A. (2003), "The Strategic Logic of Suicide Terrorism," *American Political Science Review*, 97(3), 343–361.

Patrick, Stewart (2011), *Weak Links: Failure States, Global Threats, and International Security* (New York: Oxford University Press).

Percy, Sarah, and Anja Shortland (2013), "The Business of Piracy in Somalia," *The Journal of Strategic Studies*, 36(4), 541–578.

Pew Research (2007), "A Global Look at Public Perceptions of Health Problems, Priorities, and Donors: The Kaiser/Pew Global Health Survey." Available at http://www.pewglobal.org/files/pdf/259.pdf. Accessed September 12, 2014.

Piazza, James A. (2006), "Rooted in Poverty?: Terrorism, Poor Economic Development, and Social Cleavages," *Terrorism and Political Violence*, 18(1), 159–177.

Piazza, James A. (2007), "Draining the Swamp: Democracy Promotion, State Failure, and Terrorism in 19 Middle Eastern Countries," *Studies in Conflict & Terrorism*, 30(6), 521–539.

Piazza, James A. (2008), "Incubators of Terror: Do Failed and Failing States Promote Transnational Terrorism?," International Studies Quarterly, 52(3), 469–488.

Powell, Robert (1999), *In the Shadow of Power: States and Strategies in International Politics* (Princeton, NJ: Princeton University Press).

Raffer, Kunibert (1999), "ODA and Global Public Goods: A Trend Analysis of Past and Present Spending Patterns," Office of Development Studies Background Paper, United Nations Development Program, New York.

Rapoport, Anatol, and Melvin Guyer (1966), "A Taxonomy of 2×2 Games," *General Systems*, 11(2), 203–214.

Rapoport, David C. (2004), "Modern Terror: The Four Waves," in Audrey K. Cronin and James M. Ludes (eds.), *Attacking Terrorism: Elements of a Grand Strategy* (Washington, DC: Georgetown University Press), 46–73.

Reuter, Peter, and Edwin M. Truman (2004), *Chasing Dirty Money: The Fight against Money Laundering* (Washington, DC: Institute for International Economics).

Roberge, Ian (2011), "Financial Action Task Force," in Thomas Hale and David Hale (eds.), *Handbook of Transnational Governance: Institutions and Innovations* (Malden, MA: Polity Press), 45–50.

Rodrik, Dani (1999), *The New Global Economy and Developing Countries: Making Openness Work*, Policy Essay No. 24 (Washington, DC: Overseas Development Council).

Room, Robin, and Peter Reuter (2012), "How Well Do International Drug Conventions Protect Public Health?," *The Lancet*, 379(9810), 84–91.

Rosendorff, B. Peter, and Todd Sandler (2004), "Too Much of a Good Thing? The Proactive Response Dilemma," *Journal of Conflict Resolution*, 48(5), 657–671.

Rostow, W. W. (1960), *The Stages of Economic Growth: A Non-Communist Manifesto* (Cambridge: Cambridge University Press).

Rouse, Stell M., and Moises Arce (2006), "The Drug-Laden Balloon: United States Military Assistance and Coca Production in the Central Andes," *Social Science Quarterly*, 87(3), 540–557.

Ruggie, John, G. (1972), "Collective Goods and Future International Collaboration," *American Political Science Review*, 66(3), 874–893.

Runge, C. Ford (1984), "Institutions and the Free Rider: The Assurance Problem in Collective Action," *Journal of Politics*, 46(1), 154–181.

Russett, Bruce M. (1970), *What Price Vigilance? The Burdens of National Defense* (New Haven, CT: Yale University Press).

Saideman, Stephen M., and David P. Auerswald (2012), "Comparing Caveats: Understanding the Sources of National Restrictions upon NATO's Mission in Afghanistan," *International Studies Quarterly*, 56(1), 67–84.

Salehyan, Idean (2009), *Rebels Without Borders: Transnational Insurgencies in World Politics* (Ithaca, NY: Cornell University Press).

Sambanis, Nicholas (2004), "What Is Civil War? Conceptual and Empirical Complexities of an Operational Definition," *Journal of Conflict Resolution*, 48(6), 814–858.

Sambanis, Nicholas (2008), "Terrorism and Civil War," in Philip Keefer and Norman Loayza (eds.), *Terrorism, Economic Development and Political Openness* (New York: Cambridge University Press), 174–206.

Sandler, Todd (1977), "Impurity of Defense: An Application to the Economics of Alliances," *Kyklos*, 30(3), 443–460.

Sandler, Todd (1992), *Collective Action: Theory and Applications* (Ann Arbor, MI: University of Michigan Press).

Sandler, Todd (1993), "The Economic Theory of Alliances," *Journal of Conflict Resolution*, 37(3), 446–483.

Sandler, Todd (1997), *Global Challenges: An Approach to Environmental, Political, and Economic Problems* (Cambridge: Cambridge University Press).

Sandler, Todd (1998), "Global and Regional Public Goods: A Prognosis for Collective Action," *Fiscal Studies*, 19(3), 221–247.

Sandler, Todd (2004), *Global Collective Action* (Cambridge: Cambridge University Press).

Sandler, Todd (2008), "Treaties: Strategic Considerations," *University of Illinois Law Review*, 2008(1), 155–179.

Sandler, Todd (2009), "Intergenerational Public Goods: Transnational Considerations," *Scottish Journal of Political Economy*, 56(3), 353–370.

Sandler, Todd (2010a), "Overcoming Global and Regional Collective Action Impediments," *Global Policy*, 1(1), 40–50.

Sandler, Todd (2010b), "Terrorism Shocks: Domestic versus Transnational Responses," *Studies in Conflict & Terrorism*, 33(10), 893–910.

Sandler, Todd (2013a), "Public Goods and Regional Cooperation for Development: A New Look," *Integration & Trade Journal*, 17(36), 13–24.

Sandler, Todd (2013b), "Buchanan Clubs," *Constitutional Political Economy*, 24(4), 265–285.

Sandler, Todd (2014), "The Analytical Study of Terrorism: Taking Stock," *Journal of Peace Research*, 51(2), 257–271.

Sandler, Todd (2015), "Strategic Aspects of Difficult Global Challenges." Unpublished manuscript, Center for Global Collective Action, University of Texas at Dallas, Richardson, TX.

Sandler, Todd, and Daniel G. Arce (2002), "A Conceptual Framework for Understanding Global and Transnational Public Goods for Health," *Fiscal Studies*, 23(2), 195–222.

Sandler, Todd, and Daniel G. Arce (2003), "Pure Public Goods versus Commons: Benefit-Cost Duality," *Land Economics*, 79(3), 355–368.

Sandler, Todd, and Daniel G. Arce (2007), "New Face of Development Assistance: Public Goods and Changing Ethics," *Journal of International Development*, 19(4), 527–544.

Sandler, Todd, Daniel G. Arce, and Walter Enders (2011), "An Evaluation of INTERPOL's Cooperative-Based Counterterrorism Linkage," *Journal of Law and Economics*, 54(1), 79–110.

Sandler, Todd, and Jon Cauley (1975), "On the Economic Theory of Alliances," *Journal of Conflict Resolution*, 19(2), 330–348.

Sandler, Todd, and Jon Cauley (1977), "The Design of Supranational Structures: An Economic Perspective," *International Studies Quarterly*, 21(2), 251–276.

Sandler, Todd, and John F. Forbes (1980), "Burden Sharing, Strategy, and the Design of NATO," *Economic Inquiry*, 18(3), 425–444.

Sandler, Todd, and Keith Hartley (1999), *The Political Economy of NATO* (Cambridge: Cambridge University Press).

Sandler, Todd, and Keith Hartley (2001), "Economics of Alliances: The Lessons for Collective Action," *Journal of Economic Literature*, 39(3), 869–896.

Sandler, Todd, and James C. Murdoch (2000), "On Sharing NATO Defence Burdens in the 1990s and Beyond," *Fiscal Studies*, 21(3), 297–327.

Sandler, Todd, and John W. Posnett (1991), "The Private Provision of Public Goods: A Perspective on Neutrality," *Public Finance Quarterly*, 19(1), 22–42.

Sandler, Todd, and Hirofumi Shimizu (2014), "NATO Burden Sharing, 1999–2010: An Altered Alliance," *Foreign Policy Analysis*, 10(1), 43–60.

Sandler, Todd, and John Tschirhart (1980), "The Economic Theory of Clubs: An Evaluative Survey," *Journal of Economic Literature*, 18(4), 1481–1521.

Sandler, Todd, and John Tschirhart (1997), "Club Theory: Thirty Years Later," *Public Choice*, 93(3–4), 335–355.

Sandler, Todd, John Tschirhart, and Jon Cauley (1983), "A Theoretical Analysis of Transnational Terrorism," *American Political Science Review*, 77(1), 36–54.

Sandnes, Hilde (1993), *Calculated Budgets for Airborne Acidifying Components in Europe, 1985, 1987, 1989, 1990, 1991, and 1992*, EMEP/MSC-W Report 1/93 (Oslo: Norske Meterologiske Institutt).

Schimmelfennig, Frank (2007), "Functional Form, Identity-Driven Cooperation: Institutional Designs and Effects in Post-Cold War NATO," in Amitav Acharya and Alastair Iain Johnston (eds.), *Crafting Cooperation* (New York: Cambridge University Press), 145–179.

Schinasi, Garry J. (2006), *Safeguarding Financial Stability: Theory and Practice* (Washington, DC: International Monetary Fund).

Schwab, Susan C. (2011), "After Doha: Why the Negotiations Are Doomed and What We Should Do About It," *Foreign Affairs* 90(3), 104–117.

Sen, Amartya K. (1967), "Isolation, Assurance, and the Social Rate of Discount," *Quarterly Journal of Economics*, 81(1), 112–124.

Shambaugh David, and Ren Xiao (2012), "China: The Conflicted Rising Power," in Henry R. Nau and Deepa M.Ollapally (eds.), *Worldviews of Aspiring Powers: Domestic Foreign Policy Debates in China, India, Iran, Japan, and Russia* (New York: Oxford University Press), 36–72.

Sharman, J. C. (2008), "Power and Discourse in Policy Diffusion: Anti-Money Laundering in Developing States," *International Studies Quarterly*, 52(3), 635–656.

Sharman, J. C. (2011), *The Money Laundry: Regulating Criminal Finance in the Global Economy* (Ithaca, NY: Cornell University Press).

Shearer, Matthew, and Joaquim Tres (2013), "South-South and Triangular Cooperation in Latin America and the Caribbean: Much Ado about Nothing?" *Integration & Trade Journal*, 17(36), 1–10.

Shibata, Hirofumi (1971), "A Bargaining Model of Pure Theory of Public Expenditure," *Journal of Political Economy*, 79(1), 1–29.

Shimizu, Hirofumi, and Todd Sandler (2002), "Peacekeeping and Burden Sharing, 1994–2000," *Journal of Peace Research*, 39(6), 651–668.

Shortland, Anja, and Marc Vothknecht (2011), "Combating 'Maritime Terrorism' off the Coast of Somalia," *European Journal of Political Economy*, 27(Supplement 1), S133–S151.

Simmons, Beth A. (2001), "The International Politics of Harmonization: The Case of Capital Market Regulation," *International Organization*, 55(3), 589–620.

Singer, David Andrew (2007), *Regulating Capital: Setting Standards for the International Financial System* (Ithaca, NY: Cornell University Press).

Siverson, Randolph M., and Harvey Starr (1990), "Opportunity, Willingness, and the Diffusion of War," *American Political Science Review*, 84(1), 47–67.

Skyrms, Brian (1996), *Evolution of the Social Contract* (Cambridge: Cambridge University Press).

Slaughter, Anne-Marie (2004), *A New World Order* (Princeton, NJ: Princeton University Press).

Smith, Adam (1976), *The Wealth of Nations*, edited by Edwin Cannan (Chicago: University of Chicago Press).

Smith, Richard D., and David Woodward (2002), "Global Public Goods for Health: Use and Limitations," in Richard Smith, Robert Beaglehole, David Woodward, and Nick Drager (eds.), *Global Public Goods for Health: Health Economics and Public Health* (Oxford: Oxford University Press), 214–265.

Snidal, Duncan (1985), "The Limits of Hegemonic Stability Theory," *International Organization*, 39(4), 579–614.

Solow, Robert M. (1957), "Technical Change and the Aggregate Production Function," *Review of Economics and Statistics*, 39(3), 312–320.

Sonntag, Diana (2010), *AIDS and Aid: A Public Good Approach* (Berlin: Springer-Verlag).

Sridhar, Devi, and Ngaire Woods (2013), "Trojan Multilateralism: Global Cooperation in Health," *Global Policy*, 4(4), 325–335.

Stålgren, Patrick (2000), "Regional Public Goods and the Future of International Development: A Review of the Literature," Working Paper 2000:2, Expert Group on Development Issues, Ministry for Foreign Affairs, Stockholm, Sweden.

Starr, Harvey, and Benjamin A. Most (1983), "Contagion and Border Effects on Contemporary African Conflict," *Comparative Political Studies*, 16(1), 92–117.

Steil, Ben (2013), *The Battle of Bretton Woods* (Princeton, NJ: Princeton University Press).

Stockholm International Peace Research Institute (SIPRI) (2012), *SIPRI Yearbook 2012: Armaments, Disarmament and International Security* (Oxford: Oxford University Press).

Stolarski, Richard S. (1988), "The Antarctic Ozone Hole," *Scientific American*, 258(1), 30–36.

Stone, Randall W. (2011), *Controlling Institutions: International Organizations and the Global Economy* (New York: Cambridge University Press).

Subramanian, Arvind, and Shang-Jin Wei (2007), "The WTO Promotes Trade, Strongly but Unevenly," *Journal of International Economics*, 72(1), 151–175.

Taylor, Michael (1987), *The Possibility of Cooperation* (New York: Cambridge University Press).

Toft, Monica D. (2014), "Territory and War," *Journal of Peace Research*, 51(2), 185–198.

Toon, Michael A., and Richard P. Turco (1991), "Polar Stratospheric Clouds and Ozone Depletion," *Scientific American*, 264(1), 68–74.

UNAIDS (2013), "Global Report: UNAIDS Report on The Global AIDS Epidemic, 2013." Available at www.unaids.org/en/media/unaids/contentassets/documents/epidemiology/2013/gr2013/UNAIDS_Global_Report_2013_en.pdf. Accessed March 24, 2014.

Unger, Brigitte (2007), *The Scale and Impacts of Money Laundering* (Northampton, MA: Edward Elgar Publishing).

Unger, Brigitte (2011), "Money Laundering Regulation: From Al Capone to Al Qaeda," in David Levi-Faur (ed.), *Handbook on the Politics of Regulation* (Northampton, MA: Edward Elgar Publishing), 615–628.

United Nations (2014a), "How Much Does Peacekeeping Cost?" Available at https://www.un.org/en/peacekeeping/operations/financing.shtml. Accessed May 19, 2014.

United Nations (2014b), *The Millennium Development Goals Report* (New York: United Nations).

United Nations Development Program (1999), *Human Development Report 1999* (New York: Oxford University Press).

United Nations Economic Commission for Europe (2014), "Protocols to the Long-Range Transboundary Air Pollution Convention." Available at http://www.unece.org/env/lrtap/status/lrtap_s.html. Accessed July 28, 2014.

United Nations Environment Program (UNEP) (1991), *Selected Multilateral Treaties in the Field of the Environment*, vol. 2 (Cambridge: Grotius Publications).

United Nations Environment Program (UNEP) (2013), "Year in Review: Environmental Events and Developments." http://www.unep.org/yearbook/2013/pdf/Year_under_review.pdf. Accessed July 19, 2014.

United Nations Environment Program (UNEP) (2014), "Ozone Secretariat." Available at http://ozone.unep.org/new_site/en/treaty_ratification_status.php. Accessed July 19, 2014.

United Nations Framework Convention on Climate Change (2014), "Status of Ratification of the Kyoto Protocol." Available at http://unfccc.int/kyoto_protocol/status_of_ratification/items/2613.php. Accessed July 19, 2014.

United Nations Framework Convention on Climate Change (2015), "Call for Climate Action Puts the World on Track to Paris 2015." Available at http://newsroom.unfccc.int/lima/lima-call-for-climate-action-puts-world-on-track-to-paris-2015/. Accessed January 9, 2015.

United Nations High-Level Panel (2001), "Recommendations of the High-Level Panel on Financing Development," United Nations, New York.

United Nations Office on Drugs and Crime (2014), *World Drug Report 2014* (New York: United Nations).

United Nations Population Fund (1994), *The State of World Population 1994: Choices and Responsibilities* (New York: UN Population Fund).

United States Congressional Budget Office (1997), "The Role of Foreign Aid in Development," Congressional Budget Office Study, Washington, DC.

United States Department of Justice (various years), *National Drug Threat Assessment* (Washington, DC: National Drug Intelligence Center).

United States Department of State (2003), *Patterns of Global Terrorism* (Washington, DC: U.S. Department of State).

United States Department of State (2013). "Country Reports on Terrorism." Available at http://www.state.gov/j/ct/rls/crt/. Accessed January 29, 2013.

Uppsala Conflict Data Program (UCDP) and Centre for the Study of Civil Wars, International Peace Research Institute, Oslo (PRIO) (2014), *UCDP/PRIO Armed Conflict Dataset*, Version 4-2013. Available at http://www.pcr.uu.se/research/datasets/ucdp_prio_armed_conflict_dataset/. Accessed April 10, 2014.

van de Walle, Nicolas, and Timothy A. Johnston (1996), *Improving Aid to Africa*, Policy Essay No. 21 (Washington, DC: Overseas Development Council).

Vicary, Simon (1990), "Transfers and the Weakest-Link: An Extension of Hirshleifer's Analysis," *Journal of Public Economics*, 43(3), 375–394.

Vicary, Simon, and Todd Sandler (2002), "Weakest-Link Public Goods: Giving In-Kind or Transferring Money," *European Economic Review*, 46(8), 1501–1520.

Viner, Jacob (1950), *The Customs Union Issue* (New York: Carnegie Endowment for International Peace).

Warr, Peter G. (1983), "The Private Provision of a Public Good Is Independent of the Distribution of Income," *Economics Letters*, 13(2), 207–211.

Warrick, Joby, and Walter Pincus (2008) "Reduced Dominance Is Predicted for U.S." *The Washington Post*, September 10, 2008, A02.

Watson, Joel (2002), *Strategy: An Introduction to Game Theory* (New York: W. W. Norton & Co.).

Wechsler, William F. (2001), "Follow the Money," *Foreign Affairs*, 80(4), 40–57.

Wescott, Clay G. (2004), "Promoting the Provision of Regional Public Goods in Asia," in Antoni Estevadeordal, Brian Frantz, and Tam Robert Nguyen (eds.), *Regional Public Goods: From Theory to Practice* (Washington, DC: Inter-American Development Bank and Asian Development Bank), 81–104.

Whaples, Robert (2006), "Do Economists Agree on Anything? Yes!" *The Economists' Voice*, 3(9), 1–6. Available at http://EconPapers.repec.org/RePEc:bpj:evoice:v:3:y:2006:i:9:n:1. Accessed October 7, 2013.

Wilkinson, Rorden, and David Hulme (2012), "Introduction: Moving from MDGs to GDGs," in Rorden Wilkinson and David Hulme (eds.), *The Millennium*

Development Goals and Beyond: Global Development after 2015 (New York: Routledge), 1–16.

Willem te Velde, Dirk, Oliver Morrissey, and Adrian Hewitt (2002), "Allocating Aid to International Public Goods," in Marco Ferroni and Ashoka Mody (eds.), *International Public Goods: Incentives, Measurement and Financing* (Boston: Kluwer Academic Publishers), 119–156.

Wolfson, Richard (2008), *Energy, Environment, and Climate* (New York: W.W. Norton & Co).

Wood, Duncan (2005), *Governing Global Banking: The Basel Committee and the Politics of Financial Globalization* (Burlington, VT: Ashgate Publishing Company).

World Bank (1998), *Assessing Aid: What Works, What Doesn't, and Why* (New York: Oxford University Press).

World Bank (2001), *Global Development Finance: Building Coalitions for Effective Development Finance* (Washington, DC: World Bank).

World Health Organization (WHO) (2001), *World Health Report 2001* (Geneva: WHO).

World Health Organization (WHO) (2002), *Coordinates 2002: Charting Progress against AIDS, TB, and Malaria* (Geneva: WHO).

World Health Organization (WHO) (2014) "Malaria," Available at http://www.who.int/mediacentre/factsheets/fs094/en/. Accessed February 20, 2014.

World Meteorological Organization (1998), *Scientific Assessment of Ozone Depletion: 1998*, WMO Global Ozone Research and Monitoring Project, Report No. 44, Geneva.

World Meteorological Organization (2013), "A Summary of Current Climate Change Findings and Figures." Available at www.unep.org/climatechange/publications/publication/tabid/429/langauge/en-us/Default.aspx?ID=6303. Accessed July 19, 2014.

World Resources Institute (1992), *World Resources 1992–93* (New York: Oxford University Press).

World Resources Institute (2000), *World Resources 2000–01* (New York: Oxford University Press).

World Trade Organization (2013), "WTO Website." Available at http://www.wto.org. Accessed October 8, 2013.

Wyplosz, Charles (1999), "International Financial Instability," in Inge Kaul, Isabelle Grunberg, and Marc A. Stern (eds.), *Global Public Goods: International Cooperation in the 21st Century* (New York: Oxford University Press), 152–189.

Zacher, Mark W. (1996), *Governing Global Networks: International Regimes for Transportation and Communications* (New York: Cambridge University Press).

Zacher, Mark W. (1999), "Global Epidemiological Surveillance: International Cooperation to Monitor Infectious Diseases," in Inge Kaul, Isabelle Grunberg, and Marc A. Stern (eds.), *Global Public Goods: International Cooperation in the 21st Century* (New York: Oxford University Press), 266–283.

AUTHOR INDEX

SUBJECT INDEX

assurance game, 27–9, 31, 34, 39,
41–2, 50, 53, 58, 61, 63, 65, 68,
92–4, 103, 105–6, 144–5, 156,
268, 295
asteroids, *see* planetesimals
asymmetric information, 14, 70–2,
89–90, 129, 136, 146, 171, 193
atmospheric observatories on Mauna
Loa, 2, 259
attack on U.S. embassy in Tehran,
1979, 213
Aum Shinrikyo, 214, 230
Australia, 30, 115, 198, 220, 247

balloon effect, 199, 202
bank failures, 171–2, 176–7
Bank for International Settlements
(BIS), 174, 177, 186
bargaining, 72, 108, 156–7, 159–62,
168, 295
Basel (Capital) Accords, 14, 177–91
as soft law, 188–90
Basel I, 179–84, 186, 189
Basel II, 182–7, 189–90
Basel III, 184–7, 189
its evaluation, 189–91
Basel Committee on Banking
Supervision (BCBS), 175–91
Bear Stearns, 3, 186
Belgium 114, 163, 178, 213, 236
benefit principle of taxation,
74–8, 106
benevolent chicken game, 31–2, 105–6
Beslan middle school attack, 214, 225
best-shot public good, 29, 64–6, 68,
72, 84–8, 90, 132, 135, 138–43,
146–7, 195, 199, 237, 242–8,
251, 257, 290–1, 293
better-shot public good, 66, 68, 85–8,
90, 132, 138–42, 242–8, 257
bilateral donors, 129
Bilateral Investment Treaties
(BITs), 161
bin Laden, Osama, 228
biodiversity, 30, 53, 78, 83, 86, 129,
142, 285, 288
biological weapons, 30, 214, 229,
249–51
BSL-4 laboratories, 85–7
Black September, 231
Boko Haram, 214

Bolivia, 79, 165, 199–203
borrowing short and lending long, 171
Bosnia War, 113–14, 221–4
bottom billion, 119, 146
Brazil, 79, 83, 115, 118, 129, 149–51,
160, 165, 167, 173, 203, 241,
251, 268
Bretton Woods system, 109–11,
154–5, 175
BRIC and BRICS, 129
Britain, *see* United Kingdom
British Antarctic Survey, 262–3
British Empire, 100, 102–3, 106
Bush administration, 98, 123, 129,
158, 208

Canada, 1, 38, 111, 114–15, 117, 164,
179, 223, 267–8, 271
cancer, 134–5, 142, 262
capital-adequacy ratio, 172–4, 176,
178–80, 183–6, 189
carbon dioxide, 2, 12, 129, 261,
267, 271
carrying capacity, 7, 259
Centers for Disease Control (CDC), 5,
16, 62, 77, 79, 81, 121, 136,
141, 143
Central American Electricity
Interconnection System
(SIEPAC), 79–80
Central American Free Trade
Agreement (CAFTA), 164
central banking system, 120, 124,
126–7
charitable foundations, 6, 53, 74, 93,
121, 123, 126, 128, 132,
136–44, 147
their activities, 93
Chechen separatists, 225
chemical weapons, 25, 43, 98–9, 214,
229, 244, 249–51
Chemical Weapons Convention, 250
chicken, game of, 22, 28, 30–1, 34,
42–3, 48, 50, 53, 58, 60, 68,
105–6, 257, 291
China, 3, 5, 35, 89, 115–18, 120, 129,
160, 164–7, 183, 197, 241,
248–51, 260, 268–72, 286, 294
chlorofluorocarbons (CFCs), 7, 8, 77,
95, 261–6, 269–72
Chunnel, 77

Japanese whalers, 194
joint products, 39, 53–4, 58, 82, 91,
    125, 128, 137, 154, 223, 242

Kaiser Chemicals, 265
Khan, A. Q., 248
kidnappings, 213–14, 224–5, 230, 239
Kosovo, 113–14, 221, 223–4
Kuwait, 243
Kuznets curve, 124
Kyoto Protocol, 25, 35, 260, 267–9,
    271, 287, 294

La Belle Discotheque bombings, 231
landlocked countries, 119, 124, 167, 285
Latin America, 78, 82–3, 91–2, 142,
    162, 173, 283, 286
Law of the Seas Treaty, 4, 55
leader-follower behavior, 29, 103,
    105–7
leadership, 11, 13–14, 29–32, 39, 42, 63,
    65, 68, 82–4, 87–8, 98–118, 121,
    141, 143, 155–6, 162, 220, 255,
    257, 262, 265, 270, 290–1, 294–5
    and asymmetry, 30, 36–8
    and game theory, 29–32, 103–7
League of Nations, 103
Lebanon, 223, 229, 231, 248
Lehman Brothers collapse, 3, 170,
    185–6
less-developed countries (LDCs),
    123–30
    and energy demands, 260
    and free riding, 129–30
    and growth, 123–4
    and income distribution, 119–21
Libya, 114–15, 117, 230–1, 243–4,
    248, 252
Long-Range Transboundary Air
    Pollution (LRTAP) Convention,
    275–81, 293
    and Geneva Protocol, 276, 280–1
    and Gothenburg Protocol, 276–8
    and Helsinki Protocol, 275–8
    and Oslo Protocol, 275–6
    and Sofia Protocol, 276–81

Maastricht agreement of 1992, 179
Madrid commuter train
    bombings, 214

malaria, 6, 25, 75, 83, 121–2, 128,
    133, 140–2, 285–8
marginal-cost pricing, 135, 275
marginal willingness to pay (MWTP), 51
market failures, 3–5, 14, 17, 45–73,
    75, 122, 135–6, 145–6, 172, 194
    and common property, 4–5
    and externalities, 46, 50
    and health, 135–6
    and need for collective action, 3–5,
        45–7, 50
    and public goods, 17, 45–68, 75
    and standard remedies, 52, 74–8
Marshall Plan, 111, 120
matching behavior, 60–2, 68, 131,
    139, 255
Mayo Clinic, 137
Médecin Sans Frontieres (MSF),
    141, 143
Medellin Cartel, 199
Medicines for Malaria Venture
    (MMV), 140–2
Mercado Común del Sur
    (MERCOSUR), 79–80, 165
Merck, 140, 142
metal detectors, 229–30
methamphetamine, 195
methane, 267
methyl bromide, 262–3
Mexico, 115–16, 164, 173, 181–2,
    199–200, 204, 268
Middle East, 37, 100, 203, 216–17,
    229, 283
Millennium Development Goals
    (MDGs), 15, 123, 126, 130, 133,
    284–5
money laundering, 14, 85, 192, 195,
    204–11, 240, 254, 291
    amount of, 204–5, 208–9
    and criminalization, 205–6
    its methods, 204
    and tax evasion, 205
monitoring, 1–2, 4, 16, 30, 37, 52–3,
    58, 62, 70–2, 74, 84, 88, 99, 137,
    155, 167, 172, 177, 206, 222, 245
monitoring the planet, 2, 6, 30, 66, 68,
    74, 259, 261, 280
Montevideo Convention of 1929, 100
Montreal Protocol, 8, 9, 77, 95, 260,
    263–6, 271, 281, 295–6
    its amendments, 263–4

ozone shield depleters, 8–9, 11–12, 14, 74, 95, 260–7, 271, 296

Pakistan, 129, 143, 165, 216–17, 224, 236, 248–51, 254
Palestine Liberation Organization (PLO), 72, 213, 216, 231
Panama, 52, 76, 207
Paraguay, 79, 165, 196
Pareto optimum, 22, 45
    see also social optimum
partnerships, 6, 53, 126–7, 133, 140–2, 147, 285
Pasteur Institute, 79, 81, 141, 143
patents, 134–5, 145–6, 159
pay-per-view television, 51
peacebuilding, 222–3
peace enforcement, 222–3
peacekeeping, 7, 30, 33, 40, 53–4, 63, 70, 77, 80, 93, 95, 101, 113, 167, 213–14, 220–4, 247, 292
    and assessment accounts, 33, 40, 77, 223–4
    in practice, 221–4
    publicness of, 53, 222–4
    and trends, 221, 223–4
    and troop contributions, 223
    UN peacekeeping versus non-UN peacekeeping, 95, 221–4
Peace of Westphalia, 99
Pennwalt Corporation, 265
Peru, 79, 165, 199–203, 268
pest control, 5–6, 32, 50, 63, 66, 68, 138–9, 280
    see also invasive species
petrodollars, 176
Pew Research Global Attitudes Project, 283
pharmaceutical companies, 122, 134–5, 142–3, 146, 197
Philippines, 123, 165, 236
piracy, 12, 15, 242, 253–4, 295
plagues, 121–2, 141–3
Plan Colombia, 201–4
planetesimals, 1, 17, 37, 65, 68, 75
Poland, 113, 163, 243, 276–7, 279
polio or poliomyelitis, 12, 66, 68, 143–5, 220, 254, 257, 282
polio versus smallpox eradication, 12, 143–5

political violence, 2, 13, 15, 51, 212–40, 243, 286, 289
polluter pays principle, 1
pollution, 1–2, 5–6, 10, 17, 23–6, 42, 46, 54, 59, 66–72, 77, 86, 89, 91, 101, 141–2, 146, 260, 272–5, 277–8, 280, 287, 293
population growth, 7, 120, 133–4, 288
Portugal, 3, 163, 275, 277, 279
Presidential Directive 42, 192–3
Prisoners' Dilemma, 10, 13, 18, 20–34, 36, 39, 40–2, 48, 53, 56–8, 60, 68, 92–5, 103–6, 132, 144, 153–4, 156, 232–8, 240, 256–7, 294–5
    and Nash equilibrium, 21–34, 92, 153
    n-person, 23–6, 40, 92–4, 235
    ordinal form, 21–2
    repeated, 33–4, 153–4
    two-person, 20–3, 153, 232–5
private goods, 17–18, 38–9, 47–9, 53, 88, 137, 149, 172
property rights, 3–4, 18, 45–6, 48, 54, 69, 120, 126–7, 134–5, 159, 168
prophylactic measures, 83
public good aid, see free-rider foreign aid
public goods, 14, 17–18, 20, 23, 25–7, 29–30, 33–4, 36–9, 43, 46–51, 53–5, 57, 59–68, 70–97, 102–3, 106–7, 109, 112–13, 116–18, 122, 126–7, 129–33, 136–47, 172–4, 222–3, 232, 242–6, 248, 251, 254–5, 257–8, 260–3, 274, 281, 290–1, 293–4
    and aggregate technology, 59–68
    definition of, 17, 47
    excludable, 49–59, 137
    impure, 49–51, 53–8, 84–8, 137
    pure, 17–18, 23, 25–7, 36–7, 39, 46–7, 53, 55, 57–60, 68, 70–1, 76, 84–8, 95, 128, 137, 223, 232, 242
    taxonomies, 47–68, 74–5, 84–8

quarantine, 132, 146
quotas and IMF funding, 110
    and voting rights, 110

Stackelberg leader, 103
stable macroeconomic environments, 119, 126–7
Standard and Poor's, 183–4
standard of weights and measures, 1
"Star Trek" federation, 9
state-sponsored terrorism, 16, 23, 108, 213, 225, 230, 241, 244, 248
strategic behavior, 13, 18–20, 128, 161, 190, 203, 232, 244, 257, 290–2, 294–6
subprime housing market crisis, *see* financial crisis of 2007–2008
sub-Saharan Africa, 5–6, 283, 286
subsidiarity, 14, 75, 81, 88–92, 96, 220, 290, 292
  and economies of scale, 90–1
  and economies of scope, 90–1
  and other considerations, 90
Sudan, 144, 220, 252
suicide terrorist attacks, 225, 227–8, 236
sulfur emissions, 4, 17, 47, 87, 89, 259, 261, 272, 275–9, 281
summation, technology of public supply aggregation, 59–61, 66–68, 72, 84–8, 132, 138–42, 262, 267–8
supranational institutions, 46, 69–70, 75–7, 88, 92–6, 99, 101, 163, 247, 257–8, 291
  and some design principles, 92–6
Syria, 43, 98, 101, 212, 219, 222–3, 225, 231, 248–51, 282
  its civil war, 219, 222–3

Taiwan, 120
takeoff to sustained growth, 124, 127
Taliban, 129, 235, 242, 245
tariffs, 46, 70, 78, 152, 154–9, 165, 167–8
technological progress, role of, 7, 10, 78–80, 124–5
technology of public supply aggregation, 47, 59–68, 72–3, 75, 84–8, 90, 122, 130–3, 136–9, 174, 290
  and game forms, 59–68
  definition of, 47

terrorism, 1, 5, 8, 12–13, 15–16, 23, 51, 60, 68, 71–2, 76, 85, 87, 99, 108, 114, 116, 123, 144–5, 195, 205, 208, 212–16, 224–42, 244, 248, 250–1, 253–4, 257, 282, 287, 291, 294–5
  and capital flows, 240
  and cycles, 225, 228–9
  definition of, 212–13, 224
  domestic, 224–9, 231, 235, 240
  economic costs, 240
  and effective policies, 229–37, 239
  and embassy security, 230
  and hostage taking, 214, 225, 230, 238–40
  and international treaties, 237–9
  its causes, 213, 229–30
  and metal detectors, 229–30
  and retaliatory raids, 230–1
  and safe havens, 5, 16, 71, 236, 240, 242, 251, 257
  transnational versus domestic terrorism, 12, 224–9, 240
  transnational, 8, 12, 23, 60, 71, 224–41, 248, 253–4, 257
  trends, 225–9, 231–2
terrorist networks, 99, 116, 214, 236–7
terrorists versus governments, 236–7
Thailand, 120, 165, 173, 203, 251, 286
threshold aggregator, 63–5, 68, 90, 92–4, 122, 124, 133, 138–9, 142
tit-for-tat strategy, 34
tolls, *see* club goods and tolls
trade barriers, 149, 152–62, 164, 282, 287, 289
trade boycotts, 16, 19, 222
trade, international, 7–9, 13–14, 74, 103, 126, 128–9, 148–69, 175, 204, 213, 219–20, 223, 240, 282
  and collective action, 7–8, 74, 152–4, 222
  and sanctions, 95
  and treaties, 70, 110, 154–5, 161–3, 165–6, 168, 282
trade leverage, 108, 152, 157, 161
  and linkages across issues, 107, 201–2
trade liberalization, 125, 127, 149, 152, 154–63, 165, 167–9, 287, 289, 294

War on Drugs, *see* U.S. War on Drugs
Warsaw Pact, 1, 41–2
watersheds, 2, 8, 38, 53, 55, 259, 272
waterways, 53, 74, 85, 124
weaker-link public good, 62–3, 68,
    85–8, 96, 132, 138–42
weakest-link public good, 60–2, 68,
    72–3, 84–8, 96, 122, 130–2,
    137–44, 146–7, 173–4, 194–5,
    199, 202, 208–10, 222, 237, 239,
    242, 254–8, 265, 281,
    290–2, 296
weapons of mass destruction (WMD),
    98, 241, 248–50
weighted-sum aggregator, 64, 66–8,
    84–8, 139–40, 174, 273–4, 280
Wellcome Trust, 123, 141, 143
West Germany, *see* Germany
World Bank, 9, 16, 76, 79–81, 84,
    91–2, 96, 121, 129–30,

    140, 154, 162, 174, 182,
    208, 292
  and mission creep, 89–90
World Health Organization (WHO),
    70, 79–80, 83, 91, 96, 121, 136,
    140–2, 144, 197, 257, 292
World Trade Center (WTC), 224
World Trade Organization (WTO), 46,
    101, 134, 148–9, 152, 157–62,
    167–9, 188, 292
  and GATT, 155–9
  its dispute settlement procedure
    (DSP), 158–9, 161
World War I, 1, 100, 197
World War II, 6, 37, 99–100, 102,
    106–7, 117, 243
WTO-led actions to reduce trade
    barriers, 158–61

Yugoslavia, 113, 275, 277, 279